Southern Africa Stands Up

BY WILFRED BURCHETT

Pacific Treasure Island   1941
Bombs over Burma   1944
Wingate Adventure   1944
Democracy with a Tommy-Gun   1946
Cold War in Germany   1950
Peoples Democracies   1951
The Changing Tide [play]   1951
China's Feet Unbound   1952
This Monstrous War   1953
Koje Unscreened [with Alan Winnington]   1953
Plain Perfidy [with Alan Winnington]   1954
North of the 17th Parallel   1955
Mekong Upstream   1959
Come East Young Man   1962
The Furtive War: The United States in Viet Nam and Laos   1963
My Visit to the Liberated Zones of South Viet Nam   1964
Viet Nam: Inside Story of the Guerilla War   1965
Viet Nam North   1966
Viet Nam Will Win   1968
Again Korea   1968
Passport   1969
The Second Indochina War   1970
My War with the CIA [with Prince Norodom Sihanouk]   1973
Portugal After the Captains' Coup   1975
China: The Quality of Life [with Rewi Alley   1976
Grasshoppers and Elephants   1977
The Whores of War   1977
Southern Africa Stands Up   1978

SOUTHERN AFRICA STANDS UP

The Revolutions
in
Angola, Mozambique, Zimbabwe, Namibia
and South Africa

by
Wilfred Burchett

URIZEN BOOKS   NEW YORK

© Wilfred Burchett 1978

First published by:
Urizen Books
66 West Broadway
New York, N.Y. 10007

Maps by William Jaber

Printed in the U.S.A.

Library of Congress Cataloging in Publication Data

Burchett Wilfred G., 1911-

Southern Africa Stands Up.

Includes index.
1. Africa, Southern—Politics and government.
2. Africa, Southern—Politics and government—1975-
3. Nationalism—Africa, Southern.
I. Title.
DT746.B87   320.9'68'06   78-9451

ISBN 0-916354-25-3   **ISBN 0-916354-26-1 pbk.**

CONTENTS

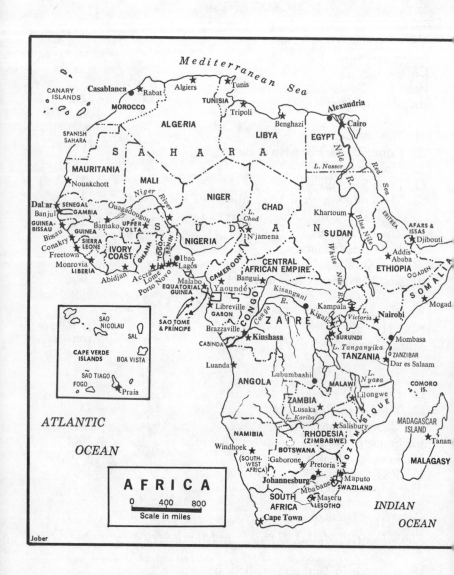

Introduction

Beginning in the late 1950s, the main western colonial powers started shedding their African colonies very rapidly. Between 1957 and 1968, Britain granted independence of varying quality to thirteen of its African colonies, from Ghana in 1957 to Swaziland in 1968. France granted independence to eleven of its colonies in 1960 alone. Morocco and Tunisia had got theirs peacefully in 1956. Algeria fought it out on the battlefield to win its independence in 1962. It was the great African independence decade.

That this came about so rapidly and relatively smoothly was not due to any sudden change of heart by the western powers towards the colonized peoples. Exhausted by World War II, and having tasted what lay ahead if they tried to defend each colony by force of arms, they decided to cut their losses. Britain had had a taste of it in Malaysia and to a certain extent in Kenya. France had had its experience in Indochina and was already bogged down again in Algeria. "Get out but save what's possible" was the mood in Britain and France as the 1950s drew to a close. So the quality of independence differed from colony to colony as the Union Jacks and Tricouleurs were hauled down and those of the newly born states were hoisted in their place.

The term neocolonialism was born together with the new states. This was teleguided colonialism in which the occupation force was replaced by local security services; the expensive colonial administration replaced by local bureaucrats—whose loyalty to the "mother-country" could usually be taken for granted—and a few strategically placed advisers to ensure that maximum privileges were preserved with minimum investment and upkeep. Thus a number of new governments which seemed to have got off to a good start soon found themselves overthrown by armed forces trained and put in place by the colonial power and left intact after the takeover. It was not always the case and there was no set pattern, but by such devices as the British Commonwealth and the Communauté Francaise and various types of currency zones and other special arrangements, the freed colonies were often bound to the former colonial powers by myriads of visible and invisible threads. And the people often found that they were being exploited by black factory and plantation owners as intensively as by the former white owners. A change of skin color at the top did not change the quality of exploitation!

However, they had got rid of that humiliating status of second-class citizens in their own country. Even if it was only the outward trappings of colonialism that had disappeared in some cases, it was still a great improvement. A modicum of human dignity had been restored even in the worst cases.

There was another element in the rapidity with which Britain and France divested themselves of their colonies. After their own traumatic experiences in World War II, there was a good deal of sympathy by the man-in-the-street in Britain and France for the sufferings of the people in the colonies, many of whom had served on the battlefields. The idea that victory and freedom were indivisible began to take hold. Those being repressed for advocating independence for their own countries found staunch advocates in the parliaments of Britain and France. Their cause was championed by parliamentarians of fame and talent. There were prestigious lawyers ready to hasten to the most far-flung corners of the Empire to defend victims of colonial persecution. Colonialism started to become a "dirty word." To a certain extent an anticolonialist public conscience was created and the merits of parliamentary democracy were well utilized.

The further the waves of independence reached south, however, where white racism was most strongly entrenched, the more perverse was the leadership resistance to change. This was the case in the African colonies which Portugal had held for nearly 500 years. A totalitarian, fascist regime in Lisbon nullified any possibility of support in the "mother country" for those who agitated for independence. There was no way in which public sympathy could be aroused through parliamentary debate or through the press. It was the case in South Africa where a type of internal colonialism held sway, where a white minority exercised a harsh dictatorship over an overwhelming majority of blacks, coloreds (the official designation of people of mixed race) and Asians. It was the case in Namibia (South West Africa) illegally ruled as a colony of South Africa under the same racist laws. It was the case in the British colony of Rhodesia (Zimbabwe), where a white, racist minority had illegally seized power and isolated the black majority from all channels of support which independence movements in other British colonies had received.

In those countries the standard response to every move, no matter how peaceful—and Gandhian-type non-violence was very much the style in South Africa, Namibia and Zimbabwe—to achieve independence or racial equality was bullets for demonstrators and the hangman's noose for "political terrorists." The rulers were of British stock, Portuguese, or Boer descendants of Dutch settlers. They were Catholic and they were Protestant, but their outlook and methods were the same. It was no accident that the greatest massacres in modern times in those racist-ruled countries took place within a few months of each other in 1960, because the victims had dared to have illusions that they were entitled to the same kind of independence that was being granted to countries the other side of their frontiers.

If the tactics of terror used by the rulers of those countries cut across geographic, racial and religious boundaries, so did the tactics of resistance to that terror. A sense of solidarity developed among the oppressed peoples, as they found by bitter experience that all avenues to achieving their modest aims had been blocked, except that of replying to violence by counter-violence. The solidarity which developed among the various national liberation struggles also cut across geographic, racial, linguistic and religious boundaries. It became a rule that as each country gained its independence, it opened its frontiers to others struggling for theirs. This has been a constant feature as the torch of liberation has been handed on from country to country, from movement to movement, literally from Cairo to the Cape. To give some examples: Algeria's first government-in-exile was set up in Nasser's Egypt and received massive financial support to carry on its national liberation struggle. Algeria in turn became host to the liberation movements of the three Portuguese colonies—among many others. As soon as Angola won its independence, it became host to SWAPO (the South West African People's Organization), as did Mozambique to the Zimbabwan liberation movements. Guinea (Conakry) did the same for Guiné-Bissau.

There was even inter-continental solidarity because the torch of national liberation in its modern phases was brought from Vietnam to Africa. It was the Vietnamese victory over the French at Dien Bien Phu in May, 1954, that inspired the Algerians to take up arms just six months later. Among the most effective F.L.N. combatants were Algerians who had deserted—or been cap-

tured—at Dien Bien Phu and who, after a short recycling course
from the Vietnamese on how to fight *against* colonialists instead
of for them—were sent back to help liberate their own country.

The book which follows is an attempt to set the background to
the liberation movements in Angola and Mozambique, how armed
struggles developed and were carried through to victory and the
impact of those victories in the surrounding countries of Zimbabwe, Namibia and in South Africa itself. Much of the material
was gathered during three visits to Angola and two to Mozambique in 1976, and through extensive discussions with today's
leaders of liberation struggles in Zimbabwe, Namibia and South
Africa.

W. G. Burchett
Paris
February 1978

CHRONOLOGY

INTRODUCTION

The chronology follows the general pattern of the book by dealing with two separate periods. The first is that of the spiral of agitation, repression and political struggle; the formation of nationalist movements which preceded the start of armed liberation struggles in Southern Africa. This period brings out the time relationships between the political ferment and launching of armed struggle in the former Portuguese colonies and what was happening in South Africa, Zimbabwe and Namibia. It covers the two decades from the time the MPLA (Popular Movement for the Liberation of Angola) and the PAIGC (African Party for the Independence of Guiné-Bissau and Cap Verde) were formed until the time that the people of Namibia and Zimbabwe took to arms.

The second part deals with the period starting with what became known as the "Captains' Coup" in Portugal and the intensive and expanding armed liberation struggles which this stimulated and which continue in southern Africa to this day.

The eight years in-between, essentially the long grinding struggle with few dramatic highlights—which brought about the collapse of the Portuguese Empire with all its implications for the people neighboring Portugal's former African colonies—is not dealt with except for a few illustrative episodes.

Thus the first part of the chronology traces the birth of the main liberation movements in order of their appearance on the stage, the second part shows them in motion, including their inter-relationships.

I

1953

Secret founding in the Angolan capital, Luanda, of the PLUA (Party for the United Struggle of Angolan Africans), the first with nationalist aims.

1956

Founding in Luanda of the short-lived PCA (Angolan Communist Party).

Formation in Bissau of the PAIGC (African Independence Party of Guiné and the Cape Verde Islands).

Founding in Léopoldville (now Kinshasa, the capital of Zaire) of the MPLA (Peoples Movement for the Liberation of Angola) by fusing the PLUA and the PCA.

Founding of UPNA (Union of the Peoples of Northern Angola) based on the Bakongo tribe.

Transformation of UPNA into UPA (Union of Angolan People).

First conference of Independent African States in the Ghanaian capital of Accra.

South Rhodesian African National Congress—the main black African movement in Zimbabwe—is banned. Five hundred national, provincial and district leaders are arrested.

Many arrests of suspected nationalists in Luanda.

Further arrests of suspected MPLA members and sympathizers including virtually the entire Angola-based MPLA leadership.

South Rhodesian (Zimbabwan) National Democratic Party formed.

Sharpeville (South Africa) massacre. Sixty-seven people killed in non-violent rally organized by PAC (Pan-Africanist Congress) protesting at humiliating pass laws under which blacks had to carry passes showing their residential, work, and tax status. World-wide protests at brutality of South African security forces.

1960, APRIL 19

Founding of SWAPO (South West African People's Organization) in Windhoek which the Namibians call Otjomuize.

1960, JUNE

Dr. Agostinho Neto, one of the founder-leaders of the MPLA, arrested in his Luanda consulting room.

1960, JUNE

Demonstrators protesting Neto's arrest in his home district of Catete, fired on by Portuguese security forces. Thirty killed.

1960, JUNE 16

Over six hundred people killed when troops opened fire on a peaceful demonstration outside the Portuguese governor's residence at Mueda in Mozambique's northern province of Cabo Delgado.

1960, SEPTEMBER

After three months in a Luanda prison, Neto is transferred to the Tarrafal "death camp" on the Cape Verde Islands.

1960, DECEMBER

MPLA members and sympathizers arrested in May and July, 1959, are sentenced to prison terms of from one to thirteen years.

1961, FEBRUARY 4

Attack on Luanda central prison, police stations and army barracks in attempt to free political prisoners. The attacks marked the beginning of Angola's national liberation struggle.

1961, MARCH 15

Indiscriminate massacre of whites, mulattos and *assimilados* (educated blacks) by UPA forces in northern Angola.

1961-62

Portuguese security forces, continually reinforced from Portugal, unleash a wave of terror throughout the country especially in and around Luanda and the northern provinces.

1961, MARCH

Meeting in Monrovia (Liberia) between the MPLA president, Mario de Andrade, and the UPA president Holden Roberto in an attempt to get unity. "Close cooperation" was the most Holden Roberto promised, but nothing came of it.

1961, DECEMBER 9
National Democratic Party of South Rhodesia is banned by the government of Edgar Whitehead.

1961, DECEMBER 17
The Zimbabwan African People's Union (ZAPU) is launched by Joshua Nkomo as a more militant version of the NDP, oriented towards preparation for armed struggle.

1962, MARCH 28
Formation of the FNLA in what was then Léopoldville (capital of the Belgian Congo, which later became Kinshasa, capital of Zaire) as a result of the fusion of the UPA with the small tribal-based PDA (People's Democratic Party).

1962, APRIL 6
The FNLA sets up GRAE (Revolutionary Government of Angola in Exile) based at Léopoldville.

1962, JUNE 25
Formation of FRELIMO (Front for the Liberation of Mozambique) in Tanganyika, by the fusion of three nationalist groups: MANU (Makonda African Union which later became Mozambique National Union), UDENAMO (Mozambique National Democratic Union), and UNAMI (National African Union of Independent Mozambique).

1962, SEPTEMBER 20
ZAPU is banned, its leaders arrested or placed under forced residence. (Those who had homes in rural areas were not allowed to move beyond the boundaries of their fields.) Nkomo, who was abroad, returned and was restricted to the confines of his rural home.

1963, JANUARY
Almost all the ZAPU detainees are released, including Nkomo, who flew to Tanganyika to enlist President Nyerere's support for preparing armed struggle.

1963, JANUARY
The PAIGC of Guiné-Bissau launches armed struggle.

1963, JUNE

FNLA starts harassing attacks against the MPLA, including the arrests of Neto and his chief aide Lucio Lara, culminating with the closing down of the MPLA office in Kinshasa in November and the expulsion of all MPLA cadres from Zaire.

1963, JUNE

South African security forces raid the Rivonia headquarters of the underground ANC which had already been waging armed struggle. Virtually all leaders were arrested and valuable archives seized.

1963, JULY 13

GRAE recognized by the Liberation Committee of the Organization of African Unity as the sole Angolan national liberation movement.

1963, AUGUST 8

ZAPU is split and a breakaway group headed by Reverend Ndabaningi Sithole forms the Zimbabwe African National Union (ZANU). There had been clashes of personality within the leadership and Nkomo had proposed a party congress for August 10. Sithole however announced the break at a press conference two days earlier. At that time ZAPU was operating under the cover name of "People's Caretaker Council."

1963, AUGUST 15

President Fulbert Youlou of Congo-Brazzaville resigns after three days of mass demonstrations. He is succeeded by Alphonse Massemba-Débat.

1963, NOVEMBER

The MPLA headquarters is transferred from Kinshasa across the Congo river to Brazzaville.

1964, JANUARY

MPLA "Cadres Conference" held in Brazzaville. A critical analysis of past mistakes is made and a definition of future aims and methods. A key decision was that of opening up a new operational front in the Cabinda Enclave which juts into territory north of the Congo river, separate from the rest of Angola and surrounded by Zaire and Congo-Brazzaville.

1964, APRIL 16

The entire ZAPU leadership, including Joshua Nkomo, is arrested by the Rhodesian Front government which had swept the polls at the end of 1962. A People's Council had already been set up in Zambia for such an eventuality. It was headed by Jason Moyo and James Chikeremo.

1964, JULY

The GRAE foreign minister, Jonas Savimbi, resigns at an OAU conference in Cairo, issuing a blistering denunciation of Holden Roberto as an American puppet as the reason for his resignation.

1964, AUGUST 26

The ZAPU-oriented "Caretaker Council" inside Zimbabwe is banned and from that time all ZAPU activities inside the country are underground.

1964, SEPTEMBER 25

FRELIMO launches armed struggle with simultaneous attacks against two Portuguese military posts in Cabo Delgado province.

1964, OCTOBER 24

Zambia receives its independence as a Republic within the British Commonwealth.

1964, OCTOBER 30

The independent republics of Tanganyika and Zanzibar fuse to become the United Republic of Tanzania.

1965, JUNE

Attempted *coup d'état* against Holden Roberto in Kinshasa by his "armaments' minister" Alexander Taty. It failed and Taty fled to join the Portuguese in Angola.

1965, JULY

Holden Roberto's "information minister," Rosario Neto, resigned.

1965, NOVEMBER 11

Prime Minister Ian Smith made a Unilateral Declaration of Independence (UDI) for Southern Rhodesia, henceforth known as Rhodesia or Zimbabwe, its original African name.

1966, MARCH

Jonas Savimbi formed UNITA (Union for the Total Independence of Angola).

1966, APRIL 30

Armed struggle launched in Zimbabwe, marked by a heavy clash between ZANU (Zimbabwe African National Union) guerillas and White police and troops at Sinoia, 130 kilometres northwest of Salisbury, the Rhodesian capital. Both sides claim to have inflicted heavy losses.

1966, AUGUST 26

SWAPO launches armed struggle for the liberation of Namibia.

1966, DECEMBER

UNITA launches some small attacks against Portuguese positions in eastern Angola from bases in Zambia. Savimbi had recruited some followers from former UPA members who had fled from Angola to western Zambia.

1967, APRIL 2-4

A "Little Summit" of militant African states is held in Cairo at the initiative of President Nasser and urges OAU support for armed struggle in Zimbabwe.

II

1974, APRIL 25

Overthrow of Portugal's fascist regime in what became known as the "Captains' Coup." A group of young officers, convinced that the colonial wars in Africa could not be won but that there was no way of ending them without overthrowing the Lisbon fascist regime, carried out a well-organized coup in the early morning of April 24, 1974. They were pledged, among other things, to a policy of decolonialization.

1974, MAY 25

Talks start in London between Portugal and the PAIGC on the transfer of power from Portugal to the independent Republic of Guiné-Bissau. After six days they were indefinitely adjourned.

1974, JUNE 5

Talks start in Lusaka (Zambia) between Portugal and FRELIMO. They adjourned the following day. Both in London and in Lusaka, the Portuguese Foreign Minister, Dr. Mario Soares, wanted to discuss a ceasefire and referendum; the PAIGC and FRELIMO delegations insisted on discussing transfer of powers for full independence.

1974, JUNE 17

Jonas Savimbi declares a unilateral ceasefire binding on UNITA forces in Angola. As FNLA forces were inactive against the Portuguese in the North, Portuguese forces could concentrate their attacks on those of the MPLA.

1974, JULY 9

Prime Minister Carlos Palma resigns as head of the first Portuguese government after the "captains' coup."

1974, JULY 12

Colonel Vasco Gonçalves appointed prime minister and pledges to strictly carry out the program of the Armed Forces Movement. In the new cabinet, Melo Antunes, one of the leaders of the Armed Forces Movement, is appointed Minister Without Portfolio, charged with Decolonialization, among other tasks.

1974, AUGUST 26

After ten days of negotiations in Algiers, in which Melo Antunes played a key role, agreement was reached on the terms of independence for Guiné-Bissau.

1974, SEPTEMBER 7

Agreement reached in Lusaka with FRELIMO leader Samora Machel on the gradual transfer of powers so that complete independence for Mozambique would be attained by June 25, 1975. The negotiating was essentially done by Otelo Saraivo de Carvalho, the military architect of the "captains' coup," and Melo Antunes who had drafted the political program of the Armed Forces Movement.

1974, SEPTEMBER 7-11

Rioting breaks out in the Mozambique capital of Lourenço Marques (now Maputo) as Portuguese and white Mozambicans opposed to the Lusaka Agreement tried to seize power and set up an "independent provisional government" along the lines of that set up by Ian Smith in neighboring Rhodesia. Official figures gave 82 dead and 479 injured. As a result of the defeat of the attempt many Portuguese started leaving for South Africa.

1974, SEPTEMBER 10

General Antonio de Spinola, appointed by the AFM to head the ruling military junta after the "captains' coup"—in an attempt to prevent the granting of independence to Angola—makes a speech appealing for a "silent majority" to assert itself in Portugal.

1974, SEPTEMBER 30

After an attempted right-wing coup had been thwarted on September 28-29, Spinola resigns his functions, equivalent to those of president. He was succeeded by General Costa Gomes. Vasco Gonçalves was re-appointed Prime Minister. Otelo de Carvalho was placed in charge of a special "anti-coup" security force, COPCON (Continental Operations Command). Melo Antunes continued to be in charge of decolonialization.

1974, OCTOBER 21
A ceasefire is signed between Agostinho Neto for the MPLA and Naval Captain Leonel Gomes Cardoso. Thus came to an end that phase of the Angolan national liberation struggle.

1974, OCTOBER 30
A draft resolution calling for the expulsion of South Africa from the United Nations for "continued implementation of *apartheid*" for refusal to withdraw from Namibia and for "support to the illegal regime in Rhodesia," is vetoed in the UN Security Council by the U.S., British and French permanent members.

1974, NOVEMBER
Delegations from the three national liberation movements enter Luanda on the basis of the separate agreements signed with the Portuguese. The MPLA delegation, which arrived on November 8, was greeted by a crowd of 300,000—by far the greatest demonstration the country had ever seen.

1974, DECEMBER 13
The UN General Assembly approves Resolutions 3297 (111 votes to nil) and 3298 (112 votes to nil), each with eighteen abstentions, demanding that Britain create appropriate conditions to enable the people of Zimbabwe to fully and freely exercise their right to self-determination, and calling for strict enforcement of sanctions against the Smith regime.

1974, DECEMBER 15
The MPLA announces the expulsion of Daniel Chipenda, leader of an anti-Neto group within the MPLA, known as the "Eastern Revolt" faction.

1974, DECEMBER 17
The UN Security Council unanimously adopts a resolution calling upon South Africa to withdraw its "illegal administration" from South West Africa and "transfer power to the people of Namibia."

1975, JANUARY 15
Signature of an Agreement between the three Angolan national liberation movements (MPLA, FNLA and UNITA) on the one side, and the Portuguese government on the other, for the complete independence of Angola by November 11, 1975. Known as the Alvor or Algarve Agreement,

after the seaside resort on Portugal's southern coast where the negotiations took place, it was the result of intensive activities by three leaders of the AFM, Melo Antunes, Otelo de Carvalho and the "Red" Admiral, Rosa de Coutinho, in seeking to harmonize the viewpoints of the leaders of the three movements.

1975, JANUARY 31
Four-party Transitional Government set up in Luanda in accordance with the Alvor Agreement, including three ministers from each of the national liberation movements and three from Portugal. Each Movement is represented on a three-party Presidential Collegiate.

1975, FEBRUARY 3
MPLA forces attack troops of the Chipenda faction which had set up an "MPLA" office in Luanda, without any legal status. After a second attack on February 13, the Chipenda faction withdraws.

1975, FEBRUARY 23
Daniel Chipenda, at a Kinshasa press conference, announces that his faction has joined forces with the FNLA.

1975, MARCH
Regular troops of the Zaire Army, together with Zaire-based troops of the FNLA, enter Angola from the North occupying Ambriz, a port-city, one hundred and fifty kilometers south of the Zaire border, Carmona (now Uije, capital of the province of that name) and other towns north of Luanda.

1975, MARCH 18
Herbert Chitepo, representative of the ANC (African National Council of Zimbabwe) is killed in Lusaka, when his car is blown up by a mine outside his home. He had been the first elected chairman of ZANU (1964) and had directed the first guerilla raids into Zimbabwe in 1966. Two other ZANU leaders, Robert Mugabe and Dr. Edson Sithole, blamed the Smith regime for the murder.

1975, MARCH 23
With reinforcements made available by the occupation of northern Angola by the Zaire armed forces, the FNLA launches a heavy attack against the MPLA headquarters area in the Luanda suburbs of Gazenga and Vila Alice.

1975, MARCH 25
FNLA gunmen round up over fifty MPLA members and cadres in Luan-

da, take them off in trucks and machine-gun them to death at Kifangondo, about twenty kilometers to the north of the capital.

A motorized column enters Luanda with some five hundred FNLA reinforcements.

Despite innumerable ceasefire agreements, the situation inside Luanda continues to deteriorate as FNLA forces, later joined by those of UNITA, try to drive those of the MPLA out of the capital.

President Kenneth Kuanda of Zambia banned ZAPU, ZANU and Frolizi (the small Front for the Liberation of Zimbabwe, headed by James Chikerema), from operating on Zambian territory.

Mozambique becomes independent. In ceremonies starting immediately after midnight, June 24, the Portuguese flag was lowered and the independent People's Republic of Mozambique was proclaimed. Samora Machel was sworn in as President.

MPLA troops, together with local MPLA supporters, attack and destroy the Luanda headquarters of the FNLA. In three days of bitter fighting the FNLA-UNITA forces were driven from the capital and the transitional government came to an end. While beating off repeated FNLA attempts to retake the capital from the north, MPLA forces pushed south to retake traditional strongholds, lost when control of them was shared on a three-way basis with the FNLA and UNITA.

Advance units of the South African armed forces enter Angola from Namibia, occupying the towns of Calueque, forty kilometers inside Angola, and Namacunde, twelve kilometers inside. *The Times* of London later reported that the entry of South African troops had been negotiated in Windhoek in early July by Daniel Chipenda in talks with South Africa's General Hendrik van den Bergh, head of BOSS (Bureau of State Security).

FNLA troops driving on Luanda are halted at Kinfangondo, twenty kilometers north of the capital. Holden Roberto, returning to Angola for the first time in fourteen years, announces he would personally direct the battle to retake the capital. His troops are beaten back.

1975, AUGUST 21
Jonas Savimbi announces that UNITA has declared war on the MPLA. MPLA cadres, members and suspected sympathizers are arrested in UNITA-controlled areas.

1975, AUGUST 29
The Portuguese Government announces suspension of further implementation of the Alvor Agreement but pledges that independence will go into effect on November 11, as promised.

1975, AUGUST 29
Vasco Gonçalves is forced to stand down as Prime Minister of Portugal.

1975, SEPTEMBER 9
A new Portuguese Government is formed with Admiral Pinheiro de Azevedo as Prime Minister.

1975, OCTOBER 23
A mixed invasion force, spearheaded by South African armored cars, artillery and motorized infantry, starts a drive to the north from the take-off positions secured by South African forces early in August. It includes elements of the ELP (pro-Spinola Portuguese Liberation Army), of Portuguese settler *vigilantes*, of Chipenda-faction FNLA forces and of UNITA troops. In titular charge of the "Drive to the North" was Daniel Chipenda. In fact, it was the South Africans who directed the operation. The maximum aim was to link up in Luanda with a mixed force of Zaire-FNLA troops before November 11.

1975, NOVEMBER 6
After a rapid advance with little effective opposition, the vanguard force of eighty armored cars, artillery, spotter planes and about six hundred South African troops is halted by MPLA forces in a delaying action on the south bank of the Queve river, seventeen kilometers northwest of Novo Redondo on the main south-north highway. Guerillas destroyed the bridge over the Queve and the advance is stopped four hundred kilometers south of Luanda.

1975, NOVEMBER 7
A first assault against the capital by the northern column is stopped on the Bengo river, less than twenty kilometers from Luanda.

1975, NOVEMBER 7

The first eighty-two Cuban combat troops leave Havana by air for Luanda.

1975, NOVEMBER 10

A second much stronger assault against Luanda by the northern column is thrown back by mid-day, the bridge over the Bengo river having been blown up by MPLA forces and the spearhead of the column—armored cars and artillery—bombarded with Soviet-made *Katyusha* multiple rocket launchers. In the afternoon the Portuguese High Commissioner, Admiral Leonel Cardoso, his staff and remaining garrison troops leave Luanda by frigate.

1975, NOVEMBER 11

In a ceremony starting at midnight, November 10, the independent People's Republic of Angola is proclaimed, the flag of the new Republic hoisted and Agostinho Neto invested as President.

1975, NOVEMBER 12

At Ambriz, 170 kilometers north of Luanda, Holden Roberto proclaims the independent People's Democratic Republic of Angola. Later Roberto and Jonas Savimbi announce the setting up of a Joint National Council for the Revolution, to be headquartered at Huambo, Angola's second largest city.

1975, NOVEMBER 20

The airlift of a reinforced Cuban special forces battalion of 650 men, which started on November 7, is completed.

1975, NOVEMBER 27

A Cuban artillery regiment and motorized battalion arrive in Luanda by sea.

1975, DECEMBER 19

The U.S. Senate by 54 to 22 votes prohibits further U.S. covert aid to the anti-MPLA forces in Angola despite urgent pleas by President Ford and Secretary of State Kissinger.

1976, JANUARY 1

MPLA-Cuban forces go over to the counter-offensive. To the north, MPLA troops with some Cuban artillery support liberated Uije (January 4), a big airbase at Negage forty kilometers to the east of Uije (January 5) and the port of Ambriz (January 12). Following their defeat at Uije and Negage, the Zaire troops pulled back across the northern frontier into Zaire.

1976, JANUARY 18

The first batch of British mercenaries leave London's Heathrow airport for the Angolan battlefront via Brussels and Kinshasa. Their main job is to replace the Zaire troops, train FNLA recruits and hold the northern sector.

1976, JANUARY 21

MPLA-Cuban forces after heavy battles retake the towns of Cela and Santa Comba (the furthest point of the South African advance) and Novo Redondo, the western anchor of the South African battle line, three days later. By then the South African "flying column" is in full retreat, destroying bridges behind them to slow up the pursuit.

1976, FEBRUARY 5

End of mercenaries on the northern front. The end came when the leader of a band of some 200 white mercenaries—almost all British—mistook a munitions truck for a tank and fired a bazooka into it. Most of the remainder of his mercenaries were killed or wounded in the resultant explosion. The leader, "Colonel" Callan (alias Costas Georgoiu), had executed fourteen of his men a few days previously allegedly for refusing to fight.

1976, FEBRUARY 8

Huambo, the UNITA-FNLA "capital" is abandoned in favor of Savimbi's military "stronghold" at Bié (formerly Silva Porto) which fell four days later.

1976, FEBRUARY 11

The OAU (Organization of African Unity) recognizes the MPLA's People's Government of Angola as the country's sole legitimate government and admits it to full membership. The FNLA-UNITA's "People's Democratic Republic" had not been recognized by any country.

1976, FEBRUARY 12

Jonas Savimbi announces that UNITA forces would regroup to wage guerilla warfare.

1976, FEBRUARY 24

Holden Roberto announces that FNLA forces would revert to guerilla warfare.

1976, FEBRUARY 27-28

President Neto and President Mobutu Sese-Seko meet in Brazzaville at the initiative of the Congolese President Marien Ngouabi. In a joint communiqué they pledge not to allow each other's territory to be used for military activities across the frontier, to facilitate the return of Angolese refugees in Zaire and Katangan "gendarmes" (who fled to Angola after the abortive Katanga secessionist war of the 1960s) to their home territories. A permanent commission would be set up at ministerial level to ensure "non-interference" in each other's internal affairs.

1976, MARCH 3

President Samora Machel announces the closing of Mozambique's frontiers with Rhodesia and the imposition of sanctions in accordance with UN and OAU resolutions.

1976, MARCH 5

The Zaire government closes the FNLA Bureau in Kinshasa in accordance with the Brazzaville Agreement.

1976, MARCH 31

South Africa withdraws its forces from Angola by the end of March. By that time SWAPO has opened a mission in Luanda and has set up training facilities, also schools and hospitals on the Angolan side of the frontier with Namibia.

1976, APRIL

The Zimbabwan People's Army (ZIPA) was formed by battlefield cadres left virtually leaderless, partly by the inactivity of the ANC (African National Council) leadership of Bishop Muzorewa and the Reverend Sithole ZANU faction; partly because some of the key ZANU military leaders like Josiah Tongogara were in jail in Zambia. The initiative to form ZIPA and to step up the fighting came from militants like Rex Nhongo, Jason Moyo, Dzinashe Machingura and others. Documents agreeing to confirm the existence of ZIPA and to set up a High Command composed of nine members each from ZAPU and ZANU, were signed by the overall commander Tongogara in his Zambian prison cell. After the formation of the Patriotic Front, ZIPA was endorsed as the military wing of the Front.

1976, MAY 1

Faced with increasing guerilla attacks inside Zimbabwe, Lieutenant-General Peter Walls, Commander-in-Chief of the Armed Forces, states that his armed forces would change from a "contain and hold" strategy to that of "search and destroy." This would involve "hot pursuit" into neighboring territories.

1976, JUNE 10-16

The Soweto massacres. At least 176 people (the official figure) were killed, and 1,222 wounded, including two whites killed and six wounded in pitched battles between mainly students and schoolchildren and the security forces. Soweto (South-Western Townships), in the outskirts of Johannesburg, with one million inhabitants represents the largest concentration of Africans in South Africa. The riots were sparked by the Government's compulsory use of the Afrikaans language as a medium of instruction. It is rejected by the blacks as the language of *apartheid.*

1976, JUNE 11-19

Trial of thirteen white mercenaries (ten British and three Americans) in Luanda. Four were sentenced to death and later executed by firing squad, the nine others were sentenced to terms of from sixteen to thirty years imprisonment.

1976, AUGUST 8

Rhodesian forces, using armored cars and artillery, attack the Nhazonia camp for Zimbabwe refugees inside Mozambique, killing at least 670 refugees and wounding twice that number. The Mozambique representative of the UN High Commissioner's Office for Refugees confirmed that the Nhazonia camp was a *bona fide* refugee camp run under UN auspices. The Smith regime claimed it was exercising the right of "hot pursuit" against guerillas. The UN's HCR representative, Mr. Idoyaga, said that the Nhazonia camp was one of three such settlements in Mozambique for Zimbabwan refugees, supported by the UN agency.

1976, AUGUST AND SEPTEMBER

Throughout this period there are widespread riots and strikes in many urban areas of South Africa. Apart from the renewed Soweto-type militancy among pupils and students, there are political strikes by black workers in Soweto, militant action—stoning of police—by colored (those of mixed race) workers in Capetown and elsewhere. In three separate actions in Capetown on September 2, 7-8 and 9, twenty-nine people are killed, according to official figures. Following the Capetown riots, a ban on public gatherings is extended until October 31.

Between August 23-25, about 200,000 workers in Soweto carried out a three-day political strike, repeated again on September 13-15 and on September 15-16, 200,000 colored workers went on strike in Capetown in an unprecedented show of solidarity with the blacks. A central target of all demonstrations was *apartheid,* but also the police brutality in suppressing what started out always as peaceful demonstrations, and unjust detentions without trial.

1976, AUGUST 26

SWAPO guerillas are reported by the Tanzanian *Daily News* as operating 480 kilometers south of the Angola border, deep into central Namibia.

1976, AUGUST 29

Sean MacBride, UN High Commissioner for Namibia, tells a Lusaka press conference that during the previous three months between 40,000 and 50,000 Namibians have been uprooted from their villages along the border with Angola and herded into concentration camp-type settlements. Many have been tortured and beaten up to extract information about SWAPO guerillas; their villages have been burned down to create a "free fire" zone along the frontier area, supplemented by a ten-foot high barbed wire fence along 640 kilometres of the Namibia-Angolan border.

1976, AUGUST 31

The *Guardian* (London) quotes a Bill Anderson, of the 6th South Africans Infantry battalion, who took part in operations described by Sean MacBride, as saying that in clearing an area of one hundred square kilometers orders were "to shoot everyone who ran and to arrest everyone who stayed. All the arrested men were beaten, tortured and interrogated without exception."

1976, SEPTEMBER 4-6

Kissinger initiates a round of "shuttle diplomacy" in southern Africa by secret talks in Zurish with the South African Prime Minister, Johannes Vorster. He pledges to consult with at least one of the leaders of the "front-line" states in forthcoming visits to southern Africa.

1976, SEPTEMBER 5-7

The five "front-line" presidents, Agostinho Neto, Samora Machel, Kenneth Kaunda, President Julius Nyerere of Tanzania and Sir Seretse Khama of Botswana meet for the first time in Dar-es-Salaam, the Tanzanian capital, together with the leaders of all factions of the various Zimbabwan nationalist movements, of SWAPO and of the South African ANC and PAC. Although all agreed on the need for stepping-up armed struggle in Zimbabwe, no agreement on unity was reached between the main Zimbabwe rival nationalist factions.

1976, SEPTEMBER 14

On the eve of Dr. Kissinger's arrival in Dar-es-Salaam, the Tanzanian Government issues a statement criticizing the U.S. Government for linking "United States support for majority rule with the struggle against communism" and the government-controlled *Daily News* comments the same day that: "If the stemming of communism is to be equated with the setting-up of puppet regimes, then Dr. Kissinger's journey is a useless undertaking."

1976, SEPTEMBER 17

The start of two days of talks between Kissinger and Prime Minister Vorster in Pretoria.

1976, SEPTEMBER 19

Meeting between Kissinger and Ian Smith at the residence of the U.S. Embassy in Pretoria.

1976, SEPTEMBER 24

Prime Minister Ian Smith, back in Salisbury, in a radio broadcast announces that after consultations with his Rhodesian Front caucus—comprising all fifty white members of the House of Assembly—he has accepted a Kissinger "package deal." According to this, "majority rule" will be granted within two years under a new constitution. In exchange, guerilla warfare would end and economic sanctions against Rhodesia lifted. On this basis, he was prepared to take part in an international conference with nationalist leaders to work out the details.

1976, SEPTEMBER 26

Meeting in Lusaka the five "front-line" presidents call upon "the colonial authority, the British government, to convene at once a conference outside Zimbabwe with the authentic and legitimate representatives of the people" to discuss the means of bringing about "majority rule" and the drafting of a constitution guaranteeing independence for the Zimbabwan people on that basis.

1976, OCTOBER 8

Anthony C. Crosland, British Foreign and Commonwealth Secretary, announces that he will convene a conference to open in Geneva on October 25 to discuss the constitutional issues involved. Three Nationalist leaders would be invited, Joshua Nkomo of ZAPU, Robert Mugabe of ZANU and Bishop Abel Muzorewa of the ANC. Ian Smith had been invited to participate or to send a delegate.

1976, OCTOBER 9

Joshua Nkomo and Robert Mugabe announce the formation of a ZAPU-

ZANU "Patriotic Front" to present a common negotiating position at the forthcoming Geneva Conference.

The Geneva Conference is opened (three days late because of procedural problems) by Ivor Richard, British ambassador to the United Nations, whom the British Government appointed Chairman of the Conference. He states the Conference aim is to ensure "that Rhodesia should become independent within two years on the basis of majority rule."

Prime Minister Smith walks out of the Conference stating he "had more important things to do at home." He had insisted that the only competence of the Geneva Conference was to discuss the implementation of the "Kissinger package deal."

Following attacks into Mozambique by Rhodesian armed forces immediately after the start of the Geneva Conference—in one of which over six hundred Zimbabwan refugees are killed—leaders of the five "front-line" states, meeting in Dar-es-Salaam, appeal for increased arms and diplomatic support for the ZIPA.

A Rhodesian military spokesman claims that 15,000 "Rhodesian African recruits" were being trained in Mozambique by "Soviet, Chinese, North Korean and Cuban" instructors and that new operational areas have been opened up by the "terrorists," now active less than one hundred kilometers from Salisbury.

All parties at the Geneva Conference agree to set March 1, 1978, as the date by which Zimbabwe should become independent. Among major problems still to be settled were the real content of "majority rule," the composition of an interim government, the personality of the Prime Minister of that Government, who would provide security during a transitional period and whether elections should be held before or after independence.

Ian Smith returns to the Geneva Conference.

1976, DECEMBER 14

Geneva Conference adjourns. Although Chairman Ivor Richard set January 17, 1977, as the date for its resumption, the Patriotic Front leaders doubted that it would be resumed. Ivor Richard announced he was undertaking a comprehensive tour of African countries involved in a Rhodesian settlement.

1976, DECEMBER 16

Joshua Nkomo and Robert Mugabe issue a joint statement accusing Britain of maneuvering to set up a "puppet government" in Zimbabwe.

1976, DECEMBER 30

Two tribal chiefs, Jeremiah Chirau of the Shona and Kayisa Ndiweni of the Matabele, resign from Ian Smith's Cabinet to form a new political movement, ZUPO (Zimbabwan United People's Organization).

1977, JANUARY 8

The ZIPA publishes five demands which Britain must satisfy if it wants to play a role in bringing about majority rule in Zimbabwe. Cease treating Smith as if he is a "respectable" politician; halt the supply of British mercenaries and arms to the Smith regime; stop the British media from slandering ZIPA and the people of Zimbabwe; stop maneuvering to set up a puppet regime and stop presenting British moves to set up such a regime as a contribution to establishing peace in Zimbabwe.

1977, JANUARY 12

Bishop Abel Muzorewa, countering a declaration by the leaders of the "front-line" states a few days earlier pledging full support for the Patriotic Front, demands a British-organized referendum for blacks to choose a national leader before the Geneva Conference resumes—theoretically on January 17.

1977, JANUARY 18

President Kenneth Kaunda accuses the British of conniving with the Smith regime to install Bishop Muzorewa as Prime Minister of a transitional government. According to Kaunda's version of the British plan five ministers would come from each party. "Smith will have his own five ministers, five from Bishop Muzorewa, five from ZUPO, and five white ministers who may come from other white political parties." The Geneva Conference was not reconvened on January 17 as Chairman Ivor Richard had planned and remained in a state of indefinite suspension.

1976, JANUARY 19

Eight Africans are hanged in Salibury for alleged "terrorist" offenses.

1976, JANUARY 19

The Patriotic Front announces the setting up of a ten-member committee to coordinate policies and strategies. It consists of the two leaders and four members each from ZAPU and ZANU.

1977, JANUARY 22

Jason Moyo, veteran ZAPU leader and one of the leading organizers of the ZIPA, is killed by a parcel bomb delivered to his home in Lusaka and sent from Botswana. Moyo had played a key role in setting up the Patriotic Front coordinating committee.

1977, JANUARY 30

The OAU, meeting in Lusaka, declares unequivocal support for the Patriotic Front. Secretary-General William Eteki Mboumoua urges all member states to give full support to the ZAPU-ZANU alliance.

1977, FEBRUARY 4

FRELIMO is transformed into a vanguard Marxist-Leninist political party at FRELIMO's Third Congress in Maputo. Till then FRELIMO had been constituted a movement.

1977, FEBRUARY 23

According to the *Times of Zambia* the Smith regime exerts pressures on Africans—especially in the tribal trust lands—to join ZUPO. These include withholding medical facilities to those who refuse.

1977, MARCH 7

The South African magazine *To The Point* summing up the result of two years' work of the Turnhalle Conference (so called because it was held in the Turnhalle Gymnasium of the Namibian capital of Windhoek) said that agreement had been reached between non-SWAPO nationalists on the following points. South Africa would grant Namibia's independence by December 31, 1978. There would be a black figure-head president and a white Prime Minister in a transitional government which would last for five years and in which South Africa would retain control of defense, foreign affairs, transport, finance and exchange, internal security and telecommunications and posts!

1977, MARCH 10

Radio Zaire announces that two days earlier several thousand "mercenaries in the pay of the Angolan Government" had invaded the country's southern province of Shaba (former Katanga). Cuba and the Soviet Union were accused of being involved. The Paris-based Congolese National Liberation Front (FLNC) claimed responsibility and said the aim was to overthrow President Mobutu's regime.

1977, MARCH 17

Radio Luanda quotes President Neto as stating that Angola played "no role in the troubles of Shaba province or of Zaire's other provinces." Later it became clear that the invaders were Katangan gendarmes to whom the Angolan Government had given trucks and fuel—but no arms—to facilitate their return to Zaire within the terms of the Neto-Mobutu Brazzaville Agreement (February 28, 1977).

1977, MARCH 21

The French-based fortnightly *Afrique-Asie* publishes sensational revelations by President Neto of a plan with the code name "Cobra 77" (or *Noël en Angola* in its French version) to invade Angola in September-October 1977. The forces would include those of the FNLA, of the FLEC (Front for the Liberation of the Cabinda Enclave), the ELP as well as white mercenaries. President Neto named some of those in charge of the first phase of the operation—the occupation of oil-rich Cabinda. Colonel Pierre Mutomo (nationality not given) trained at Saint Cyr in France and Fort Bragg. Colonel Mike Brown, American, Colonel Johnson, American, who commanded U.S. "Green Berets" in 1966-67 against Bolivian guerillas, Colonel William Thompson, of the U.S. 82nd Airborne Division who had 1,200 men at his disposal. "The plan envisages a large-scale operation with the use of air, naval and tank forces. . . ."

1977, APRIL 7

Mobutu requests aid from King Hassan of Morocco to repel the invaders of Shaba province.

1977, APRIL 10

The French Government in response to urgent requests from Zaire and Morocco delivers eleven transport aircraft and crews to airlift Moroccan troops and supplies to Zaire.

1977, APRIL 10

President Mobutu in a rally at Kinshasa declares that the original invasion could never have succeeded "without complicity at the highest level of the Zaire Army." The Soviet Union and Cuba strenuously deny any involvement.

1977, APRIL 16

The Smith regime calls up males in the 38 to 50 age group for military service (whites, Asians and coloreds).

"Maputo Declaration" adopted at an international conference in the Mozambican capital, attended by 92 U.N. member-states. The opening session was presided over by U.N. Secretary-General Kurt Waldheim. A program of action was adopted aimed at bringing majority rule to Zimbabwe and Namibia.

Attempted coup against the MPLA leadership in Luanda. Led by two members of the MPLA's Central Committee, Nito Alves and José van Dunem, the coup w˄s put down after eight hours. Among six leading MPLA officials executed by the rebels were Finance Minister, Saydi Mingas, and Antonio Garcia Neves, director of economic affairs at the Foreign Ministry. The coup leaders were eventually arrested and executed.

South Africa abandons its plan to set up an interim government in Namibia as recommended by the Turnhalle Conference—under South African pressure. (SWAPO boycotted the conference).

President Samora Machel reveals that 1,432 civilians have been killed in Mozambique by Rhodesian security forces between May 1976, and June 1977.

South Africa appoints Mr. Marthinus Steyn, a Supreme Court judge of the Orange Free State as Administrator-General of South West Africa. Steyn was a substitute for the previously-proposed interim government to rule the territory between the granting of independence and the holding of elections. The appointment was immediately denounced by SWAPO leader Sam Nujoma.

A meeting of "front-line" states' leaders in Lusaka, attended also by Joshua Nkomo, Robert Mugabe and Oliver Tambo of the ANC of South Africa, endorses the Patriotic Front's decision to have a single armed force, ZIPA, and urges that everything be done to strengthen ZIPA's military capacity.

Afrique-Asie (Paris) reveals that the Zaire government has granted one tenth of its territory (an area as great as almost the whole of Western

Germany) for missile testing and "space research." The huge territory runs along Zaire's frontiers with Tanzania and Zambia and about 250 kilometers from the Angolan frontier. Overall director of the project is a Dr. Kurt Debus, who directed the secret Peenemunde testing ground during World War II, developing the V1 and V2 guided missiles which wreaked havoc in England.

1977, SEPTEMBER 1

The British Foreign Secretary, Dr. Owen, and the U.S. Ambassador to the U.N., Andrew Young, present to Ian Smith in Salisbury another Anglo-American plan, designated by the British as a White Paper. It contained the most detailed proposals until then as to how power was to be transformed into that wielded by majority rule. Among the seven essential points are provisions for "The establishment by the British Government of a transitional administration, with the task of conducting the elections for an independent government" and "A United Nations presence, including a United Nations force, during the transition period."

1977, SEPTEMBER 2

South Africa incorporates Walvis Bay, Namibia's only commercial and fishing port, into Cape Province, declaring that it will remain South African even after independence. Walvis Bay adjoins the richest uranium fields in South West Africa. All U.N. and OAU resolutions relating to Namibian independence refer to it as an integral part of Namibian territory.

1977, SEPTEMBER 12

Steven Biko, outstanding 30-year-old black leader, dies of "extensive brain damage and severe bruising" in a Pretoria prison cell. His death provokes heated protests inside South Africa and abroad. It was widely accepted that he had been beaten to death.

1977, SEPTEMBER 23

Meeting in Maputo, the leaders of the "front-line" countries declare that the Anglo-American plan of September 1 can be taken as "a basis for further negotiations." But Patriotic Front leaders demand the dismantling of the Rhodesian army and police and object to wide powers being given to the British Commissioner, as envisaged in the plan.

1977, SEPTEMBER 25

Secret talks between President Kaunda and Ian Smith in Lusaka.

1977, SEPTEMBER 26

Joashua Nkomo and Robert Mugabe announce conditional acceptance of the Anglo-American plan but state that armed struggle will continue until "final victory."

1977, OCTOBER 19
South African Government arrests seventy leading Africans, bans eighteen black organizations, closes down the two main African newspapers and places a number of whites, including Donald Wood, editor of the East London (South African) *Daily Despatch,* under restricted residence.

1977, OCTOBER 21
United States withdraws its ambassador from South Africa for "consultations" following the crackdown on black leaders and their organizations.

1977, OCTOBER 27
President Kaunda reveals that in his secret talks with Ian Smith, the Rhodesian Prime Minister has asked for talks with Joshua Nkomo, who was also in Lusaka at the time, but Nkomo had refused.

1977, NOVEMBER 5
The U.N. Security Council unanimously imposes mandatory sanctions on the supply of arms to South Africa. A seven-point resolution expresses the Council's view that the acquisition of arms and related material by South Africa "constitutes a threat to the maintenance of international peace and security." Three proposals later presented to apply a trade ban on all exports to South Africa were successively vetoed by the three western permanent members of the Security Council, the U.S.A., Britain and France, each time supported by the two other non-permanent western members, Canada and West Germany.

1977, NOVEMBER 10
Field Marshal Lord Carver, Britain's Resident-Designate Commissioner to Zimbabwe, returns to London after a futile eight-day visit to Rhodesia and Zambia in an attempt to get all-round support for the Anglo-American plan.

1977, NOVEMBER 24
Ian Smith announces that the Rhodesian Government accepts the principle of majority rule based on "one man, one vote" and that he would start negotiations with the three nationalist leaders, Bishop Muzorewa, Reverend Ndabaningi Sithole and the head of ZUPO, Chief Jeremiah Chirau for talks aimed at an internal settlement. Joshua Nkomo and Robert Mugabe could also take part, the Prime Minister said, on condition that they renounce "terrorism."

1977, NOVEMBER 25

A spokesman for the Patriotic Front in Lusaka warns the internal nationalist leaders that they would become "as much a target as the enemy" if they cooperated in setting up what would be a puppet government. A spokesman for the "front-line" states states that any proposal which excluded the Patriotic Front from elections was unacceptable.

1977, NOVEMBER 29

Bishop Muzorewa appeals to guerillas to return home from their bush training camps and bases and from neighboring states because the war's objectives had been attained. But he rejected ZUPO taking part in the talks proposed by Ian Smith, as its leaders represented Smith's ruling Rhodesian Front.

1977, DECEMBER 3

A leading South African economist states that South Africa is listed by experts in the "highest moderate risk" category (exceeded only by Indonesia) for investors. Within three years it will move into the "prohibitive risk" category, and within seven years to the "highest prohibitive risk" of all countries.

1977, DECEMBER 6

President Kaunda disassociates himself from the Anglo-American peace plan. Pointing out that all peace initiatives were a product of the Patriotic Front's guerilla war, he insisted that the focus must first be on independence "that is the transfer of power to the majority under the leadership of the Patriotic Front."

1977, DECEMBER 9

Ian Smith opens talks with Muzorewa, Sithole and Chirau. A number of issues immediately emerge. The value of one man and one vote. Smith wants the white vote weighted so that the composition of a 127-seat assembly would be 84 black and 45 white members, enough for the whites to block any constitutional amendments. Smith wants segregated electorates in which "whites only" would stand in white constituencies and "blacks only" in black constituencies. The Africans wanted commando units such as the Selous Scouts and the Special Air Service disbanded before elections.

1977, DECEMBER 10

Security Council votes unanimously to set up a watchdog committee to ensure strict adherence to the mandatory arms embargo against South Africa.

1977, DECEMBER 11
Angola's MPLA transforms itself into the Angola Workers' Party, following a three-day congress. Agostinho Neto is elected president of the new Marxist-Leninist party.

1977, DECEMBER 16
The U.N. General Assembly votes 113 to 0, with ten abstentions, to impose an oil embargo on South Africa. The abstentions included the five western members of the Security Council as well as Belgium, Italy, Luxembourg, Israel and Iran.

1977, DECEMBER 19
Ivor Richard, British ambassador to the U.N., claims there are only three obstacles to Namibia's independence, the size of the South African force to remain during transition, where they should be located, and the size of their presence. (In subsequent negotiations with the "contact group" Sam Nujoma agreed to leave the question of the size of a U.N. force to Secretary General Kurt Waldheim, but suggested a force of 5,000 troops with an administrative force of 1,000. South Africa wanted to limit the total to 2,000.) The three days of talks were inconclusive but the patriotic front leaders conceded a U.N. role in a final settlement and Owen and Young agreed that no agreement was possible without a "substantial role" for the Patriotic Front.

1977, DECEMBER 24
The Mozambican People's National Assembly, chosen through an electoral process which started on September 25 with the election of village assemblies, then district and provincial assemblies by December 4, holds its first session in Maputo. It unanimously adopted a resolution confirming the People's Assembly as the country's supreme organ of power.

1977, DECEMBER 28
The South African appointed Administrator-General for South West Africa, Marthinus Steyn, asserts that whether the U.N., the Western Powers and SWAPO agreed or not, elections would be held under his authority and Namibia would obtain independence by the end of 1978. (The Western powers in this case were the so-called "Contact Group" comprised of the five western powers in the Security Council who had taken the initiative of trying to mediate a settlement with Pretoria on the issue of Namibia's independence.)

1978, JANUARY 30
Meeting at Malta between British Foreign Secretary David Owen and the U.S. Ambassador to the U.N., Andrew Young, and the two leaders of the

Patriotic Front, Joshua Nkomo and Robert Mugabe in an effort to salvage something of the Owen-Young, Anglo-American plan for Zimbabwan independence under one-man, one-vote, majority rule.

1978, FEBRUARY 13

Ian Smith, Muzorewa, Sithole and Chirau reach an eight-point agreement on broad constitutional outlines for majority rule in Zimbabwe. The "internal settlement" is denounced by the Patriotic Front leadership, treated with "reserve" by British Foreign Secretary Owen and skepticism by U.S. ambassador to the U.N., Andrew Young who commented that it "could lead to civil war similiar to that in Angola."

1978, MARCH 15

The "internal settlement" for Zimbabwe is rejected as "illegal and unacceptable" by the U.N. Security Council in a 10 to 0 vote with the five western members abstaining.

Part I

Angola and After

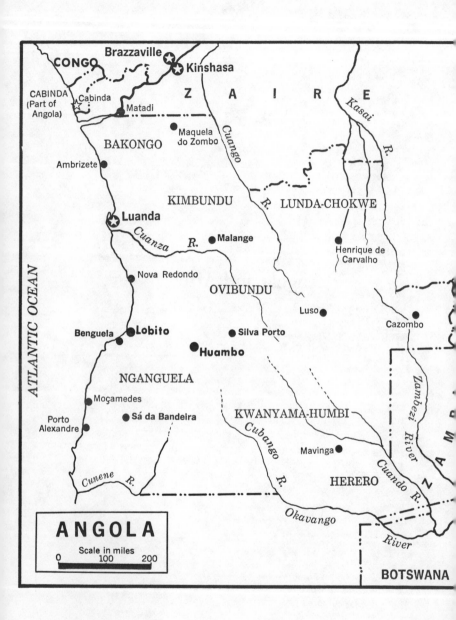

I How It Started

How does a liberation struggle get off the ground these days when the most lethal weapons in the hands of the liberators are, at first, jungle knives, clubs, and stones? That was the question I put to Mendes de Carvalho, a tiny, merry black with twinkling, deep-set eyes in a face which ended in a pointed beard who, from his prison cell—and through a misunderstanding—had sparked off the first armed action in Angola. The date, February 4, 1961, is now celebrated as the start of Angola's armed struggle for independence from the Portuguese.

At the time that I met him, he started to answer my question by explaining that in the late 1950s there was rising discontent in all the Portuguese colonies, because the end of World War II, which had brought such great changes elsewhere in the world, promised nothing for those under Portuguese rule.

> When we heard that Britain, France, Holland, and Belgium were preparing to give independence to their colonies—or that the colonized people were preparing to seize their independence—we said: "Why not us?" But how should we prepare our people for this? It was a question that many of us discussed. . . .

Not only in Luanda, but in Lisbon as well, a brilliant group of students from Portuguese Guinea, Mozambique, and Angola debated the same problem. Centered around Amilcar Cabral from Guinea, they included Agostinho Neto and Mario de Andrade from Angola and, later, Marcelino dos Santos from Mozambique. All had one common idea—to rid their peoples of 500 years of Portuguese rule. In the Portuguese colonies there were special problems, as Mendes de Carvalho explained:

> They were different from those of other European countries. The old "divide and rule" device had been developed in a more subtle fashion. A white was considered superior to a mulatto, a mulatto superior to a black; and even blacks were divided into two categories, *assimilados*, who had to renounce their Africanism to get a minimum of education and escape what was virtually slave status, and inferior ordinary blacks—natives. This system even split families down the middle. A younger brother was oppressed by his older *assimilado* brother. In some areas the *assimilados* had to live separated by a few

3

hundred meters from the "native quarters" to prove they had acquired "civilized status." Under such conditions how could we develop the sense of unity vital for a national struggle? Such a movement had to be linked with the masses, but the people, from bitter experience, were highly suspicious of anyone trying to organize them.

We started forming sporting and cultural movements to have some common meeting ground. In the sense that the real aims were secret, these were clandestine movements. The most successful from an organizational and propaganda viewpoint was the Movement of Angolan Nurses.

At the period he was describing, Mendes de Carvalho, like Samora Machel, subsequently president of FRELIMO and then of Mozambique, was a male nurse. The importance of male nurses as a transmission belt for the national liberation struggles in Angola and Mozambique seems to have escaped the Portuguese authorities. Nursing was one profession to which male *assimilados* had relatively easy access and it was a well-paid one. With Aghostino Neto—in between prison terms—a practicing doctor in Luanda, it had other advantages, as Mendes de Carvalho pointed out:

There were other organizations of intellectuals who were more politically active, but because of this they were under PIDE [Portuguese Gestapo] surveillance. It was very difficult for them to move about. But in each administrative zone, province, and district, the local Portuguese administrator had the right to a nurse to look after his family. The same thing at every military post. Local Portuguese settlers and traders also came to the nurses with their health and family problems. Male nurses had freedom, and even a certain priority, of travel throughout the country. So it was decided to organize them for the liberation struggle.

At first, fairly innocuous circulars were sent out to the "Nurses Network" asking for financial contributions to aid "patriotic organizations." Those who responded favorably got a second circular of a more political nature—suggesting they organize politically. Within a short time nurses in Luanda and other urban areas were starting to distribute political literature. The central theme was independence.

A big boost in the early stages of organization was the conference of independent African states in the Ghanaian capital, Accra, in April, 1958. Mendes de Carvalho, as a member of the clandestine Angolan delegation, stopped off at Kinshasa and Brazzaville on the way to organize Angolan exiles in those capitals. The Accra conference was the first of its kind. One of the resolutions adopted called on the colonial powers "to set definite dates for granting independence to their African colonies"; another denounced all forms of racial discrimination. This was a propaganda bonanza and the "Nurses' Network" worked overtime to get the good news to their rapidly growing circle of activists. Since the Portuguese had never bothered to learn the local language, a nurse could spread the word to a provisional governor's staff while he dealt with the great man's ingrown toenails or massaged his back. A mass propaganda campaign started on the basis of the Accra decisions to promote the idea that, first, Angolans had the right to independence, and second, they had good friends all over Africa—including governments—who felt the same way. The PIDE began to take notice.

> Their agents started to follow some of us. On March 29, 1959, we sent a comrade to Kinshasa with propaganda material. He collected other material there but was arrested by PIDE agents at Luanda airport when he returned four days later. A few days later I and several other comrades were arrested. Then there were wholesale arrests of all persons suspected of any contact with us. It was tough, but on the other hand it was a major breakthrough.
> The arrests caused indignation throughout Angola. The PIDE as usual had struck out blindly. The divisions between blacks and whites, mulattos and *assimilados* were much reduced because we were all hit. Progressives all over Europe started protesting the arrests. Portugal started to get worried about the effect on its international image.

The March arrests were followed by another wave in July; the three lists of names published bear out Mendes de Carvalho's remarks about all sections of the population being hit. Although Dr. Neto was not on the published lists, he was arrested in June, 1960, in his Luanda consulting room, and after three months in prison, was shipped off to the Cape Verde Islands. Villagers from Neto's home village of Bengo and the neighboring one of Icolo, who went to the district center of Catete to protest the arrests, were fired on by Portuguese troops. Thirty were killed and about two hundred wounded out of a crowd of about one thousand. The following day troops were dispatched to the two villages where they killed or arrested everyone they could lay hands on, then burned down the villages. Mendes de Carvalho continued his account:

> Members of our group were finally sentenced in December, 1960. As I was held to be the chief culprit, I was sentenced to thirteen years, the others getting from one to six years. When the sentences were announced, the comrades outside stepped up their political work—in Angola as well as in Lisbon. Then came the *Santa Maria* incident, which excited all our activists.[1] After all the arrests and terrible repression, our militants wanted action. I got word that plans were being made to attack the prison and the PIDE headquarters, but I did not know the date.

Among those who planned the attack was Antonio Lourenco, a tall, gaunt man with a polished dome of a head when I met him fifteen years later. Together with three other survivors of the attacking force—still banded together in what is known as the February Fourth Group—Antonio Lourenco explained what happened:

> From 1958 onward our MPLA group started clandestine struggle, editing and distributing pamphlets, and mobilizing the masses. By 1960, Agostinho Neto had returned, and this inspired us, and our comrades inside the prison—they represented the majority of our activists by that time. But with the arrest of Neto after a few months, and the escalating repression, our group decided that no advance could be made through political struggle alone. We had to go over to armed struggle. We started to gather the most determined among the militants to carry out an armed coup. We originally planned it for January 28, 1961.

From other sources it is clear that the fixing of the date was influenced by the arrival in Luanda of a large number of journalists, who speculated that the *Santa Maria* was heading that way. From the time Captain Galvao and his men had seized the liner on January 23, they had played hide-and-seek with the navies of the world. On January 25, however, a U.S. Navy plane claimed to have spotted the vessel on a southerly course about one-third of the way across the Atlantic from the Caribbean, where the seizure had taken place, heading toward Angola. Hence the concentration of journalists in Luanda. The publicity value of Captain Galvao's coup was not lost on those planning one of a different nature in Luanda. Eventually the U.S. Navy intervened and "persuaded" Galvao to turn about and head for Recife in Brazil. The timing of the attack on the prison thus lost its urgency, and perfection of preparations became more important, as Antonio Lourenco explained:

> Altogether we were 3,128 men pledged to launch the attack. Our method was to buy the same sort of trousers, shirts, and shoes so it would be easy to recognize friends from foes. But we didn't have enough money left over for everyone to spend twenty-five *escudos* (roughly one U.S. dollar) for a machete. Those who could, bought them; others armed themselves with axes, clubs, and even stones.
>
> Once we had the arms, we started training in the offensive and defensive use of machetes, axes, etc. We went on foot and in small groups to Cacuaco, twenty-two kilometers from Luanda, and trained there for eight days. On February 3, we heard some disturbing reports and decided our attack must be made the following day—so we returned to Luanda.

As to the origin of the disturbing reports, Mendes de Carvalho filled in the details. He had managed to set up communications with the outside world through the improbable combination of a sympathetic prison guard and a progressive priest. Such personalities, relatively rare but impressively courageous, proved to be a constant throughout the national liberation struggles in the Portuguese colonies. It explains why there are a sprinkling of Portuguese, or white Angolans, among the officers and ranks of the FAPLA, the military wing of the MPLA—often described as Cubans by Western journalists. De Carvalho described how the date for the attack was finally fixed:

> On February 3, I managed to get a message out through the progressive priest, Neves Bendinha, to my younger brother asking him to come to the prison because I had a document I wanted to send to Lisbon. My brother misunderstood the message and thought that I was to be sent to Lisbon. He informed my wife and family—and other comrades. Everybody started to get excited. They thought we were all to be transferred to Lisbon, which could be like a death sentence. Our wives and families started preparing suitcases with food and clothes.

The PIDE couldn't understand what was going on. The whole town was in a state of confusion. Most of the taxis had been requisitioned by families and friends rushing to consult each other and decide what to do. The prison guards sent for me to ask what it was all about. I couldn't explain because I didn't know myself.

In the meantime the February Fourth Group had contacted their leader, Comandante Imperial Santana, who assigned specific targets to the various units—the São Paulo prison, where Mendes de Carvalho and the others were being held, the PIDE headquarters, military barracks, naval facilities, mail and telegraph and radio stations, etc. Comandante Paiva was charged with firing a rocket at midnight to signal the start of the attack. He fired it bang on midnight.

Our main aim was to free the political prisoners. After our first attack the guards fled—but they took the keys of the cells with them! We had no way of opening the doors. Our axes and machetes were useless to deal with the doors and iron grilles. The fiercest fighting was at the prison and the PIDE headquarters. It continued till about 5 A.M., by which time seven Portuguese guards had been killed. At 6 A.M., they brought up artillery and armored cars and our forces withdrew. We did not have a single wounded man. Although the situation was very tense and the Portuguese made a big display of heavy weapons our morale was high and we were determined to press on. It was in this spirit that we attacked again on February 11. But this time the PIDE and the armed forces were well prepared. We had the troops ahead of us and the PIDE behind, so we had lots of dead and wounded men.

By that time the authorities knew the rumor that the political prisoners were to be sent to Lisbon had caused the attack. In fact an uprising would have taken place anyway, but the rumor fixed the date. Mendes de Carvalho was accused of having given the signal. The only witness to the harmless message sent to his brother had been the sympathetic guard who was present when the priest telephoned. Unfortunately he had been killed in the attack. De Carvalho was further accused of having given instructions to kill the only witness to his story. He was threatened with public execution. But after days of torture and interrogation by the PIDE and prison police he and the other political prisoners were sent back to their prison cells to serve out their sentences which, for Mendes de Carvalho, included eight years in the notorious Tarrafal "death camp" in the Cape Verde Islands. No prisoners were released and the Portuguese started a massive and savage manhunt:

> A terrible wave of repression started all over the country. The Portuguese changed their tactics. Before, they arrested people and threw them into prison. Now they tortured and killed them. There were indiscriminate killings all over the country, one effect of which was to further forge national unity. Another effect was to convince the Angolan people that the only solution was generalized armed struggle. It was this spirit that led to the formation of the FAPLA [Angolan Peoples' Liberation Armed Forces] in February, 1962.

The ferocity of the Portuguese repression in 1961-62, which sent hundreds of thousands of Angolans fleeing into the Belgian Congo (later Zaire), was not only the result of the Luanda uprising. Perhaps it was inevitable anyway—the classical reaction of a colonial power when the colonized take up arms. But a tragic and appallingly convenient pretext was offered by the indiscriminate massacre of Portuguese settlers and their families, which started in the northern areas of Angola on March 15, 1961. (One of the main centers of these massacres was Maquela do Zombo, later to make world headlines as the scene of the execution of fourteen British mercenaries on the orders of their commander, "Colonel" Callan, in early February, 1976.)

The difference between the February Fourth uprising with its avowed aim of freeing political prisoners, and the March Fifteenth uprisings—both in that fateful year of 1961—is fundamental to an understanding of much that happened later in the Angolan independence struggle. One was politically motivated, the other was racist with tribalist overtones. Among the victims were many mulattos, *assimilados*, and Angolan women married to Portuguese, together with their children. A puzzling and tragic feature, from which Angola still suffers today, was the extermination by both the Portuguese and those that took part in the March Fifteenth uprising, of any Angolan who could read and write. On the part of the Portuguese such an act could be explained by their colonialist, racist logic. The mulattos and *assimilados* had used their privileged status to acquire modern ideas about indepen-

9

dence and even revolution! Certainly only a tiny minority had been infected by such dangerous ideas, but better to strike at many to stamp out the few! But why Angolans should strike down compatriots because they were literate was a more complex question. The incidents are well documented by many sources, including Western missionaries. It is freely testified to by survivors in the northern regions today and is a subject to which this author paid much attention in his travels in those areas.

Among the nationalist movements which proliferated in Angola in the mid-1950s, was UPNA (Union of the Peoples of North Angola) founded in July, 1956, by Barros Necaca and José Eduardo Pinnock. This movement had the very limited and separatist aim of restoring the ancient Kongo kingdom in the northwestern part of Angola, based on the Bakongo and Zombo tribes, with San Salvador as its capital. The claim, eloquently promoted at the U.S. State Department and UN headquarters by Necaca's Kinshasa-based nephew, Holden Roberto, was that the Kongo kingdom had been unjustly lumped together with the rest of Angola at the Congress of Berlin (1884-85) when the imperialist powers arbitrarily carved up Africa among them. Barros Necaca claimed he was a direct heir to the San Salvador throne. A formal plea to the UN Secretary-General in June, 1956, demanded a change in the name and status of the area as "an ex-independent territory having no treaty with Portugal."[2]

Thanks to the discreet advice of a U.S. State Department official that it could be difficult to stimulate much support for a revived Kongo kingdom, a view which was much more vigorously expressed when the subject was raised at the 1958 Accra conference, the idea was—at least temporarily—shelved. Shortly after the Accra conference, UPNA was dissolved in favor of UPA (Union of the Peoples of Angola) with Holden Roberto as its effective head. But although the change of name was intended to give the movement an all-Angolan flavor, it did not mean any change of tribalist and secessionist ideas, as subsequent events were to prove. Holden Roberto, at the time UPA was formed, had spent less than five of his thirty-seven years in Angola—the first year after his birth in San Salvador, three years as a pupil at a missionary primary school, and brief visits in 1940, 1951, and 1956. UPA had neither program nor ideology apart from an indiscriminate hatred for all things Portuguese. The movement first attract-

10

1961, when tribal bands armed with machetes and cutlasses simultaneously attacked homes and farmsteads, hacking to pieces men, women, and children. The first victims were whites but soon included African wives of Portuguese and their children, whatever their color. The killings quickly spread to mulattos, *assimilados*, and anyone who was literate. Five weeks after the attacks started, the official Portuguese press service, Lusitania Agency, announced that 267 persons, "mainly Europeans," had been killed and seventy-two were missing. Non-Europeans obviously did not count!

Paratroops and commandos were rushed to the spot; troop reinforcements were sent from Portugal and a wholesale and barbarous extermination of African Angolans started. Visiting the area fifteen years later, I found the horrors of those years, especially 1961-62, still fresh in people's minds. An oft-quoted figure is that of 20,000 Africans killed. According to UN statistics some 600,000 fled the country, most of them going to Zaire.

Why did the insurgents turn against the mulattos, the *assimilados*, and the literate? As part of the preparation for the March Fifteenth uprising, the UPA had sent so-called "prophets" into the northern areas. Among other tasks they had to persuade UPA followers that by wearing certain charms and keeping one's face toward the enemy, the latter's bullets would dissolve into water. Thus no reason to be afraid of the enemy's monopoly of firearms! A variant of this same myth was used three years later by warriors of Pierre Mulele, a follower of the murdered Congolese leader Patrice Lumumba, in the Simba uprising against Moïse Tshombe. They stormed into battle with spears and the war cry: "Mai Mulele! Mai Mulele!" (Water of Mulele) and were mowed down by the hundreds as the bullets of Tshombe's white mercenaries failed to dissolve into water. Portuguese journalists reporting on the March Fifteenth uprising in northern Angola described the attackers with "scarlet-painted faces . . . as if demon-possessed, dancing and singing, shouting that the bullets of the whites do not kill. . . ."

MPLA members and sympathizers with more experienced views of the realities of warfare tried to dissuade the UPA followers from believing such rubbish. In any case they were against the indiscriminate slaughter of whites. Point Three of the MPLA's

Minimum Program, adopted when the movement was founded, had stated among its aims:

> To unite all political parties, all people's organizations, all the armed forces, all eminent personalities in the country, all religious organizations, all minorities, all ethnic groups, all social strata, and all Angolans, irrespective of political tendencies, economic circumstances, race, sex, age, and all Angolans living abroad.

When the UPA combatants were decimated by Portuguese bullets, the word was passed around that this was because MPLA skepticism had neutralized the protective spells. So the UPA machetes were turned against those who should have been their brothers-in-arms, leaving irreparable scars despite many initiatives by the MPLA and friendly African leaders to heal them.

Working in a government hospital in San Salvador at that time was Manuel Quarte, who later became a famous guerilla leader under the name of Comandante "Punza." At the time of the uprising he was part of the "Nurses' Network." When I met him, he was Commissioner of Uije city, a big, cheerful *assimilado* with powerful shoulders and a radiant smile. After the February Fourth uprising and the subsequent manhunt, he headed a group fleeing from Luanda, attempting to escape across the frontier into the Congo. They ran into a group of UPA combatants who were killing "whites, mulattos, *assimilados*, even their own people who had become Catholics. . . ." "Punza" explained that he escaped only because there were UPA people who disobeyed the official line and hid him. Another former member of the "Nurses' Network," Luis Felipe, in charge of refugee affairs at Uije when I met him, told of similar incidents. He was one of those who had done his best to debunk the idea of bulletproof spells and had narrowly escaped with his life.

A year after the March Fifteenth massacre, the UPA fused with another northern movement, the PDA (Angolan Democratic Party) which had been formerly known as the Aliazo (Alliance of the Zombo People) to form the FNLA (Angolan National Liberation Front). Nine days later the GRAE (Revolutionary Government of Angola in Exile) was set up in Kinshasa with Holden Roberto as its president. The next move was to form ELNA (Angolan National Liberation Army) as opposed to the FAPLA.

Whatever else had been achieved at the cost of a staggering loss of Angolan lives, the February Fourth and March Fifteenth uprisings marked a historic point of no return in the fight for national liberation. The armed struggle was well and truly engaged. But the fact that it had been launched by two movements—later to be joined by a third—with widely differing aims and concepts, was to have tragic consequences.

II Comandante Margoso's Story

Comandante Margoso Wafuakula is about as tough-looking a guerilla as I have ever come across. That includes some very tough ones—from the veterans of Vietnam and Laos to Palestinians along the Lebanon-Israel border, and from other wars in between. Short and stocky, with a dark-brown leathery face dominated by a broad, hooked nose that looks as if it had been smashed into his head, Margoso wears a permanent ironical, skeptical sort of expression, and it took some persuasion, including repeated perusal of my credentials, to start him talking. But it was worth the effort. His experiences explain much of the otherwise inexplicable in the Angolan liberation struggle. I met him in March, and again in July, 1976, in Holden Roberto's former stronghold of Carmona (now Uije, capital of the province of the same name). I knew that he had taken part in both the February Fourth and March Fifteenth actions; that he had subsequently been one of Holden Roberto's most efficient commanders but had later led a revolt against the FNLA leadership and had become one of the most valued MPLA commanders. How did it all come about?

Immediately after the February Fourth assault on the prison, my brother was killed. We had both taken part. We had played together in the Bravo football club, one of the few places where whites and mulattos got on well together. After they killed my brother, the PIDE turned their attentions to me. I was warned by friends to get out of Luanda. I went first to my father's home at Caxito, 40 kilometers to the north. A week later the PIDE started snooping around and I left for Nambuangongo, seventy-five miles northeast of Luanda where my mother's family lived. I didn't know that it was a stronghold of the UPA, nor did I know very much about the politics of the North. At the beginning of March people started coming from San Salvador and Zaire, speaking Kikongo [one of several names used to describe the language of the Bakongo people who lived on both sides of the Angola-Zaire frontier—W.B.]. They were from the UPA and started by demanding 250 *escudos* per head as "contributions to the patriotic independence struggle." They were fiercely hostile to the MPLA and I could not reveal that I was an MPLA supporter. On March 15, everything exploded. Whites, for the UPA, meant colonialists and colonialists meant whites. In our area they were all killed. Even women and children. This was absolutely contrary to what we had been taught by the MPLA. As I was one of the few who had had some guerilla training, I was elected to command a Youth Group of 400 young people to defend the area from Portuguese reprisals.

We fought well against the Portuguese forces sent to repress the uprising. For the first six months none of their troops dared enter the Nambuangongo-Dembos forest area. My father was a headman there and at the end of that first six months when the Portuguese started to make some headway, he and some other headmen got together and decided that I should be sent to Zaire to bring back arms and equipment for the MPLA forces. They had confidence in my revolutionary experience and the results of the military activities of our Youth Group, which by then was known to be MPLA. Local people contributed 50,000 *escudos* to buy arms. In mid-August, 1961, with some other comrades, I set out on foot, reaching the Zaire frontier twelve days later. We got as far as Songololo—twelve miles inside Zaire—when we were arrested by the Congolese police. After a week in prison we were escorted to the UPA headquarters in Kinshasa. There we were very relieved to meet "Johnny" Eduardo Pinnock—a comrade-in-arms we thought—fighting like us against the Portuguese colonialists. But he cursed us, confiscated our 50,000 *escudos*, and had some of his men beat us up.

We quickly found that even to mention MPLA in Kinshasa was to risk being killed. After being held under close surveillance for two months—we could not walk a hundred yards from the barracks without being followed—Pinnock asked us if we really wanted to fight the Portuguese. Of course we did. On October 26, twenty-two of us were sent to Tunisia and after that to Rome, where we stayed one week. Holden Roberto and Jonas Savimbi were also there. Then we were sent back to Tunisia and received by officials from the Ministry of the Interior, who looked after us for another week. After that we went to the frontier area near Algeria, carrying out guerilla activities and military and political training.

It is necessary to interrupt this account of some unwritten history to explain matters of which Comandante Margoso and some other MPLA cadres are probably unaware even today. They form part of the extremely complex background to the Angolan revolution and related movements. Margoso, for instance, had no inkling as to why his group was sent to Rome for a week. In fact they were there to "prove" that Holden Roberto and the UPA were yearning for armed struggle and the MPLA was not! They were there to prove a point being pushed—erroneously in the view of many specialists on the subject—by the Martinique-born revolutionary theoretician, Frantz Fanon, that if general conditions existed for armed struggle, the main thing was to get it started. According to this theory, even without political preparations the masses would participate once the first shots were fired.

Fanon, for reasons which may be valid, was critical of orthodox Marxists in his native Martinique, whom he accused of following the then-current French Communist Party line of applying brakes to national liberation movements in the French colonies because such activities could prejudice the chances of the

15

party being elected to state power. Once that happened—or so the argument was said to run—the colonial question would be settled by constitutional means!

Armed struggle in Algeria was reaching its climax at the time of the February-March 1961 uprisings in Angola. Fanon, then in Algeria, saw the possibility of opening up a second front to take some of the heat off the Algerian FLN. He fervently believed that the main revolutionary force in a colonial country like Angola was the peasantry, but doubted that the MPLA leaders whom he met in Algeria agreed. According to some of his intimates at that period, he transferred his suspicions of Marxist intellectuals in Martinique to the MPLA intellectuals he met in Algeria and elsewhere, including the Marxist leader of the MPLA at that time, Viriato da Cruz. Because of this, he jumped to the conclusion that Holden Roberto—apparently skillful at grasping what others wanted to hear and giving them satisfaction if this was to his advantage—shared his views and was the only Angolan leader capable of waging armed struggle. The presence of Margoso and his group was the living proof!

At the Rome meeting, faced with opposing views, Fanon proposed that Algeria should also provide training facilities for MPLA guerillas. Amilcar Cabral, one of the founders of the MPLA, was mandated to go to Angola and return with the first group of such trainees. He came back empty-handed because the MPLA felt that the best training ground was under combat conditions on Angolan soil. For Fanon, however, this was one more proof that the MPLA was only a group of intellectuals without roots among the people or any stomach for armed struggle. In those days Fanon's opinions carried much weight with the leadership of the Algerian NLF, especially with Ben Bella.

After the cease-fire in Algeria in March, 1962, Margoso was sent first to Tunisia for a short course in military topography, following which he was sent back to Kinshasa:

> There I met Holden Roberto again and he explained that the FNLA was now going to make an alliance with the MPLA. He had asked the Zaire president, Kasavubu, for a military training base, and this had been granted at Kinkuzu. On August 14, 1962, I was sent to this base, in barren country about twelve kilometers from the Zaire river. We had no uniforms, no weapons, and no conditions for training. We made a start by appealing to young Angolans in Zaire territory to

16

come to Kinkuzu and be trained for the national liberation struggle. Between August and December, 1962, about 3,000 young people were trained by us as well as was possible without any military equipment. When training was finished these young people were eager to get into action against the Portuguese. I told Holden Roberto: "These are good young fighters, ready to go into the maquis—but they have no equipment."

Holden Roberto contacted the Algerians who sent a batch of old weapons used in their own struggle. We divided them up, split up our forces into units, each unit under one of the commanders who had been trained in Algeria, and took up positions on the Angolan side of the frontier, gradually pushing south from there. We came down into the Dembos forest area again but the atmosphere there was quite different from when I had left. Most of those who were UPA before had now joined the MPLA. I tried to keep my forces away from theirs and only attack the Portuguese. While I never spoke out against the MPLA at political meetings, I could also not display my real feelings because of my previous experiences with Holden Roberto, Pinnock, and some of the other leaders. We settled down to guerilla warfare, ambushing enemy convoys. One of our best successes was blowing up an enemy supply train in April, 1964. But we never received supplies or anything else from Holden Roberto and by mid-1965 we were running desperately short of equipment while the Portuguese were pressing us very heavily. I asked to go back to Zaire to get fresh supplies. This was agreed. I was very angry when I met Holden Roberto and told him frankly of our difficulties due to total lack of support from the base. He promised he would raise some heavier equipment and told me to go to the Kinkuzu headquarters and wait.

While I was sitting on my backside at Kinkuzu, a delegation arrived from the maquis asking for uniforms and weapons. Roberto sent them also to Kinkuzu, where we exchanged experiences.

The exchanges between Margoso, a man of blunt tongue and peppery temper, and Holden Roberto were apparently brutally frank. But things had developed favorably on the international front for Roberto. For a while, President Ben Bella, who had excellent personal relations with Mario de Andrade, one of the founder members of the MPLA, and its representative in Algiers, recognized both the MPLA and the FNLA as legitimate Angolan national liberation movements. Later when Zaire recognized only the FNLA-UPA, Ben Bella, intent on being on the winning side in his African policies, decided to give unconditional support to

Holden Roberto. President Ahmed Sékou Touré of Guinea went even further and took Holden Roberto and the GRAE under his personal sponsorship, something he was to regret bitterly years later. The upshot was that in July, 1963, GRAE was recognized by the Liberation Committee of the newly formed Organization of African Unity (OAU) as the sole Angolan independence movement. A major victory for Holden Roberto and a major defeat for the MPLA!

Once Holden Roberto had secured the recognition of the GRAE by the OAU, he seriously set about the attempted extermination of the MPLA and any waverers within the FNLA who opposed this new policy. Comandante Margoso makes this clear in the next part of his account:

While we were waiting, with everyone terribly demoralized, at the Kinkuzu base, demanding arms to get into action against the Portuguese, Holden Roberto persuaded Mobutu to get weapons from Tunisia. Tunisia sent some, but Mobutu grabbed them all for his own war against Mulele. Eventually we scraped together some weapons. I was nominated commander of the First Military Region [which covered the whole of the area between Luanda and the Zaire frontier, the only place where FNLA forces had any activity—W.B.] and we crossed the frontier again on December 18, 1966. We got to the Ambriz river on December 24, but it was in flood and we couldn't cross it. We had to stay there for twenty-four days until the waters receded—eating grass when we ran out of food. Finally we got across and pushed south again. When we got to a point north of the Dembos—Nambuangongo area, we found that all the fighting was between MPLA and FNLA forces, and local FNLA commanders told me their instructions were to concentrate all efforts on wiping out the FAPLA.

There it was. Instead of fighting the common enemy, Angolans were killing Angolans. Because of this constant fighting, I could not push through to where I was supposed to set up my headquarters without clashing with the MPLA. Eventually I set up my operational base in the Bulapipa forest in Uije province.

Once we got the base organized, local FNLA commanders started sending me MPLA prisoners to be executed. I was the one who had to decide which were to be executed. My reply was the only possible one: "These men are MPLA. Therefore they are Angolans. You ask me to kill them? No! Bring me Portuguese—I will kill them. Not Angolans."

The years dragged on and we did little against the Portuguese. But the prisoners sent to be executed accumulated until I had over 400 of them. By all I had seen, I knew that it was only the MPLA who ·were fighting the Portuguese colonialists. So I armed the 400 prisoners and they turned out to be my best fighters. But there was a "trusty" of Holden Roberto, Pedro Vida, responsible for the Nova Caipemba area[also in Uije province centered about fifty kilometers northwest of the provincial capital—W.B.], who sent a letter back to Holden Roberto to the effect that not only was I refusing to execute MPLA prisoners, but I was using them on the battlefield. By then they were really my best shock troops, many of them with fourth-grade education. I realized that they were not only needed on the battlefield against the Portuguese, but also later as teachers for our children. In the latter part of 1968, a Swiss journalist was brought into our territory and with his escort was a letter ordering me to return to Kinshasa.

The origin of the visit of journalist Pierre-Pascal Rossi, in Margoso's view, which may or may not be correct, was that throughout 1967 and 1968, the MPLA had been pressing its views ever more insistently on the OAU's Liberation Committee. Word was beginning to get through that, as Margoso had discovered, it was only the MPLA that was fighting the liberation struggle. There was also documentary evidence that Holden Roberto had given orders that all MPLA cadres remaining in Zaire were to be exterminated. The MPLA was pressing for the OAU to send in a mission to inquire into the real facts of the situation. There was a meeting of the OAU scheduled for September, 1968, and all the signs indicated that the MPLA request would be granted. (As indeed it was!) Holden Roberto wanted to plant some favorable reports in the press first. Therefore the visit of Pierre-Pascal Rossi was arranged—without his necessarily being informed of the reason. He reported having walked for seventeen days through mainly unpopulated countryside, until he entered the area where Margoso had his headquarters, an area stretching in a triangle with its base centered on Bembe in Uije province, about one hundred kilometers northwest of the provincial capital, and its apex at Nambuangongo. He told of a meeting with Margoso, "who claimed to have a total of about 1,800 guerillas."[1] Margoso said his instructions were to make everything sound and look as impressive as possible. He gave the total number of FNLA soldiers in the field as about 10,000. Holden Roberto was claiming 30,000 "fully-trained soldiers" in the field by that time. It was agreed to send an OAU observer mission, but Margoso says they only got as far as Songololo, where they were told officially to wait for guides. The guides never did turn up and despite being liberally plied with palm wine and other drinks, the mission returned to report very unfavorably on the FNLA. Margoso in the meantime had started back to Kinshasa:

It was the rainy reason and the going was slow. I set out on December 29, 1968, and did not get to Kimpangu [just across the Zaire frontier from Maquela do Zombo—W.B.] until January 25, 1969. I sent a telegram to Holden Roberto asking for transport. I was not alone—I had brought some of the MPLA comrades to prove that they were willing to cooperate with us in the anti-colonialist struggle.

Holden Roberto sent a Mercedes car, with the Assistant Chief-of-Staff, Sengele Norberto. I dropped the MPLA comrades off at a place where my mother was living, because Norberto's attitude toward them was very hostile. When we got to Holden Roberto's headquarters, it was reported that I had brought MPLA people and left them at my mother's house. Holden Roberto didn't react to that and only said that I had better have a rest. January and February I spent with my wife, expecting to be convoked at any time. On March 27, Roberto sent a jeep to bring me to his headquarters and there he informed me that I was under arrest. "You are a ruffian," he said, but he didn't explain why I was being arrested. "One ruffian and another makes a ruffian and a half," I replied as I was put under guard. There was an FNLA council meeting a few days later at which it was decided I should be executed for having brought MPLA members into Angola and leaving them in my mother's house. (By that time they were safely across the river in Brazzaville!) The jeep was fueled up and I was to be taken to a frontier area and shot. Holden Roberto wanted it done quickly before anyone outside would know. But while the jeep was being prepared, someone in his headquarters leaked the news and very soon there was a big crowd demonstrating. Some of them—including a man with a gun—pushed their way into Holden Roberto's office and demanded that I be freed.

In the end it was decided that I should be tried. The idea was to prove that I was an agent of the MPLA. But there was no proof. Holden Roberto's Minister for Information spoke up for me. "If there has been any real fighting in northern Angola since 1967," he said, "this is because of Margoso. Who captured Portuguese prisoners? Margoso. That's why the OAU continues to support us. I don't agree to his being killed." That saved me.

20

Later I was put in solitary confinement for one year, in a cell at the Kinkuzu base. No visits, no letters. From my cell I wrote a letter to Holden Roberto asking whether I was going to be left to die only because I had served the Angolan people.

When Margoso was released, he was seriously ill with hemorrhoids and it was due only to the intervention of Holden Roberto's brother, Dr. Sebastian Roberto, that he was hospitalized and, after lengthy medical treatment, gradually regained his health. By 1971, he was rehabilitated—physically as well as politically—by the FNLA. He was sent back to Kinkuzu as deputy chief-of-staff of the FNLA armed forces.

There was the same state of demoralization. Officers and men only wanted arms and a chance to get into the fight. On September 13, 1971, after having contacted men and officers, I held a meeting at which I told them the true state of affairs. Holden Roberto was not interested in fighting the Portuguese, but only in exterminating the MPLA—in Angolans fighting Angolans. I was able to convince them through my own experiences. The decision was taken to convoke Holden Roberto to the base. As soon as he entered he was to be shot. But two officers from Roberto's home town, San Salvador, Donda Afonso and Matir, tipped him off and said: "If you come bring plenty of force."

Holden Roberto came on October 14—together with the Zaire armed forces. The latter immediately encircled the base. Roberto had with him "Johnny" Eduardo Pinnock, Pedro Viola, Luis Angles, and some others. When the meeting started, we denounced the miserable conditions inside Angola. No uniforms, no arms, no real combat against the colonialists. Roberto shouted back: "You people have been corrupted by the Communists. I don't want to talk to you anymore. I will go back and talk with President Mobutu. You can send your officers to talk with the President."

The soldiers shouted back? "No! Our officers won't leave the camp. If Mobutu wants to talk with us, he can come here. We are Angolans. We know what's going on in Angola. If Mobutu wants to know, he should come here."

Holden Roberto got into his car and drove back to Kinshasa. From that moment we severed all relations with him and hauled down the FNLA flag. We contacted some refugees in the frontier area and got them to go into Angola and explain about the situation at Kinkuzu. Our supplies were cut off, but local people sent in fish and rice and we ate better than at any time under Holden Roberto. A local doctor gave us free medical aid. Mobutu and Roberto saw we were doing quite well without them, so they sent in some truckloads of food. We seized both trucks and drivers and held them.

On November 26, [1971], Holden Roberto and some top Zaire officers arrived by helicopter. Roberto's idea was to try to divide the officers from the men. Everyone was in a very angry mood. Stones were thrown at Roberto; he was spat at while the Zaire officers looked on open-mouthed. We spoke in Kikongo dialect and in French so they could understand. The only point that Roberto tried to make was that the officers should go and talk things over with Mobutu. The troops said: "You're not going to take our officers. You'll only kill them."

Eventually five of us agreed to go. The Chief-of-Staff, Eugenio Jaime Agosto, the Deputy Chief-of-Staff, Elias Fernando Pia do Amaral Cruxeiro, Regimental Commander, Benito Manuel Fernando Fernandez, myself as Adjutant to the Chief-of-Staff and the adviser to the headquarters staff. We met with Mobutu at 9 A.M. on November 26, together with Holden Roberto and four top Zaire staff officers.

Mobutu wanted to know what was behind the revolt. We said: "We have no food, no weapons, no uniforms, no medical aid. Everyone wants to fight the colonialists but we are cooped up in a prison. Reports sent back to Holden Roberto are simply ignored."

Mobutu looked straight at Roberto and said: "This is simply a lack of organization. You understand—I don't want Angolan blood shed in my country."

He decided to give us two small trucks and two jeeps so that the Kinkuzu staff could maintain liaison with our bases inside Angola. He gave us some money to buy essential medical supplies and sent us back to Kinkuzu in a helicopter. When we reported back everyone agreed that we must stick to our positions. One of the officers who had betrayed our original plan was shot. The other escaped with a bullet in his leg. Holden Roberto took this as the final proof that we had really rebelled and set out to crush us. With the three chiefs of the Zaire armed forces, he worked out a plan which was approved by Mobutu on March 17, 1972, the day after he returned from a visit to Switzerland.

When we saw four jet fighters circling overhead early on March 18 we knew what we were in for. We had prepared statements for the local and international press and sent two messengers to deliver them. But they were caught and executed. Word then came of sixty armored cars moving toward the camp and I advised all the officers to withdraw to positions from which we could cross over to Brazzaville. They didn't agree and thought the display of force was only to improve Roberto's bargaining position. We had already buried our arms—pledging they were for use only against the Portuguese.

The planes made low passes and it seemed obvious they wanted us to fire on them so they could have the pretext to open up on us. I withdrew to a position about one kilometer south of the base. Behind the armored cars were artillery pieces drawn by trucks. But there was no fighting. Some shells were fired, then the troops moved in and arrested all forty-five officers. Most of them were brought back only two months later—to be executed by firing squads in front of their men. The others were burned to death in an electric oven in the Binza suburb of Kinshasa.

Roberto had completely decapitated his armed forces. The entire professional officer corps had been liquidated. The reserve troops were completely demoralized. There were no more instructors to train replacements for the latter. It was because of this that Holden Roberto turned to China for instructors.

Specialists on the Angolan liberation struggle—including Basil Davidson, by far the best informed among them—agree with Margoso that the FNLA forces never recovered from the Kinkuzu revolt. And it will be seen that Margoso did his best to ensure this! That this was the reason for the dispatch of Chinese instructors is obviously Comandante Margoso's own opinion. But certainly Holden Roberto was forced to look elsewhere for support. At that time Chinese instructors were helping to train FRELIMO guerillas in Tanzania. It is generally believed that President Julius Nyerere of Tanzania interceded for the same help to be extended to the FNLA. Mobutu had made a first visit to Peking in January, 1973— and was received by Chairman Mao Tse-tung. Holden Roberto soon followed in Mobutu's footsteps and secured a promise of 250 Chinese instructors, who started arriving in Zaire in mid-1973.

Margoso had not yet finished with the Kinkuzu affair. Although he must have been the most wanted man in Zaire at the time, he remained on the Zaire side of the frontier for almost six months. Together with another MPLA cadre, Margoso crossed over to Brazzaville on September 5, 1972. This was precisely the date of the OAU meeting in Kampala (Uganda). Margoso and his companion sent a document explaining the situation with Holden Roberto and the FNLA and the highlights of what had happened at Kinkuzu. According to Margoso:

Roberto's delegation was headed by "Johnny" Eduardo Pinnock and N'Gola Kabango [later the FNLA's nominee as Minister of the Interior in the three-movement Transitional Government—W.B.]. When they saw the letter we had circulated, they abandoned the meeting and returned to Kinshasa.

Margoso remained in Brazzaville for almost one year, by which time he had withdrawn some 2,000 of the original 2,600 soldiers from the Kinkuzu base, bringing them across the Zaire river in groups of twenty to thirty at a time.

Most of the other 600 had left the base to get jobs in Kinshasa. With those that came across the river, we crossed the Congo-Brazzaville border into Cabinda province, the MPLA Second Military Region, where we activated the struggle again.

Here Comandante Margoso contributed to the defeat of foreign-backed secessionist attempts in oil-rich Cabinda province. Subsequently he was transferred back to his home battleground in the First Military Region—but this time as Commander of FAPLA forces. With his knowledge of the terrain—and his contacts with the FNLA forces—he played an invaluable role there. One of the important tasks assigned to him just prior to my first meeting with him was dealing with the white mercenaries— mostly British—and the regular troops of the Zaire army which had formerly occupied many key centers in the north.

III Holden Roberto

The following extract from a *New York Times* article by Leslie Gelb was read into the U.S. *Congressional (Senate) Record* of October 28, 1975, by Senator Edward Kennedy:

> The CIA cash-funneling operations in Portugal were said to have revived dormant but traditional connections between the agency and anti-Communist West European socialist and labor movements. And the operation in Angola, the sources said, led to the reactivation of Holden Roberto, head of the FNLA, the man chosen in 1962 by President John F. Kennedy and the CIA to forge a link between the U.S. and the indigenous groups that were expected to drive Portugal from Angola one day. . . .

It is worth noting that Leslie Gelb cited "four official sources in Washington" as the basis for his information and that the story was not officially denied. It continued:

> The sources said that from 1962 to about 1969, the CIA supplied Mr. Roberto with money and arms, but to little avail. At that point he was deactivated and put on a "retainer."
>
> Mr. Roberto was reactivated this spring, according to these sources, at about the time it became clear that the then Communist-leaning government in Portugal ordered its armed forces in Angola to give active support to the Soviet-backed Popular Movement for the Liberation of Angola headed by Agostinho Neto.
>
> But the sources said that CIA operatives and American diplomats judged that U.S. support should also be thrown behind Jonas Savimbi, the leader of the UNITA.
>
> It could not be learned whether Chinese and American officials had ever discussed or sought to coordinate their efforts against Mr. Neto. What was learned was that American funds were being used to buy arms for both Mr. Roberto and Mr. Savimbi, and that the Chinese were providing military advisers for Mr. Roberto and perhaps for Mr. Savimbi as well.
>
> It could not be learned whether any CIA operatives were also acting as military advisers.
>
> At stake in Angola, besides the enlargement of Soviet influence, is a region deemed rich in copper, industrial diamonds, and oil. Of particular interest to the United States and to President Mobutu, the sources said, is Cabinda, an oil-rich area bordering on Zaire and separated from Angola by the Congo river. There, the sources re-

lated, the Gulf Oil Corporation continued to pump over 100,000 barrels a day. The sources said that Mr. Mobutu would like to annex Cabinda in the likely event of a Communist take-over in Angola. . . .

Leslie Gelb also quoted "authoritative sources" for the information that the CIA maintained its largest African station in Zaire. This revelation from one of America's most responsible journalists in one of the country's most highly responsible newspapers came as no surprise. No more did a follow-up news item in the *New York Times* of December 20, 1975, revealing that since 1961, Holden Roberto had been receiving a salary of $10,000 a month to supply information to the CIA and that the "Forty Committee," presided over by Henry Kissinger, had supplied Roberto with $300,000 to help him in his struggle with the MPLA. Some months later, the report stated, important sums of money were given to Jonas Savimbi, funneled through Zambia and Zaire.

My mind went back to a conversation in Algiers in mid-1963 with a professor of physics, Aquino de Braganza, whom most specialists consider one of the best-informed minds on everything concerned with the national liberation struggles in the Portuguese colonies. A Portuguese-Goan of Indian origin—his real name is Desai—he studied physics at the University of Grenoble where his closest friend was Marcelino dos Santos, a founder member of both the MPLA and FRELIMO and now Vice-President of Mozambique. Aquino de Braganza has been closely associated with all national liberation movements in the former Portuguese colonies. He helped set up the World Conference on Nationalist Movements in the Portuguese Empire which later developed into CONCP, the very important Conference of Nationalist Organizations of the Portuguese Colonies. An intimate friend of Agostinho Neto, Samora Machel, and the late Amilcar Cabral, he now directs the Institute of African Studies in Maputo. At our meeting in Algiers, Aquino de Braganza told me some of the basic facts of what was going on in Portugal's African colonies. He mentioned names which till then had meant nothing to me—Cabral, Neto, Andrade, Holden Roberto, personalities I might encounter in Algiers. "Be careful of Holden Roberto," he said. "I know for a fact that he is a CIA agent." It meant little to me at the time, and in fact I met none of them in Algiers. Cutting short my visit I returned to Southeast Asia to make my first visit into the liberated zones of South Vietnam.

In the summer of 1976, however, I sought out Aquino de Braganza in Maputo to ask why he had been so certain in September, 1963, that Holden Roberto was a CIA agent, and how he had been recruited.

Because I knew the man who arranged it. He even boasted about it to me—he took me for a friend. He was one of the right-hand men of Irving Brown of the International Department of the AFL [American Federation of Labor, the International Department of which had long previously been listed as a CIA-subsidized organization—W.B.] His name is Carlos Kassel, an anti-Castro Cuban who had worked for the dictator Trujillo in Santo Domingo and was later placed by Irving Brown in the ILO [International Organization of Labor] headquarters in Geneva.

The first contacts with Holden Roberto were made in 1960, when John Kennedy was preparing an African policy in view of the great surge for independence that was sweeping the whole of the continent. Roberto was recommended as his "man in Angola." The first move was made through American Protestant missionaries in Kinshasa [then Leopoldville—W.B.] Most active in the affair at that time was a certain George Hauser. The deal was clinched in 1962, through Ahmed Tlili, the general-secretary of the Tunisian Trade Unions and Carlos Kassel. After it was finalized, Kassel strutted around in Algiers as a full-fledged leader of the FNLA. The CIA by then had established a solid bridgehead within the FNLA.

Confirmation of this came from an unusual source. Jonas Savimbi, an *assimilado* from the powerful Ovimbundu tribal grouping centered at Silva Porto (Bié) in central Angola, educated in political science at the University of Lausanne, had decided to throw in his lot with the FNLA. He had hoped for a leadership position, but had settled for the post of foreign minister in Holden Roberto's GRAE government in exile. He resigned in a spectacular fashion in July, 1964, during an OAU meeting in Cairo. The reasons he gave added up to the accusation that the FNLA was nothing but Holden Roberto who was "flagrantly tribalist." He portrayed a picture of the Kinkuzu training base not very different from that described to me by Comandante Margoso twelve years later. Above all he complained that the FNLA was in the hands of "neocolonialists" and "notorious agents of imperialism." He named Carlos Kassel, "a militant anti-Castroist"—Savimbi had always presented himself as a great admirer of Castro and for a

27

time could count Che Guevara among his supporters—a certain Bernhard Manhertz, an American who had served in South Vietnam and now directed FNLA military affairs, and another American named Mr. Muller, who had been a public relations officer for the anti-Lumumbist government of Cyrille Adoula in Zaire, and who Savimbi claimed was a personal adviser to Holden Roberto. Savimbi repeated these charges in much greater detail in a letter dated October 18, 1964, to the magazine *Remarques Congolaises et Africaines* which was published in their issue of November 25, 1964.[1]

The letter was in reply to an article in a previous issue, signed D.D.D., attacking Savimbi because of his desertion from the FNLA. Savimbi started his reply by pointing out that the initials D.D.D. stood for Diop Djibril Demba, a cousin of Holden Roberto who was employed at the GRAE Ministry of Information. His letter was divided into five headings: American imperialism inside the UPA and GRAE, the unity of Angolan nationalist movements, the so-called "democratization" within the UPA and GRAE, the reasons for the military setbacks, and "my position regarding Angolan nationalism." Under the first heading, he dealt with Holden Roberto:

> The political career of Holden Roberto started in 1959 with his departure for the United States, where he made numerous friends. After his return to the Congo in July, 1960, he became friends with Messrs. Kandolo, Nondaka, and Mobutu—just those who handed Lumumba over to Tshombe in 1961. Kandolo, who handed over Patrice Lumumba's documents to American spies, is the one who later defended Holden Roberto when he was accused of having been linked to Patrice Lumumba. It is paradoxical that the same hand which killed the patriot Lumumba should protect Holden Roberto—without any reason to do so!
>
> The UPA and GRAE have always enjoyed unconditional support from the Adoula government, of which Messrs. Kandolo, Nondaka, Albert N'Delé, and Mobutu were the pillars. The pro-Americanism of the Adoula government was no secret for anyone.
>
> The American government has always been interested in trying to impose Holden Roberto on the Angolan people as leader. During a month's stay in New York at the end of 1961, I noticed that the Americans were determined to push for Holden Roberto as the leader and in case of a setback in this, then to use him as a buffer between divided Angolan nationalists. . . .

It is hard to avoid the suspicion that Savimbi was piqued that Roberto seemed to be "the chosen one," when he would gladly have undertaken that role himself. That he was inordinately ambitious and chafed at having to play second fiddle to anyone became very clear later on. His account continues:

> It was in this spirit that Holden Roberto, among other things, engaged Carlos Kassel, a militant anti-Castroist. Kassel worked in Tunisia, alongside Ahmed Tlili, then General Secretary of the Tunisian Trade Unions, who passed him on to Holden Roberto as his adviser on trade union affairs. Carlos Kassel succeeded in setting up the LGTA [General League of Angolan Workers] in 1962, which in no way represented the Angolan proletariat. The LGTA then became allied to the ICFTU, thus facilitating powerful material support from the AFL-CIO in the U.S.A., of which Irving Brown was one of the directors in contact with Holden Roberto. This aid went directly to the UPA-FNLA. Carlos Kassel carried out several missions in the name of GRAE, notably that of its adviser to the GRAE mission in Algiers, alongside "Johnny" Eduardo Pinnock.
>
> When the visit of Fidel Castro to Algiers was announced last year, Kassel was asked to leave and since then he has maintained his job in Leopoldville (Kinshasa).

Among other evidence of Holden Roberto surrounding himself with Americans, Savimbi cites him having hired as a personal adviser Professor John Marcum, director of the African program at Lincoln University, as well as some of the other names mentioned earlier—Manhertz (from April 1964 to head of ELNA) and Muller (also as personal adviser, and refers to Muller's help in setting up an Angolan section in the U.S. Embassy at Kinshasa). He remarks also that Roberto sent eleven Angolans to Israel for counterespionage training, using them later to set up his own personal security unit. In concluding this section of his letter, Savimbi makes an admirable statement which only shows his own later activities in a more inexplicable light:

> The experience inside the movement, a profound knowledge of the behavior of individuals, and the materialist analysis of revolutions have all convinced me that no progress is possible with individuals whose allegiance is to the Americans; who can have no other logistics base but Leopoldville in the hands of neocolonialists and notorious agents of imperialism. With such a situation how can one take seriously Holden Roberto's declarations on the eve of his visits to Moscow and Peking?

Yet Holden Roberto had made statements which seemed to place him among the staunchest anti-imperialist leaders and at least some people in high places seem to have been impressed!

On the question of the unity of the nationalist movements, Savimbi writes briefly that he had sent letters to both the MPLA and the UPA in February, 1961, stating that he would not join either movement until unity had been achieved between them. He referred to various meetings, conferences which had all failed to bring this about. Finally, he had joined the UPA at the end of 1961, as he estimated they had the best chance of waging armed struggle on a national scale. Under the heading of the third question of "democracy" within the UPA-GRAE leadership, Savimbi lists the twenty-one members of the Executive Committee of UPA and their origins. Twelve were from San Salvador; six—including Holden Roberto—were close relatives; nineteen were from the Bakongo regions of Angola's extreme northwest. "For your information," Savimbi writes, "here are the names of the five main tribal groupings which make up Angola, in order of importance: Ovimbundu, Kimbundu, Bakongo, Lunda-Kioko-Tchokué, and Ganguela. It is obvious that tribalism must not be exploited by leaders, for it is the whole people that must make the revolution. The flagrant tribalism of Holden Roberto is demonstrated by those who make up his government."

On the question of the reasons for the military setbacks, Savimbi used his heavy artillery:

I will start by recalling that President Ben Bella in September, 1963, sent a hundred tons of arms to GRAE. Since then no one has heard of any stepping up of armed struggle in the interior of the country. A revolution is not a mechanical act which depends exclusively on outside aid. Our analysis of the dismantling of the ELNA, and the end of its military activities, leads us to these conclusions:
(1) Holden Roberto's collusion with the American imperialists who placed Bernhard Manhertz at the head of the Liberation Army.
(2) American infiltration into the maquis which formerly existed. I cite the arrest in his headquarters of Comandante Antoine Muandazi by Portuguese troops a few days after he had given an interview to an American journalist, Lloyd Garrison.
(3) Total lack of political work in the army which is nothing but a personal propaganda instrument of Holden Roberto. I cite the example of photos taken at the Kinkuzu base by American journalists and

distributed to the Western press with great success. I also cite the case of the twenty-five soldiers sent to Tunisia in 1962 [Margoso had said twenty-two—W.B.] to be trained with the Algerian Liberation army and of whom only five were not Bakongo and only ten had completed primary education, the others being illiterate. Later it was these who constituted the general staff of the Angolan National Liberation Army [ELNA].

(4) Introduction of a mercenary spirit among the soldiers, paying their wages only when they return to Leopoldville after a sally into Angola. This is one of the mistakes which has led them to fear pushing too far into the interior and not being able to return to collect their pay. It is because of this that they hang around the Congo-Angolan frontier, becoming a frontier army. I cite the example of the mission sent at the end of 1962, with the consent of the Adoula government and the United Nations command—which supplied the transport, arms, and money—in order to attack the Benguela railway and thus end the Katanga secessionist movement, because the arms Tshombe was getting passed along this Angolan railway.

This mission included three Angolan [ELNA] army officers and returned two months after it left, having spent all its money in the frontier area without engaging in any military activity whatsoever. One of the three officers, Pirois, is today a member of the ELNA general staff.

Many of the points Savimbi was making were almost exactly those of Comandante Margoso, but seen from the opposite side of the frontier. The main difference was that the conclusions they drew were different, at least as interpreted by their actions. The fifth point which Savimbi made was perfectly valid—that a guerilla force must have the total support of the population in order to live and come to grips with the enemy.

This was a realistic assessment of the situation at that time and a correct dissection of the spurious nature of the UPA-FNLA and Holden Roberto's role and motives. Perhaps Jonas Savimbi was sincere in his criticism of Holden Roberto at that time and in his reasons for abandoning him. But how can his vehement denunciation of imperialism and neocolonialism and those who collaborated with them be squared later on, not only with his collaboration with Portugal, South Africa, and the United States, but with his renewed alliance with Holden Roberto against the MPLA?

IV Jonas Savimbi

Forty-eight hours after UNITA forces fled their main stronghold of Bié (formerly Silva Porto), I accompanied an official MPLA search team trying to discover what had happened to MPLA cadres arrested months earlier by UNITA. The missing included Joaquim Kapango, member of the MPLA's political bureau, and two members of the Huambo Provincial Administrative Committee. The prisons were empty when MPLA forces entered the city on February 12, 1976. After an hour of fruitless digging in the courtyard of Komarko prison in the city outskirts, the search team found nine freshly dug pits behind the squat, white-walled prison on the edge of a field of young maize. A human foot was sticking out of one of these. The grass around the pits was trampled flat and stained with blood. Lying on the ground were a half-dozen blood-stained iron bars, some with bits of human hair sticking to them.

As exhumation started, it quickly became clear that in the pits were the bodies of some hundred MPLA cadres known to have been detained in the Komarko prison. The still-fresh bodies had been thrown pell-mell into the pits, the sandy soil shoveled in on top of them. Toilet bowls in the washroom were covered with blood where the executioners had apparently tried to wash off the traces of what they had done before joining the headlong flight of UNITA forces from the city. When the body to which the foot belonged turned out to be that of a young woman whose face had been battered out of recognition, one of the search team muttered bitterly: "There is the true face of Savimbi." Savimbi had been in his Bié headquarters to the end. One of his final acts had been to go on the radio and order all inhabitants to flee because: "The MPLA are at this moment massacring every man, woman, and child in Huambo" [the former Novo Lisboa, the UNITA-FNLA capital, 165 kilometers to the west, liberated by MPLA-Cuban troops four days earlier—W.B.].

On the main street of Bié, an emaciated group of some twenty-five people were straggling along with a banner: "Welcome the glorious FAPLA. We are the survivors of the Bié Angola Police Corps Training School." I spoke with twenty-four-year-old Domingo Antonio Neto, emaciated and in rags. He explained that the Transitional Government, formed of all three movements plus the Portuguese under the terms of the Alvor Agreement of

January, 1975,[1] had agreed to set up several such schools for training a national police force for service after the departure of the Portuguese. Each of the three movements contributed an equal number of trainees and others were selected from the local population. The Bié school had 720 trainees.

When UNITA and the FNLA joined forces against the MPLA, they drafted about one hundred each of their own nominees into their respective armed forces. The remainder were arrested as pro-MPLA, or suspected sympathizers, and jailed at a former Portuguese concentration camp at Capolo, about eighty kilometers from Bié. A few days previously, as MPLA forces got closer to Savimbi's headquarters city, they were taken out in batches of ten and twenty and shot, their bodies falling into, or being thrown into, the nearby Quequema river. Firing squads were unable to finish their work before the arrival of the MPLA-Cuban forces. Domingo and his little band were among about seventy-five survivors of the original 500-odd detainees.

In Huambo, there were similar stories as survivors limped back into the city. There were moving scenes as mothers and wives rushed to hurl themselves into the arms of sons and husbands recognized from afar, many of them survivors of UNITA prisons and death squads. Others collapsed on learning from survivors the fate of those they had hoped to welcome. One thin wreck of a man, Pedro Fancones, told me of the daily executions at a prison where he was held just three miles from Huambo until a few hours before UNITA officers fled the city on February 8. As at the Komarko prison, victims were beaten to death. When the officers fled, UNITA prison guards told those still alive that they could go. Fancones said he was one of a dozen survivors from 110 prisoners who had fled in different directions from the looting UNITA troops. He considered himself lucky to limp home with nothing worse than a bullet in his foot.

Huambo, incidentally, was a ghost city. There had been warnings broadcast by a top UNITA officer that Savimbi would send planes to raze Huambo to the ground and, in any case, anyone found in the city would be massacred by the MPLA.

The executions could only have taken place on this scale—something like 10,000 in the Bié-Huambo area was the official estimate once all reports had been collated—on Savimbi's direct orders. But was that his "true face"? It certainly was not his only face. Many who should be good judges of character, including Che Guevara, recommended him to their friends as sincere, intelligent, a true revolutionary and a patriotic Angolan, a natural leader, and other such eulogistic terms. And perhaps he was at the beginning. He certainly gained the confidence of many anti-imperialist African leaders. But so did Holden Roberto! Those I have met who knew him personally agree on one thing—that at first Savimbi wanted to fight for Angolan independence, but he vacillated from the beginning as to which group to join.

Aquino de Braganza, for one, was convinced that after Savimbi's break with Holden Roberto, he decided to have his own tribal and clan base. This was made easy for him by some pressure groups inside Portugal and elsewhere, interested above all in keeping open the vital Benguela railway, which linked Angola's Atlantic ports of Lobito and Benguela with Mozambique's Indian Ocean ports of Beira and Maputo (formerly Lourenço Marques). It was the sole means—in those days—of getting Zambian copper and the mineral wealth of Katanga (Zaire) to the sea and onto the world markets. The Benguela railway runs through the heartland of Savimbi's own tribal group, the Ovimbundu. The center of the Ovimbundu is Bié, Savimbi's birthplace. When the "specter" of independence for Angola loomed over the horizon, Portuguese and other international interests were eager to ensure that the Angolan section of the Benguela railway and the regions known to possess rich mineral resources would remain in "friendly" hands.

In any case, and for whatever reason, Jonas Savimbi formed his own UNITA (Union for the Total Independence of Angola) movement in March, 1966. In a reference to the founding of UNITA in his most informative book on the Angolan national liberation struggle, Basil Davidson comments:

This group was the first to profit from Zambia's October, 1964, independence. Savimbi was able to collect UPA supporters among refugees in western Zambia and send some of them into eastern Angola in 1966-67. These eventually raised a number of actions against the Portuguese, including an attack on the frontier town of Teixeira de Sousa, on the Katanga border; but these actions were marked by what appears to have been a very inadequate political preparation and an even less adequate supply of arms. Sporadic operations seem to have occurred after that, whether in northern Moxico or, as claimed, in eastern Bié, but on a small scale.

In October, 1969, a UN survey noted: ". . . there has been no mention of UNITA in the Portuguese military bulletins since 1968," while reports by Finnish, Italian, West German, and OAU observers in eastern districts, as well as those of the present writer, were unanimous in concluding that UNITA had become, by 1970, little more than another distracting sideshow. Its bulletins in Western Europe continued to make large claims which were increasingly hard to believe; often they were impossible to believe. . . .[2]

Lucio Lara said that the first armed action by FALA, UNITA's Armed Forces for the Liberation of Angola, took place on December 25, 1966 and that it was a disaster with heavy FALA losses. After that, Lucio Lara, veteran MPLA leader and secretary-general of the MPLA's Central Committee, said: "There was practically no military activity except to prevent our troops from operating in what Savimbi claimed was 'his' territory."

Again one can not do better than quote Basil Davidson to illustrate the significance of the operational reports which Lucio Lara was to quote from:

Supplies flow in from the Indian Ocean. Or rather, they do not *flow* in—a word suggesting ease and regularity of motion; they are delivered from across the seas in sudden and erratic bursts, their precise contents seldom known in advance, often unexpected, sometimes practically useless. Boxed or baled, they arrive in such trucks as can be found and kept on the road. They are driven day and night from the Indian Ocean, discreetly, even secretly, by men with needful papers and few words for the curious. MPLA transport crews perform extraordinary feats of physical and moral endurance. Until late in 1969, the whole two thousand miles and more of road will be entirely bad; then the eastern Zambian sector will be tarred, afterward the Tanzanian sector, afterward again the fearful western Zambian sector, where the road, till then, will often be a trail deep in sand.

Zambia remains a transit country; here the MPLA have no facilities for training or long-term logistics. Supplies have to go through as quickly as they can be taken. The taking is a long affair of jagged nerves and small disasters. Trucks break down far from help; weeks will pass before they can be rescued. Rivers must be crossed on ferries; sometimes these ferries are little more than rafts of timber built for walking folk and rural carts, platforms that lumber from one bank to the other in a slewing motion that gives no guarantee of safe arrival. When the rains are down, these rivers swell into moving lakes that suck at anything they can catch. . . .[3]

Comandante "Punza" illustrated what happened if MPLA units tried to transit through Zaire with supplies which reached Brazzaville the "hard way" but which could conceivably reach the place where they were needed by a "softer way":

I was with quite a big group of well-trained cadres. We were well-equipped and were known as the "Bomoko" squadron, on our way to link up with comrades who were isolated in the Malange area [an old MPLA base area, a little over 400 kilometers due east of Luanda— W.B.]. It was in late 1967. Everything went smoothly at first, but we were arrested by FNLA troops at Songolongo. All our supplies were confiscated; we were imprisoned for thirty days, then had to return to Brazzaville. After that it was decided that the group would have to return to the borders with Zambia, await supplies there and make another attempt to get through to Malanje from Zambia. In my case, it was decided I should go to Tanzania for further training.

From the Zambian border to Malanje was just about 1,000 kilometers, all of which had to be covered on foot, each man usually carrying arms for two and supplies for an indefinite future. If the war seemed to drag on interminably, it was due to such conditions. But if it wore down the resistance forces, it wore down the Portuguese even more. Like the drip-drop of water wearing away a stone, convoys of supply trucks grinding across stretches of sand, toiling up and down mountain tracks or up to their middles in mud and water; columns of men with seemingly impossible burdens on their backs plodding along through forests and swamps, pausing to do battle where they must, but inexorably pushing the struggle to where it hurt the enemy most, were eroding the morale of the Portuguese. And the savagery of the reaction of the fascist leadership in Portugal itself and those running the war on the spot only speeded up the demoralization process. This became clear only later when the revolt of the Armed Forces Movement exploded in Lisbon on April 25, 1974. But at any given moment for those engaged in the liberation struggle, for all but the stoutest of hearts, things must have looked almost impossibly difficult. Lucio Lara, with his lean, brown, almost Vietnamese face—the similarity accentuated by his Ho Chi Minh-type beard and sensitive features—confirmed this. The situation-report cards in his hand spoke for themselves.

1968-69 were difficult years for us. It was essential to push ahead and establish bases in the more highly populated west. To do this we had to cross the Cuanza river which runs north-south and in Central Angola cuts the country in two. With great difficulty an advance column had pushed its way from the east—from bases in Zambia and with arms and supplies that had come from Tanzania—and reached the east bank of the Cuanza. That represented an effort of six months. As they crossed the Cuanza they were attacked by UNITA forces. There were quite fierce clashes and although they did not lose many men, by the time these attacks were beaten off, all the ammunition and supplies, transported so painfully for use against the Portuguese, were used up fighting those who should have been our comrades-in-arms. Had the advance group got through to the target areas, supplies would have been captured from the enemy. As it was, they had to turn round and march all the way back to the Zambian border and await fresh supplies for another attempt. One can say that a whole year of our revolution was lost by this.

He selected one of the white cards, covered in neat but tiny handwriting. (All the place names referred to are just east or west of the Cuanza river, at points about eighty kilometers east of Bié, except where otherwise mentioned.)

We have two sections. One is commanded by Comandante "Furioso,"[4] in the Umpolo region: four detachments each with twenty guerillas, but they were attacked by a counterrevolutionary group of about sixty men who had been hiding in a place called Zona, near the N'ginga river. In the suburbs of Quite, there is a sawmill of António de Figueiroso and inside the sawmill are about thirty Portuguese troops. We captured a Commander Chicolo there, sending him back to Cassemba [an MPLA base over 300 kilometers to the east—W.B.]. South of Lungubongo are 300 UNITA troops, who cooperate with the thirty Portuguese troops in the sawmill. Their main base is at Cuemba [145 kilometers to the east on the Benguela railway—W.B.]. Part of their force when they are on operations stays behind "to defend the area against Communist infiltration." The rest execute missions against our forces. Some of them were at Chimbandiango, others on the banks of the Lunga river. We expelled them from these two positions. They have two men for every weapon and do everything to save ammunition. They do their training at Lungobungo. They have a force of three hundred, plus the local population. They attack us, so we attack them.

We had one man wounded when we wanted to cross the Cuanza south of Mutumbo. First of all we had to beat off the Portuguese. We were obliged to go still further south to try to cross in order to establish a bridgehead for the follow-up force. We established contact with the column which was following with the main arms and supplies, but Portuguese units attacked us before we could cross. We were obliged to exhaust the munitions that had taken one and a half months to bring, turn round, and march back.

This report referred to events in the early part of 1969. Later that year another column did succeed in crossing the Cuanza and pushing through, fighting both UNITA and Portuguese troops all the way to the Atlantic coast. But the nature of the obstacles that had to be overcome in forcing the gateway to the Atlantic was revealed on another of Lucio Lara's white cards. Again the FAPLA vanguard units had to fight UNITA and Portuguese forces at every decisive step in their western drive:

We attacked at Sanga [about 200 kilometers northwest of Bié and 180 kilometers due west of Novo Redondo on the Atlantic coast—W.B.] on September 21, 1969. UNITA forces attacked us on October 15, on the Couvala river; we lost the very good comrade Monoueilolo. They attacked again on January 1, at the M'bulu, a tributary of the Quito river. On January 15, they attacked us again at the M'bulu; we had one comrade wounded. On February 17, they attacked us at Samelil; one of our comrades was killed. On February 22, we counterattacked at Samuelene. We wounded some of them, but lost two comrades, Diku and Kambembe. On March 23, we were attacked at Kassampua, during which we lost two comrades. On April 17, we attacked them at the source of the Queimi and routed them, losing one comrade. The counterrevolutionaries have Portuguese arms, F.N. rifles, machine guns, and Portuguese hand grenades. They have no bazookas.

The report was dated April 30, 1970. It shows that about four months were lost in skirmishing between Angolans, which meant in effect that UNITA was doing in the Center-South exactly what the FNLA was doing in the North. Had UNITA really been fighting the Portuguese, Savimbi should have welcomed MPLA reinforcements for a common struggle. The reason why he did not was made clear by some documents extracted from the PIDE archives by the then Captain Otelo Saraivo de Carvalho, the military architect of the "Captains' Coup" in Lisbon. Handed by him to Aquino de Braganza, these documents were published in the July 8, 1974, issue of *Afrique-Asie*. Professionally mistrustful of "secret documents," I was one of many journalists skeptical of the contents until I learned of their origin—for obvious reasons not revealed by *Afrique-Asie* at the time of publication. For Otelo de Carvalho, an honest officer with the courage of a lion, was one of those best placed to know that such documents existed and the truth of what they revealed. Two of his three African tours of duty had been in Angola, the first in 1961, the second in 1973. (In an interview shortly after the coup in which he had played such a decisive role, he told me of his deep disgust with what had been going on in Angola, especially in the years immediately preceding the Lisbon coup.)

The documents consisted of: a memorandum addressed by Savimbi to General Luz Cunha, Portuguese commander-in-chief in Angola, and General Bettencourt Rodriguez, commander of the Eastern Military Zone, dated September 26, 1972; a letter sent on October 25, by Savimbi to Lt. Colonel Ramires de Oliveira, chief of staff to General Rodriguez; Oliveira's reply to Savimbi, dated November 4; and another letter to Oliviera from Savimbi, dated November 7, 1972. The first Savimbi letter congratulates "their Excellencies" on the fourth anniversary of the accession to the premiership of Portugal of "his Excellency, Professor Marcelo Caetano" and congratulates also General Luz Cunha, "for his nomination to the high responsibility as commander-in-chief of the armed forces in Angola." After a long analysis of the dangers of a rapprochement between the MPLA-FNLA and the "annoying consequences of official recognition of the OAU by the United Nations," especially the fact that a UN delegation had "claimed to have visited Guiné-Bissau" (which it had indeed done in 1972) and that the same delegation "was planning to visit the liberated zones of the MPLA and FRELIMO," Savimbi makes a major statement of UNITA policy:

> Our position is irreversible. We are no longer interested in either the OAU or today's Zambia and less still in any alliance with the MPLA.

If certain aspects of UNITA policy are still not sufficiently clear for the Angolan governmental authorities and the nation, there is one irrefutable fact: we have actively participated in weakening the MPLA in certain of the eastern regions. And we can not entertain any sort of illusions on any type of alliance whatsoever with the men whom we have fought against, and continue to fight against, without any letup. Whatever may be the intentions of the [Portuguese] government, we will never again be deluded into taking up arms against the authorities. We will use them till the end to force the MPLA one day to withdraw from the East.

Peace in the East, in our opinion, should take into account, among other things, the following factors:

(a) The weakening, up to the liquidation, of the MPLA forces in the interior of Angola. This task can perhaps best be carried out by the combined efforts of military and paramilitary forces together with those of UNITA.

(b) Liquidation of the MPLA camps in the frontier region between Angola and Zambia. That can easily be carried out by UNITA. . . . Our plans have already passed the preliminary stage.

(c) A campaign to discredit the MPLA. Our target for this is the OAU, at least as far as liberation movements are concerned. Once the MPLA is weakened, or liquidated, in the East, the road will be opened for much broader horizons for us.

We greatly thank you for the unofficial note from the Portuguese government of July 4, 1972. UNITA will try to reach agreement with the authorities of Moxico [the province in which the Portuguese Eastern Military Command had its headquarters at Luso—W.B.] to facilitate the transit of persons between the UNITA regions and the posts so that the local people do not run unnecessary risks. With documents recognized by both sides, the local people who will be returned to the posts can come and collect their food left in the forest, as long as they have not committed any reprehensible acts while they were in the forest. [This apparently refers to peasants whom the Portuguese authorities by that time were trying to herd into *aldeamentos*, "strategic hamlet"-type concentration camps, but who were allowed out to gather food in the forest.—W.B.]

Savimbi offered intelligence-gathering services to the two generals, proposing in exchange that UNITA forces be granted a non-attack transit corridor leading toward MPLA bases near the border between Angola's most southeastern province of Cuando-Cubanga and Zambia. As a sample of how advantageous such an arrangement could be, he listed a number of MPLA bases in that area, with the exact number of men and types of arms in each. Hospital facilities were not omitted, as the following bit of intelligence shows:

> There are other camps at Nguvu, with twenty guerillas armed with "PPxes" [apparently Soviet automatic arms] and hand grenades. This camp has also a field hospital under the responsibility of Dr. Eduardo dos Santos. [Eduardo dos Santos is one of the founder members of the MPLA—W.B.] On the Kalabo line toward the Cuando-Cubango frontier there are several camps; the best-known is that of Shikongo which has at least fifty elements armed with the usual arms used by the MPLA. It has a military instructor, a doctor and several nurses, a political commissar, three schoolteachers. This is where they are going to build a school with Danish aid. . . . We had the occasion to send into Shikongo some of our men disguised as MPLA members to take part in meetings organized by Daniel Chipenda,[5] or another MPLA leader. Daniel Chipenda had already left Shikongo, but a *métis* arrived there who, by the description, must be either Carreira or Jorge, but who they called "Diaquité." ["Carreira" refers to "Iko" Carreira, veteran guerilla leader and now Minister of Defense; "Jorge" refers to Paolo Jorge, now Foreign Minister of the People's Republic of Angola.—W.B.]

There is mention of a request from the two Portuguese commanders for guides to MPLA encampments. Savimbi agreed to provide them but only when a camp had been located, in which case he suggested "joint operations" to wipe it out. Finally, he had a few material requests—1,500 cartridges of 7.62 mm., and some cloth for camouflage uniforms, including "at least two uniforms of good and real camouflage cloth, one for me and one for Puna," (Miguel Nzau Puna, secretary-general of UNITA).

The most interesting portion of the much shorter, first letter to Lt. Colonel Ramires de Oliveira, apart from information as to MPLA military movements and a proposal to "infiltrate the First Congress of the MPLA . . . to know what is discussed and decided," is the disclosure that UNITA had a liaison unit permanently in contact with Oliveira's headquarters.

> I have in my possession an OAU document which I consider of extreme importance. I have just received it. It deals in great detail with the supply of arms to the MPLA, as well as to other movements

active in the Portuguese territories; quality, quantity, finance, transport methods, etc. I think it is useful, in so far as it reflects the spirit that dominated that last meeting of African heads of state in Rabat last June. As soon as I have finished studying it I will send it *by the usual channels.* . . .

As to the possibility of a meeting with me, I have always been disposed to meet more responsible persons to discuss by word of mouth what I think and what the position is of the local and national authorities about what we are doing. But this meeting should be prepared *by our delegation.* . . . In any case I think that *our delegation* could, starting from the next meeting, bring concrete proposals as to the installation of a receiver-transmitter for us. I don't think I can fix the date for the next meeting, as several points of my memorandum are still being studied by the responsible local authorities. . . . [Emphasis added]

The reply of Oliveira also dealt with the questions raised by Savimbi in his memorandum to the two generals, which had been "duly studied and greatly appreciated," the view expressed "in its broad outlines coinciding with ours. . . ." In what amounted to a thirteen-point memorandum, Oliveira encouraged Savimbi in his espionage activities, confirmed that they were informed about the forthcoming MPLA congress, and that there was "a very special interest in infiltrating the latter to know what is discussed and decided." He rejected any permanent corridor in the region proposed by Savimbi, but said that temporary attack-free transit could be arranged through prior notification. He suggested that cooperation between UNITA forces and "our troops should be secretly strengthened." Oliveira proposed that a face-to-face meeting be arranged at which the following agenda would be discussed:

(a) UNITA activities against the MPLA and FNLA-UPA in the interior of the national territory.
(b) Activities of cells of UNITA militants in Zambia.
(c) Utilization of the Luanguinga corridor by UNITA.
(d) UNITA attacks on MPLA bases outside Angola (Zambia).
(e) Installation of a transmitter-receiver at UNITA headquarters.
(f) Aid requirements of the civilian population in the Lungubongo (UNITA-occupied) area.
(g) Procedures to adopt for exchange of information.

The extent of tactical cooperation sought by Savimbi, but about which the Portuguese seemed suspicious, is revealed by the following passage dealing with Savimbi's request for the transit corridor and related matters. It is dealt with under Point Five of Oliveira's reply:

(5) The secret nature of these contacts unfortunately—but it is a drawback that must be accepted—causes certain inconveniences.

(a) One of these inconveniences consists in the impossibility of granting the authorization for the free use of the corridor situated between the Lufuta-Luanguinga and Luanguinga-Luvo rivers. On each occasion that this needs to be utilized, the [Portuguese] Command must be informed, so that our troops can be withdrawn from the region under some pretext for the necessary period. Outside that period, it will be impossible to ensure your security in the use of the corridor.

(b) In the same way, Zones 1, 2, 3, 4, and 5, cannot be used without prior request or, in case of extreme necessity, immediate notification. UNITA carried out activities on October 12, against the UPA in Zone 1 and only informed us on October 21. It carried out another operation in Zone 2 which has only now been communicated to us. As these are zones into which our troops go frequently, sometimes with helicopters, the risks run by your troops are obvious. . . .

The first half of Savimbi's reply of November 7 consists of an obsequious apology because of a missed rendezvous with a doctor sent from Oliveira's headquarters to treat some heart and liver ailments from which Savimbi said he was suffering. He was too ill to go on foot, and being carried in a stretcher was not possible "because of the secret nature of our meetings." But he referred to Oliveira's letter of July 20, 1972, "No. 1,457/2 p 215,07, in which with all possible clarity it was stated that 'periodical medical aid will be provided by a military doctor who will travel by road with escort by arrangements with the wood merchants to a central point designated by you.' " (There is also frequent reference to the wood merchants who apparently maintained liaison between Savimbi's headquarters and one of the nearby Portuguese posts.)

Then follows a peculiar passage which suggests that the "reward" for what was clearly the deepest treachery to the Angolan independence struggle was that Savimbi's forces were transferred from fertile regions to others where not only was it impossible for them to feed themselves, but they could move about only at the pleasure of the Portuguese military command!

> The occupation of the sector which has been placed at our disposal will, in practice, depend on a greater tolerance by the authorities for the movement of our forces in Zone 1. This problem should be discussed with all the lucidity that the situation requires. . . . But I am disposed to follow your instructions while always presenting my own viewpoint. My own strategy is more adapted to the movement of small forces than the big units which their Excellencies have at their disposal.
>
> Wherever UNITA has been stationed since my arrival in Angola, we have cultivated the local fields which has enabled us to fulfill our food needs without being a charge on the people. But when our groups are to be stationed in desert areas, it is frankly impossible for them to support themselves there, which leads to lack of discipline. The map of the areas allotted to UNITA has been drawn up taking into account the global strategy against subversion in the East rather than the contribution that UNITA could make to the struggle against the MPLA and UPA [FNLA]. I have accepted the situation and have not demanded anything more. . . .

The letter concludes by thanking "his Excellency, the General commanding the military zone, for his kindness in having authorized the repair of our machine gun. . . ." No mention is made of the face-to-face meeting or the agenda to be discussed.

At what point did Jonas Malheíro Savimbi become a traitor to the Angolan national liberation struggle and to the Angolan people? The tone of the communications cited in the above documents suggests that they started long before the earliest date—July, 1972—mentioned in the correspondence. Aquino de Braganza believes they started, at the latest, in 1970 when General Francisco da Costa Gomes was appointed commander-in-chief of Portuguese armed forces in Angola, bringing with him General Bethencourt Rodrigues as commander of the Eastern Front. De Braganza believes that Costa Gomes was not personally involved in the affair, but that Bethencourt Rodrigues, who was relieved from all military posts on April 25, 1974, was. But some "softening-up" had obviously gone on before. In his book former dictator Marcelo Caetano relates how he instructed Costa Gomes to approach UNITA and that this was done by Bethencourt Rodrigues![6]

Objectively, Jonas Savimbi was Portugal's man from the moment he founded UNITA, and actively so from the moment he launched armed struggle. It was no accident that he incorporated the band of green from the Portuguese national flag into that of UNITA, nor that he placed in its center the celebrated Portuguese national symbol—the cock rampant.

Armando Dembo, veteran FAPLA guerilla commander and political officer, from 1965, in Moxico district (now Angola's biggest province) where the military actions described on Lucio Lara's white cards took place, told me: "Savimbi's troops undertook no action whatsoever against the Portuguese. Only against us." Dembo—a powerfully built Angolan African, who was Provincial Commissioner of Moxico province when I met him in Luena (formerly Luso), the provincial capital, in November 1976—was speaking of the period starting in 1965, when he had been sent there to prepare the political ground for opening up the eastern front in the area. "The people were very cooperative," he said, "and by the time we were ready to start armed struggle, we had their total support. But we had to fight off UNITA attacks almost as often as those of the Portuguese." As he had been active in the area uninterruptedly from 1968 onward, Dembo obviously knew what he was talking about.

In the light of what is now known of Savimbi's long collaboration with the Portuguese colonialists, his switch to an alliance with the South African racists—which so shocked his left-wing supporters abroad—is seen to be a natural transition!

V The Long March of Agostinho Neto

A socially timid man with a shy, almost apologetic smile, Dr. Agostinho Neto has that good "bedside manner" considered essential for a successful medical practitioner. If his exercise of the profession for which he was trained was brief—in terms of formal practice—it stood him in good stead in helping comrades in the jails and concentration camps and jungle battlefields through which he passed on the long march to final MPLA victory. The gentle smile and often hesitant speech conceal a dogged stubbornness of character and singleness of purpose which some of his admirers, and most of his detractors, claim make him impossibly withdrawn, aloof, stern, and inflexible. Other admirers argue that it was precisely these qualities that enabled Neto to drag the MPLA up to its feet again after what seemed to be irreparable defeats.

There were plenty of examples of "one step forward, two steps back" during the fifteen years of armed struggle but there was also the inexorable push of the political and military front lines from the sparsely populated perimeter areas in the east into the heartland and finally to the vital Atlantic coast.

He is a poor public speaker who reads much better than he sounds—a drawback in a country where illiteracy is at least eighty-five percent and virtually one hundred percent in the areas where Neto did most of his work. Yet the flame of his innermost convictions burned brightly enough to inspire a dedicated group of men and women to follow him to the end. Like so many other illustrious revolutionary leaders—Mao Tse-tung and Ho Chi Minh, for example—Agostinho Neto is a poet. His language is economical, but his ideas come through sharp and clear. His closest comrades-in-arms say that he is an eloquent and convincing debater.

What makes people so stubborn? What turns them away from the prospect of a privileged life such as Agostinho Neto could easily have had as a medical practitioner in Lisbon or Luanda? It was a question to which the United States devoted much attention in Southeast Asia. Teams of psychologists and psychiatrists were sent to South Vietnam to interrogate "Vietcong" prisoners and establish what motivated them. According to the distinguished Dr. Erich Wulff, who served years in a West German hospital unit in Danang and listened to many tape recordings of the interrogations, they almost invariably started with: "What were your relations with your mother," proceeding to whether the subject ever masturbated and if so: "What did you think about at that time?" The astounded Dr. Wulff dryly remarked: "Had they asked the prisoner what his relations were with the local landlord, or what he thought about when American planes napalmed his village, the replies might have been more conclusive."[1] The results of this research in Vietnam proving inconclusive, the United States then dispatched an international team of anthropologists to Thailand to discover what there might be in the racial, physical, and cultural background of a Thai peasant or Meo tribesman that could possibly make him a "Communist"—the only term acceptable to the CIA and Pentagon for anyone who resorted to armed struggle against "authority."

Agostinho Neto's first brush with "authority" was in 1951 when, as a medical student in Lisbon, he showed too much interest in a presidential election in which an Admiral Quintao Meirales dared to oppose the dictator Salazar. When it became clear that the election was to be rigged without even an impartial check on the counting of votes, Quintao Meirales withdrew. Historically, his withdrawal was less important than the fact that a young Angolan medical student received his first lesson in the impossibility of changing the fascist regime and therefore—and even more so—changing the fascist-colonial overlordship in his native land by legal, constitutional means. Active in a students' organization imprudently supporting the opposition candidate, Neto was picked up by the PIDE and jailed for a few weeks as a warning that even privileged blacks, such as *assimilados*, had no right to take part in politics.

Together with a small group of like-minded nationalists from the Portuguese African colonies—Amilcar Cabral of Guiné-Bissau and Mário de Andrade, an Angolan poet and literary critic, among the most outstanding of them—Neto helped to set up in Lisbon a Center of African Studies aimed at combating a condition to which they themselves had succumbed—de-Africanization. Intellectually they revolted against the concept of the *assimilado*, the legal act by which they renounced their Africanism and in Portuguese eyes lost their status of "savage" and became "civilized" in the terminology of the colonizers. By awakening national consciousness, these outstanding pioneers of the independence movements

47

in the Portuguese colonies had taken the first steps toward creating national liberation movements. They were conscious of the need to close the gap between themselves and the illiterate masses and to re-Africanize themselves. Although their strivings were at first expressed in cultural forms, the seeds of the future militant movements germinated in their poetry and prose, inevitably assuming more political undertones. The Portuguese were not unaware of this and soon closed down the Center of African Studies.

By the time the MPLA was formed in Leopoldville in December, 1956—with Amilcar Cabral as one of the founder members—Neto was again in jail. Arrested for political activities in February, 1955, while still a medical student, Neto was released in June, 1957, by which time the MPLA was six months old. In late 1959 he returned to Luanda and set up practice as a doctor, only to be arrested a few months later—in June, 1960—to be eventually shipped off to the Tarrafal concentration camp in the Cape Verde Islands, and still later to prison in Lisbon.

In the meantime a fresh crop of students was absorbing progressive and nationalist ideas in Lisbon. They included Lucio Lara, later to become general secretary of the MPLA's Central Committee, Eduardo dos Santos, first foreign minister of the People's Republic, and Déolinda Rodrigues de Almeida, an outstanding women's leader who died of torture and ill-treatment in a Zaire prison, a victim of the Zaire-Holden Roberto persecution of all MPLA cadres who fell into their hands. In Lisbon and for those who were in the prisons and concentration camps, the only political support the young nationalists received was from the harshly persecuted and clandestine Portuguese Communist Party. And even these furtive and spasmodic contacts caused some problems. Speaking of that period (the early 1960s) Lucio Lara responded to my question as to whether the struggle in Vietnam had any influence on their own movement:

> Yes. A very positive influence. We had a similar problem when we started to organize. We found, as had the Vietnamese comrades, that even the most revolutionary forces in the Metropole do not always understand the needs of the militants in the colonies. In 1959, when the Portuguese started arresting our leadership in Luanda, it was we students who had to continue the struggle. In 1959-60, we were much influenced by everything we could learn about the Vietnamese struggle. . . .

(At that point in our conversation, he produced a battered, dog-eared copy of *North of the 17th Parallel*, my first book on Vietnam, published in Hanoi in 1955, many of its pages with lines underscored in pencil—and asked for an autograph!)

> The Portuguese Communist Party wanted us to join them, as the French Communist Party had wanted the Algerians to join them— which we knew about. But we said: "No. Our problems are different. We must be independent as the Vietnamese comrades remained independent." Later the Portuguese comrades agreed that we had been right. They never wavered in their support for us.

A constant of the MPLA struggle, already referred to several times, was the terrible handicap of the denial of base and supply facilities in Zaire. This led to many initiatives by the MPLA to come to terms with the FNLA. There were many discussions and several agreements were signed—including one which because of MPLA concessions provoked the revolt of some of its leading members. But none of these agreements ever went into effect because, as only became clear much later, Holden Roberto had become a CIA agent less than one year after the launching of armed struggle. Late in 1962, Neto, having escaped from jail, turned up in Leopoldville and tried once again to achieve some sort of operational unity with the FNLA but it was impossible for reasons which Neto could not know about at that time. Even that staunch MPLA supporter, Basil Davidson, admits that in the year which followed Neto's reappearance on the scene, he thought the MPLA was finished. Writing in *West Africa* magazine (December 14, 1963) he commented: "Initially the more influential of the two big nationalist movements, the MPLA has fractured, split, and reduced itself to a nullity. With Holden Roberto's UPA steadily gathering strength and allies, the MPLA has ceased to count." Quoting this article in his great classic on the Angolan liberation struggle, Davidson writes: "The judgment was my own . . . and it was singularly wrong. But that is what things looked like at the time."[2]

Neto and the rest of the MPLA leadership had been expelled from Leopoldville by that time, their bases closed down, stocks of arms seized, numerous cadres arrested and killed. For months prior to their expulsion in November, 1963, they had been persecuted and harassed by the government of Cyrille Adoula, with Holden Roberto instigating the total destruction of the MPLA. In August, 1963, however, there was a ray of unexpected light. After three days of stormy demonstrations in Brazzaville, the reactionary government of Abbé Fulbert Youlou in Congo-Brazzaville was overthrown and replaced by that of the relatively enlightened Alphonse Massemba-Débat. A feature of the independence struggles in Africa has been that newly independent countries have placed facilities and sanctuaries at the disposal of neighboring peoples still fighting for their national liberation. Thus Algeria's National Liberation Front had found political sanctuary in Cairo and later training and base facilities in neighboring Morocco and Tunisia and, once having achieved its own independence, Algeria was generous in according political bases and training facilities for the liberation movements of the Portuguese colonies, among others.

Now, in its hour of need, the MPLA leadership also found sanctuary across the frontier from what is now Zaire, in Congo-Brazzaville which, together with Zaire, has a common border with Angola's vital Cabinda province. In Brazzaville, Neto, Lucio Lara, and a few other stout hearts among the MPLA leaders started rebuilding from the wreckage left by the 1961 decapitation of the Luanda leadership and the treason of Holden Roberto and his immediate protectors, the Kasavubu-Adoula regime in the former Belgian Congo.

There were further favorable developments on the African scene. The independent republics of Tanganyika and Zanzibar were united in the single progressive state of Tanzania in April, 1964. Shortly afterward, Neto received permission from the staunch anti-imperialist president, Julius Nyerere, to open a MPLA bureau in the capital and port city of Dar es Salaam. For years to come it was to be the main point of entry for FAPLA military supplies from the Soviet Union, China, and other socialist countries. Later that same year, in October, Zambia received its independence and despite some initial difficulties due to president Kenneth Kaunda's visceral anti-Communism and his belief that the MPLA was a "Communist" movement, the way was opened for supplies to transit across Zambia from Dar es Salaam to Angola's eastern frontier areas.

But if things at the end of 1963 looked hopeless to so experienced an observer as Basil Davidson—who had been with Tito's partisans in Yugoslavia in World War II—they must have seemed even more hopeless to many of those fighting inside the country. Especially to those in the First Military Region, the survivors of the 1961 massacres, who were still battling in the Dembos forest north of Luanda. Repeated attempts to get arms and supplies to them from the North had been blocked. Without any outside support, they fought off attacks by FNLA and Portuguese troops, ambushing the latter's convoys to get arms and supplies, disrupting communications, and forcing the Portuguese to disperse their forces. They were entirely on their own for five years before the first FAPLA relief column, in July, 1966, battered its way through from the east, each man carrying weapons and supplies for two.

A decisive landmark of the liberation struggle was the "Cadres' Conference" in Brazzaville in January, 1964—just two months after the arrival of Neto and the rest of the available MPLA leadership. It was an extremely frank and critical session of as many cadres as could be mustered. Past mistakes and shortcomings were mercilessly analyzed and criticized and a new course was charted for stepping up armed struggle in a more organized and realistic way. One of the major decisions was to use the new possibilities opened up by the Congo-Brazzaville sanctuaries to create a Second Military Region in Cabinda province. For a start this meant mobilizing nationalist elements there for the political work which the MPLA, like the Vietnamese, recognized was the essential precondition for armed struggle. The "Cadres' Conference" was the watershed between isolated, heroic insurrectionary activities and planned, revolutionary armed struggle on a national scale. It marks the start of the dogged, step-by-step thrusts forward which were so much a reflection of Neto's own character—the refusal to admit the permanent nature of reversals or that there were any obstacles that could not be surmounted.

Following the opening of the Second Military Region in Cabinda in 1964, a third front was opened in Moxico on March 18, 1966, when a convoy of Portuguese trucks was halted by a tree across the road near the village of Kakweje, about two-thirds of the way between the provincial capital and the Zambian border. It was an ambush and the Portuguese realized to their cost that a new front had been opened up. This took place after a year's careful political preparation directed by Armando Dembo. "They vaguely knew we were around," Dembo was to tell me later,

> but they didn't know where. The motorized patrol was looking for traces of us, but they thought the tree across the road was an accident. Our ambushing party had just seven weapons—but plenty more after that first action. By the time the Portuguese realized we were there in force, the province had been split up into six operational zones—from A to F. Zones were split up into sectors and sectors into groups. Each new sector was opened up only after careful political preparation.

In January, 1968, the MPLA transferred its headquarters into the liberated areas and five months later, on May 8, 1968, the Fourth Military Region was opened up by armed action in Luanda province, adjoining Moxico to the north. The Portuguese reply was to launch a strong offensive, backed up by intensive air bombardment, against all known bases and liberated villages in Moxico province. "At one point we were intensively bombed for twenty days on end," Armando Dembo recalled, "but we took very few losses. Four dead and seven wounded, including civilians."

These were the country's most sparsely populated provinces, with a density of less than four inhabitants per square kilometer. Although it strained the muscles and staying power of the guerillas and their back-up supply forces to the utmost, it also put a heavy strain on the Portuguese armed forces and their logistics services. Patiently the MPLA organizations in groups, sectors, zones, and military regions were consolidated and preparations were made to make of each consolidated area a jumping-off point for the next target.

Although the necessity of advancing across those impossibly long supply lines from the Indian Ocean toward the Atlantic and establishing the main base areas in the most sparsely populated areas of the country was a terrible handicap for the MPLA guerilla forces, it also had its positive side and may even provide a lesson for those advocates of urban guerilla warfare who argue that small rural communities spread over large areas cannot provide a secure base for guerilla activities. Obviously factors of terrain, topography, and natural cover are of essential importance, but political preparation has proven to be the decisive factor. The accident of adverse circumstances in Angola, however, favored the full deployment of what Vo Nguyen Giap, Vietnam's greatest exponent of "people's war" considered vital to success—namely to catch the adversary in the contradiction between concentrating his forces to deal decisive military blows at the guerillas forces, or dispersing his forces to defend territory. Also the gradual encirclement of the urban centers by the countryside. By the time the MPLA was gradually pushing its spearhead political units across the Cuenza river to open up the Fifth Military Region in Bié province, where the population density was about fifteen per square kilometer, in the second half of 1969, the Portuguese forces were severely overextended. They were kept off balance by the explosion of widely separated fronts which they could not afford, militarily, to ignore. The MPLA picked up strength as it advanced into the enemy's natural centers of strength—the urban centers where it had its garrisons, police, and espionage systems. Its facilities for exploiting this built-in corruption were infinite—had that been the main battlefield.

As the relation of forces changed in favor of the MPLA on the internal front, there were international repercussions. The truth gradually dawned on even those OAU member states which had been sincere supporters of the FNLA and its government in exile (GRAE) that it was only the MPLA which was solidly implanted inside the country and waging an unyielding struggle against the Portuguese. In addition, the fact that it was only the MPLA which was represented in CONCP together with the PAIGC of Guiné-Bissau and Mozambique's FRELIMO, the recognized national liberation movements of the latter two countries, weighed heavily with the progressive member states of the OAU. Recognition of GRAE was finally withdrawn by the OAU at its Addis Ababa summit meeting in June, 1971, and the MPLA was recognized as the legitimate national liberation movement. By this time the FAPLA guerillas had advanced close enough to the Atlantic seaboard for MPLA Action Committees to step up their activities in their old strongholds of Luanda, Benguela, and other major urban centers. Military activities close to the real centers of Portuguese power meant a heavy demand on supplies and, once again, a big effort was made to come to terms with the FNLA, this time through the government of Sese Seko Mobutu, who had seized power in Zaire in 1975. There were strong pressures on Agostinho

Neto from OAU member states to patch up differences and form a united fighting front with the FNLA, an aim which the MPLA leadership heartily supported. Lucio Lara explained to me how these efforts developed:

> In fact, we started a campaign accusing the Zaire government of sabotaging our struggle against the Portuguese. Mobutu, who wanted to preserve an anticolonial posture, was rather sensitive to this but it was difficult for him to give us transit facilities because of Holden Roberto. Eventually he said he would agree, but only if the MPLA and FNLA got together. Of course we wanted this. After a number of exchanges Holden Roberto came to Brazzaville in August, 1972, and negotiated an agreement with delegates from Zaire, Zambia, Tanzania, and Congo-Brazzaville which provided for a MPLA delegation to go to Kinshasa in December of that year to sign the agreement. Our delegation went and in an extraordinary effort to achieve unity, on December 13, 1972, President Neto signed an agreement with Holden Roberto to merge our two movements and set up a "Supreme Council for the Liberation of Angola" with Holden Roberto as president and Agostinho Neto accepting the post of vice-president, but retaining for the MPLA the right to handle military affairs.

It was a surprisingly conciliatory gesture at that time, especially as Neto conceded responsibility for administering the liberated zones, propaganda, and diplomatic representation abroad to Holden Roberto. It was the most spectacular of many efforts made by Neto in the name of national unity—but it was to cost him dearly. In fact the "Supreme Council" never functioned. Lucio Lara explained why:

> When we studied the draft agreement, it was clear that Mobutu had been manipulated by Portugal through some of the parties to the Brazzaville negotiations. While we were prepared to make many concessions of form to get unity, we could not sacrifice principles. We suggested that, as the overall agreement had been negotiated without the presence of the directly interested parties, there should now be direct negotiations on the details and implementation of the "unity" agreement. This was agreed. The first direct MPLA-FNLA meeting on implementation took place in Kinshasa in February, 1973, and talks continued throughout February and March. The stumbling block was the categoric refusal of the FNLA delegation to

54

include any reference to "armed struggle" in the final agreement. As the intensification of armed struggle was central to everything, our talks reached an impasse. Our delegation left—with two members remaining to maintain liaison—and we raised the reason for the impasse at the May, 1973, meeting of the OAU at Addis Ababa. The OAU accepted our position. Mobutu promptly arrested our two liaison officers as "spies" and things went from bad to worse.

Using Neto's concessions to Holden Roberto as a pretext, one of the MPLA leaders, Daniel Chipenda, broke with the Neto leadership. Like Jonas Savimbi, Chipenda was of the Ovimbundu tribal grouping of the Center-South, the largest—with an estimated two million adherents—single group in the country. At times a contender for the tribal leadership, Chipenda took with him in his anti-MPLA "Eastern Revolt" group many commanders and fighting men in the Mbunda southeastern regions near the frontier with Zambia. Despite the pretext of Neto's over-generous concessions to the FNLA, many observers interpreted the Chipenda defection as having been maneuvered by Zambia's leadership, who were eternally suspicious of the MPLA's ideological orientation. In any case it was a heavy price for Neto to pay for a completely fruitless attempt at reconciliation with the FNLA. But, as with Vietnam's delicate balancing act with China and the Soviet Union at the most critical moment of its national liberation struggle, Neto had to contend with pressures from even his closest supporters within the OAU, and give evidence—sometimes against his better judgment—that it was not the MPLA which was responsible for lack of unity. Lucio Lara, always in the center of the decision-making storms, commented:

> It was a very difficult time for us. We were attacked from all sides. For having made too many concessions. For not having made enough. For a time, even Congo-Brazzaville was against us. It did not last for long and President Ngouabi soon resumed his all-out support for us. But at the moment it hurt.[3]

If it was a difficult time for the MPLA and a period of enormous strain on the Neto leadership, it was an even more critical moment for the colonial-fascist regime in Lisbon. The MPLA thrust into the heavily populated centers of the Atlantic seaboard, together with the advance of the PAIGC in Guiné-

Bissau and of FRELIMO in Mozambique shook the regime to its foundations. The bankruptcy of the hopelessly outmoded colonial empire was exposed with brutal clarity. Even some of Portugal's European allies—especially where social-democrat governments were in power—recoiled from having to justify to their electorates attempts to prop up such a tottering edifice. And the cost of attempts to sweep back the tides of change—even with NATO-financed brooms—was clearly beyond the capacity of Portugal.

Through total control over information the regime could conceal the real situation from the people at home and abroad, but the truth could obviously not be concealed from the troops on the spot. Demoralization set in at all levels. There were barbarous massacres by leading fascist commanders, battlefield desertions (partly in revolt at the massacres, partly because of the hopelessness of the military situation) and massive departures of men of military age from Portugal itself to avoid the call-up. The press in Lisbon continued to issue "victory" communiqués and statistics of "terrorists" wiped out, but the real word came back through the discreet "killed in action" notices and the accounts of wounded and survivors.

VI April 25 and the Alvor Conference

Three days after the April 25 coup which ended half a century of fascism in Portugal, I asked a young artillery captain participant what had pushed him and his comrades into such a risky and perilous adventure. (He must remain anonymous because in those early days it was a breach of discipline for anyone but an authorized Armed Forces Movement spokesman to talk to the press. And under Portugal's new military president, General António Ramalho Eanes, breaches of discipline—even old ones—are sternly punished.) His reply was as follows:

> Once the armed independence struggles started in Africa, soldiering became a dirty and dangerous affair—a low-prestige profession. The military academy was no longer stuffed with the sons of the rich upper class. Because of battlefield losses and draft-dodging there was a real shortage of officers, and of candidates for the military academy. Entrance standards were lowered—even sons of the lower middle class were welcomed. Because social standards were lowered a big class differentiation developed between the captains—even some majors—and more junior officers, and the colonels and generals. This meant that in the Overseas Territories the junior and medium-grade officers began to feel considerable sympathy for those waging their independence struggles as well as a feeling of hopelessness as to any chances of a Portuguese victory.

In an attempt to stimulate interest in a military career, in July, 1973, the Caetano government offered any university graduate six months of militia-type training in Portugal followed by commissions with privileges and pay on the same scale as those who had done several tours of duty in Africa. This proved to be the stone that upset Caetano's applecart! A conspiratorial meeting of about 150 officers took place on September 12, 1973, in a house on the outskirts of the lovely old town of Evora, some hundred miles almost due east of Lisbon. They included the artillery officer:

> The September 12 meeting was to protest against the idea that youngsters with six months home training could be promoted over the heads of those with four and more years of training and overseas service. Apart from anything else, this would have a terrible effect on the battlefield. We mainly discussed the new decree, but also the

deterioration of the military situation in Africa. We elected a committee from the different branches of the armed services to bring pressure on the Caetano government to withdraw the decree.

At that time we had no thought of making a coup. There was no unified political viewpoint. We were naïve, thinking it was enough to point out the injustice and the government would correct it. We wanted the decree repealed and the standing of career officers safeguarded. Our leverage, we felt, was that the government needed us, but we also recognized the dangers. The PIDE was bound to be informed. But with the wars going so badly we felt that if our movement was united enough the government would not dare to arrest us. . . . We continued to meet secretly, always in different places. At the beginning we did not know each other's viewpoints. Because of built-in loyalties, there were those who reported everything discussed, back to the Ministry of Defense. The minister became worried and started some shadow-boxing. A document was circulated setting forth all the great things that the government had done to improve the lot of the armed forces. We were all supposed to sign this, but refused. This was the first act of open defiance.

As members were posted overseas, the movement was exported with them. To Guiné-Bissau—where Captain Otelo Saraiva de Carvalho was very active—to Angola and Mozambique. Discussion groups started there at the same level. It was the captains, as company commanders in the field, who were taking the greatest losses in Africa. So it was natural that they should be most active in discussing and clarifying the situation.

The reaction of Caetano to the alarm signals he was getting was very typical of the man and the system. Things were changed in form but not content. Even the PIDE (International Police for State Security) was changed into the DGS (Directorate of General Security), but the men and methods remained the same. Salazar's "National Union" party became the "People's National Action" party, but the leadership and fascist policies remained unchanged. A civilian, Dr. Joaquim Moreíra da Silva Cunha replaced General Alberto Viama Rebelo as Defense Minister, but the offending decree remained in force. A new post, Minister for the Army, was created, with a General Alberto de Andrade e Silva in charge. His solution was to give a small pay hike to the lower officers and sergeants. The artillery officer commented:

This may have impressed some of the sergeants, but it was too late to have any effect on the captains. The discussions had gone far beyond the repeal of the July decree by this time. The whole question of the African wars had been posed and, in the light of that, the nature of the regime at home. Beyond that, we had discussed the war in Vietnam, the role of the United States in global politics—the whole world situation.[1] We were getting more ideologically motivated. In these discussions and analyses, those with the most logical answers were those most listened to. . . .

The new Minister for the Army knew what the captains were up to and that the discussions had taken on a specific political character, and he was not the only senior officer to know of this. On December 20 [1973] the Spanish prime minister, Admiral Carrero Blanco was assassinated. Caetano went to Madrid for the funeral. General Kaulza de Arriaga,[2] former military commander in Mozambique, who knew about our discussions, approached us and offered his services to head a coup while Caetano was away in Madrid. We refused. A rightist military putsch aimed at prosecuting the wars in Africa more efficiently was the last thing we wanted. Not only that, but one of our officers [it was Captain Carlos dos Santos Fabiao, later chief of staff of the post-coup Portuguese armed forces—W.B.] stood up in the military academy and denounced Kaulza de Arriaga's move. But by January, 1974, we were unanimous that the fascist regime itself had to be changed and, given its nature, this could be done only by a military coup. . . .

We came to this decision reluctantly. In 1969, when Caetano replaced Salazar as prime minister, we had some hopes that he would change things . . . but he had turned into a jellyfish and would have to be overthrown. A much smaller committee was elected to replace the original *ad hoc* one and it was entrusted specifically with the task of organizing a coup. The new committee was given full powers to plan whatever action it considered most effective. By this time we knew that all telephone conversations between members of what had already become the Armed Forces Movement were tapped by the DGS. Communications from then on were by personal contacts, the wives of AFM members often acting as couriers. And, although the new committee was smaller, it was more representative as far as units were concerned and it covered all of Portugal.

In the meantime another incident had added fuel to the flames. There had been student troubles at Coimbra University, the country's oldest and most prestigious school. These were partly in protest at the undemocratic nature of the October 28, 1973, National Assembly elections and vaguely at the continued prosecution of the war. The most militant of the student leaders

59

were punished by being drafted into the military academy. While some officers secretly welcomed the injection of radical and ideologically motivated students as reinforcements to the movement, the general feeling was resentment that the armed forces and the military academy were regarded by the government as some kind of penal institution. It was the final straw which apparently persuaded a few waverers that direct action was the only way out. The coup planning committee was divided into two parts: a military subcommittee to work out the tactical planning for the coup and coordinate military action between the various branches of the armed forces, and a political subcommittee to draw up a political program. Captain Otelo Saraiva de Carvalho was in charge of the military subcommittee; Major Melo Antunes was in charge of drafting the political program. What specifically motivated them? It was an obvious question at my first meeting with Otelo de Carvalho. He replied as follows:

I spent three tours of duty in Africa. Two in Angola, one in Guiné-Bissau. For me and many of my comrades, an anti-colonial consciousness was formed during such tours of duty. Why were we fighting? Why were our comrades dying? Why were African patriots being massacred? For the big Portuguese monopolies. So they could keep their hands on the raw materials and exploit the cheap labor of the Africans. So that the privileges of the rich settlers could be maintained.

In my first tour of duty we worked off some of our frustrations by trying to help the population by building roads, schools, hospitals, sanitation works. . . . But by my second tour, I understood this was all useless. To really bring happiness to the Angolan people their country had to be returned to them. We were involved in an unjust war. I first went to Angola in 1961. The officers and sergeants used to whip up morale by urging troops into battle with such slogans as: "Angola Is Ours!" . . . "Save the Motherland!" and other jingoistic appeals. When I returned in 1965, the atmosphere had changed completely. There were still not many desertions at that time, but you couldn't whip up enthusiasm any longer with the old slogans. From then on things went from bad to worse because all the junior officers and lower ranks understood that it was an unjust war.

By 1973, at the end of my last tour of duty, in Guiné-Bissau, the hope of the officers' corps was that we could hold on and create conditions for the government to find a political solution. But the inefficiency and immobility of the government was terrifying. That is why we decided the only way to end the war was to end the regime. And that is why I agreed to play a leading role.

Born in Mozambique, Otelo de Carvalho comes from a relatively modest background. Certainly the daily injustices meted out to the Africans helped condition Otelo's feelings as to the unjust nature of the war. Melo Antunes, however, comes from an extremely rich patrician Lisbon family, yet his reaction to my question as to how he got involved in such a hazardous adventure, which might easily have cost him the rest of his life in prison, was very similar to Otelo's. There seemed no objective reason why he should have thrown in his lot with the conspirators. He came close to admitting this:

My development was perhaps not typical for the others. As a student, I was somewhat autodidactic, delving into things beyond the requirements of my formal studies. Although I was in the literary faculty at the university, I became very interested in social and political problems. I went into the army only because this was a family tradition. Soldiering did not stop me from thinking, or exercising the critical faculty which I had developed toward things in general.

But during my fifteen years in the army, I found it impossible to exert any criticism either against the army or the regime. Still, I maintained contact with my left-wing friends and was active when this was practicable. I read everything I could lay hands on and tried to prepare myself for when the time was ripe. The formation of the Armed Forces Movement provided the occasion.

When I asked whether there was anything particularly decisive that pushed him to play the role he did, Melo Antunes said:

My three terms of service in Angola—two years each—made the strongest contribution to my real understanding of the colonial question. Those experiences defined my attitude toward colonialism and the fascist regime. Reality comes from practice. Practice in the army—as in other fields—taught me reality. And in all those years of military service I never lost my critical faculty—although exerting it was another matter.

I thought I would try constitutional means. In the elections of 1969, I wanted to stand as a candidate of the CDE opposition.[3] After all, there were officers in the National Assembly representing the fascist National Union Party—why not officers for the legal opposition movement? I was a captain at the time. The authorities made me withdraw my candidacy. I was subject to military discipline and had to stand down. Systematic persecution followed—continual transfers and other punishment. This was decisive in proving to me that other means had to be found to change the regime. When the Armed Forces Movement was formed, it was obvious that this was the instrument for those "other means."

In view of the attitudes of officers like Otelo de Carvalho and Melo Antunes, it was not surprising that the AFM program stipulated, among other points, that there must be: "Recognition of the principle that the solution to the wars overseas is political and not military; conditions must be created for a frank and open debate at the national level of all the overseas problems aimed at a new policy that will lead to peace." Nor was it surprising that it was these two officers who played a key role in thwarting the schemes of the first post-coup president, General Antonio Sebastiao Ribeiro de Spinola, to sabotage the decolonialization process. (In this, Spinola was ably supported by the then foreign minister, Socialist Party leader, Mário Soares.) It was only after the decolonialization negotiations were taken out of the hands of Soares and entrusted to Melo Antunes that things really started to move.

If the London negotiations on Guiné-Bissau which started on May 25, 1974—one month to the day after the coup—had an atmosphere of complete unreality, those on Angola, at the resort town of Alvor on Portugal's southern coast, were marked by a business-like practicality which provided for Portugal's withdrawal from by far its richest African colony. The Alvor Agreement (January 15, 1975) was the high-water mark of the AFM pledge to accord independence to the African colonies. I was present at both the London and Alvor conferences, and it was impossible not to note the difference in style between a delegation headed by Mário Soares, with right-wing Palma Carlos as prime minister, and that headed by Melo Antunes, with the progressive Vasco Gonçalves as prime minister. From the London conference, I reported:

This is a conference of apparent good will and the atmosphere seems good. But the Guiné-Bissau delegation is far more conscious of the historic nature of the talks here than the Portuguese delegation.

Soares is mandated to negotiate a military cease-fire and discuss a form of "self-determination" to be decided by a referendum. The mandate of Major Pires of the PAIGC (African Party for the Independence of Guiné-Bissau and the Cape Verde Islands) is to get an agreement which will be a model for those later to be concluded between Portugal and its southern African colonies of Mozambique and Angola. Also to get Portugal's new government to see that "self-determination" and "referendum" in this context are old-fashioned terms which have lost their meaning.

It is a replay of the old record that has been heard from Panmunjom in 1951 . . . of the side in the wrong wanting a purely military disengagement to get its troops out of an untenable situation, while the other side wants an overall, lasting political-military settlement. . . .

Mário Soares had told a group of us in Lisbon on the eve of his departure for London that he expected to sign an agreement within two days. He returned to Lisbon for consultations on the fourth day of the talks without any agreement. After two days in Lisbon he returned to London, where the meeting was adjourned after two more days of fruitless talks. " 'Self-determination' would have sounded wonderful in 1945," Major Pires told me.

"But not in 1974. We have been recognized as an independent state by nearly ninety countries. We have observer status at the United Nations. Over two-thirds of our country is solidly liberated. Why should we discuss Portugal supervising our "self-determination"? Our people have already "determined" what they want. Full and total independence with no strings attached.

But that was part of the unreality within which Spinola and Soares dictated that "decolonialization" should be negotiated. A further meeting between Mário Soares and Major Pires in Algiers in mid-June got nowhere. It was the same situation with Mozambique. Despite the public and well-photographed heartiness with which Soares greeted Samora Machel at the opening session of "decolonialization" talks on June 5, 1974, the talks immediately bogged down and were adjourned the following day. A brief communiqué noted that "both sides recognized that the establishment of a cease-fire depends on prior global agreement related to fundamental political principles." Which indicates that what most interested Soares was a cease-fire, whereas Samora Machel had reaffirmed the position that he had outlined in a speech three days before the talks started: "It is not the contents of independence that we are going to discuss with the Portuguese. Independence is our inalienable right. We intend to discuss the transfer of powers."

Some of the most militant officers in the AFM by this time (mid-June) were muttering doubts as to their choice of Spinola as president and were wondering aloud whether they might have to start all over again. On June 7, Spinola made a speech in Lisbon which sounded like an obituary for the Armed Forces Movement. "It is impossible to exaggerate the debt of gratitude the country owes to those valiant workers of the Movement of April 25. Now that its task has ended, let me express the appreciation of the nation to all those who acted without pressures or conformism in the higher interests of the community. . . ." You've done a great job, lads, now back to the barracks, was the sense. The captains, however, were far from feeling that their "task was ended." Above all, it had not ended on that key issue of decolonialization—the only way to end the African wars.

On July 5, Premier Palma Carlos issued an ultimatum: either he must be granted far wider powers or he would resign. The extended powers would include authority to hold presidential elections within three months to confirm Spinola as the head of a presidential-type regime; postponement of the elections to a Constituent Assembly scheduled to be held by March 31, 1975, until November 1976; and authority for the prime minister to choose his cabinet without reference to the president—all three clear violations of the AFM program. After an all-night session on July 8-9, the State Council, comprised of seven members of the ruling junta set up after the April 25 coup, seven members of the Coordinating Committee of the AFM, and seven citizens of "recognized merit," turned down the Palma Carlos ultimatum. Only three of the twenty-one members supported him. So he resigned. Three of his supporters in the cabinet went with him, including a Spinola protégé, Lt. Colonel Firmino Miguel. Two days later, most of Lisbon's morning and evening papers announced that the president had chosen Firmino Miguel as the new premier. But on July 12, it was announced that the new prime minister was Colonel Vasco dos Santos Gonçalves, which meant that the Armed Forces Movement was digging in its heels: Firmino Miguel had never been associated with it, whereas Vasco Gonçalves had lent it his full support from the moment of its existence.

Things on the decolonialization front moved swiftly from that moment on. On July 17, a small "rectification" to the Constitution appeared in the *Government Gazette* recognizing that people in the Overseas Territories had the right to "self-determination *with all its consequences.*" (Emphasis added.) A few days later, at the demand of the AFM leadership, President Spinola declared that the "consequences" included the "right to political independence to be proclaimed in terms and on dates to be agreed. . . ." In the new cabinet, Melo Antunes was appointed Minister without Portfolio charged with Decolonialization, among other tasks. New talks were held with Guiné-Bissau in mid-August and on August 26 complete agreement was announced in Algiers on the terms of independence. On September 10, 1974, Portugal recognized *de facto* Guiné-Bissau as a sovereign and independent country and, as a good will gesture, sponsored the admission of the new republic to the United Nations. There were parallel talks with the FRELIMO leadership, in which Otelo de Carvalho joined Melo Antunes and Mário Soares in trying to get a reasonable and realistic settlement. After one of these sessions, which took place in the Zambian capital of Lusaka, Otelo told me how he had accompanied Mário Soares to the Belem presidential palace in Lisbon to report to Spinola. He had asserted with typical soldierly bluntness that there was only one thing to do—accept the FRELIMO proposals "which seem to me to be the only correct and possible ones" if Portugal wanted to withdraw with her "head high." But Spinola was furious and threatened to ask President Nixon to send American troops to Mozambique. With Soares a glum but silent onlooker, Otelo objected that Nixon would not be interested in a Vietnamization of the war in Mozambique. Spinola retorted that if Nixon refused, South Africa was sure to oblige.

Otelo published this version in an interview with the weekly *Portugalia* on December 12, 1974. Spinola issued a communiqué denying he had said any such thing, but Otelo stuck to his version, noting the curious silence of Mário Soares on the whole affair. At a press conference on December 31, a spokesman for the Coordinating Committee of the AFM, replying to a question about the Spinola denial, said: "We have no doubts whatsoever as to the veracity of the statement made by Brigadier Otelo Saraivo de Carvalho, as the matter was known to the Coordinating Committee at the time it occurred. . . ."

Despite Spinola's active opposition, and the spinelessness of Soares, an agreement was reached on September 7 for a gradual transfer of powers so that complete independence would be achieved by June 25, 1975—the thirteenth anniversary of the founding of FRELIMO. "The independent state of Mozambique," states the agreement, "will exercise complete sovereignty in the internal and external domain, establishing political institutions and choosing the social system which it considers in the best interests of the people." Spinola's reaction, three days after the signing of the agreement, was a speech in Lisbon calling for a "silent majority" to assert itself against "totalitarian extremists working in the shadows." Immediately after Spinola's September 10 speech, glossy, expensively produced posters began to appear all over Portugal portraying a man's face, lips stitched together, exhorting "silent majority" support for Spinola and a "No" to "extremists." The word was passed around that there would be a monster "Silent Majority" rally in the Lisbon *Pequeno Campo* bullring on September 28. Foreign journalists who followed up literature slipped under their hotel room doors, with invitations to contact the MFP (Portuguese Federalist Movement), received free tickets for a bullfight in the same arena on September 26. The tickets were handed out with a few words that something sensational could be expected and a nod and a wink to the effect that it would be something super-sensational. As the ostensible aim was to raise funds for the Returned Soldiers' Association, the bullfight was virtually an official event, with President Spinola and Prime Minister Gonçalves due to attend.

Spinola, who arrived first, was greeted with unusually enthusiastic applause and ecstatic cries of "Long live the President." The first "sensation," however, was when Gonçalves was greeted with boos, derogatory shouts against the Armed Forces Movement and cries of "Long live the Overseas Territories." It turned out that large blocks of seats had been reserved for special groups. Foreign journalists, as the Lisbon press noted next day, were not the only ones to have been offered free tickets! Little notice was given to the bullfight, attention being focused on an energetic discussion between Spinola and an obviously angry Gonçalves.

66

What was gnawing at Spinola's vitals was the specter of Angola, with all its oil, diamonds, coffee, and other riches going the way Guiné-Bissau and Mozambique had gone. The only way to halt the trend was to get rid of Gonçalves and send the Armed Forces Movement back to the barracks. While the bullfight and argument between president and prime minister continued, word was passed around that after the event was over there would be an attack against the headquarters of the Communist Party, only a few hundred yards away from the *Pequeno Campo*. By the time the "Silent Majority" activists started streaming toward the Communist Party headquarters, however, the way was blocked by hastily assembled pro-Communist militants. Members of some of the organized groups from the bullring suddenly appeared in helmets, with iron bars and even an occasional knife and pistol in their hands. There was a short sharp clash in which the knives and pistols were flourished with threats that they would be used "later." The iron bars were wielded, but the attackers were easily beaten off. All this was just a full-dress rehearsal for what was planned for the "Silent Majority" rally two days later.

The left-wing parties—for once the Communists and Socialists were on the same side—demanded the rally be banned. They were backed by the civilian governor of Lisbon who pointed out that such a rally was "unauthorized." Spinola insisted, in the name of "freedom of expression," that it be held. The Armed Forces Movement at first held a "neutral" position, but leaders of the left-wing parties produced evidence of arms entering the country from Spain and of plans to infiltrate commando groups into the capital as "participants" in the rally.

After the *Pequeno Campo* incident, the AFM leadership began to prick up its ears, especially when on September 27, virtually the entire Lisbon press demanded that the rally be banned. Throughout that day barricades and checkpoints were set up all over the country—especially at the approaches to Lisbon. The trade unions responded to the "Ban the Rally" appeal. Engineers halted their Lisbon-bound trains, drivers stopped the buses which were to transport tens of thousands of people, mostly from the politically backward areas of the country, provided with free tickets to converge on the Lisbon bullring.

Activists from the Communist and Socialist parties and the MDP (Portuguese Democratic Movement, which originally grouped the Communist, Socialist and Progressive Catholic movements, but from which the Socialists later withdrew) went to the barricades and checkpoints and were later joined by local units of the armed forces, on instructions from the AFM leadership. Patient explanations were given as to why people were being turned back and cars searched for arms. That such vigilance was justified was shown by the search of a hearse on its way to Lisbon. Despite the protests of the driver and his companion, activists at the barricade even opened the coffin. It was found to contain machine guns and bazookas. There were many similar discoveries. Such arms were handed over by the controllers to the AFM representatives who, in most cases, handed them back to the activists.

It was by far the most dramatic moment since April 25. And not only at the barricades. A cabinet meeting which started at the São Bento governmental palace late on the evening of the 27th, and at which a majority demanded the banning of the rally, was transferred to São Belem, the presidential palace, with Spinola instead of Goncalves presiding. Otelo (by then Brigadier Otelo de Carvalho and deputy head of the newly created nation's security forces, COPCON, popularly known as the anti-coup command) was also convoked to the presidential palace. He later described the atmosphere as he walked in:

> Around two o'clock on the morning of the 28th, I was summoned to Belem Palace to find everyone in a state of great tension. An atmosphere you could cut with a knife. . . . I was aware that the grave problem of the moment was that of setting up the barricades and how to dismantle them as soon as possible. The fact was that despite tremendous discussions no one had turned up with a solution. I was called in to the council chamber, where I found General Spinola deeply shaken and in a state of great excitement. Prime Minister Vasco Gonçalves was also there and I learned later that he had been attacked and insulted by those elements of the Junta of National Salvation [the seven-member ruling body, headed by Spinola— W.B.] who were later purged. I also learned later that when they started to insult him, he wanted to leave the palace, reacting violently against an order to resign, to quit his post.

To his great astonishment, Otelo de Carvalho found that he, like Vasco Gonçalves, was virtually under arrest. He had left his

COPCON headquarters, saying he would be back in forty-five minutes at most. With the country on the verge of civil war and the effective commander of its security forces under detention, together with the prime minister, it was obvious that flashpoint was being reached. (The titular head of COPCON was General Francisco da Costa Gomes, but as he was concurrently chief of staff of the armed forces, Otelo de Carvalho was the operational head.)

At a certain point, the fact of my being detained at Belem Palace started to worry my comrades whose units were in a state of alert. . . . An hour went by, a second hour, and then every minute telephone calls started to pour into Belem Palace, all of them asking for me. I started then to centralize my command post there where I was, especially for those units which were the most excited. Anxiety grew like a snowball. Calls poured in from all over the country—from Porto, Coimbra, Caldas da Rainha, from the navy and air force—calls that took on an ever more alarmed note—asking what was going on? Had I been arrested? If not when would I be returning to headquarters? There were units which wanted to march on Belem—even against my orders—because they noticed that I wasn't speaking freely over the telephone. It was clear to them that I was under constraint. In fact there was always an officer from the president's staff at my side at the telephone. I spoke mainly in monosyllables: yes, no, okay, I'm all right, no problems. But tensions continued to build up.

News reached the palace, via the radio of a mobile detachment of the Republican Guards [a very reactionary urban security unit which was a hangover from the fascist regime, still in being despite left-wing demands that it be deactivated—W.B.] that two artillery units from the [leftist-commanded] Light Artillery Regiment were moving on Belem. There was then a counterorder from the palace to reinforce its defenses with a squadron from the Seventh Cavalry Regiment. . . .

All these events led me at one point to turn to General Costa Gomes and say: "General, things are in such a state that I'm afraid my comrades start to believe that I really am arrested. The best thing would be for me to return straight away to COPCON while you stay here commanding the forces. You set up your headquarters here; I will send you a senior officer to maintain liaison with COPCON, while I return to quiet down our people there."

Costa Gomes agreed, but when Otelo started to leave the palace an officer from the president's staff prevented him on some vague pretext that his presence was still needed. He started to leave a second time and was again prevented. This time Spinola's choice for prime minister, Firmino Miguel, intervened to explain: "I'll tell you something that nobody else has the guts to say: President Spinola summoned you here in order to detain you." Otelo replied that he would not be responsible for the consequences. The telephone calls continued to pour in. At one point, with Otelo's COPCON chief of staff on the line, Spinola stepped up to the telephone and said: "Otelo is right alongside me. He has not been arrested. We are working in close cooperation. He is perfectly all right."

In the end it was agreed that Otelo should leave for COPCON together with Spinola and his entourage, plus Costa Gomes and his staff. When most of them were already in their cars, Otelo was summoned again by Spinola who informed him that he would not go personally to COPCON, but that he should convince the COPCON headquarters staff that everything was "all right" and they had the complete confidence of Spinola.

Spinola, in fact, was the first to crack. In the meantime he had been issuing all sorts of orders for units to move. But the units demanded that the orders come from Otelo. Spinola had also issued arbitrary orders that no newspapers should appear on the 28th, while the radio continued to broadcast a presidential communiqué to the effect that the rally would go ahead as planned. Instead of confirmation that units loyal to him—so he thought to himself—were marching to his defense, the palace was bombarded with calls from units wanting to rush to the rescue of Otelo de Carvalho, who personified the Armed Forces Movement. The true relation of forces in the country at that time was revealed by those telephone calls early on the morning of the 28th, and by the determination of those manning the barricades.

At midday on the 28th, a communiqué was issued in Spinola's name canceling the rally. By mid-afternoon a communiqué was issued by the MDP with a first list of those arrested in what was proven to be a well-organized plot to seize power. Apart from the notorious General Kaulza de Arriaga, there were two other well-known fascist generals, Pereira de Castro and Barbieri Cardoso, plus a dozen lower-ranking officers. Civilians included a son of Caetano and a member of the Champalimaud family—the country's second biggest monopoly grouping. The following day it was announced that nineteen members of the Espirito Santo family—the third biggest monopoly and owners of the bank of the same name—had fled to Madrid. In the small hours of that fateful Saturday morning a COPCON unit—acting on a tip-off—had raided the headquarters of the MAP (Portuguese Action Movement), one of the innumerable small parties operating under a "nationalist center" label. In a room on the first floor they found—and arrested—seven men, one with a rifle mounted with a telescopic sight. He turned out to be a qualified sharpshooter. A small pane in a window which overlooked the residence of Vasco Gonçalves had been broken sufficiently to give a clear view of the prime minister's movements around his home, well within range of the rifle. Apart from other arms there were copies of a MAP manifesto warning of the threat which the present situation posed "to Portuguese permanent values and traditions." By detaining Vasco Gonçalves during those hours when his movements would normally have brought him within range of what the Lisbon press referred to as the "Dallas rifle," President Spinola probably unwittingly saved the prime minister's life!

At eleven o'clock on Monday morning, September 30, Spinola appeared on television to announce his resignation as president in a tough, defiant speech obviously aimed at further encouragement for the "silent majority." One of the original "captains" who was standing by my side at a television set commented: "He was never really with us. He joined the movement in order to cancel it out. As a military technician he knew he couldn't win. But he couldn't bring himself—and much less the social-economic forces he really represented—to accept decolonialization on the only possible basis: total independence."

Just how serious the coup attempt had been was apparent when COPCON forces raided the headquarters of the Federalist Movement (which had changed its name to Progress Party just prior to September 28) on Avenida Infante Santo, in the very heart of Lisbon. It turned out to be a military-political headquarters and arsenal. Apart from a certain quantity of arms seized on the spot, there was an inventory of others ordered from abroad. Some of them were later found in caches inside the country. These included fifty 60 mm. mortars and five thousand mortar shells; fifty bazookas with incendiary, armor-piercing and explosive rockets; two hundred light automatics with 100,000 rounds of ammunition;

nine hundred hand grenades of various types; one hundred Mauser and other type pistols; cartridge belts and magazines to equip two thousand men; two hundred Molotov cocktails and chemical equipment, on the spot, for thousands more. The headquarters section included sophisticated equipment supplied by ITT (International Telephone and Telegraph Company of sad notoriety during the Chilean coup, and owners of Lisbon's Sheraton hotel) for intercepting telephone and radio communications; maps of strategic nerve centers of Lisbon and other cities; duplicated extracts from a book which set out the step-by-step preparation and execution of the anti-Allende coup in Chile; lists of Portuguese to be summarily executed and others to be arrested and concentrated for investigation in the Lisbon football stadium and bullring à la Chile!

Costa Gomes replaced Spinola as president, Vasco Gonçalves was reconfirmed in his post as prime minister, Otelo de Carvalho became the titular head of COPCON. Three right-wing members of the military junta were dismissed; Firmino Miguel was removed from his post as Defense Minister as was the Monarchist, Sanches Osorio, from his post as Minister of Social Communications (Information). (It was ironic, to say the least, that it was Mário Soares, as prime minister, who restored Firmino Miguel as Minister of Defense in his first cabinet, announced on July 23, 1976.)

In looking back and scratching below the surface of those first six months of AFM power, one finds—despite everything that was written in the Western press at the time—that the central issue was always that of the dismemberment of Portugal's colonial empire. While the press went on about conflict of personalities, Gonçalves's authoritarianism, Communist take-over of the trade unions, freedom of the press, "political pluralism," and whatever, the main question being passionately discussed at cabinet meetings and other behind-the-scenes debates was always the pros and cons of an honest and sincere decolonialization policy. And if the July crisis paved the way for the independence of Guiné-Bissau and Mozambique, the September crisis paved the way for that of Angola—the bitterest pill that Portuguese reaction was forced to swallow.

With many of the leading opponents of decolonialization in Portugal itself in jail, and others like Spinola neutralized, ardent decolonializers like Melo Antunes, Otelo de Carvalho and the "Red Admiral," Rosa de Coutinho, worked hard to harmonize the views of the three proclaimed national liberation movements, the MPLA, FNLA, and UNITA. Leaders of neighboring countries and members of the OAU also did their best to bring about what turned out to be an unnatural alliance among the three, or at least get them to agree on a common negotiating position solid enough to secure a Portuguese withdrawal from Angola.

Thus it was that on January 17, 1975, the three Angolan leaders affixed their signatures, alongside those of the three Portuguese ministers responsible for the decolonialization process, to a document which provided for independence for Angola by November 11 of that same year. It was a moving and solemn ceremony, reflecting the thoughts of Portuguese and Angolan leaders alike that there were almost certainly stormy waters to be navigated before what was an excellent agreement on paper would become reality.

The difference between the atmosphere at the Alvor Conference and the other decolonialization conferences I had attended was that there was sincerity and good will on the part of those representing the colonial power toward the former colony. There was no tricky corporation-lawyer approach, no attempt to cheat "the natives." The traditional "divide and rule" formula had been transformed into a "unite and be free" counsel to the three movements, with the Portuguese negotiators playing a major role in bringing the rivals sufficiently close together to speed up production of the final document of Angolan independence. History will accord due merit to Prime Minister Vasco Gonçalves for his courage and stubborn integrity on that vital and emotion-charged issue of decolonialization, as embodied in the Alvor Accord. But it was his unyielding stand on this issue, together with his equally firm decisions later on nationalizing the banks and major monopolies and presiding over the expropriation of the great estates of the absentee landlords in the Alentejo, which earned him the bitter, unforgiving hatred of reaction at home and abroad. The intensity of the campaign later waged against him, especially in certain sections of the Western press enraged at the prospects of multinational interests falling into black hands in Africa and "red" hands in Portugal itself, subsequently led to a fatal split within the AFM leadership. First Melo Antunes, then Otelo de Carvalho,

73

joined with those demanding the ouster of Gonçalves, something both of them later were to regret bitterly. It must be recorded that Mário Soares, with the backing of Western Europe's Social Democrats, played a leading role, in the name of "democracy" and "plurality," in dragging Gonçalves down and thereby wrecking the progressive leadership of the Armed Forces Movement. But among the things which the successors to the four governments presided over by Vasco Gonçalves were *not* able to do was to put the former Portuguese empire together again. Not only did Gonçalves preside over the dissolution of that empire, he also blocked very serious attempts to impose neocolonialist solutions aimed at keeping the wealth—especially that of Angola—in multinational and Portuguese monopoly hands.

VII The Portuguese Exit

The delegations of FNLA, MPLA, and UNITA, led by their respective presidents, Mr. Holden Roberto, Dr. Agostinho Neto, and Dr. Jonas Savimbi, met at State House, Mombasa, Republic of Kenya from January 3 to 5, 1975, thanks to the good will and availability of the government of the Republic of Kenya.

The meeting evolved in an atmosphere of mutual and perfect understanding. As a result the delegations fround a common political platform in the light of the negotiations with the Portuguese government for the formation of a Transitional Government which will lead Angola to independence. The three delegations analyzed all problems related to the decolonialization process and to the future sovereign state of Angola.

The delegations agreed on a common political platform which includes, among other questions, those related to the formation of the Transitional Government, to the question of the armed forces in Angola and to the creation and installation of future institutions. Within the same spirit of understanding and unity, the three liberation movements decided that from now on they will cooperate in all spheres and especially on that of decolonialization for the defense of the territorial integrity as well as for the national reconstruction. . . .

So stated the splendid "Final Communiqué" of the three presidents which made the Alvor Conference and speedy agreement with the Portuguese possible. Prior to this—and subsequent to it—such "understanding and unity" had been distinguished by its absence. As an example, less than two months after the "Captains' Coup," Jonas Savimbi had declared a unilateral cease-fire—on June 17, 1974. The MPLA leadership was in a state of deep crisis. In addition to the "Eastern Revolt" of Daniel Chipenda, a group of highly influential intellectuals—nineteen in all—headed by Mário de Andrade and his brother, the Reverend Joaquim da Rocha Pinto de Andrade, launched from Brazzaville in May, 1974, an "Active Revolt" faction directed at what they called Agostinho Neto's "presidentialism." They criticized the MPLA-FNLA agreement on setting up the "Supreme Council of the Revolution," with Holden Roberto as president, although by that time it was clear this was devoid of any practical significance. This defection had little influence on the military situation since the "Active Revolt" members had not been "active" on the battlefield, but it greatly complicated matters on the international front, as did Chipenda's defection. (In 1973, the Soviet Union had switched its support from Neto to Chipenda, switching back again only after learning, and warning Neto of Chipenda's plans to assassinate him. These dissensions led to various OAU mediation attempts which objectively weakened the military struggle more than the defections themselves. Speaking of the period immediately after the "Captains' Coup," Lucio Lara said:

The local Portuguese military authorities used the FNLA and UNITA to try to destroy us, counting on the MPLA having been mortally weakened by internal dissensions. The FNLA and UNITA made their separate and unilateral cease-fires and concentrated their efforts with the Portuguese forces to do just this. But despite the Chipenda military defection, the vast majority of the rank and file in the Mbunda zone remained loyal to us and we were solid on the ground in all our liberated areas. We beat off attacks on all fronts because no one on the enemy side had much stomach for the battlefield by then. One day our headquarters radio operator was twirling the knobs of a set freshly captured from the Portuguese. By chance he raised the Portuguese military headquarters in Lisbon. "Who's that?" came the query. "The enemy," replied our operator once he realized who was on the line. "Which enemy?" By then we were alerted. "The MPLA." "Hang on" came the reply. Both sides were quick to exploit this unexpected contact. Lisbon suggested an immediate meeting, but President Neto was in no hurry. Then Rosa Coutinho came on the line and a rendezvous site was fixed for three weeks later.

Thus, on October 21, 1974, a cease-fire agreement was signed by Agostinho Neto on behalf of the MPLA and naval Captain Leonel Gomes Cardoso on behalf of the Portuguese armed forces, and that stage of the armed struggle came to an end. Lucio Lara noted that during the negotiations the Portuguese side was "interested in projecting UNITA and tried to impress us with the need for coming to terms with Savimbi."

It was on the basis of the three cease-fire agreements that delegations from the FNLA, UNITA, and the MPLA arrived in Luanda in November, 1974. The MPLA delegation was greeted by the greatest mass demonstration the capital had ever seen. But while the MPLA arrived without troops or weapons, the FNLA brought in substantial quantities of both. As part of the Alvor Agreement, each of the three movements was to contribute 8,000 of its troops which, together with 24,000 Portuguese troops, would form a mixed force of 48,000 troops, surplus Portuguese troops to be withdrawn between October 1, 1975, and February 29, 1976. Three representatives of each of the movements, presided over by the Portuguese High Commissioner, would act as a ten-member National Defense Commission. This never worked. Regular forces of the Zaire army, plus Zaire-based regular FNLA troops which had taken no part in the national liberation struggle invaded Angola in the north in March, 1975, first occupying Ambriz, a coastal town 150 miles south of the Zaire border, then Carmona (now Uije, capital of the province of that name) and other key points in the northern areas. This released reinforcements for the FNLA troops already in Luanda and these started pressure and provocations to try to drive the MPLA delegation out of the city.

According to Comandante "Juju," spokesman for the general staff of the FAPLA at the time, we discussed the situation (March, 1976), and whose version was confirmed by countless residents who were in Luanda at the time:

It was after troops of the Zaire army invaded the North with continuous armed provocations against our cadres that some of our troops entered Luanda. During March, there were three or four incidents every day. We made cease-fire agreements but each was followed by an escalation of the attacks. On March 23, there was a heavy attack against MPLA headquarters installations at Cazenga and Vila Alice in the outskirts. The following day FNLA gunmen rounded up over fifty MPLA cadres and members, took them off in trucks and machine-gunned them to death at Kifangondo, about twenty kilometers to the north of the capital. At the end of the month the FNLA brought into Luanda a motorized column comprising five hundred troops. . . .

By this time, UNITA had joined forces with the FNLA, the latter having taken advantage of the withdrawal, passivity, or tacit support of the Portuguese to take over many towns in the Center-South, aided by armed Portuguese vigilante groups from the local settlers. On the eve of May Day, the pro-MPLA trade union headquarters had been attacked in Luanda. Despite further cease-fires, fighting continued throughout June and the first days of July. On July 9, a funeral procession for an MPLA woman cadre, Lilia Celina, was attacked with heavy machine-gun fire from the nearby FNLA headquarters. This was the last straw. On July 12, in an organized mass action directed by MPLA militants, the FNLA headquarters was destroyed. After three days of bitter skirmishes, the FNLA-UNITA forces were driven from the capital. That was the end of the Transitional Government and the start of what the MPLA leadership considers the "Second War of Resistance."

While content to defend the capital from repeated FNLA attempts to recapture it, the FAPLA launched a vigorous offensive to retake former MPLA strongholds farther south, control of which had been shared with FNLA-UNITA forces of the Transitional Government.

Confirmation of this admittedly MPLA version of events in Luanda during the period described comes from two well-known—and by no means pro-MPLA—British journalist specialists on southern Africa, Colin Legum and Tony Hodges, in a booklet published in 1976. In the section entitled "How the MPLA Won," Hodges writes:

> In the early months of 1975, the FNLA was acutely conscious of its political weakness in the country, above all in MPLA-dominated Luanda. The Front's support (until the fusion with Chipenda's forces) was concentrated almost exclusively among the northern Bakongo, half of whom were living abroad in refugee settlements in Zaire. The FNLA tried to overcome this unfavorable relation of forces, particularly in the strategic capital area, by setting up a well-financed political apparatus and sending in well-armed contingents of its armed wing, the ELNA, into Luanda and other important centers. With funds supplied by Zaire and the U.S. the FNLA bought up the country's major means of communications, acquiring a TV station and the leading daily newspaper. . . . More important, the FNLA began to move large numbers of heavily armed ELNA troops from its base camps in Zaire into Angola, including hostile Luanda. On a simple level, the FNLA had a distinct advantage over its rivals at this time. While the MPLA had built up a relatively small guerilla army of about 6,000 soldiers (UNITA had an even smaller guerilla force of, at most, 1,000), FNLA had trained a regular army of about 15,000 troops in its Zairean camps. In addition, it was well supplied with arms, having received 450 tons of Chinese arms in 1974, and it had the assistance of 125 Chinese military instructors. . . . Indicative of the FNLA's military buildup in Luanda was the arrival of a motorized column of 500 ELNA troops on March 30.[1]

The FNLA made desperate attempts to retake Luanda and on July 21, Holden Roberto announced he was personally taking charge of ELNA troops to lead them into the capital—his first entry into Angola in fourteen years! By then it was claimed that Holden Roberto had 17,000 troops under his command. They were halted at the gates of the capital on August 8. By that time the numerically inferior and more lightly armed FAPLA, in bitter battles from Luanda all the way back east to the Zambian border, had ejected ELNA troops and forced them to withdraw to whatever base areas they held in the northwest. The strength and vitality and the popular support they enjoyed is demonstrated by the fact that while defending the capital and cleaning the ELNA troops out of all those areas they had occupied as participants in the three-movement Transitional Government, they also chased UNITA out of a whole string of vital towns and positions in the south. On August 21, Savimbi formally "declared war" on the MPLA, arresting all MPLA cadres, members, and suspected sympathizers the UNITA police could find. Within a few weeks, UNITA had been driven out of such key cities as Lobito, the headquarters of the Benguela railway on the coast 400 miles south of Luanda; from Pereira de Eca, another 500 miles to the south near the Namibia border; from Luso, 400 miles to the east of Lobito on the Benguela railway. This could only be accomplished through the strength and popular backing of the local MPLA action committees and groups backed by guerilla units.

It cannot be emphasized strongly enough that this was done exclusively by MPLA's own combat units. There were some Cuban military advisers, as there had been for years past with a number of African national liberation movements. There was virtually no military transport, no artillery. Some military supplies had arrived from the Soviet Union, Yugoslavia, and Algeria between March and June. But by all accounts—except that of Dr. Kissinger—these were light arms suitable for the guerilla-type units which was all the FAPLA had at that time. Savimbi's reaction was to turn to South Africa for help. By early August, vanguard South African units had entered Angola from Namibia and occupied Calueque and Namacunde, twenty-four and eight miles, respectively, inside Angola. The pretext was that they were there to protect hydroelectric installations at Ruacana on the Cunene river. In the booklet referred to above, Colin Legum, in the section headed "Foreign Intervention," states that: "The South African army, as is now known, was no stranger to the Angolan terrain; the Portuguese had allowed them to send in their forces up to a depth of 200 miles to root out SWAPO guerillas and to study Angola's guerilla operations."[2]

In a document published by the UNITA information office in

December, 1975, Savimbi reported that South African troops had invaded Angola in July, 1975, defeating both MPLA and UNITA attempts to block them, and the Manchester *Guardian* quotes South African Defense Minister Pieter Botha as telling Parliament that "from July 14, 1975, to January 23, 1976," twenty-nine South African troops had been killed in action in Angola and fourteen in "accidents."[3] On August 12, the South African government officially informed the Portuguese government that because Portugal seemed incapable of protecting South African workers at the Ruacana hydroelectric installations, South Africa had sent in a small force to Calueque to protect them. The chronology of all this is important in view of Kissinger's strenuous efforts to persuade a U.S. Senate investigating committee that South African troops entered Angola only after the arrival of massive numbers of Cuban combat troops. The only foreign troops in Angola at the time of the massive FNLA and UNITA defeats were those from Zaire, South Africa, and elements of the Spinolist fascist ELP (Portuguese Liberation Army, originally formed in Spain for the overthrow of the Gonçalves government). FAPLA Comandante Farrusco was in charge of guerilla groups on the southern border. We met in Sa da Bandeira a few days after the South Africans were forced to withdraw.

I was an eyewitness from the time the South Africans, with support from UNITA, the FNLA-Chipenda faction, and ELP forces started to invade our country at Calueque. This was at the beginning of August, 1975. The enemy knew we were weak there, which is one of the reasons they picked it as the invasion point. When the first group arrived, their slogan was "FNLA-UNITA-Chipenda!" With their armored cars and artillery, there was little we could do but observe and report back. They started their drive north on October 23. When they arrived here at Sa da Bendeira [now Lubango] I saw how they started to massacre the population. About two hundred, including women and children, were killed in the first days. Chipenda, who came from South Africa, brought with him members of the BRJ [Brigade of Revolutionary Youth, indoctrinated along the lines of the Hitler Youth] and these were used to identify MPLA members or sympathizers. Denunciation by the BRJ was the equivalent of the death sentence. When I was doing resistance work in Vila Ariago [about twenty-five miles south of Lubango] I saw the ELP, protected by South African troops, kill twenty-seven cattle-people [a semi-nomad pastoral people living in Southern Angola, vaguely related to the Hottentots—W.B.]. They just herded them into a freight car, shunted it down the line a few hundred yards, machine-gunned them and threw the bodies into the river. An acquaintance of mine, who thought they must be queuing up for work, joined the queue and was also thrown in and shot. There are hundreds of witnesses to such massacres.

Carlos Mangas, a tall young Angolan of Portuguese parents, a schoolteacher from Benguela, happened to be on his way to Lubango airport on the second day of the South African drive north. With him was the Angolan pilot of a light plane waiting at the airport to take them back to Benguela, the pilot's Swiss wife, who had just returned from leaving their three children in Lisbon, and an Angolan chauffeur.

We pulled onto the side of the road when we saw a column of armored cars coming. We saw a machine gun swing round as one of the cars passed. The next thing was a terrible burst of fire. My three companions were killed immediately. I was blown out of the car with a bullet through my hand and lay alongside the others as if also dead. I lay there for three hours until the column and following troops passed. Meanwhile I swallowed my MPLA membership card and threw away an MPLA emblem that I wore round my neck. Then some infantry came by. One of them threw a grenade at the car and although it landed on the opposite side from where I was lying, I instinctively reacted. One of them, an Angolan, shouted: "That bastard's still alive," and he pointed his gun. But it only clicked. Some South Africans who were setting up a mortar position nearby came over to see what was happening. As I am white and speak good English, we could converse. I said I was a school inspector and had just been checking up on schools in the region. An officer scribbled out a note and told me to go on to a medical station at the airport and get my wounds fixed up. By now I had grenade fragments in my left side and leg. At the medical station my wounds were dressed. Everybody was quite friendly and I was told I'd be put on a supply plane to Johannesburg next day and from there flown to Portugal. But next morning the whole atmosphere had changed. When I asked about a plane an officer snarled, "There's no place for FAPLA commanders in South Africa." It seems that during the night I had been denounced by a BRJ spy. I was beaten up around the face and knee-kicked in the stomach and then submitted to electrical torture under the supervision of a South African major. Electrodes were fitted into my ears and current generated through a hand-operated set. "We are South African volunteers," said the major. "We have come to fight Communism. We will never let Communism get a foothold in southern Africa." They had discovered that my spectacles were made in Benguela and the major wanted to know where the military positions around Benguela were. "Where are the Cubans?" There was a special device which projected what I think must have been a photo taken from a space satellite onto the ground, with an exact scale in meters, and he asked me to identify positions. In between the torture treatments I gave what I believed were the most misleading answers. After the interrogation was over I was held at the dressing station for several days and saw huge unmarked transport planes landing several times a day and unloading military supplies. . . .

Carlos Mangas—who had given a false name—was later transferred to a hospital where he met Farrusco, who had been picked up in civilian clothes with a bullet in his lung. Taking advantage of a brawl among the hospital guards when UNITA expelled the FNLA-Chipenda faction from Lubango, they both escaped. On November 3, ten days after occupying Lubango, the South African column, together with ELP troops, arrived within three miles of the center of Benguela, about two hundred miles to the north.

Comandante Augusta Rosa, a big full-bearded white Angolan born in Mozambique of Portuguese parents, took up the story. Part of the column had sped west from Lubango to Serpa Pinto (now Menongue), the terminal point of the Moçamedes railway, 350 kilometers due west from Lubango.

A column of eighty South African armored cars and one company—about 120 men—of ELP troops attacked the Benguela airport on November 5. We started hitting back immediately, as we had tried to harass them in the outskirts. But we had no weapons to match theirs. They occupied the airport and by the night of the 5th we were completely encircled. There were about 600 South African troops, three to each of the the armored cars, the rest artillery, infantry, and other support troops. We had lost seven of our original ten companies in that area, mostly in clashes with ELP and Portuguese vigilantes in the Huambo area to the west. We fought our way out of the encirclement on the night of the 5th and withdrew toward Novo Redondo, 120 miles north of Benguela. There we made a determined stand four miles south of the city. After eight hours of continuous bombardment, during which we took heavy losses, we withdrew to the banks of the Queve river, seventeen kilometers to the northwest. There we made a last stand. Most of our men were wiped out—even a few who wanted to surrender were shot down to the last man. But the stand there gave us time to dynamite the bridge over the Queve and this was a serious blow to the South Africans.

The destruction of the bridge over the Queve was a most decisive action, carried out by Comandante Rosa and a small group of specialists. The South Africans were obliged to withdraw and make a long deviation, gaining valuable time, or the FAPLA to consolidate their defenses around the capital. The South Africans had suffered far higher losses than expected and their timetable was seriously upset. The very heroic and costly delaying action from the Angola-Namibia frontier to the Queve river was fought exclusively by FAPLA guerillas and greatly contributed to shattering the master strategy of the South Africa-UNITA-Chipenda forces advancing on Luanda from the south and the Zaire-FNLA forces advancing from the north. Their maximum objective was that the north-south columns would link up in Luanda before November 11 so that the Portuguese would hand over independence to an UNITA-FNLA coalition. The minimum was that the Zaire-FNLA column would occupy the Luanda water-pumping station at Kifangondo 18 kilometres north of the capital and the South African-UNITA-Chipenda-FNLA faction would occupy the Cambambe hydroelectric station which was the main supplier of electricity to Luanda, about 200 kilometres southeast of the capital. Thus, even if the MPLA still controlled the capital on November 11, the city would be completely paralyzed—without water or electricity—and the Portuguese could not hand over independence to "one faction" under such conditions. Lucio Lara described to me the situation in the capital during those crucial days:

On November 6, with the South Africans advancing north of Benguela, the Portuguese high commissioner, Admiral Leonel Cardoso, called on our leadership. He was very worried about the situation due to "MPLA obstinacy," as he put it. "You are in great danger. All forces in Angola are against you." But the Portuguese had never warned us that Zaire forces had invaded Angola months previously as had South African forces. We pointed this out. He replied: "UNITA and the FNLA have powerful forces at their disposal. They will crush you." He urged us to come to terms with them. We refused. On the morning of November 7, we stopped the first Zaire-FNLA attack, at the Bengo river, just 18 kilometres north of Luanda. In the afternoon we had a visit from Rear Admiral Victor Crespo heading the Ministry of Coordination, formerly Minister of the Colonies]. He had just come from Huambo where he had seen Savimbi's second-in-command, Nzau Puna [UNITA's secretary-general]. It was a very dramatic moment, especially as we knew that a second Zaire attack would be coming very soon. "It's your last chance," said Crespo. "You must come to terms with UNITA." We asked how he could suggest such a thing when Savimbi had brought in South African troops which were already pushing north from Benguela. Crespo put his head in his hands: "But they are very strong. I was today in Nova Lisboa [Huambo]. They said they were ready to make an alliance with the Devil if necessary! You must settle with them." "No, never!" we replied. "You will be crushed," he insisted. "The MPLA will never be crushed. Perhaps we ourselves will be liquidated, but the MPLA will never be crushed. Angola will never be crushed." Crespo left.

A few days earlier we had prepared to declare independence on the 7th. The text was ready. The enemy advance had been so swift and they had such superior strength of arms that some thought the defense of the capital was impossible without outside aid. It was quite possible that we would no longer be in the capital on the night of November 10-11. But there were other considerations. The 7th was the anniversary of the Bolshevik Revolution and for us to choose the same date might be misunderstood. Also the 11th had been the date set by the Alvor Agreement for the transfer of powers. We reversed the original decision and decided to defend the capital, come what may. We decided to appeal for outside help, but only as a sovereign, independent state and from our own capital. From the 7th onward Portuguese forces and part of the Portuguese population inside Luanda became very aggressive and provocative. Anti-MPLA banners suddenly appeared and the situation was very tense.

Cuban advisers had certainly been informed of the original decision to declare independence on the 7th and immediately ask for stepped-up Cuban aid, proposals urged by Cubans on the spot and with which Fidel Castro was entirely in accord. This explains why on November 7, before the People's Republic was officially proclaimed, the first eighty-two Cuban combat troops left Havana on an ancient Bristol-Britannia, bound for Angola, as the result of a decision taken by the Cuban leadership two days earlier. They were part of a reinforced battalion of 650 special forces to be ferried into Angola within the following thirteen days. Comandante "Juju" described what was happening in Luanda in the meantime as follows:

The all-out assault that we had been expecting began on the morning of November 10. It started at 6 A.M. from a point ten kilometers north of Kifangondo, with Holden Roberto and the Zairean general in charge to supervise the operation. A column started to move down the sixteen miles of road that lead to Luanda. It was spearheaded by nine French-made Panhard armored cars. These were followed by forty-eight truckloads of troops. There were about one thousand Zairean troops divided into two battalions, one reinforced company of Portuguese commandos, forty Portuguese sappers, about one hundred FNLA troops, and ten South Africans—replacing French mercenaries who had failed to show up—to handle a 130 mm. artillery piece and a couple of 122 mm. mortars. The armored cars, with the motorized troops following on behind, moved two hundred yards at a time, stopped, raked the surrounding area with machine-gun fire, then moved on again. At 11 A.M., they entered our field of fire. There were two surprises awaiting them. First, after their November 7 attack, we had blown up the bridge over the Bengo river. Second, we had just received some Soviet *Katyusha* multiple rocket launchers. When most of the column was within range the *Katyusha*s opened up. There was terrible panic. The noise and streaks of fire were terrifying enough. Several armored cars and trucks, packed up tight at the destroyed bridge, were knocked out in the first lightning salvos, others as they tried to turn around or reverse and speed back out of range. Those that survived never stopped until they got to Porto Quipiri, their advance base about 15 kilometers back along the road to Caxito [about 50 kilometers north of Kifangondo where the column had been stopped and the Zaire-FNLA main logistics base—W.B.]. Unfortunately we had no means of crossing the Bengo river and following up our victory. It took us about twelve days to rig up a bridge and follow them back to Caxito, which we captured on November 22 almost without a fight.

In the area around Porto Quipiri we captured hundreds of tons of valuable equipment, scattered around on both sides of the road. They had forced the local population to load it onto trucks for their advance, but there was no one to help them during their retreat. Some of the attackers, at least, had no idea what had hit them when the *Katyusha*s opened up. We found a note scrawled on the wall of one of the Porto Quipiri arms storehouses: "We're pulling out. The Russians are using atom bombs."

Thus neither maximum nor minimum objectives of the anti-MPLA forces were attained. The northern column did succeed in putting the Kifangondo pumping station out of order by artillery fire and Luanda was without water for a couple of days before the damage was repaired. But the southern column was blocked on the southern bank of the Queve river, 240 kilometers short of their minimum target of Dondo and the Camambe hydroelectric station and 400 kilometers short of their maximum target—Luanda. There was no alternative on the afternoon of November 10, 1975, but for the Portuguese to lower their flags over Luanda for the last time and for High Commissioner Admiral Leonel Cardoso, his staff, and remaining troops to step aboard a frigate and steam out of Luanda harbor, marking the formal end of almost 500 years of Portuguese rule in Angola.

Angolan independence and the establishment of the People's Republic of Angola was formally proclaimed at midnight on November 10. In a moving ceremony, the flag of the new republic was hoisted by Comandante Imperial Santana, who had led the uprising in Luanda nearly fifteen years earlier and who had miraculously survived the attack, the terrible repression which immediately followed, and the arduous years of liberation struggle. In the small hours of the morning of the 11th, Lucio Lara, as General Secretary of the MPLA's Central Committee, invested Agostinho Neto as President of the People's Republic. In his inaugural speech, President Neto accused the FNLA and UNITA of having systematically sabotaged the Alvor Agreement and reproached the Portuguese for their "constant disregard" of the agreement and, among other things, "for the fact that it has systematically remained silent over the invasion of our country by regular armies and mercenary forces."

Twenty-four hours later at Ambriz, about 170 kilometers north of Luanda, the disembarcation port for the hapless invasion force which was licking its wounds at Caxito, Holden Roberto proclaimed the independence of the "People's Democratic Republic of Angola." On November 12, Holden Roberto and Jonas Savimbi announced the formation of a "Joint National Council for

86

the Revolution" with its headquarters at Huambo, as the provisional governing organ of the "People's Democratic Republic." Giving his version of the liberation struggle which had led to the exit of the Portuguese, Holden Roberto warned the Angolan people to be vigilant against the designs of "Soviet social imperialism." Referring to the countries on whom he was counting for immediate recognition, he continued:

> All these friends—Zaire, the People's Republic of China, Tunisia, the Central African Republic, Nigeria, Ivory Coast, Senegal, Cameroon, Liberia, Uganda, Kenya, Togo, Ghana, Lesotho, and other African and Asian states—all these truly friendly countries which know that we are neither acrobats nor utopians but simply proud nationalists who are attached to the proud realities of our country— these brothers and friends should know that we are convinced that we can always count on the warmth of their affection. . . .

It was a valiant, but vain, effort. While the People's Republic was immediately recognized by some thirty countries—including such unlikely ones as Brazil—the "Democratic People's Republic" was neither then, nor later, recognized by a single country—not even by Zaire or South Africa!

VIII Enter the Cubans

What are Cubans? It was a question I put to Nicolás Guillén in the summer of 1976 in Havana. A short, stocky man with a massive head and a brown, humorous face, he is Cuba's outstanding national poet and one of the most prestigious writers in Latin America. "We are a nation of mulattos like me," he said.

When the Spanish colonizers came to Cuba, the native population was very weak numerically and culturally, living in the Stone Age. They were quickly exterminated. Cuba was discovered by Columbus in 1492. The Spanish conquest started in 1511 and within forty years there was scarcely one of the original population left. But the Spaniards who came had no taste for hard work. They needed African labor for their farms. They had already acquired a taste for slaves in Spain. From 1517 onward large numbers of slaves were imported, continuing until 1880. Official statistics give a figure of some 800,000, but in reality it ran into millions. Apart from official imports, there was a huge black market by which the slaves were smuggled in.

Cubans are almost exclusively a mix of Spaniards and Africans, descendants of the original conquerors and their African slaves. The mixture took place over a period of centuries. Spanish culture started to merge with African culture, with African culture extremely important.

Guillén, who is still young and full of energy at seventy-four, has been president of the Union of Cuban Writers and Artists since 1961. I asked him how he evaluated a recent description by Fidel Castro of Cuba as a Latin-*African*, and not a Latin-American, country.

It is absolutely correct. Fidel was referring to this merger of two races, two cultures. Our music, our dance, our food, our temperament, everything, is based on the fusion of these two cultures. It is the basis for all my poetry. There has been a long process of the merger of the two races, but not in isolation from the process of the formation of our nation. Today we never speak of Africa in the abstract. The reality is that Africa is comprised of many different nations, peoples speaking different languages and with different characteristics. But we are especially conscious of those parts of Africa from which so many of our ancestors came. Angola is one of them. Very many slaves were brought to Cuba from Angola, also to Brazil and other Caribbean islands. It is in the Caribbean that the racial and cultural influence of Africans is strongest because in bigger countries like the U.S.A., Brazil, and Canada, the colonizers could not completely wipe out the local population. In the Caribbean it was relatively easy to destroy the indigenous population to get their land and replace them with slave labor for the colonizers' plantations. That is why black influence is strong, almost total in some places.

He produced a photo of himself with Agostinho Neto, taken during a secret visit by Neto to Cuba in 1966. The two great poets were sitting at the same table in the headquarters of the Union of Writers and Artists where we sat now to discuss Angola. Affectionate smiles played on both their faces.

What better symbol that we are Cuban-African, Latin-African! Because of our antecedents we have great sympathy for Spain and for Africa. These are the two forces which decided the character and way of thinking of the Cuban people. During the Spanish Civil War, many thousands of Cubans went to fight—many of them to die—with the Republicans. Spain is the country of our white ancestors, just as Angola is one of those of our black ancestors. It is part of the roots of our life. Sympathy for the Angolan resistance struggle is part of our revolutionary nature, as was also our sympathy for the Spanish Republicans and for the Vietnamese and others fighting wars of national liberation. But it is also because Angola is part of us. It is the great pride of our people that we are able to do something for one of the lands of our ancestors.

Don't forget that we are also indebted to the newly freed slaves who fought side by side with Cubans in our own war of independence from the Spaniards.

One did not have to be long in Cuba to realize that there was a great feeling of pride that Cuba was helping the Angolan "brothers" or "comrades," according to whom one spoke. When word got around at an inland rest resort where I was having a brief holiday that I had recently been in Angola, people gathered around to ask how the Cubans were doing. There were broad smiles when I praised the modesty of the Cuban troops and their popularity among the Angolan people.

One of the first public references to historical people's links between Cuba and Angola was on March 11, 1976, when Oscar

Oramas, Cuba's ambassador to Angola, presented his credentials to President Neto:

> If Cuban blood was spilled to liberate Angola we do not forget that African blood was also spilled in other lands struggling for their independence. In fact African slaves, our brothers, fought with arms in hand for the liberation of Cuba. Africa was the gateway for our nationality, for our culture, for our psychology; and constitutes a fundamental factor of our nationhood. It was for this reason that Comandante Fidel Castro said we are a Latin-African country.

At the time that Oscar Oramas presented his credentials it was still a secret that "Che," with Castro's support, headed two hundred Cuban guerillas in training and fighting alongside the forces of the post-Lumumbist National Revolutionary Council, headed by Gaston Soumialot in the former Belgian Congo against the forces of Moise Tshombe and the swashbuckling white mercenaries of Major "Mad" Mike Hoare. As in Angola, it was only after counterrevolutionary forces intervened from the outside to crush revolutionary forces, that Cuba sent combat troops to the rescue.

A large proportion of the Cuban troops who came to Angola were black. As the nondescript uniforms of the FAPLA were gradually replaced by standardized Cuban jungle greens, it was impossible for an outsider to distinguish between Cuban and Angolan blacks. (As indeed it was very difficult to distinguish the white Angolans of Portuguese origin who had thrown in their lot with the FAPLA from white Cubans.)

November 5, 1975, when the decision was taken to send in Cuban combat troops, was the 132nd anniversary of one of the numerous slave uprisings in Cuba. On that occasion the leader of the uprising was a woman known as Black Carlota, a worker at the Triunvirato sugar mill in Matanzas province. With a machete as her only weapon, she had led her fellow workers in revolt. Who in 1843 could have imagined the manner in which her death would be revenged? It was in keeping with the temperament of Castro that he gave the name "Operation Carlota" to the military rescue mission in Angola. It was typical also that Castro escorted the commanders of the "first eighty-two" in his own jeep to the steps of the plane that was to take them on their long and hazardous flight from Havana to Luanda.

No objective observer would contest the fact that, within a month of having expelled the FNLA and UNITA from Luanda, the MPLA controlled twelve out of Angola's sixteen provincial capitals—which meant they controlled the provinces as well. This they had done entirely by their own efforts. There were Cuban military instructors—238 was the precise figure I heard—whose main task it was to teach the use of modern, shoulder-fired weapons to which the MPLA had access after supply by sea became possible in early 1975. There is no question that if the FAPLA had bridging equipment they would have pursued and destroyed the greater part of the Zaire column which drove toward Luanda on November 10 and would have captured Caxito by their own efforts much earlier than November 22. Because they were hopelessly outclassed in firepower, the FAPLA had to resort to passive defense measures such as dynamiting bridges. But with Cuban help on the way, Castro cabled to advise no more destruction of bridges—it would only hamper pursuit of the enemy. (When the pursuit got under way, it was the South African and Zaire troops who were blowing up bridges in their flights to the south and north respectively.) It is highly probable that when they arrived on November 9, the "first eighty-two" were rushed to the front-line positions on the Bengo river to handle the *Katyushas* which dispersed the Zaire motorized column advancing on the capital the following morning. But the airlift of the full reinforced special forces battalion was only completed on November 20. It was quickly reinforced by an artillery regiment and a motorized battalion which left Havana on November 9. After considerable U.S. naval and air harassment, the three transport vessels dropped anchor in Luanda harbor on November 27. Then followed intensive preparations to push the South African and Zaire invaders back and deal the *coup de grace* to the forces of the FNLA, UNITA, ELP, and the Portuguese vigilantes. Among the first tasks was the repair of thirteen bridges, north and south of Luanda, within twenty days of the arrival of the airlifted battalion. There was a crash program for training FAPLA specialized units to handle the equipment the Cubans had brought with them, which was far in excess of what their own troops needed. Plans were worked out with the FAPLA general staff for integrated and coordinated operations

There had been a very great numerical expansion of the

FAPLA from the moment the MPLA had been able to enter the urban centers within the framework of the Alvor Agreement. Young people flocked to the colors faster than they could be trained and armed. But, as I had witnessed in Vietnam, revolutionary conviction and enthusiasm provide remarkable shortcuts in mastering the techniques to push ahead with the revolution and, in the final analysis, to save one's life in combat. "Courage" is the watchword, "but courage with intelligence." Fight to win, not to die.

The combination of a battle-tempered hard core of FAPLA troops, greatly reinforced by new recruits who had been through a crash training program under Cuban instructors, Cuban armored and artillery units to outgun and outpace the South Africans, and clandestine MPLA Action Committees in every town occupied by the invaders paved the way for the counteroffensive launched by the MPLA in December, 1975, and January, 1976. Cuban armor and artillery were used almost exclusively against the South Africans still halted on the Queve river in the south, short of their targets of Porto Amboim, Gabela, and Quibala. In the north, the counteroffensive was carried out almost exclusively by the FAPLA, using a few tanks, transport, and heavy weapons brought in by the Cubans, with some Cuban specialist units. Carmona (Uije) was liberated on January 4; the big airbase at Negage, 25 miles to the east, on January 5; and Ambriz, on January 12. As the Zaire-FNLA forces depended on supplies flown in to Negage, or shipped by sea to Ambriz, these were disastrous losses. It was after the loss of Carmona—the Zaire occupying troops fleeing in panic when they realized they were almost surrounded and that FNLA troops supposed to be guarding the approaches were nonexistent—that the Zaire units pulled back nonstop across the border into their own country. It was at this point that British and other mercenaries were hurriedly flown out to try to stop a complete collapse on the northern front.

On the southern front, the counteroffensive got under way in the third week of January. The eastern anchors of the South African defense line, the towns of Cela and Santa Comba, were taken on January 21, the western anchor at Novo Redondo on January 24; and after that South African armored and artillery units started speeding south considerably faster than they had advanced, blowing up all bridges behind them. On February 8,

Huambo, the capital of the FNLA-UNITA "Democratic People's Republic" was abandoned in a retreat to the UNITA stronghold at Bié, 160 kilometres to the east. It was taken by FAPLA-Cuban forces four days later. After having consistently denied that there were any South African troops in Angola—until some South African prisoners were presented to the press in Luanda on December 16, 1975—Defense Minister Pieter Botha announced on February 3, 1976, that South African troops had withdrawn to the border areas and that some 4,000 to 5,000 were patrolling a "buffer zone" to a depth of 60 kilometres on the Angolan side of the frontier with Namibia.

Jonas Savimbi tacitly admitted defeat on February 12 by announcing that UNITA forces would revert to guerilla warfare and on February 24 Holden Roberto made a similar announcement on behalf of the FNLA. A decisive factor in this was not only the fact that their military strength rested almost entirely on that of South Africa and Zaire, which had respectively withdrawn their forces, but that the OAU on February 11 had recognized the MPLA's People's Republic of Angola as the sole government and admitted it to full membership.

Having played a decisive role in a shortcut to the end of the war and an MPLA victory, above all by expelling the South Africans, what were the Cubans to do next? Certainly they were not all going to pack their bags and return home because South Africa had pulled back its troops to the Namibian side of the frontier by the end of March, 1976. At the Conakry summit meeting between Fidel Castro and the presidents of Angola, Guinea, and Guiné-Bissau (March 14-15), it was agreed between Castro and Agostinho Neto that Cuba would withdraw part of its military forces, but would continue an accelerated training program for building up a modern Angolan army and provide various other types of aid. (The very insistence with which Henry Kissinger was demanding a total withdrawal of Cuban forces aroused suspicions of impending attempts at "destabilization.")

While fighting was still continuing in the southern frontier regions, civilian Cuban medical teams started arriving, their places in the transport planes being taken by departing military personnel. In a remarkably short time, a fully equipped Cuban hospital with seven doctors and an appropriate number of nurses and service personnel was set up in fifteen of Angola's sixteen

93

provinces. As the total number of doctors left in Angola after the mass Portuguese withdrawal was sixty-eight—with more than half of them in Luanda—this was no mean contribution. And no small sacrifice from a country which is itself short of public-health personnel.

By the end of 1976, Cuba was training some 6,500 Angolans—500 of them in Cuba, the rest in Angola—to become doctors, engineers, schoolteachers, specialists in sugar and coffee production, transport, bridge-building, housing construction, public-health work, various branches of industry, agriculture, and fishing. The Cuban experience in fighting illiteracy was also placed at the disposal of the Angolan government. Angolan slaves had been used to promote the Spanish plantation economy in Cuba just as, after they could no longer be exported abroad, the Portuguese used them to promote a colonial Portuguese plantation economy in Angola. Sugar and coffee were essential products in both countries. It was the same with cattle. But an independent Cuba had advanced by leaps and bounds in scientific and technological developments. It was natural for the Cuba of Fidel Castro to use its experience to shorten the road to economic development in Angola in all those areas in which it had expertise. And it was not just a question of passing on scientific and technological know-how. Cuban troops were out in the fields alongside Angolan volunteer workers on weekends and holidays to cut sugarcane, pick coffee, help with the rice harvest, and in general to extend a helping hand at all levels.

At the MPLA Congress which opened in Luanda on December 4, 1977, President Neto paid a special tribute to Cuban specialists and technicians. "Cuba did not merely supply equipment, which we could not have used at that time . . . but hundreds of civilian technical experts came to help . . ." Referring to the almost total lack of technicians after the Portuguese withdrawal, Neto said that about 3,500 Cuban technicians and skilled workers came to Angola during 1977. He referred specifically to the rehabilitation of the sugar industry—both production and refining—which would have been impossible without Cuban help. 250 Cuban specialists worked in the Coffee Institute and on the plantations. Cuban doctors and public health workers carried out over one million consultations and 16,000 surgical operations in the first nine months of 1977. About 500 Angolan transport workers had graduated in Cuban-run technical courses and Cubans temporarily provided crews for Angola's modest coastal merchant fleet.

On the question of Cuban troops in Angola, Fidel Castro told visiting U.S. Congressmen (Frederick W. Richmond, Democrat of Brooklyn and Richard Nolan, Democrat of Minnesota) on December 5, 1977, that Cuba had withdrawn about 60 per cent of its forces following the victory over the South African and Zaire troops at the beginning of 1976. But following the Katangan invasion of the Shaba province of Zaire, which Neto regarded as a provocation to get Angola involved in a shooting war with Zaire and foreign powers supporting that country, Cuba had been asked to send some of its troops back. As this period—April-May 1977—coincided with a South African build-up on the Namibia-Angolan border, Cuban reinforcements were sent.

"If we had continued to withdraw at that point," Castro said, "Angola would have been invaded by Zaire and South Africa. This has not happened, and the Cuban presence in Angola is the reason." (/) Ann Crittenden in the *New York Times*, December 7, 1977.(/)

South African armored cars did make an incursion into Angola on August 27, 1977, at a point close to where the original invasion had taken place just two years earlier. They withdrew after a sharp class with FAPLA forces. In his talk with the U.S. Congressmen, Castro made it very clear he had no intention of buying American friendship at the expense of that of Angola. Commenting on the view inherited by the U.S. State Department from the days of Henry Kissinger, that only Cuban willingness to withdraw from Angola could lead to a normalization of relations with the United States, Castro remarked that Cuba's relations with Africa grew out of the American-imposed blockade of Cuba's trade with Latin America: "How can we be asked now to destroy those links? If we were to negotiate this with the United States, it would destroy our relations with Angola. No country that respects itself could do that."

A Cuban exit does not seem likely in the foreseeable future!

IX The Kissinger Version

As an example of trying to fool U.S. lawmakers on questions of peace or war, it is difficult to surpass Henry Kissinger's testimony at the hearings of the U.S. Senate Subcommittee on African Affairs regarding "U.S. Involvement in Civil War in Angola" (January 29-February 6, 1976). For a Harvard Ph.D. it was a lamentable performance; for a Secretary of State it bordered on the impeachable. Before a court of law, perjury could possibly have been invoked. To the credit of the Subcommittee, Kissinger's considerable eloquence and brilliance of argument fell, if not on exactly deaf ears, at least on those sharpened by such deceits as the Tonkin Gulf Resolution and by other denials of reprehensible activities in which U.S. involvement was later proved. Kissinger had long been a master of turning the truth upside down and getting away with it. His testimony was permeated with contempt for the intelligence and knowledge of the Subcommittee members. Witness, for instance, his version of the development of the national liberation struggle in Angola and the U.S. attitude toward it:

> In 1961, the United States declared its support for self-determination in Portugal's African territories. At the time the National Front for the Liberation of Angola, FNLA, was a leading force in the struggle for independence. [In fact the FNLA was formed on March 28, 1962] Looking to the future, we sought to develop a relationship with the FNLA through providing it with financial, nonmilitary assistance. The U.S.S.R. had already established links with the Popular Movement for the Liberation of Angola, MPLA, through the Portuguese Communist Party. The MPLA began military action against the Portuguese in the mid-1960s. The National Union for the Total Independence of Angola, UNITA, an offshoot of the FNLA, also began to fight in the late 1960s. Although these various uncoordinated insurgency efforts caused considerable difficulties for Portugal, they posed no serious military threat to the dominance of Portuguese military forces in Angola.
>
> However, the overthrow of the Portuguese government in April, 1974, and the growing strength of the Portuguese Communist Party apparently convinced Moscow that a revolutionary situation was developing in Angola. The Soviet Union began to exploit this situation in the fall of 1971 through the shipment of arms and equipment to the MPLA. The United States at the same time re-

ceived requests for support from other Angolan elements but turned them down. . . .

This might have gone down with primary-school students who never bothered to read the newspapers. Kissinger would never have even tried to get away with such gibberish at Harvard. How could he expect to get away with it before a Senate subcommittee? It is a measure of his contempt for the U.S. legislative process that he attempted it. The importance of the hearings, incidentally, was that it represented an attempt by Kissinger to reverse Congressional decisions taken a few weeks earlier to halt all U.S. aid, overt and covert, which might risk U.S. involvement in the Angolan war.

It was obvious from Kissinger's testimony before the Subcommittee that he was enraged that Congressional action had blocked the process of the United States moving into Southern Africa. It is difficult to imagine more misinformation (to use a polite term) packed into such a short space and at such a high level than that contained in the two paragraphs quoted above.

Perhaps there is some obscure verbal confirmation that the United States in 1961 supported "self-determination in Portugal's African territories." In practice, within the framework of NATO, the United States provided the necessary material support for Portugal to wage its war of suppressing such self-determination. Talk of a "relationship with the FNLA through providing it with financial, nonmilitary assistance" is merely a euphemism to cover up the fact that the CIA had bought up Holden Roberto as the "U.S. man in Angola"—although in fact he was in Kinshasa. The attempt to equate the buying up of Holden Roberto with any aid the Soviet Union was giving the MPLA at that time—and it is doubtful that there was any at all—is dishonest to say the least, and that this was done through the Portuguese Communist Party is nonsense. The MPLA had rejected that sort of relationship with the Portuguese Communist Party and Kissinger offered not a shred of evidence to the contrary.

The following sentence, that the MPLA "began military actions against the Portuguese in the mid-1960s," is an offense to anyone who has studied the public record of events. At the latest, MPLA military actions began on February 4, 1961. This is a matter of fact, recorded in any reference book worthy of the name dealing

97

with that period. The next sentence describing UNITA as an "offshoot of the FNLA" would also be disputed by most students of the Angolan national liberation struggle. It is true that Jonas Savimbi had been the FNLA "foreign minister" and had broken with Holden Roberto. But to describe UNITA as an offshoot of the FNLA is a shoddy bit of scholarship unworthy of anyone with Kissinger's academic qualifications. What he was clearly trying to do, by falsifying dates and distorting events, was to place the FNLA, the MPLA, and UNITA on a more or less equal footing, with a slight edge for the FNLA as the pioneer resistance movement, therefore qualifying for United States backing.

The next passage can be qualified as political chicanery. That it should have been practiced at such a high level—the second highest in the land—merits special attention. It is on a par with Watergate or the Tonkin Gulf Resolution for duplicity. The various "uncoordinated insurgency" efforts (note that the FNLA as a "leading force in the struggle for independence" had been downgraded before the end of the sentence to an "insurgent") "posed no serious military threat to the dominance of the Portuguese military forces in Angola." It was the "overthrow of the Portuguese government in April, 1974, and the growing strength of the Portuguese Communist Party" which "apparently convinced Moscow that a revolutionary situation was developing in Angola. . . ." Here Kissinger really outdid himself. The mind boggles at the fact that he actually went on record with such evidence of intellectual and political dishonesty. The "Captains' Coup" was the cause and not the result of the national liberation movements in Angola and the other Portuguese colonies! The evidence of every participant in the April 25 coup in Portugal from Spinola down, whatever their ideological options, was that a change at the top was necessary because of the military bankruptcy of fascist Portugal's situation in the African colonies. It is nothing short of incredible that Kissinger, alone of all world statesmen, should have tried to prove the opposite. To sum up his original thesis: The Soviet Union, through the Portuguese Communist Party, staged a coup in Portugal, then inspired the Portuguese colonies to stage a revolt in Angola supported by Moscow! He continued in the same vein:

It is no coincidence that major violence [in Luanda] broke out in March, 1975, when large shipments of Soviet arms began to arrive—thousands of infantry weapons, machine guns, bazookas, and rockets. On March 23, the first of repeated military clashes between the MPLA and FNLA occurred. They increased in frequency in April, May, and June, when deliveries of Communist arms and equipment, including mortars and armored vehicles, escalated by air and sea. In May, the MPLA forced the FNLA out of the areas north and east of Luanda and, in June, took effective control of Cabinda. . . .

This too is sheer dishonesty. The version of these events described in an earlier chapter was confirmed by documents of the Portuguese authorities in Luanda at the time. There were "repeated military clashes" from March onward, but the initiative was exclusively that of the FNLA. Evidence of this may be found in a document signed by twelve Portuguese doctors from the Portuguese military hospital in Luanda, on March 28, 1975, and submitted to the Portuguese high commissioner. As they were also integrated into the armed forces, subject to military discipline, it was clear that only exceptional circumstances could Fhave moved them to act:

We, the undersigned, military doctors of the Portuguese army, while in the service of the Luanda Military Hospital, on March 28, 1975: (1) Were present at the arrival at this hospital, and rendered first aid to scores of people wounded by firearms, the majority of them civilians. (2) From all the victims we collected identical evidence, namely: (a) They were people of diverse origins and ethnic backgrounds, of whom the number at the beginning exceeded one hundred and who had been arrested at various points on the public thoroughfares of Luanda on March 22 and 23 by elements of the ELNA. (b) They had been accused of belonging to the MPLA or of having taken part in disorders between the civilian population and the ELNA; they were incarcerated in the ELNA Information Center and then transferred to the Sao Pedro de Barra fortress.[2] (c) From there they were transferred to places in the region of Caxito, where summary executions took place. (d) Some of the victims who were shot down remained where they fell but had survived and could later make good their escape. In face of the gravity of what we have set forth, and of the ample evidence of genocide being perpetrated against the civilian population of Luanda, of which this report is perhaps only one example, we request an urgent and rigorous inquiry into these events, and the adoption of more energetic measures, before such acts of Nazi bestiality become generalized and institutionalized within a climate of fascist terror.[3]

One can obviously excuse Dr. Kissinger for not having been aware of this particular document and the details to which it refers. But whichever of his hats he was wearing at the time, he was morally, politically, and professionally—especially as an academic—bound to check the facts and report accordingly to the Senate subcommittee. As it turned out he was only interested in deceiving the members for his own devious purposes.

Regarding Cabinda, nobody should have been better informed than Henry Kissinger. The Cabinda Enclave, separated from the rest of Angola by a broad strip of Zaire, has the good fortune—or misfortune according to how things go—to be rich in oil, exploited by the Gulf Oil Corporation of the United States. Within two months of the "Captains' Coup," Nixon had a mysterious *tête-à-tête* with Spinola in the Azores. Following a historic speech by Spinola on July 27, 1974, in which he was forced by the progressive elements then at the head of the Armed Forces Movement to state the principle of complete independence for the African colonies or "territories," there was a meeting at Sal, in the Cape Verde Islands between Spinola and President Mobutu of Zaire. Accompanying Mobutu were two of the most trusted aides of Holden Roberto, Vaal Neto (later Minister of Foreign Affairs in the Huambo-based Democratic People's Republic of Angola) and N'Gola Kabangu, FNLA Minister of the Interior in the three-movement Transitional Government, Minister of Industry and Energy in the Huambo-based government,

According to details later revealed in the Lisbon press, an eight-point secret agreement was signed: (1) Spinola would support Holden Roberto. (2) Cabinda would be ceded to Zaire. (3) Spinola would place at the disposal of Mobutu an Angolan team loyal to himself. (4) Cabinda would be handed over to another team, dependent on Mobuto and Spinola but which would be directed by FLEC—the artificially inspired Cabinda secessionist movement. (5) Support by Spinola for Mobutu's concept of a Zaire-Angola-Cabinda Federation of which Mobutu would be president and Holden Roberto vice-president. (6) Help by Mobutu in mobilizing some other African heads of state to promote the image of Spinola and his associates in Portugal as "genuine anti-colonialists of a new type." (7) A guarantee that Portuguese and multinational companies operating in Portugal could freely exploit, for a minimum of twenty years, the natural resources of Angola, Cabinda, and Zaire. (8) Aid by Mobutu for Portugal to "recuperate" Mozambique and Guiné-Bissau, not only by help in provoking *coups d'état* and assassinations but by the infiltration of mercenaries and the corruption of certain cadres of the PAIGC and FRELIMO.

It is hard to believe that such an exponent of "destabilization" as Henry Kissinger was unaware of this compact. History has proved over and over again that oil is always mixed with blood. In securing the Cabinda Enclave, the MPLA—well aware of Mobutu's designs on the area—was defending Angola's patrimony against all comers. As early as November 10, 1974, fifty commandos of Zaire's "Special Forces" under the command of a notorious French mercenary, Jean Kay, and supported by some local armed members of the FLEC, had tried to stage a coup. Two Portuguese sentries were killed. Portuguese troops were flown in from Luanda five days later, the coup attempt put down, and Jean Kay arrested.[4] It was not the only attempt at a French-backed take-over. On July 25, 1975, a Paris-based secessionist group headed by a certain N'Zita Henrique Tiago announced that it had set up a "Provisional Revolutionary Government" for Cabinda. Six days later, the head of the rival FLEC, Luis Ranque Franque, announced from his Kinshasa headquarters that henceforth Cabinda was an "independent territory." Happily, despite Henry Kissinger's regrets, Cabinda was firmly in MPLA hands, having been one of their strongholds from the early days of armed struggle. The MPLA leadership was determined that Cabinda should not become another Katanga or Biafra, the scene of another secessionist war in which outside powers fought for the right to exploit the area's natural resources.

The Kissinger version continues:

In August, intelligence reports indicated the presence of Soviet and Cuban military advisers, trainers, and troops, including the first Cuban combat troops. If statements by Cuban leaders [which Kissinger did not quote] are to be believed, a large Cuban military training program began in Angola in June, and Cuban advisers were there before then. By September, the MPLA offensive had forced

UNITA out of several major central and southern Angolan cities.

In early September, the poorly equipped UNITA forces turned in desperation to South Africa for assistance against the MPLA, which was overrunning UNITA's ethnic areas in the south. South Africa responded by sending in military equipment, and some military personnel—without consultation with the United States.

The UNITA forces launched a successful counteroffensive which swept the MPLA out of the southern and most of the central part of Angola.

In October massive increases in Soviet and Cuban military assistance began to arrive. More Cuban troops were ferried to Angola. Cuba inaugurated its own airlift of troops in late October. And the MPLA declared itself the government of Angola, in violation of the Alvor Accord.

Kissinger seemed incapable of getting anything straight—even dates available from a perusal of the daily press. And if one source of information is discredited more than another in the Western world, it is U.S. "intelligence sources." Such sources were capable of reporting a nonexistent naval clash between North Vietnamese patrol boats and American destroyers in the Gulf of Tonkin, in August, 1964. But with the most sophisticated gadgetry of detection that the world has ever known they were incapable of discovering the approach of at least one battalion-sized "Vietcong" unit around each of 140 cities, towns, and U.S. bases, or a company of commandos around the U.S. embassy on the eve of the 1968 Têt offensive in South Vietnam! About the only fact which stands up in the previous four paragraphs from Kissinger's testimony is that "Cuban advisers were there before then" (June, 1975). Everything else is wrong—in context, in chronology of events, in facts, in interpretation.

If one takes the last point of the fourth paragraph first, Kissinger might have mentioned that on August 29, 1975, Portugal formally declared the Alvor Agreement *null and void* and dissolved the Transitional Government. It was on this basis that Portugal decided on the total withdrawal of its forces by November 11, 1975, instead of the phased withdrawal under the terms of the Alvor Agreement, by the end of February, 1976. There was no Alvor Agreement left when the MPLA set up the People's Republic on November 11, 1975, or the FNLA-UNITA set up the Democratic People's Republic on November 12, 1975. A Secretary of State is surely supposed to know about such matters! The UNITA "successful counteroffensive" was simply the famous "drive north" of the South African column of armored cars and artillery units, with more Portuguese ELP troops than UNITA, which put UNITA in charge of many southern and center towns and cities, but by no means "swept the MPLA out of the southern and most of the central part of Angola." Curious also that Kissinger thought it necessary to mention that the South African dispatch of military equipment and "some military personnel" was done without consultation with the United States. In a famous interview which the Senior Editor of *Newsweek*, Arnaud de Borchgrave, had with the South African prime minister, Balthazar Johannes Vorster (see *Newsweek*, May 17, 1976), the following exchange took place:

> *De Borchgrave*: Would it be accurate to say that the U.S. solicited South Africa's help to turn the tide against Russians and Cubans in Angola last fall?
> *Vorster*: I do not want to comment on that. The U.S. government can speak for itself. I am sure you will appreciate that I cannot violate the confidentiality of government-to-government communications. But if you are making the statement, I won't deny it.
> *De Borchgrave*: Would it also be accurate to say that you received a green light from Kissinger for a military operation in Angola and that at least six moderate black African presidents had given you their blessings for the same operation?
> *Vorster*: If you say that of your own accord, I will not call you a liar.

True, Vorster later denied the statement and De Borchgrave was banned "for life" from visiting South Africa. De Borchgrave threatened to sue Vorster for libel and the "ban for life" was suddenly cancelled. De Borchgrave, an old acquaintance from several wars, personally confirmed to me that his version was accurate and I believe he is too much a professional to make an error on such a crucial question. The implication is that Kissinger gave Vorster the green light but Congressional action a few weeks later switched it to red, which is the color that the faces of Kissinger and Vorster must have assumed when they realized the decision was irrevocable.

The reference to the MPLA having overrun UNITA's "ethnic areas in the South" also requires some analysis. Especially as it was backed up by Kissinger under questioning. He maintained

103

UNITA had by far the greatest popular support. This was supported by one of those splendid maps the Pentagon was so expert in producing to prove the war was being won in Vietnam, or to prove any other point the Pentagon wanted to make. Such a map was produced at the hearings by the Deputy-Secretary of Defense, Robert Ellsworth, and is included in the published record. It shows certain shaded areas as those under MPLA control. These include Cabinda, and then a stretch running from Ambrizete down to Novo Redondo on the west coast more or less extending east straight across Angola to the Zaire border. A much bigger area stretching to the border with Namibia in the south and Zambia in the west was classified as UNITA-controlled territory, the area to the north of the shaded area up to the frontiers with Zaire was said to be FNLA-controlled.

The map and what it was intended to prove amounted to a monumental exercise in deception. The Pentagon—and Kissinger—seemed to have accepted that the three movements were tribal-based, true enough as far as the FNLA and UNITA were concerned but not in relation to the MPLA. The map very roughly represented the distribution of the three main ethnic groups. Various figures have been given as to their respective size and one can take Colin Legum's figures[5] as being roughly correct, at least in their proportions. Seven hundred thousand Bakongo in the north; two million Ovimbundu in the south, and one and a half million Mbundu in the north-central region. It was this ethnic map which was presented by Ellsworth to back up Kissinger's arguments on the proportionate political influence of the three movements. But the MPLA was never tribal-based. It had all-Angolan solid roots all over the country and from the moment of its foundation had fought against tribalism, racism, and regionalism. It is true that Holden Roberto belonged to the Bakongo and Jonas Savimbi to the Ovimbundu, but to suggest they were accepted as the sole leaders of those tribal groupings, or that there were not all-Angolan aspirations among the Bakongo, the Ovimbundu, and the Mbundu was sheer nonsense.

The reference by Kissinger to the "first Cuban combat troops" arriving in August, 1975, is also unfounded and as it is based on U.S. "intelligence sources" it can be discarded. It was presumably thrown in because of the evidence that South African troops had entered southern Angola in late July and early August.

104

During three visits to Angola and extensive travels starting in February, 1976, I never heard any evidence of the presence of Cuban combat troops before the arrival of "the first eighty-two" on November 9, 1975. Nor could one find any evidence of Kissinger's assertion at the hearings that, at the time the OAU held its emergency session on January 13, 1976, the FNLA-UNITA forces "still controlled about seventy per cent of the territory and seventy per cent of the population."

For eloquence and a sense of "morality," it was hard to fault Dr. Kissinger's performance:

> The United States must make it clear that Angola sets no precedent; this type of action will not be tolerated elsewhere. This must be demonstrated by both the Executive and the Congress in our national interests and in the interests of world peace.
>
> To the Soviet Union and Cuba, the administration says: We will continue to make our case to the American public. We will not tolerate wanton disregard for the interests of others and for the cause of world peace. To the American people, the administration says that the time has come to set aside self-accusation and division. Our own country's safety and the progress of mankind depend crucially upon a united and determined America. Today, as throughout 200 years, the world looks to us to stand up for what is right.
>
> By virtue of our strength and values we are leaders in defense of freedom. Without us there can be neither security nor progress. . . .

The published record makes no mention of any "amens" at this point although Kissinger seems to have thought they were called for. Perhaps some of the Senators had irreverent thoughts that every dictator from Thailand to Chile knew he could count on U.S. executive support in any emergency. Certainly the more perceptive of the Senators would know that an international public opinion poll as to whether the United States was seen as the global champion of freedom and progress would not sustain Kissinger's claim!

X The Nito Alves Coup Attempt

At 4:30 A.M. on May 27, 1977, Luanda residents were awakened by machine-gun fire and the sound of exploding grenades from the direction of the city's Sau Paolo prison. Almost immediately afterward, small-arms fire was heard from the vicinity of the government radio station, which soon started broadcasting exhortations, in the name of its "Action Committee," for everyone to hasten to a "mass demonstration" in front of the People's Palace, where President Neto and Prime Minister Nascimento had their offices. The only response within the next few hours was the arrival of a few dozen youths—obviously curious as to what was going on—in front of the palace. Nothing resembling a "mass demonstration." About 9 A.M., another broadcast was made, this time in the name of the Ward Committee of Sazimbanga, one of the poorest of Luanda's *museque* (literally, "sand slum") suburbs. For the perplexed Luanda residents and others within range of the capital's underpowered radio transmitters, this set the real tone for what was going on. It said in part:

> In an emergency meeting to analyze the situation, the Sazimbanga Ward Committee decided on new revolutionary forms of struggle. The Neto government, using open cynicism, ordered the forces of repression to act against the revolution under the most criminal propaganda it has ever known. Nothing can save the revolution unless the people rise up. The FAPLA have joined the people's masses to bar the road to the alliance of right-wing and Maoist forces which have conspired against the victories of the people's revolution. . . .

Another broadcast urged all "those who have felt humiliated because of the color of your skin" to join the demonstration. How wise the MPLA leadership had been to wage a campaign against racism, tribalism, and regionalism of the FNLA and UNITA. The appeal to racism fell on deaf ears, but it pointed the finger at who was behind the whole affair—Nito Alves, former Minister of the Interior. No crowds gathered for the demonstration. On the contrary, people were staying indoors, awaiting some clarification of the situation. The streets were virtually deserted. By 11 A.M., the radio announced that various "corrupt ministers" had been arrested and would be executed in Revolution Square for "betraying the

106

confidence of the masses." Again gunfire was heard from the direction of the radio station, and toward midday radio listeners could hear a brief argument during a further exhortation, then the announcement: "*Radio Nacional* is with President Neto. Comrades, the Angolan radio is in the hands of the revolutionaries. The situation is normalized. . . ."[1]

What had been going on? A full reply to that involves many of the factors which have led to such tragic consequences in many of Africa's independence movements, especially after power had been won. After the Alvor Agreement, Nito Alves was sent into Luanda to prepare the arrival of the MPLA representation in the Transitional Government. He did his work well, but for himself as well as the MPLA. In creating the embryo People's Power organizations, he was exceeding MPLA instructions and setting up his own political power base. In distributing tens of thousands of weapons and never giving an account of to whom they had been distributed, he was giving muscle to that power base. At first Nito Alves had flirted with the self-styled Maoist group in Portugal, the MRPP (Movement for the Reconstruction of the Party of the Proletariat) and had supported parallel groups in Luanda, including the Amilcar Cabral Committees. Later, seeing that the wind was not blowing in that direction, he turned on them and was most zealous—once he became Minister of the Interior—in ensuring that they were suppressed and the ringleaders arrested. As he needed an outside power base—if not China, why not the Soviet Union? Heading the MPLA delegation to the 25th Congress of the Soviet Communist Party (February 24-March 5, 1976) there is no doubt that Nito Alves used the occasion to seek Soviet support. Whether he succeeded is another matter, but he acted as if he had. From about that time onward, he covertly, and in some cases almost overtly, set about challenging Neto's leadership of the MPLA.

A case in point, of which I was an eyewitness, was during the trial in Luanda of thirteen British and American mercenaries. The MPLA leadership had decided that the trial must be held under the most impeccable conditions of judicial impartiality. It was not intended as just a punishment trial of the captured mercenaries, but as an exposure trial of the whole sordid business in the hope of getting international action to stop this practice once and for all. In so doing the Angolan government hoped to exercise an immediate deterrent effect on the recruitment of mercenaries by the Smith regime in Zimbabwe and their use in Namibia and elsewhere. It was to this end that the government had invited legal experts from thirty-nine countries and representatives of the world press to observe and report on the trial. In the early stages, the opinion of the international legal observers and press was unanimous as to t e admirable serenity and fairness of the proceedings. But suddenly there were street demonstrations with organized marching columns with banners demanding death for all the mercenaries. There was extensive radio coverage and also coverage in one of the capital's two daily newspapers, *Diario de Luanda*. Inquiries made by myself and other journalists showed that MPLA and UNTA (Trade Union) representatives tried to stop the demonstrations but were met with objections that these were people's "spontaneous" demonstrations and remarks such as "whose side are *you* on." They lasted just one day. Next morning, politically minded readers of the government-owned *Jornal de Luanda* understood what was going on when there was a front-page article stressing that Agostinho Neto was not only president of the Republic, but also commander-in-chief of the armed forces.

Another incident occurred when the people's prosecutor at the trial of the mercenaries, Manuel Rui Alves Monteiro, made his summation. The court was packed with people who had not previously attended the proceedings. They burst into cheers and wild applause when he demanded the death penalty for all thirteen accused. The street and court demonstrations did what they had been intended to do—cloud the atmosphere of judicial impartiality in which the trial was held and challenge the leadership of Agostinho Neto. It was no secret for any well-informed observer in Luanda that Nito Alves, as Minister of the Interior, was the guiding hand in both these incidents. A born opportunist with an obsession for power, he was appealing to racist emotions to enhance his own popularity. There is every reason to believe that, because of his manipulations of public opinion, the sentences passed on the mercenaries were severer than they would otherwise have been.

Whether Nito Alves believed he had Soviet support in all this cannot be known. He certainly did not have the support of the two Soviet legal experts at the trial. Leaving, like most of those on the International Commission of Inquiry on Mercenaries, before the sentences were pronounced, the two Soviet members, Vladimir Kudriatsev and Aran Poltariak, took me aside before they got into their car for the airport and said: "We want to make it clear to you, and through you, to the world press, that in the event of any blanket death sentences, we, the Soviet representatives on the International Commission, are opposed to this. We uphold basic principles of international law—no punishment without a crime and individual sentences according to the degree of guilt." (Four of the thirteen were in fact executed.)

Nito Alves, however, fired another shot about the time of the Luanda trial. In late June, 1976, he made a long speech to mark the holding of the first election for People's Power Committees in Luanda. The speech was written by Edgar Vales, whose sister Cita Vales had been his mistress. Together with another brother, Edmond, these three white Angolans, born in Cabinda, formed a sort of inner and ultra-leftist advisory council to Nito Alves. Some parts of the speech, which I heard over the radio, would perhaps have been appropriate for a meeting celebrating the anniversary of the Bolshevik Revolution—for example, its detailed history as to how the Bolsheviks came to power. It also contained a blatant black-racist remark, written in, as we learned later, in his own handwriting by Nito Alves to the effect that racism will disappear in Angola on the day that the comrades sweeping the streets will be not only blacks but also whites and those of mixed race.

I later asked the Soviet Tass correspondent what he thought of the speech and he replied: "I don't know what was in it. My interpreter refused to translate." That Nito Alves courted the Soviet embassy was well known; one Soviet diplomat was recalled for having responded too openly to the courtship.

Obviously the activities of Nito Alves—and his aspirations—had not gone unnoticed by President Neto and top aides such as Lucio Lara, "Iko" Carreira, and others. There had been a meeting of the MPLA's Central Committee in October, 1976, at which a number of key decisions were made. The Ministry of the Interior was abolished in favor of a security body answerable directly to the MPLA and Nito Alves was dropped as a co-opted member of the Political Bureau but remained a member of the Central Committee. It was decided to appoint a "commission of inquiry" on "fractionalism," its effect as a "destabilizing influence" on the economic, political, and social life of the country, and to find out

109

who was responsible. The report on the results of the inquiry was to be presented by Comandante Saydi Mingas (Finance Minister) at a meeting of the Central Committee, at the Museum of the Revolution, at 10 A.M. on May 20, 1977. Fifteen minutes before it was due to start, President Neto changed the meeting place to Futungo de Belas, ten miles south of Luanda near his personal residence. Two members of the Central Committee, Nito Alves and José van Dunem, deputy to "Balakoff," political commissar of the FAPLA, protested at the last minute change. They had good reason to do so, as was learned later.

The scenario as defined by the chief plotters was somewhat similar to that enacted during the trial of the mercenaries. "Spontaneous" mass demonstrations outside the Museum of the Revolution against the government and MPLA leadership, for a start. Then armed units, faithful to Nito Alves and Van Dunem, called in first to encircle the demonstrators on the pretext of protecting the Central Committee, but in fact to isolate them from units loyal to the MPLA leadership. Then an ultimatum for the immediate dissolution of the Central Committee and Political Bureau. In case of refusal, the immediate arrest and execution of all members opposing the dissolution. Perhaps an offer for Neto and a few others to go into exile which they would certainly have refused.

The sudden change of meeting place upset these plans. There was just enough time to cancel those that had been made, but none to organize new ones. Nito Alves and José van Dunem could not do otherwise but attend the meeting. The report of Saydi Mingas was devastating. Alves and Van Dunem had succeeded in setting up a parallel organization to that of the MPLA, deliberately aimed at sabotaging the economy and causing mass discontent among the population and, by withholding their salaries and their rations, within the armed forces. To all complaints, their standard response was: "Complain to the whites and mestizos who run the government." (Agostinho Neto's wife is white, Lucio Lara and "Iko" Carreira are of mixed race.) After listening to the report there was no doubt in the minds of the overwhelming majority of the Central Committee members as to who the "fractionalists" were. There were demands ranging from expulsion of Nito Alves and José van Dunem from the Central Committee to their arrest and immediate trial. Nito Alves counterattacked by demanding that a thirteen-point "thesis" which he had prepared should be the basis of the Central Committee discussion. This was refused because the meeting had been called to discuss the report of the Commission of Inquiry. But Alves was allowed to present his thirteen points, the last of which contained the essence of what all his activities had been about: "If there is any fractionalism within the MPLA," he said, "it is among you, the present leadership, that it is to be found. I am the incarnation of the revolution. History has reserved for me the role of carrying out the revolutionary process. The conditions which I demand are the only possible ones. Immediate resignation of the Political Bureau, suspension of the Central Committee and the appointment of a revolutionary political-military committee to assume the leadership of the country." Alves was thus demanding nothing less than the liquidation of the Neto leadership. A point of no return had been reached.

Neto, who had not intervened in the discussions, suspended the meeting at midday to hold private talks with Nito Alves and José van Dunem in a last-minute appeal for unity in the face of what he considered another impending attempt from outside to "destabilize" Angola. It was useless; the positions were irreconcilable. When the session resumed, Neto pointed out that the Central Committee had in its hands concrete evidence of the participation "of these comrades, if I can still call them 'comrades,' in a widespread conspiracy against the state, the government, and the MPLA." He called for their expulsion from the Central Committee. Alves and Van Dunem vigorously protested, claiming that the president's role should be restricted to that of an "arbiter between various tendencies," to which Neto replied that to limit himself to such a role would be "to abandon my fundamental prerogatives of leadership of the state, the MPLA, and the government."[2]

Alves argued that in any case the Central Committee only had the right to "suspend" and not to "exclude" and demanded that the session continue for at least another three days. This was refused, but it was agreed that a further session would be held the following morning. By that time there were street demonstrations in favor of the Neto leadership, with the main slogans: "Long Live the MPLA" and "Down with fractionalism." In a short meeting on the morning of May 21, the Central Committee voted overwhelmingly to expel Nito Alves and José van Dunem. On the afternoon of that same day, at a hastily assembled meeting at the Luanda sports stadium, as reported by Sara Rodriguez, Neto took his case to the people of Luanda:

"Although the Alves-Van Dunem faction put on a revolutionary cloak, they were in fact helping the counterrevolutionaries by their splitting tactics and by their practice of operating secretly while refusing to debate questions openly. During our history we have several times seen that those who practice factionalism—evoking ideological or tribal, or even class issues—always end by allying themselves with our enemies. In order to fight the MPLA, any group must ally itself with some force. Since we have the support of all the progressive forces in the world, such a group will . . . end up allying itself with the reactionaries. . . ."

The factionalist tendency has also been accused of trying to gain support from the Soviet Union. The leading Angolan newspaper, *Jornal de Angola*, commented: "During a trip of a few days . . . Nito Alves tried to draw into his adventure a country with whom the MPLA has solid relations of friendship and international solidarity. The maneuver was well thought out. It is part of imperialism's technique to try to set revolutionaries in contradiction with each other."

A flood of crude pamphlets were circulated in Luanda in the past few weeks accusing the MPLA of "anti-Sovietism." At the May 21 meeting, President Neto replied: "There are no militants more faithful to the socialist cause than the traditional MPLA leadership—not for sentimental or subjective reasons. We know what the Soviet Union is," he said, recalling the Soviet Union's support for the MPLA in the difficult days of armed struggle.

Brushing aside the "anti-Soviet" charges, he noted ironically that: "Outside Angola they criticize us for being under Soviet guidance. They say it is the Soviet Union that is ruling Angola. These are lies. As long as this political leadership is ruling the country we will always defend our independence and our nonalignment. And if the Soviet ambassador comes to me with some difficult problem, the first thing I say is: 'Wait a few hours,' and as usual I consult with the Political Bureau to discuss whether or not we should accept proposals made to us. It is we who make the decisions. This is the fundamental principle of our independence. We do not accept orders from anybody, whoever they are." President Neto also refuted imperialist allegations that Angola is under Cuban control.

In Luanda, following house-to-house searches in some residential areas, arms caches have been found—though it is not yet certain whether these arms supplies were being hidden by factional elements or by other counterrevolutionaries. . . .[3]

112

The conspirators went ahead with their plans to stage an armed coup. Part of their activities was known to Neto and other MPLA leaders, but the depth and breadth of the plot was not known. When Simon Malley, editor of the authoritative Paris-based fortnightly Afrique-Asie asked why, even in view of what was known, they were not arrested, Neto replied that he had so often been accused of arbitrary acts in dealing with opposition and fractionalist elements that he preferred the risk of letting things take their course. Let the enemies fully expose themselves before the public. Doubtless he was right, but the exposure of the lengths to which the Alves-Van Dunem group were prepared to go was to have tragic consequences.

Within half an hour of the first shots being fired at the Sao Paolo prison, the commander of Cuban troops in Angola was at Neto's side. He had already been in telex contact directly with Fidel Castro. "If you need any help you have our total support. Fidel's instructions!" Neto picked up the phone and called "Iko." "Great," was his reply. "But we have our 9th Armored Brigade which assures the defense of Luanda so it shouldn't be necessary." The Cuban commander remained at Neto's headquarters in case his services were needed. And as tangible evidence of the level of Cuban support, he announced that Fidel's brother, Raoul, Minister of Defense and Second Secretary of the Central Committee of the Cuban Communist Party, was ready to leave immediately for Luanda if Neto so desired. Neto did so desire, and Raoul Castro was on his way within hours.[4]

What even the usually well-informed "Iko" did not know was that the commanding officers of the 9th Brigade were in cahoots with the plotters, as was the Deputy Chief of Staff of the Armed Forces, "Monstro Imortal." (I had always wondered what sort of personality would choose such a *nom de guerre*!) Nor was it known that "Bakaloff," Political Commissar of the armed forces, Pedro Fortunato, Commissioner of Luanda province, and David Aires M'achado, Minister of Trade, were among the ringleaders of the plot. (Participation of the latter explained why imported consumer goods were left to rot in storage depots while the shelves of the cooperative shops were empty of goods.)

The Sao Paolo prison was easily taken over and most of the prisoners, including nine supporters of Nito Alves, were freed. Oddly enough, the only ones not to take advantage of the situation despite the exhortation of the "liberators" were some leaders of the "Active Revolt" and the nine white mercenaries, imprisoned there since their sentencing almost a year previously. The 9th Armored Brigade was the only major military unit to have its headquarters inside Luanda. Its commanding officer—loyal to Neto—was away on a military training course in North Korea; his replacement was with Nito Alves. It was the ten tanks and armored cars of the 9th Brigade which were used to seize the prison and radio station. They then took up positions around the presidential palace. How all this could happen was related by "Iko" to Simon Malley:

> Immediately after the Central Committee decision of May 21, we knew that Nito Alves and José van Dunem would try something. They stopped living at their homes and moved from place to place for fear of being arrested. I set up radio patrols on the night of May 26. These kept me informed as to what was going on in the city. The "Nitists" were knocking on the doors of houses in the residential areas, asking people to turn out next day to demonstrate against the Central Committee and Political Bureau and to demand the reintegration into the Central Committee of Nito Alves and Van Dunem. We learned also that street barricades were being set up to prevent the MPLA leadership from moving from their residences in Miramar [a Luanda city district where most of the MPLA leadership—including Nito Alves and Van Dunem] to the presidential palace.
>
> When the first shots were heard, around 4:30 A.M., we did not quite know how many military units were involved. Above all we had no idea that the 9th Armored Brigade was implicated. We always had confidence in this unit which had fought in the north against the FNLA and the Zaire troops and had behaved very well. I managed to get to the Defense Ministry about 5 A.M. where I found several of our military commanders. Each was charged with a mission to contact the various units and garrisons—to sound out the whole situation and determine what action should be taken. The Comandantes Bula and "Dangereux" from staff headquarters should go to the 9th Brigade garrison headquarters at Dos Dragoes. Meanwhile the brigade's deputy commander, Comandante Nguianda, had also gone there. He was received with a volley of shots. He escaped but did not succeed in warning the FAPLA Chief of Staff, Xietu, who was also on his way there together with Comandantes "Dangereux," Bula, and Nzaji [head of the FAPLA security services]. On the way, they met a tank of the 9th Brigade, coming from the residential areas.

Not knowing that this was an "enemy" tank, they followed it with their cars into the garrison courtyard.

The tank turret swiveled round immediately and threatened them with its cannon. They were forced to get out of their cars. Disarmed and heavily guarded, they were taken into the room of a young officer. Only Xietu, whose car was last in the convoy, managed to escape by threatening the troops who surrounded him with a grenade which he pulled out of his pocket. It was in the young officer's room that the Comandantes, Bula, "Dangereux," and Nzaji found the Minister of Finance, Saydi Mingas. Three other comrades—"Eurico," head of personnel at the Defense Ministry, Comandante Gato, the recently named Commander of the Port of Luanda, and the director of the Economic Affairs Section of the Ministry of Foreign Affairs, Garcia Neto, who had been arrested in the city—were also brought into the same room.[5] In all, there were about a hundred persons arrested at the barricades because they had documents indicating that they belonged to various government services.

In the meantime, "Iko" had received word from Helder Neto, one of the heads of the DISA (Internal Security Agency), that a tank had burst into the courtyard of the Sao Paolo prison. Shortly after came the word that Helder Neto had been killed, together with some prison guards; and that, apart from the nine Nito Alves activists, about thirty other FNLA, UNITA, and FLEC prisoners had been freed. His account continued:

When we understood that the 9th Armored Brigade and several units of the military police were involved in the conspiracy, intervention by tanks of the Presidential Guard and of the Reconnaissance Brigade of the army staff headquarters became absolutely indispensable.[6]

It was then found that communications with the headquarters of both the Presidential Guard, twenty kilometers north of Luanda at Cuaco, and the Reconnaissance Brigade in the southern outskirts of the city, had been cut. Comandante Onambwe rushed off by jeep to the Presidential Guard and put himself at the head of their eight tanks in a dash to the People's Palace where they joined forces with the seven armored cars of the Reconnaissance Brigade, which had already spearheaded the re-occupation of Sao Paolo prison and the radio station. There remained the key question of the 9th Armored Brigade. It was known that some other army units had been tricked into reinforcing this unit but its real strength was an unknown factor. "Iko" recommended that President Neto accept the offer of Cuban help. Within minutes four Cuban tanks rumbled out of their garrison headquarters at Viana, about twenty kilometers south of Luanda. At this moment Cita Vales, who was together with Van Dunem in a temporary headquarters near Viana, wrote in her diary: "All is lost. The Cubans are moving."

The Cuban tanks met up with those of the Presidential Guard and the armored cars of the Reconnaissance Brigade at the radio station. The combined force then set out for the Headquarters of the 9th Armored Brigade. Onambwe, acting on direct instructions from Neto, gave the mutineers just twenty minutes to free the prisoners, lay down their arms, and "unconditionally surrender." The twenty minutes proved to be too long. While most of the prisoners were being released, the six most important ones were removed to a house in Sazimbanga. Their hands tied behind their backs with nylon cord, they were machine-gunned, their bodies then placed in two cars, gasoline poured over them and the two cars set alight. Miraculously, Gato was left for dead on the floor of the bathroom where the machine-gunning took place and was found by the crew of an armored car which raced to the spot once it was found that the main hostages were missing. He testified that some of his comrades were still alive when they were carried to the cars and burned to death.

By 1:30 P.M. on May 27, just nine hours after it had started, the coup attempt had been crushed. The commanders of the 9th Armored Brigade, the only real muscle on which Nito Alves counted, had accepted the ultimatum. The public had not responded to the plotters' exhortations for mass demonstrations. Had they done so, Agostinho Neto and other MPLA leaders would have suffered the same fate as Finance Minister Saydi Mingas, Garcia Neto, "Eurico," and the others. By the time it was over, however, about two hundred people had lost their lives, almost all of them in opposing the plotters.

Among those captured immediately after the showdown with the 9th Armored Brigade, was Pedro Fortunato. He gave some very frank testimony to a preliminary Commission of Inquiry set up immediately after order was restored—but while the main plotters were still at large. Extracts of testimony given to the commission were published in the *Jornal de Angola*. Thus, in summarized form, Fortunato explained as follows:

> Once the projected demonstration had reached the People's Palace, a "delegation" would have gone forward and arrested the president. At that moment, Alves was to have read a proclamation over the national radio announcing the new regime had taken over.
>
> Had more than a couple of hundred people shown up, or had the army sided with the plotters, [Monstro] Imortal was to have followed up the proclamation by arresting and "eliminating" government leaders. Among those scheduled for elimination, according to Fortunato, were MPLA Secretary-General Lucio Lara, Minister of Defense "Iko" Carreira, Comandante Onambwe (who took part in recapturing the radio station), Comandante Nzaji (who was murdered May 27 when he tried to negotiate with the plotters on behalf of the government), Comandante Ludy, head of state security, and Comandante Xietu, chief of the army general staff headquarters. President Neto, he said, was to have been arrested but allowed to leave the country in exile—although other evidence indicates the popular physician-poet-political leader was to have been assassinated.
>
> Additional witnesses testified that the murder plans were more widespread. According to conspirator Domingos Francisco, who had the task of providing arms and ammunition for the coup attempt, "the meetings [to plan the take-over] began eight months ago on my farm. They were to prepare a *coup d'état* in order to eliminate the MPLA. There was to be physical elimination of all the members of the Central Committee, of the president and all members so they could take over the government. On May 26, I was contacted by Major Bage and told the operation was to take place the following day, and that the government had been appointed. Alves was to be president, Van Dunem prime minister, Imortal minister of defense and "Bakaloff," chief of staff of the armed forces. We were trying to finish with the MPLA. . . ."[7]

Some accounts in the Western press made it appear that it was Cuban military intervention that was decisive in saving the situation for the Neto leadership. But while it was of enormous importance that Castro immediately announced total support and Neto knew he had this powerful card up his sleeve, it was not the four Cuban tanks that caused the collapse of the Alves-Van Dunem plot. It was the lack of any popular support. Had tens of

117

thousands of people swarmed into the square before the presidential palace demanding a change of government and MPLA leadership, the position of Neto—and the Cubans—would have been very difficult. But not even the two hundred which the plotters had set as the minimum to justify the arrest of President Neto turned up. Nito Alves and his co-plotters had completely misjudged their support at every level, displaying an almost infantile naïvete which is often a distinguishing mark of an ultra-leftist mentality that has moved so far around the political spectrum that it merges with that of the ultra-right.

After the Cuban tanks moved and the radio had already started denouncing the plotters, Cita Vales sent a message to a contact of Nito Alves, planted within the secretariat of President Neto: "It is absolutely necessary that you immediately contact the Soviet embassy and convince them to help us flee the country by any possible means. . . ." The message was intercepted and Cita Vales, together with José van Dunem—who had succeeded Nito Alves as her lover—were among those arrested in the first few days. There is no evidence of the Soviet embassy having lifted a finger to help any of the plotters.

From captured documents, avowals of those first to be arrested among the chief plotters and the conversations which Simon Malley had with Agostinho Neto, Lucio Lara, "Iko" Carreira, and others, it became clear that Alves-Van Dunem-"Bakaloff" had adopted an "all things to all men" policy. They had set up three distinct contact teams to approach the socialist camp, the Western world, and certain African states. They had a different "sales talk" for each. For the socialist world the "line" was to the effect that the Neto leadership was preparing a "turn to the right" and the policy of "nonalignment was a cover for setting up a social-democratic type regime." The new leadership would ensure the closest relations with the Soviet Union, offer air and naval bases and guarantee that the Soviet Union would have a privileged position in the political, economic, social, and cultural spheres in Angola. President Neto, Lucio Lara, and "Iko" Carriera were accused of having organized the invasion of the Shaba region of southern Zaire by the former Katangan "gendarmes."[8]

To the Western world, the assigned contact team offered the withdrawal of all Cubans within eighteen months of Nito Alves-José van Dunem taking over and the repudiation of all agreements with the Soviet Union. To ensure some "scare support" the story was spread that NATO was about to place Angola within COMECON (the East European equivalent of the Common Market) and that the FAPLA was training commando groups for intervention in Namibia, Mozambique, Tanzania, and Zambia and preparing to send a force of between 15,000 and 20,000 troops to fight in Zimbabwe (Rhodesia) and South Africa.

To frighten the Arab world, there were stories of "Zionist" advisers in the Angolan security services and a strong rumor that Neto was about to allow the Soviet Union to set up three major military bases in Angola in exchange for sixty million dollars annually, and so on. There was an infinite variety of concoctions to cater for every suspicion. In some cases it worked and there is evidence of considerable sums of money being placed at the disposal of the plotters. Support from outside however was more easily organized than that from inside.

The fundamental error that was to cost the lives of Nito Alves and all the chief plotters was to have underestimated the political maturity of the people, especially those of the capital who had been through so many trials by fire. From February 4, 1961, to May 27, 1977, much blood had been spilt in the streets of Luanda in an attempt to wipe out the leadership of the MPLA. Nito Alves was strong and could rally popular support only when the people believed he was acting as a loyal supporter of Agostinho Neto and the leadership which had proved capable of leading the Angolan people through an impossibly difficult national liberation struggle. The people of Luanda had seen with their own eyes that leadership stand up to the Portuguese; deal with the FNLA and UNITA when they went on the rampage inside Luanda. Who was Nito Alves in comparison? Doubtless the results of his organizational work in preparing for the triumphal arrival for the MPLA in Luanda in November, 1975, went to his head. But the people had not turned out for Nito Alves. They were there to render homage to Agostinho Neto and other veteran leaders of the MPLA.

Alves and his supporters also overlooked the extent to which racist and tribalist concepts had given way to national concepts during the prolonged military-political struggle, accompanied from the beginning by a conscious effort of the MPLA leadership to promote all-Angolan sentiments. The appeals to rally to the putschists' banner on the basis of black racism fell flat. As did also

Nito Alves's belief that by having the heavy weapons of the 9th Armored Brigade and a few prestigious commanders at his disposal, rank and file supporters of the MPLA would rally to his side. Doubtless he would have had outside support had he been able to prove successful. But in just nine hours it was all over. All that remained was to round up the ringleaders.

Nothing could be more symbolic of the lack of popular support than the manner of the capture of Nito Alves himself. He dared not seek shelter in the Luanda *museques*, although it was there that he had always claimed he had massive support. He fled to the forests north of the capital. Hiding by day and moving by night, fearing to ask anyone for help, he slowly made his way back to his home district of Piri in Uije province, not far from the Zaire border.

To an old woman squatting over a cooking fire in the tiny hamlet of Velho Eduardo (Old Edward), he introduced himself by his real name, Alves Bernado Baptisto, "son of Mario Joao and Bernardo Pango. . ." He begged for food saying that he and his companion had eaten nothing for fourteen days. On the pretext of fetching a chicken, the woman contacted Velho Eduardo, whose son Adao Eduardo set off at full speed to contact the forward headquarters of none other than Comandante Margoso (see Chapter Two). Alves had narrowly escaped capture by Margoso's men a week previously by abandoning his vehicle under a volley of fire and plunging into the forest. Margoso had sworn to bring him "alive or dead" to Luanda.

The old woman, Joaquina N'Gongo, returned to the hut without a chicken but she grilled some bananas and served them with *funji*—flour ground from manioc roots and cooked with water, the staple diet of most Angolans, followed by coffee. The three then lay down to sleep. Joaquina related what happened:

"I heard the noise of a motor. From my bed I could see Nito Alves coming closer, closer—trying to hide the pistol in his hand. I pretended to be asleep. When he got to the foot of the bed I threw off the blanket so that it landed over his head. 'There are troops . . . Troops are coming . . .' he yelled. 'It's only my brother coming from Luanda,' I replied.

"I got up and reached for the door which he hid behind as I opened it. It was only half-opened when he fled, the others behind him. The FAPLA opened fire. I thought he was dead, but no. The bullets whizzed past without hitting him . . .[9]

For a while it seemed that Nito Alves had made good his escape again. But by daybreak the entire people had turned out to support Comandante Margoso and his men. From Piri and neighboring Quibaxe and other villages they came bearing whatever weapons they had—mainly the fearsome *machete*. As if hunting some dangerous animal they advanced in long lines combing the forest tree by tree, bush by bush, clump by clump of vegetation. Finally they found the would-be president of Angola hiding up a baobab tree. Margoso's men had to protect him from the local people who were demanding summary justice. The fact that he had plotted to decapitate the entire leadership of the MPLA and was responsible for the brutal murder of some of the most popular veterans of the liberation struggle had turned his closest relatives and neighbors against him. But Margoso's men brought him back to Luanda where he was tried before a military tribunal and executed by firing squad.

No defeat could have been more total. Lack of support in the initial uprising, failure to find refuge in the Luanda *museque* which was supposed to be his main power base, hunted down like a wild beast in his own home district. The whole episode proved once more that people's support is not an abstract, demagogic term. It is a living reality without which neither the Angolan, nor the Vietnamese, nor any other national liberation movements could have survived. But to have faith in this requires a rare quality of leadership, strong nerves and continuing renewal of the people's faith in that leadership.

The Nito Alves coup attempt ended one more dramatic phase of the Long March of the Angolan revolution. "Bakaloff," the last of the ringleaders to be captured, was rounded up a few months after Nito Alves and was also executed. That none of them could find a corner of the country in which to hide speaks for itself.

It would be unrealistic to think that the crushing of the Nito Alves coup attempt meant that the MPLA leadership could lean back and relax. The oft-repeated slogan: *A Luta Continua* (The Struggle Continues) remains valid.

FNLA-Zaire forces can still make commando raids across the

northern frontier to wipe out a village or destroy some economic objectives. The UNITA forces are still active in the Center-South and along the Namibian border.[10] The timing of the coup attempt was related to the MPLA Congress, which opened on December 4, 1977, but which was originally scheduled for much earlier. It was postponed because of the coup attempt. This was the Congress which was to decide on the formation of a Marxist-Leninist Party and elect the leadership of that Party. Alves had hoped to maneuver within the MPLA Central Committee to ensure his own leadership before the Congress took place. But his expulsion, together with that of José van Dunem, from the MPLA Central Committee ended that possibility.

At the December Congress, it was decided to set up a Marxist Party of Labor from the most active MPLA militants—drawing largely on the Action Committees which had long fulfilled the role of Communist Party cells. A 45-member Central Committee was elected and it in turn elected an 11-member Political Bureau, headed by Agostinho Neto. It included all those on the Nito Alves list for execution: Lucio Lara, "Iko" Carreira, Lopo do Nascimento, José Eduardo dos Santos, Carlos Rocha and others. The Party of Labor is charged with playing a vanguard role in building a socialist society in Angola based on the country's traditions and concrete conditions.

PART II

Mozambique

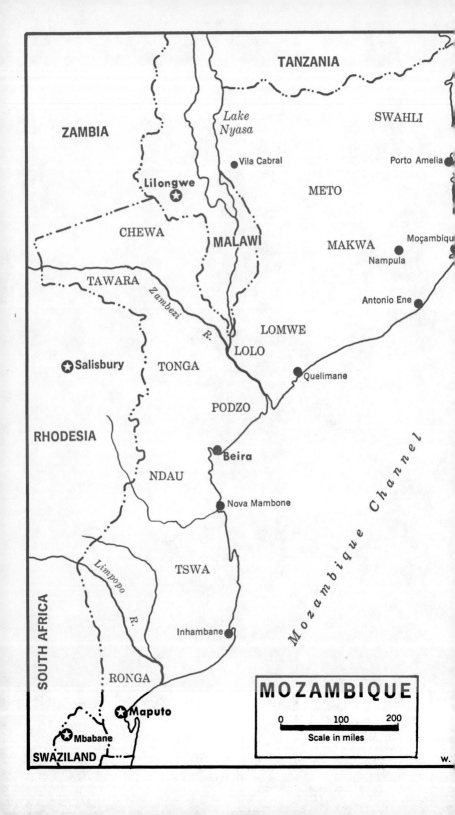

XI The Mozambique Detonator

Mozambique was the last of Portugal's mainland African colonies to rise up in armed revolt. Angola, 1961; Guiné-Bissau, 1963; Mozambique, 1964. That was the timetable. It is tempting to think that there was some super-body who pressed the buttons to bring each of them on to the battlefield against Portuguese colonialism according to a pre-arranged plan. But armed liberation struggles do not work like that. People can be brought to take up arms only when every other means of obtaining independence has been exhausted. A feature common to each of the three struggles was popular reaction to some especially revolting act of repression by local, bloody-minded military commanders of the Portuguese fascist government—a government determined to stamp out any sparks carried into the Portuguese colonies from the fires of independence burning elsewhere in Africa at that period.

The reaction of Lisbon and the strong-arm generals in the African colonies was a standard reflex of maximum terror to crush even the most innocent signs of yearning for the independence that was being granted, or had been wrested by force of arms, in neighboring British, French, and Belgian colonies. The distribution of pro-independence tracts in Luanda in March, 1959; a dockers' strike at the Bissau Pidgiguiti docks in August, 1959, and a peaceful pro-independence demonstration at Mueda, in northern Mozambique in June, 1960, were all suppressed with unbridled ferocity. They had been in the past, too. But the winds of successful armed resistance were blowing strongly from several parts of the world—especially from Vietnam and Cuba—and produced a cross-fertilization of ideas among a group of ardent patriots from the Portuguese colonies who were later to lead their peoples to victory. They had come to a conclusion best summed up by Amilcar Cabral, the founder and leader—until he was assassinated by PIDE agents—of the PAIGC (Party for the Independence of Guiné-Bissau and the Cape Verde Islands):

> It is obvious from all the facts that violence is the essential means of imperialist domination. If, then, we accept the principle that national liberation equals revolution, and is not simply a matter of raising a flag or singing an anthem, we shall find that there is and there can be no national liberation without the use of liberating violence on the part of the national forces.[1]

The example of what happened at Mueda on June 16, 1960, will remain a classic illustration of Amilcar Cabral's words. Due to the accelerated process of Portuguese colonialist repression in Mozambique after World War II—the eviction of peasants from the most fertile lands to make way for Portuguese peasant settlers, the sale of labor to South Africa to work under slave conditions in the Rand gold mines—there was considerable flight into exile in neighboring countries such as what was then Tanganyika, Nyasaland, Northern and Southern Rhodesia, South Africa. The more politically minded among the exiles—and they were numerous—identified themselves with the independence movements in those countries. They supported UNIP (United National Independence Party) in Northern Rhodesia, which was soon to become Zambia; TANU (Tanganyika African National Union) in what was to become the ruling party in independent Tanzania; the Malawi Congress Party in Nyasaland, which was to become independent Malawi; ZAPU (Zimbabwe African Peoples' Union) in Southern Rhodesia (ZANU [Zimbabwe African National Union] was not yet in existence at this time). In South Africa, they worked underground with the ANC (African National Congress). They rejoiced and identified themselves with the success of some of these movements when Tanzania, Zambia, and Malawi won their independence; as well as black African countries further afield in Kenya and Uganda. The exiles saw that it was possible to have political activities and organizations and to work for a peaceful transition to independence. They started to organize themselves to this end.

In Tanganyika, they formed the MANU (Makonda African National Union) based on a large tribal grouping in northern Mozambique, which later changed its name to Mozambique African National Union. In Northern Rhodesia and Nyasaland, UNAMI (National African Movement of Independent Mozambique) was formed; and in Southern Rhodesia, UDENAM (Mozambique National Democratic Union). Once they successfully developed political activity outside Mozambique, the big problem was how to get an independence movement going inside the country. What should the aims be? How to present them and get people organized? The leadership of MANU felt it was necessary to send a delegation to Mozambique, take the temperature of the situation and express their views to the Portuguese that as independence was in the air all over eastern Africa—why not for **Mozambique?**

128

At that time the idea that national liberation implied armed struggle was far from their minds. The idea was to start a dialogue—as their friends had done with the British in Tanganyika. How to improve the precarious living conditions which sent people like them into exile? How to deal with the questions of arbitrary arrest, forced labor, unemployment? There was a lack of schools and hospitals and a need for lower taxes. The idea was to use these claims as a platform around which to organize political struggle in case the Portuguese proved difficult. A first group was sent in to the district center of Mueda, in the heart of Makonda country. Heading it was a popular MANU leader, Faustino Vanomba. The local administrator refused to see him, or to accept the list of claims which had been put down on paper. He returned empty-handed to Tanganyika.

A second group was sent to Mueda—this time seven persons headed by another popular MANU leader, Simao Chucha. They were promptly arrested by the local administrator and deported to southern Mozambique. A single third delegate, Tiago Mula, was sent to find out what had happened to the second group. He was also arrested. Back in Tanganyika, the MANU leadership had no idea what was going on, whether anything had even been discussed, why their delegates had not returned. The head of MANU, Quibaite Duane, decided to come in person together with Faustino Vanomba of the first delegation. This time they took the precaution of infiltrating some of their members to alert the local people as to their visit and its purpose. Apparently the word spread like wildfire that "the men from Tanganyika are coming to solve our problems." People started pouring into the district center. It was decided to organize a big welcoming meeting and in view of the popular excitement the local authorities gave permission for the meeting.

This time they were received and the Portugese administrator listened to their claims—the same ones that Vanomba had brought in written form the first time. It was June 9, 1960. The reply was: "I have no competence to settle such matters, but I will transmit your claims to the provincial governor. You may return in a week's time. In the meantime, if you have families here, go and visit them and return on the 16th." It seemed that the delegation and claims had made a big impression. Preparations went ahead for a big meeting on June 16. Throughout the whole of Cabo Delgado province the word spread to converge on Mueda for a mass meeting outside the district headquarters. Even the local police encouraged people to participate. The following description, and the essential parts of the background information, came from a young schoolteacher—twenty-two years old at that time—who was an eyewitness:

There was great excitement. The delegates arrived early on the morning of the 16th, but people had been gathering in front of the district headquarters for two or three days, eager to see how their problems were going to be solved. The governor arrived from the provincial capital of Porto Amélia [now Pombo] at about 3 P.M. Thousands of people applauded when the delegates were invited into the secretariat. Soon they came out again. Then the governor came out and started to walk down the steps, escorted by the *cipaios* [local police]. Everyone was ordered to stand to attention while the flag was hoisted. People started shouting: "We haven't come to salute the flag but to learn how you are going to solve our problems." The governor stopped and said: "I've come to examine the situation in this province. The government thinks you can do much to solve the problems yourselves by working harder, by intensifying the cultivation of peanuts and the harvesting of cashew nuts."

The people shouted back: "We haven't come to discuss peanuts and cashew nuts. You called us here. We want to know what you discussed with our two leaders—what decisions have been taken."

The governor went back up the steps and into the building. But the people wouldn't leave. Some of them went into the secretariat with the two leaders. We didn't know what was discussed, but we heard sounds of a scuffle and blows. The delegates then came out again, surrounded by police who handcuffed them in front of the crowd. None of us could understand what was happening. The governor came out again and everyone started shouting: "We want to know what is going on." The governor said that anyone who wanted to speak should step forward. A few volunteers stepped forward and were taken into the secretariat. Again, we didn't know what happened. A few minutes later they came out into the hall—also handcuffed. The governor then signaled for some Land-Rovers lined up in front of the administration buildings and the police started pushing the delegates and the others toward the Land-Rovers.

The people—I also—started advancing toward the Land-Rovers shouting: "Why have they been arrested? You can't take them to prison. What have they done? You invited us to come. We won't leave until our demands are met." The *cipaios* started hitting people with rifle butts and bayonets and the people struck back with stones. The *cipaios* then started firing and troops who had been hidden among shrubs and trees behind the headquarters started advancing and firing from behind with automatic weapons. As the people fled, troops and police fired into the crowd. People were just mowed down—women, children, old people—there were piles of dead and wounded everywhere. Over 600 people were killed. That was Mueda!

Why was the schoolteacher there? And how did he react?

From 1957, I had been following the political situation. The activities of the movements outside the country had their repercussions inside. MANU had more influence in Cabo Delgado and neighboring Niassa province; UDENAMO had more influence in Manica, Sofala, Gaza, and Lourenço Marques in the south; UNAMI also had some influence in Niassa, but was stronger in Tete and Zambezi provinces. At that time I was more attracted by MANU. My contacts were with them. I had started to do underground work for them—often receiving their cadres at night, carrying out small tasks. The Mueda massacre only confirmed what had been building up in the minds of many of us for years—the only way forward was by armed struggle. The following year, I went as a delegate from Cabo Delgado to a conference in Tanganyika where, on May 25, 1962, the three movements decided to unite in a single national liberation front. A protocol was signed by each of the three leaders to this effect and just one month later, on June 25, the three organizations dissolved themselves to form FRELIMO—Front for the Liberation of Mozambique—with Eduardo Mondlane as its president. I thus became a founder-member of FRELIMO. The other Cabo Delgado delegate Joai Namimba, like Eduardo Mondlane, was later assassinated by the PIDE.

Writing of this period later in his fundamental and masterly work, *The Process of the People's Democratic Revolution in Mozambique*, Samora Machel, who succeeded Eduardo Mondlane as FRELIMO president, summed up the situation, starting with the difficulties of getting a unity of viewpoint among the three movements:

These elements had lived for a long time outside of Mozambique without direct contact or real knowledge of the existing situation. Their political experience was acquired in close association with

131

nationalist organizations of Rhodesia, Malawi, Zambia, Tanganyika, Kenya—organizations which through demonstrations, strikes, and other nonviolent actions created a situation which led the colonial power to negotiations resulting in an initial phase of internal autonomy and ultimately independence.

These elements confused the situation of a developed colonial power like Great Britain with the situation in Portugal, an underdeveloped, nonindustrialized country with the status of a semi-colony. They ignored the distinction between a bourgeois democracy—where, after all, national and international public opinion play a role, where issues can seriously be raised in parliament—and a fascist country where censorship and political repression prevent any display of opposition. . . .

Writing about the course of events which led to acceptance of armed struggle, Samora Machel cited the massacres at Xinavane (1949) and at Mueda; the brutal repression of strikes by miners, railway workers, and others; the contempt by Portugal for various anticolonialist resolutions at the United Nations and other factors which, taken together, "clearly showed that the only way to liberation was armed struggle." The fact that this was not clear to everybody, including some of the leaders of the three movements united together in FRELIMO, was proved by the subsequent course of events.

It was clear enough however to the Mueda schoolteacher who, like another schoolteacher later to become famous as General Vo Nguyen Giap, drew the right conclusions and reached for a gun. At the time I talked with him, former schoolteacher Alberto-Joaquim Chipande was Minister of Defense of the People's Republic of Mozambique. Like Giap, he led the very first armed action which led into the full-fledged armed liberation struggle. As Giap and Ho Chi Minh had done with the cream of the French, and later the American, Generals Chipande and Samora Machel ran rings around the best generals that Portugal could field.

It was appropriate that the former schoolteacher received me in the briefing room where Portugal's most prestigious—and most ferocious—military leader, General Kaulza Oliveira de Arriaga, used to brief his officers on his latest "win the war" plans. But how did he come to be there? It was an obvious first question and the first part of the reply was his account of the Mueda massacre.

After FRELIMO was formed, I was sent to Algeria to get some military training. In June, 1964, I got orders directly from President Mondlane to start military action. Eduardo Mondlane's instructions were very precise: "You were sent by the people. You are a son of the people. You should now return to the people to start armed struggle." It was a period of great persecution. The PIDE was very active and even though I quickly got close to our frontier, it took me and my group of about thirty, two months to actually cross the border. People were demobilized and demoralized because of the great wave of repression which had followed the Mueda massacre, including the bloody suppression of strikes. Eduardo Mondlane had instructed us to "clearly define who is the enemy." Arms are to be used against whom? Against the Portuguese army, police, and the whole administrative machinery which oppresses and massacres our people. On the other hand, all civilians, whoever they are, are part of the people. "You will protect them, whatever their race or religion. Civilians are not our enemies—they must be protected. Advance, and we will tell you when to start the war. Create suitable conditions." Once we crossed the frontier, we advanced. I was told to go to Cabo Delgado [Mozambique's northernmost province with a frontier of over 250 kilometers with Tanzania, extending from Niassa province to the Indian Ocean].

We continued to advance, dropping off small groups to organize support, so we could attack on as many fronts as possible. It was up to me, as head of the group, to choose the first target. The Portuguese controlled all the highways so it was quite difficult to continue advancing. We marched by night, mainly barefoot through the forest, so as not to leave any traces. However, for all our care, by the time we got to Macomia—about one hundred kilometers southeast of Mueda—the Portuguese got wind of our presence. Their vigilance was stepped up and there were arrests in the areas through which we had passed. I sent word back that it was difficult to advance farther and asked for permission to attack where we were, so as to mark the date of launching armed struggle as soon as possible. A messenger arrived on September 15, [1964] with the word to attack on September 25.

We held a meeting of group commanders on the 20th to work out plans and tactics. It was agreed that as this was to be the historic signal for launching people's war, the very first attack must be made in cooperation with the local people. All clandestine FRELIMO workers in the area were contacted and we explained that on the night of September 24 bridges should be destroyed and roads blocked by felling trees or digging ditches across them.

My group of twelve was to attack Chai, a small administrative center about forty kilometers northwest from where we were at Macomia.

We marched the whole night of the 23rd and slept in the forest, without anything to eat. The same on the night of the 24th. We were in position at 3 A.M. on the 25th. But how to attack? The Portuguese had defense units, sentries. We didn't even know how many or how they were disposed. I gave orders to call off the attack for that night and withdraw. Some of our comrades objected strongly. I said: "We've had nothing to eat or drink for three days. We'll withdraw and rest up." Others objected: "After coming so far, we can't stop now." My reply was: "We don't know the real situation. Perhaps we will kill civilians by mistake." So we marched back fifteen kilometers and rested alongside a small lake. There at least we had water, also dense forest for protection.

We decided to send a scout into Chai early next morning. He was in civilian clothes, a valid identity card in his pocket, and bandages around one leg—pretending he had to enter the hospital. We had given him money to buy some peanuts and manioc for us. He got into the administrative courtyard and was able to contact some prisoners. They told him where the police were stationed and how many, and where the sentinels were posted. He came back and drew a map of the situation. We worked out a plan, ate some manioc and peanuts, and set out immediately after sundown. We surrounded the building and advanced to within fifteen to twenty meters of the positions guarding the barracks. At just 9 P.M., one of our men tried to grab a sentry from behind, but there was a pillar in between and he just couldn't get his hands right around him. There was a scuffle and I ordered that the sentry be shot. He was killed and that was the first shot in our armed struggle. There was a sharp gun battle and the Portuguese started hurling grenades from inside the post.

We withdrew without loss. The armed struggle had started. The next day many people fled to join us in the forest, including one of those in the post when we attacked. He said we had killed the head of the post and five others and that there was tremendous panic. He immediately asked to join our unit—and was accepted.

By one of those fortunate coincidences with which diligent journalists are occasionally rewarded, I met another of the "Chai Twelve," Comandante Martinis Mola Muainkongua. He is an enormous man, at least six feet tall and well proportioned, with a massive head and jaws, and his face is entirely covered with tattoo scars of the Makonda tribe. At the time I met him, he was in charge of a re-education center in Inhumbane province. At the end of the visit, as is my custom, I asked where he had been during the armed struggle. "I was a battalion commander, from 1964, in Cabo Delgado," he replied. I asked if he had been there at the time of the attack on Chai. "Yes, I took part in it." His account was similar to that of Defense Minister Chipande, with a few extra details.

"We were only a small group with very few arms. But we had one French light machine gun. Some of the local population joined in. The Portuguese were taken by surprise but started firing back and throwing hand grenades very quickly. We dispersed singly and regrouped at the agreed rendezvous point later. A second group attacked a post at Diaca [less than 50 kilometers east of Mueda—W.B.] and fared better than us because they captured two 7.7 cm. elephant guns. The main thing was that the armed struggle was launched."

"How did the Portuguese react?"

"They started thrusts into the jungle to find us. At first in two or three truckloads. It was easy to ambush them and get plenty of weapons. We gradually built up a stock of arms. But our first work was political—getting people ready for the idea that we were going to fight. We had to persuade them to move back with us into the forest—away from roads and built-up areas."

"When you attacked at Chai did you think that it would take ten years till final victory?"

"We never even thought about that. All that mattered was that we had decided to fight. Better to die on our feet than live under colonialism."

"How many of the original twelve survived?"

"All of us, starting with our leader, Alberto-Joaquim Chipande."

A ludicrously modest beginning, many FRELIMO members must have thought, even a hopeless, reckless venture. After all the political preparation and training, after all the marching and risks—two elephant guns! And an irrevocable challenge flung down to an experienced colonial power with a modern army and powerful Western friends. But, by the very conditions which force patriots to such a desperate enterprise, national liberation struggles have to start from zero—at least materially. From nothing except revolutionary vision and optimism but based on a clear and realistic appraisal of what comes next.

Total Portuguese control of information at home and abroad prevented news of the armed revolt in Mozambique from getting to the outside world for a long time, but the word spread like wildfire inside Mozambique and, from that viewpoint, the attacks against Chai and Diaca achieved precisely what the FRELIMO leadership intended.

XII Lighting Fuses

The echoes of the shots fired at Chai and Diaca reverberated through the forests and mountains of Cabo Delgado and the neighboring northern province of Niassa, arousing hope in the minds of some and fear in others. Firing the first shot is a solemn and irrevocable step. Not one for faint hearts to take. Once firearms are used, you have to be prepared to go through to the end. The enemy's reaction is predictably swift and savage, especially in the case of a long-established colonial power trying to put down an armed revolt. Even within the leadership of national liberation movements there are always those who, fiery and militant as they may be in debate, shrink from the ultimate decision to launch armed struggle. These dive for cover, hands over their ears, when the first shots ring out. FRELIMO was no exception, as Samora Machel pointed out. There were those who wanted only political struggle, as in the former British colonies.

Opposition to armed struggle blocked the liberation process. To solve this contradiction in the interests of the masses, erroneous conceptions had to be dealt with. . . . A first group with Baltazar Chakonga and other former leaders of UNAMI and MANU withdrew from FRELIMO because they were opposed to the principle of armed struggle. Another group with Gumane and former leaders of UDENAMO and MANU underestimated the real strength of the enemy because they had not studied it. They thought that some violent and terroristic actions would be enough to push the enemy to capitulate. In reality this was also opposition to the principle of armed struggle because they wanted armed actions to be launched without any prior mobilization of the masses, without any preparation of cadres who would orient and direct the process.

The process was carried out by careful preparation of cadres and the meticulous work of those cadres in winning over the people and getting them to accept and support armed struggle. The following account from a gnarled old veteran, Mueva Macuta, from the village of Muidumbe in Mueda district, is typical of scores I heard:

One day I was contacted by a FRELIMO militant. He gave a long and detailed explanation about the aims and organization which would lead our people to freedom. A few days later I told my wife I had some "very important secret information." This was that there would be armed struggle. We decided to flee from the colonialist-controlled village. It was the most important moment in our lives. We were going to take to arms for the liberation of our people. We knew that the only way to avoid another Mueda-type massacre, in which many of our friends were murdered, was to go deep into the forest.
Then we heard about the attacks on Chai and Diaca on September 25. We felt we had to organize to help the comrades who had done this. But what could elderly people like us do? In fact everyone could do something. My weapon was a mattock to help feed the

soldiers. Of course there were difficulties. We had to cut down trees to make cabins in the forest. At first there was no water; we went for days without drinking anything. We had practically no clothes. But we had sworn that we would never return to live under colonialist domination and that we would put up with anything to bring off victory.

Mueva Macuta and his wife were thus psychologically and ideologically and even organizationally prepared for those first shots. They were ready to stay with the fight till the end. At Mataca, a hilly, forested area in the southwestern corner of Niassa province, Comandante Laitone Dias, a stocky, powerfully built cadre charged with implanting the first communal villages in the area when I met him, explained how this preparatory work was done. In 1965, at the age of twenty-six, he had been sent by FRELIMO into the Mataca area, to prepare for the extension of armed struggle into Niassa province the following year. His functions were those of a political commissar.

My task was to arouse the political consciousness of the people, to prepare them psychologically for armed struggle. It was not easy. The first difficulty was to persuade people that FRELIMO really intended to fight. Once that was accepted—and many were scared—I had to persuade those who would listen that not only would we fight, but we would win. That was still more difficult to accept. But it was normal. People could see the strength of the enemy, it was more difficult for them to see our latent strength. We never tried to create illusions. We were prepared ourselves, and we set out to prepare the people for a long, hard struggle. And mine was a long, hard task. But people started to believe in our determination; that we were not alone. The fight was going on not only in neighboring Cabo Delgado, and not only in Mozambique, but in Angola and Guiné-Bissau as well. And in Vietnam and other parts of the world. We had the support of progressive forces everywhere and the socialist world.

Gradually people came round to the idea that we would fight and win. Then came the toughest part. To persuade them to leave their villages and move deep into the forest, away from roads and built-up areas, so as to avoid reprisals once the fighting started. To do this meant real commitment. Some could not face the prospects of life in the forest. They abandoned the villages but fled over the borders into Tanzania and Malawi.

In Niassa, there was no attack on Portuguese posts, as there had been in Cabo Delgado, to initiate the armed struggle. It started in the Mataca area, when one fine morning the Portuguese found a number of villages completely deserted. Mataca is an area of seemingly endless, silvery forests of trees which grow to a remarkably uniform height, then seem to spread out at the top rather than push any higher. From the air, the forest gives the impression of a well-clipped lawn; and although it is infinitely less dense than the Vietnamese jungle, protection from aerial reconnaissance is almost as great. The armed action started when Portuguese patrols were sent to locate the vanished villagers. According to Comandante Dias:

The first phase was when they started sending columns on foot to find the new villages. We ambushed them and grabbed weapons and ammunition.

The next phase was that of sending in armored cars. We planted mines and blew them up. Each phase was separated by a long period while the Portuguese decided what to do next. This gave us time for training and consolidation and to get production going in the new villages. Also to get fresh supplies of better weapons down from the frontier areas.

The third phase was when the enemy used reconnaissance planes to locate the villages, then bombing those they managed to find. We fired at their planes and occasionally brought one down.

The fourth phase was divided into two parts. The Portuguese started using heliborne troops to encircle the villages.

At first they had a regular pattern of operations. A reconnaissance plane would come over. If it found something, it would be followed by three fighter-bombers to bomb and strafe. Then seven to eight helicopters with troops. We hit back and often managed to knock down a helicopter. Later they used a "recce" plane, four bombers, and twelve to fifteen big helicopters. By that time they had started setting up *aldeamentos* [Vietnamese-type "strategic hamlets"] in which they herded any villagers they could grab. They would just bundle anyone they could lay hands on into the copters and fly them off to the nearest *aldeamento*.

This started a tug-of-war. Our troops, supported by the people living in the area where an *aldeamento* had been set up, and by those inside, would attack to help them break out. They would go back into the forest and the Portuguese would try to round them up again. This phase lasted until the end, with the Portuguese pushing in toward our strongholds and establishing posts while we attacked their posts and cut communications. By the end of the war they had twenty military posts ranging from platoon to battalion strength, but by then we either controlled or had cut all the roads between these posts. Then we started encircling them and wiping them out one by one. Nothing of this would have been possible without the total support of the people in the new villages—which were our bases and local headquarters.

One of the rather moving aspects of the struggle in Mozambique was the illustration it afforded of solidarity of neighbor states—in this case, Tanzania and Zambia—as soon as they were in a position to help. Tanzania, for instance, only gained its independence in December, 1961, becoming a republic within the British Commonwealth a year later. Very shortly after FRELIMO was founded, it was able to open an office in Dar es Salaam. Later on, bases for military training were opened up; and once the armed struggle in Mozambique started, it was nourished with arms which had been transited through Tanzania. Thus, the first two provinces to begin armed struggle were Cabo Delgado and Niassa, which between them have over 600 kilometers of frontier with Tanzania.

Similarly, once Zambia had consolidated its independence, gained in October, 1964, and the armed struggle had developed sufficiently in Cabo Delgado and Niassa, it was possible to open up a new front in the vital Tete province, which has some 400 kilometers of frontier with Zambia. (It goes without saying that in its turn, Mozambique, within a year of winning its independence, was providing the same sort of base, training, hospital, supply, and other facilities for the Zimbabwe freedom fighters as Angola was providing Namibia); and militant black solidarity of this type was clearly a source of enormous encouragement to militants across Mozambique's southern frontier in South Africa.

The importance of this support for FRELIMO can be judged from the pattern of military developments. The first actions took place within about one hundred kilometers of the northern frontiers. Gradually the areas in which the actions took place were denied to the enemy and consolidated into bases from which the liberation forces could steadily push south. This was how it was, first with Cabo Delgado, then with Niassa. Four years after Chai and Diaca, something similar started in Tete. If the pace seemed agonizingly slow, what were a few years when the stake was ending 500 years of colonial domination? The opening of a front in

Tete province was a bitter pill for the Portuguese to swallow. Rich in minerals, including uranium, gold, copper, titanium, beryllium, bauxite, coal, iron ore, manganese, and wolfram, it is also the province of the Cabora Bassa Dam (which ties with the Grand Coulee in the U.S.A. for fourth place in the world's great hydroelectric complexes). The Portuguese believed that Cabora Bassa, and the heavy South African investment in its construction, plus the importance of Tete's largely unexploited minerals, could be a means of internationalizing the war if FRELIMO pushed things too hard. In the provincial capital—also called Tete—was the headquarters of the Zambezi Planning Council, which was controlled directly from Lisbon, bypassing the Mozambique colonial administration. Ostensibly its competencies were an ambitious development scheme for the valley of the Zambezi, which flows through Tete, virtually cutting the province in half. Ten thousand square kilometers bigger than the whole of Portugal, the population of Tete was only 600,000—about one tenth that of the colonial power. From the rugged mountains which lead up to the frontier with Malawi in the east, heavily forested hills and plains stretch almost 600 kilometers to the frontier with Rhodesia. The whole of the territory north of the Zambezi river stretching up to the Zambian border is excellent for guerilla activities as far as cover is concerned, although water is a problem in the dry season.

António Hama Thai, a big handsome man with a gleaming smile, now Governor of Tete province and the dynamic leader of FRELIMO's armed forces there during the war, explained the general strategy and tactics of the guerilla forces:

We divided the province up into four operational sectors, three north of the Zambezi and one to the south. The two northernmost sectors, leading to the frontiers with Zambia and Malawi respectively, were opened up first and then consolidated for the transiting of supplies and as bases for advance into the other two sectors. Once the latter two were consolidated, they were to serve as base and transit areas for advances further south and east.

The enemy had relatively strong forces stationed in the provincial capital: around the Cabora Bassa Dam site, which they turned into a formidable fortress with a military headquarters at Estima; and also at Changara—a road junction ninety kilometers southwest of Tete and only fifty kilometers from the Rhodesian border on the Tete-Salisbury highway. There were regular Portuguese army, navy and air force units, commandos, special force units, PIDE, and volunteer companies formed from local Portuguese settlers.

We had to dispose our forces according to those of the enemy, although not in the same numbers. Our main activities were road-cutting operations and ambushes. Guerilla units operated under each of the four sector commands. They could operate as single units, or several together in a coordinated action.

For instance, to deal with a convoy of thirty to forty trucks escorted by twenty to thirty armored cars or other military vehicles, we would use several units amounting to between seventy-five and 150 men, disposed along the estimated length of the convoy. After a sharp coordinated attack, the units would withdraw immediately and rush to other positions along the route of the convoy. In this way we could hit the same convoy four or five times, by which time there was usually not much left of it.

Apart from the losses in men and weapons inflicted on the enemy, it slowed them up tremendously. After we got more experience, it would take the enemy up to fifteen days to cover the 147 kilometers from Tete city to Cabora Bassa. For longer hauls it would take them up to ninety days. We cut all subsidiary roads so the only ones left open were those leading from Tete to Cabora Bassa, and from Tete to the Rhodesian and Malawi frontiers respectively. This made it easier to concentrate our forays for ambushes on those roads.

After two years of consolidation in the northern sectors, we were able to cross the Zambezi and extend our operations into the southern sector. That was in 1970. Two years later, we had pushed the armed struggle into Manica and Sofala province [of which the port city of Beira is the capital]. By that time, the Portuguese only controlled Tete city, the Cabora Bassa construction site, and the three main highways along parts of which they had established *aldeamentos*, into which they herded whomever they managed to round up in their helicopter raids. All the rest was a liberated zone in which an entirely new type of life was being built up. For the first time people knew what it was to live without foreign oppressors on their backs. And if the highest level of free life until that time was in the liberated zones, the highest level of oppression was in the enemy-controlled *aldeamentos*. Our people well understood the contrast!

In the name of "fighting terrorism" colonial powers and local dictators go over to the highest stage of terrorism, one aspect of which is the concentration camp village. Another is the My Lai type of massacre. A standard type of reprisal was described by

142

N'dlovo Chaca, another of the old veterans of the struggle in Tete. He was from Furancungo, a district town less than fifty kilometers from the border with Malawi, on the Tete-Malawi highway. He had joined FRELIMO in January, 1968, as he explained: "Because I felt the urge to fight against those who rounded us up for forced labor and arrested people for no reason at all." The preparatory political work seems not to have been as successful in his town as in other places, because people stayed where they were, even after the armed struggle started.

Shortly after the first shots were fired in Furancungo we were attacked. The Portuguese invaded our settlement, burned our houses and barns, killed our goats and pigs. On June 15, 1968, two helicopters attacked us. On that day, ninety-nine people in our village were killed. After that we fled and settled in another place close to the Zambia frontier. For some years, as was the aim of the massacre, there was no more resistance from our villagers. But later, the shot came back through the breech. It had only added to people's hatred. To see their families and friends gunned down only because they wanted to help the combatants—their children—this was something they could never forget. When we got settled in the new village, people started saying: "We have to pay them back." Word was sent to a local FRELIMO headquarters to send arms and soldiers and we would help them. We even formed a women's detachment and set up a special unit to transport arms from the frontier.

The Furancungo massacre was one of many such at the start of the armed struggle in Tete. They were obviously aimed at stamping out from the beginning any sparks of struggle wherever they appeared. Terror tactics were stepped up as more and more territory eluded Portuguese control and the carefully laid fuses of revolt led to explosions farther south and toward the Indian Ocean in the east. More and more, the massacres began to express the frustrated rage of the Portuguese command rather than any hope of a deterrent effect.

This seems the only explanation for what happened at Wiriamu, a village some twenty-five kilometers southwest of Tete city, on December 16, 1972. It was just a few months after the first explosions of revolt had been detonated in Manica and Sofala province, well to the south. On December 14, a small Portuguese plane flying from Beira to Tete was hit by ground fire, which the authorities believed must have come from the general area of Wiriamu. The following day a Portuguese patrol sent to investigate the incident fell into a FRELIMO ambush. Portugal's most prestigious soldier, General Kaulza Oliveira de Arriaga, in his advance headquarters at Tete, considered this too much. The war was getting too close. All that remains of Wiriamu today is a bare, elevated piece of land bordered by a few dead trees with burn marks on the lower part of their trunks, a mound of stones to mark the spot where the inhabitants were buried by neighbors from nearby villages and a small wooden chest under a shelter, which contains a few skulls and bones found after the mass burial.

One of three known survivors of Wiriamu, João Xavier, a slim young farmer who has rebuilt a cabin on the outskirts of the former village, was working in the fields on Saturday morning, December 16. This is what he told me:

Around 11 A.M., I heard the sound of planes, then I saw trucks. They came right into the village and troops started jumping down and moving into positions all around the village. I dropped to the ground and hid in some bushes. The trucks pulled back and the troops moved around to join up with others which had arrived by helicopters. The Portuguese commander was accompanied by a Mozambican called Kangolongondo whom everyone knew was a PIDE agent. He went from hamlet to hamlet, roaring out that everyone must assemble in the center of Wiriamu. Almost everyone went, from the fields as well. After they were all assembled, the commander said, through Kangolongondo: "Today you will all die because you have been the 'kitchen' of the terrorists."

By then they were surrounded by the troops, who opened fire on them. People started running in all directions. The troops stopped firing and rounded everyone up again. The villagers were then tied up, men, women and children, their arms and legs bound and carried into the huts. Incendiary grenades were thrown in and I could hear the terrible screams and see the red flames and black smoke. [While this happened planes came and shot at all the cattle.] Almost everybody was killed on the spot, but a few who managed to flee were shot down by the planes and died trying to cross the river or of wounds even if they managed to reach the forest. After the Portuguese left I found two others alive and together we headed for the liberated zone.

Those who came from neighboring villages to discover what had happened buried the remains of 328 bodies, but it is believed that the real figure of those killed is closer to 400, many bodies having been carried away in the river into which scores of the wounded, according to João Xavier's eyewitness account, collapsed.

In June, 1970, General Kaulza de Arriaga, who could roughly be compared to France's General de Lattre de Tassigny in the first Vietnamese resistance war against the French, or to General William C. Westmoreland in the second resistance war against the United States—that is, their respective countries' most prestigious military strategists—announced the launching of the "Gordian Knot" war-winning operation in Mozambique. In the same briefing room in which the great man had announced this absolutely unbeatable strategy, I asked the former schoolteacher, Alberto-Joaquim Chipande, what it was all about and why it had failed.

It was Kaulza's reaction to the impasse in which the enemy was already finding himself. Until then, one must admit, the Portuguese did not use very sophisticated weapons. But in June, 1970, more modern weapons were supplied by Portugal's NATO allies. The French provided Alouette helicopters which Kaulza used as troop carriers. The Americans supplied jet planes. Our leader, Eduardo Mondlane, had been assassinated a few months earlier. Kaulza calculated that FRELIMO would be demoralized and that one powerful offensive could finish us off.

He had succeeded in infiltrating agents into our ranks to sow confusion and sap our confidence, to create dissensions and divisions. But the enemy never learns. Massacres and the assassination of Eduardo Mondlane only stiffened our resolve.

"Gordian Knot" was a "kill all, burn all, destroy all" type of operation aimed at penetrating the liberated zones, destroying not only FRELIMO bases, our armed forces, cadres, and organizations, but at the wholesale massacre of everyone within the liberated zones and everything that had been built up there. But Kaulza was too late. If "Gordian Knot" had been launched at the beginning of our struggle it is possible we would have been crushed. It was a well-prepared operation; from a professional military viewpoint it was well executed.

But we were ideologically far stronger—a point the importance of which the enemy never could grasp. We had come through an important ideological crisis—a struggle between the revolutionary line originally launched by Eduardo Mondlane and strongly defended by Samora Machel, and the reformist line defended by Reverend Uria Simango and Lázaro Nkavandame.[1] The revolutionary line had won out. It was a question of for whom the war was all about.

We were somewhat fewer in numbers, but stronger and more united than ever. Kaulza had plenty of material—everything from planes and helicopters to bulldozers to push into our positions. But we gave them all a real hearty welcome. By the time "Gordian Knot" was launched we had accumulated six years' experience of armed struggle under the most varied and impossible conditions. We beat it back and from then on we kept advancing until the end. We carried the battle into the enemy-controlled areas. No longer was it a question of just cutting roads and ambushing convoys, but of wiping out his fortified positions and garrisons. Kaulza's offensive aimed at creating dissensions within FRELIMO had the opposite effect. We started our counteroffensive and never stopped until we had won the final victory.

XIII The Green Revolution

If peasants could be talked into abandoning their homes and hamlets and moving back into the unknown, deep into the forests, forewarned that life would be tough and dangerous, there must have been deep and compelling reasons. It was not the glib tongues of the FRELIMO cadres which made people say that the start of armed struggle was the "happiest," "most important" day of their lives.

In the past any changes in their lives proposed by the Portuguese authorities had always been for the worse. They found that even when they thought they had reached the rock bottom of hopeless misery, there was still a lower depth being prepared for them. If they could be mobilized to risk their lives in ambushing convoys hauling material to the Cabora Bassa Dam, it was because the FRELIMO cadres could explain that one of the schemes of the Zambezi Planning Council was to use the waters of the dam to irrigate the Zambezi valley, expel the Africans living there, and settle up to one million Portuguese peasants in their place.

In their blood, in their legends, and as far back as family and clan memories could reach, it had always been like that. For five centuries they had been pushed around by the white overlords, more precisely pushed off the more fertile lands, pushed off those which had access to rivers and streams into marginal lands where only a starvation existence was possible. And the reward for generations of hard work in developing the marginal lands was to have them expropriated once their productive potential had been demonstrated. It was not quotes from Marx or Mao that persuaded people to join in or support armed struggle, or abandon their traditional lands to carve out new *machambas* and build new stick-and-mud cabins in the wilderness. It was because of what their lives had been for as long as any could recall.

The Portuguese masters were content—as far as the agricultural techniques of the Mozambicans were concerned—to let things remain as they had found them when Vasco da Gama dropped anchor at Mozambique Island, from which the country takes its name, in March, 1498. A simple fact illustrates this. When a UN mission arrived in Mozambique almost 500 years later, on April 7, 1976, to assess the type and quantity of economic aid needed to compensate for the severe losses incurred by the

147

People's Republic of Mozambique in implementing UN sanctions against Rhodesia, the request, as far as aid to agricultural production was concerned, was not for tractors or modern harvesting machinery. It was for one million hoes, one hundred thousand shovels, half a million jungle knives and machetes, two hundred thousand sickles and scythes, and fifty thousand axes! In traveling several thousands of kilometers through the country I saw only two plows, one drawn by a horse, the other by oxen. My interpreter was so excited in seeing the first of these that he asked the driver to stop so that we could take a picture. To illustrate progress!

Cultivation in the *machambas* was by the slash-and-burn method. Members of a clan move around in the same general area recognized by other clans as theirs, cutting down trees and burning clearings, which are cultivated in the best of cases by hoes and mattocks, but often enough by holes made in the ground with pointed sticks, into which the maize or other seeds were dropped.

The first colonists had been adventurers who grabbed as much land as they could, mobilized the Africans who lived on the lands they had seized into their private armies, and went to war against similar adventurers to decide whose domains should be the greater. These were replaced by royal charter companies somewhat similar, apparently, to the East India Company of notoriety which was the spearhead of British imperialist penetration of India. Since Portugal itself was not sufficiently developed economically to digest such huge colonies as Angola and Mozambique, the capital in the charter companies was mainly British, but also Belgian and Swiss, and of course partly Portuguese. Such companies, known as *companhia magistratura*, not only had the right to exploit the land granted to them, but the local population was considered in every respect as their "property," to be taxed, exploited as slaves, recruited into private armies—whatever the certified owners thought fit and profitable.

After the fascist regime took power in Portugal in 1926, Salazar—first as minister of finance, then prime minister—launched some new policies in an attempt to gain greater control over the colonies. He reduced the holdings of the charter companies and passed a law under which Portuguese peasants were encouraged to migrate to Mozambique, where they could have land for the asking. It was the start of real colonization, a colony of settlers who would farm the land, export some of Portugal's own problems of population pressure in the overcrowded Tras-os-Montes region in the north, and the militant unemployed laborers from the latifundia in the south. From Salazar's viewpoint, this was a means of ensuring effective Portuguese control over the colony at a time when the first stirrings of demands for independence in Africa had become discernable.

Joaquim de Carvalho, a veteran FRELIMO militant who was appointed Minister for Agriculture when the People's Republic was set up, and who had made a profound study of the country's land problems, explained the consequences of the Salazar settler policy:

When the Portuguese settlers arrived, they looked around for land that they thought suitable and simply applied to the government for ownership rights. Government approval was virtually automatic and the settlers then had the right to governmental help to expel the "natives" in case they refused to leave voluntarily. That was the sort of situation with which FRELIMO was confronted when we started to launch our national liberation struggle. An exact statistical analysis showed that 0.2 per cent of landowners, virtually all Portuguese, owned 49.9 per cent of the cultivated land in holdings of over twenty hectares; another 23.6 per cent, mainly Portuguese, owned 26.4 percent of the rest in holdings of from two to twenty hectares. The remaining 76.2 per cent of cultivators, working fields of well under two hectares, accounted for 23.7 per cent of the cultivated land. The actual figure was 1,258,000 familes holding 1,184,000 hectares. The statistics by no means reveal the true situation, because the land held by the African cultivators was in the poor, infertile regions to which they had been expelled by the Portuguese settlers.

Of course we did not have these statistics at our disposal when we launched our struggle. But we had the picture of the acute misery, the conditions of almost permanent famine, the weight of the oppression if they raised their voices, in which the rural population lived. They were our natural allies once they grasped the fact that we were going to fight to change all that.

After Salazar came Caetano in 1968, but by then the armed struggle was launched and was sufficiently vigorous for Caetano to modify the land policy. His idea was to create a rural bourgeoisie—Portuguese mixed up with Africans—in farms of a hundred up to one thousand hectares, the proprietors of which would have a vested interest in defending their properties against our armed struggle.

Fortunately for us, they started too late. The Portuguese immigrants were poor people. They had neither machines, capital, nor farming know-how to work big holdings. Because of us, they could no longer use the old slave labor methods. Any attempt at forced recruitment of labor ended up in swelling the ranks of enthusiastic volunteers for our armed forces. The writing was all too clearly on the wall for Africans to want to become part of an African-Portuguese barrier against national liberation.

Tens of thousands of Portuguese *colon* families were, however, settled in the valley of the Limpopo river, which runs roughly parallel to the South African border in Mozambique's southern province of Gaza. African farmers were simply expelled from their lands. And over half a million Mozambique African farmer families were forced to abandon subsistence farming for their own consumption to grow cotton for the big, multinational companies which had acquired huge cotton-growing concessions. Dealing with the situation in agriculture at the time FRELIMO started armed struggle, Samora Machel made the following comment in the booklet referred to earlier:[1]

It is certain that the unleashing of the armed struggle forced the colonial government to . . . step by step abolish forced agriculture in an attempt to win over the peasant masses and persuade them to abandon their demands. But the needs of the concession companies, which in the final analysis controlled the government, rapidly reasserted themselves and again started the system of compulsory crops within the framework of the *aldeamento* concentration camps, set up to isolate the population from FRELIMO. As a result more than a million and a half Mozambicans, about one sixth of the population—according to government statements—were interned in such camps where, under the threat of colonialist arms, they were forced to produce these products [essentially cotton, sugar, and sisal] later acquired at low prices by the companies which enjoy a purchasing monopoly.

Samora Machel pointed out that in 1961, producers in Israel received the equivalent of 12 *escudos* per kilogram of first-quality cotton, those in neighboring Rhodesia 6.97 *escudos*. Producers in Mozambique were at the bottom of the list with only 3.70 *escudos* for cotton of the same high quality. It was this that enabled the hopelessly antiquated Portuguese textile industry—with fifteen per cent of the spindles over fifty years of age and the average well over twenty years—to compete on the home and international markets. He continued:

> The implantation of European communities on lands expropriated from the African population is one of the constants of Portuguese colonial policy. There is a double objective: to absorb the unemployed rural manpower in Portugal; and to transform the European farmers into defense bastions of the colonial order. Various regions of our country have been the object of this practice—the Limpopo valley, Montepuez [Cabo Delgado], Marrupa and Gurué [Niassa], Vila Manica, and others. But because of its proportions, the plan to install over a million Europeans in the Zambezi valley acquires a special significance because this is a matter of modifying the ethnic composition of our country and of erecting a human barrier to the development of the liberation struggle. In this way conditions are prepared to distort the real content of our struggle, transforming it into a racial confrontation.
>
> The creation of such settlements is radically opposed to the interests of the African rural communities. Plunder of the land and the transfer of the rural population to new zones systematically reduces them to misery and augments the supply of cheap labor for the companies and *colons*. A typical example was the creation of the Limpopo settlement in the second half of the 1950s, which blocked and destroyed the development of a prosperous African rural community, which was already integrated into the market economy, and which had laid the basis for mechanized agriculture.
>
> Forced labor on company plantations, which is the basis for the fabulous profits of companies monopolizing sugar and sisal production, for instance, constitutes a particularly brutal form of exploitation of the rural workers. They are forced to abandon all their agricultural and handicrafts activities for a wage of less than five *escudos* for a working day of twelve to fifteen hours. More than a hundred thousand workers are subjected to such conditions every year.

Despite the expropriation of their lands and forced labor at token payments, a direct head tax of about twenty-five per cent of their annual revenue was imposed on the rural population and, together with indirect purchase and excise taxes on everything they purchased, it was this most impoverished section of the pouplation, according to Samora Machel's survey, which contributed 29.8 per cent of revenue to the Mozambique colonial administration. They were financing their own repression. The FRELIMO president was basing his figures on the situation in 1970, when Kaulza Oliveira de Arriaga took over as Portugal's proconsul in Mozambique. In that year 45 per cent of government expenditure went for the war, 3 per cent for education and 2.6 per cent for public health. Obviously this meant education and public health mainly for the urban centers, which meant essentially for the white population. The magnificent sum of 1.5 per cent was allotted for "rural development." In the harsh light of such realities, Samora Machel explains that:

> National liberation for the broad masses of the peasantry means a radical change in the situation of the peasantry; the abolition of forced labor; an end to the plunder of the land and its exploitation by company concessions; an end to the big plantations; liquidation of the practice of selling workers abroad; restructuring the tax system in favor of the workers. These demands amount to the dissolution of the colonial state; the state of compulsory crops and plantations; the state of dependency on imperialism as represented by the multinationals and of subservience to the South African mining interests and Rhodesian plantation agriculture.

Obviously it was easy for FRELIMO, or any other organization, to offer a more attractive alternative. It is equally obvious—as shown by the outcome of the struggle—that FRELIMO was able to convince the rural masses that they would abide by their pledges to transfer real power in the countryside to them. They did this in the liberated zones because it was the only way the FRELIMO armed forces—and the peasant producers who went deep into the forests with them—could survive. But history is rich in examples of the peasantry being used to win someone else's battles—notably those of the bourgeoisie in Europe against the feudal lords, or those of the feudal lords against absolute monarchs—and then being crushed in turn. An outsider with access to the history books can be excused a certain skepticism as to the rewards of peasant loyalty to a revolutionary cause. How is it working out in Mozambique? Perhaps in that first year of independence it was too early to say.

In any case the creation of communal villages was FRELIMO's concept of the reward. The first definition I heard of

152

what a communal village is, was during an impromptu halt on a remote road in the central coastal province of Zambezi. A group of mainly elderly people were constructing some buildings. Some were cutting slim saplings into even lengths; others were ripping strips of bark from freshly cut branches. These would be used to lash together the pointed poles that had been stabbed into the earth to form walls; and these walls would be plastered over with the mud which was already being softened up from nearby soil. Barefoot and bare-chested, trousers in tatters, these men with wrinkled, knobby faces as if roughly hewn from coal dropped their poles and strips of bark (but not their knives, I noted) and gathered around the Land-Rover as we stepped out.

To my somewhat obvious question as to what they were doing, the reply was: "We want to construct something good for the people."

"What exactly?"

"A communal village."

"What does that mean?"

"It means a village where we will live together and have our own hospital, a school, bathhouse, maternity clinic, a small orphanage for those who lost their parents in the war, a people's shop, a water tower, and a big hall for public meetings."

A wizened old man whose ribs could easily be counted, ticked off the various projects on his fingers as he replied. There was a mirthless sort of laugh when I asked if they did not have such elementary facilities before.

"For any of these we had to walk fifteen kilometers to Namacurra—the nearest district center—and if we carried someone who was seriously ill, we had to wait for hours at the hospital until the last white had been treated, even if he only had a sore finger or headache."

The group of fifty represented the "construction brigade" for that particular week of a scattered collection of peasants in the area who would soon move into the new communal village of Mutanse. Other brigades were out harvesting rice. For that season they still had individual *machambas* but they had been cultivated and were now being harvested collectively. Next season there would only be big cooperative fields. About 600 people would comprise the new village. Symbolic of a new outlook was the fact that the first building completed was the big meeting hall, capable at that time of standing several hundred people. It was simply a big, thatched, sharply sloping roof, propped up by poles.

I saw similar scenes of building activity in my travels all over the country. In February, 1976, FRELIMO's Central Committee had approved a decree on establishing communal villages, the most audacious decision since that of launching armed struggle. It entails the complete restructuring of the countryside, a total break with old life styles and production methods. But like every other such measure it is not new for that part of the population which lived in the liberated zones where conditions of survival imposed such a collective style of life and work. Compared with the work of persuading peasants to abandon their homes and hamlets to start a new wartime life in the forest, the work of persuading them to abandon old individual habits for the promised land and benefits of collective life was clearly much easier. As part of the motivation for this revolutionary decision, an introductory part of the decree states:

> The great mass of the Mozambique peasantry are dispersed all over the country, practicing subsistence farming. In agriculture the peasant family generally carries out its activity with poor-quality soil, practicing the hacking down of trees and undergrowth on small *machambas*, burning them down so as to proceed to sowing. The soil is not properly worked, the seed is not selected. Because no technical or financial assistance whatsoever is available, it is impossible to wage an effective struggle against various scourges such as rats and insects, or natural calamities such as flooded fields from torrential rains, which are far beyond their power to handle.
>
> All this leads to an extremely low productivity of labor; to very small harvests providing only subsistence for the family and, in some cases, a small surplus. The latter is in general sold in its entirety to the *cantineiros* [literally, "innkeepers," almost exclusively Portuguese who held a monopoly on rural trading] who, representing the only commercial organization to which the peasants had access, imposed their well-known methods of exploitation. The *cantineiro* was the center of all commercial life in the countryside, buying at the lowest prices the surplus products of the peasant masses and selling at the highest possible prices essential products such as salt, pepper, textiles, etc.
>
> This situation was aggravated by the isolation of the peasants in relation to each other, preventing them from organizing and combining their forces in the sense of controlling nature on the one hand,

and, on the other, constituting a force capable of resisting capitalist exploitation.

Another result of this dispersal is the difficulty of developing and diffusing political, technical, and scientific knowledge to permit an organized struggle against superstition and reactionary traditions. It is for all this that the peasant, feeling himself crushed and incapable of changing his status, tried to flee from this vicious circle of misery and stagnation by emigrating to the cities or across the frontier to try to improve his way of life.

It was to change all this that the nationwide drive was launched to create the *aldeais communais*, or communal villages. Eleven criteria were laid down as the minimum requirements for a communal village. They could be summarized as providing for decent housing which would "guarantee protection against the sun, rain, heat, wind, or cold, which means that each family should build a house with hygienic conditions and security." Facilities for the storage and marketing of produce, and for the manufacture and repair of farm tools. A school and clinic in every village with emphasis on prevention of disease as far as public health is concerned. Crèches and nurseries to free parents for production. Decent streets within a village and roads to link them with neighboring villages, and "to facilitate easy circulation and the disposing of produce." Cultural and sporting activities, "with the affirmation and development of Mozambique culture and personality," provision for public meetings, discussion and recreation for all sectors of the population, and finally and most importantly: "Carrying out administrative tasks related to different aspects of life in the village, in coordination with different government branches."

Nothing very dramatic in Western terms, but an enormous leap into the future for a Mozambican semi-nomad peasant. Such units could be established either "on the basis of existing villages which can be adapted providing the locality has good conditions for productive activity," or "on the basis of a completely new locality, in which is selected a place most suitable for housing, production, and the rest of the planned activities." It was considered advisable, the decree stated, that a communal village should have a minimum of fifty families, "a figure which can be increased according to conditions in different regions and the development of the village itself."

To give the scheme a good start, the Ministry of Agriculture sent teams to help lay out three pilot villages which would establish guidelines for the others. One of these was at Mataca, in Niassa province, mentioned earlier as the locality where Comandante Laitone Dias had persuaded the peasants to follow the resistance into the forest. I had arrived at Mataca late at night after a seven- or eight-hour drive in a Land-Rover from the provincial capital of Lichanga. Early next morning, people were coming out of their huts, rubbing their limbs in front of small fires in front of each house. Women lowered shoulder shawls to feed their babies, others fanned fires to heat water. Mataca is in the highlands; the air was chilly but the sky clear and blue. Young women were warming themselves up by pounding at cassava in wooden tubs hollowed out of bits of tree trunks, with six-foot-long poles. A dozen or so cabins bordered a large clearing which had been the site of the first village abandoned and which, Comandante Dias explained, would be the new administrative center. Alongside his own neat, mud-plastered house were drum-shaped pigeon coops on top of sawed-off tree trunks, and behind them were rabbit hutches—an example to others that each family should raise some private livestock.

I asked how people were reacting to the new ideas and Comandante Dias replied:

> For those who have come back from Tanzania and Malawi, it is a new type of life. They are used to individual work. People have to be politically educated to the new ways. Such things are discussed in many meetings, people putting forth their ideas, asking questions, until we get answers that everyone agrees to. Many of the older people point out that what we are doing is a continuation of what we did in the liberated zones during the war. In the old days some groups went to the Rovuma [the river which forms the northern frontier with Tanzania—] for arms. Now a group of over three hundred has left to get building materials. Others have chosen the place for the housing settlement and started building, while still others are doing the farm work.

When I asked whether they were producing for their own food needs or for a marketable surplus, Inacio Muava, a short, stocky man in charge of overall production, replied: "Because much of the labor power is diverted into building work, we don't have conditions for producing surpluses. The main aim is to make the center self-sufficient, then produce surpluses for exchange with other centers. We have a large proportion of refugees—mainly from Tanzania—who came a little late for us to have good results this season." Mataca was going to be a big communal village with a population of about 3,000.

Although all the work was still being done with hoes, the fields were laid out on the basis that one day tractors would be available. One field of 250 hectares, selected for maize for the following season, was already cleaned of the stumps and roots which are a feature of the traditional *machamba*. A brick-making brigade was at work, some patting moistened earth into molds, others emptying the molds of embryo bricks to dry in the sun. At the site selected for housing, dried bricks were being built into the walls of houses such as no Mozambican peasant had ever dreamed of occupying. Each had four bedrooms and a sitting room—with chicken coops and rabbit hutches behind—and plenty of space for trees and gardens between the houses.

Provisions were made in the construction for the unbelievable day when electricity and piped water would be available. And, in accordance with the Central Committee's decree, land had been set aside for a strip that could land a light plane. (At least a helicopter pad must be provided, according to the decree.) Lines of young women—almost every one with a baby tucked into a shawl on her back—were hacking away with mattocks, singing in rhythm with their work, doubling the area of a hectare-sized vegetable plot. The older women were watering lettuce, carrots, cabbages, and beans—the first fruits of their collective work. Students from Maputo University, doing their annual monthly stint of practical work, discussed plans with Inacio Muava to dam the stream from which the women were drawing water in kerosene cans, and irrigate the vegetable plots by gravitation.

The atmosphere indicated that Mataca had got off to a good start. Formation of the communal villages has to be voluntary according to the decree, which means that the success of building them up in the old liberated zones will be a crucial factor in stimulating their formation elsewhere. Peasants all over the world are slow to change their habits. They have to be convinced by practice or example to take a new step. But once they have taken that step—provided it was a voluntary one—there is usually no retreat. The idea of moving a whole country from an archaic rotating slash-and-burn type of agriculture to one of large, stable fields, soon to be cultivated by plows, with tractors and helicopters over the horizon, represents a tremendous leap into the future. "We will start by rotating crops instead of fields," said Inacio Muava.

The idea of houses with windows, villages with running water and electricity, crèches to take the babies off the backs of their working mothers, clinics, granaries, shops—none of this figured even in the dreams of the vast majority of Mozambique's peasants, not even at the moment of independence. But all this is swiftly taking shape in a handful of pioneer villages which will doubtless become focal points for inspection delegations from all over the country as they start to function. But it needed a bold and confident leadership to project such visions and press on with their materialization.

XIV Cabora Bassa Dam

As an illustration of the Portuguese concept of using Mozambique as a gigantic servicing station for South Africa and Rhodesia, the Cabora Bassa Dam and hydroelectric complex is the most impressive. One of the world's great engineering projects, its setting is fit for a Wagnerian opera. Wild, towering mountains split into a huge rugged gorge along which the Zambezi used to flow. Their tree-covered slopes now form the banks of an enormous man-made lake of 2,700 square kilometers—270 kilometers long. The calm lake waters converge on a dam higher than the Eiffel tower and, shaped like a crescent moon, curve inward to restrain the pressure of this enormous body of water. At the time of my visit at the end of May, 1975, the waters were just creeping up to the full mark—323.5 meters. At 325 meters they would be diverted to a spillway.

With a total capacity for 3,600,000 kilowatts, Cabora Bassa is by far the biggest such complex in Africa and is exceeded by only three others in the world, two of them in the Soviet Union, at Krasnoyarsk with 5,000,000 kilowatts and Bratsk with 4,500,000, the other in Canada at Churchill Falls, also with 4,500,000 kilowatts. One might well ask what need has Mozambique, with a population of a little over 9,000,000 and virtually no industry, of such a gigantic power-producer. The answer is that she has no such need. Present power consumption of Mozambique and her two neighbors, Zambia and Tanzania, could absorb only about fifteen percent of the Cabora Bassa output.

In a vast underground hall, carved out of the bowels of a mountain on the southern bank, were five turbines in various states of installation. Number 1 was already whirring and purring away, its performance being studied by a group of Portuguese and Angolan technicians through red and green lights on a control panel. Number 2 was also in place awaiting its turn for the test run. Number 3 was awaiting a giant rotor to be lowered into position— it had been held up because there had been a rockfall in the transport gallery which killed six Africans, bringing the new total to sixty dead. The gleaming overhead transmission lines disappeared into purple mist and swirling clouds on their way eventually to deliver their charge to distant South Africa.

The transformer station converts Alternate Current into Direct Current; the mono-polar high-tension lines stretched some 1,400 kilometers across Mozambique to bring Cabora Bassa power to South Africa. The transformation and transmission systems are so designed that Mozambique can not tap a single kilowatt hour of energy for itself. It was South Africa that put up the money and Portugal pledged repayments in electric energy over fifteen to twenty years. But the original estimate of costs had been far exceeded and the period of repayments which Mozambique had inherited could well run into thirty years.

As things stand Cabora Bassa represents a whole herd of white elephants which Mozambique will be obliged to feed at great expense for decades. The only immediate benefit was that the station could serve as a higher institute of training for a large number of Mozambican electrical engineers!

With considerable investment, the lake could be tapped for irrigating the lower reaches of the Zambezi valley as the Portuguese had intended, to further their plan of implanting one million Portuguese settlers. One might well ask what the Portuguese government hoped to gain from such a grandiose scheme that promised no financial benefits for decades. The plan to replace African farmers by Portuguese settlers in the Zambezi valley was only a by-product of the main scheme. Portuguese engineers at Cabora Bassa assured me there had not even been preliminary studies for irrigation and possible navigation prospects. The main Portuguese by-product was the use of Cabora Bassa Dam as bait to get South Africa heavily involved so that the guerilla war could be internationalized and South Africa would acquire a powerful vested interest in the extermination of the national liberation forces.

The South African leadership was in a very swaggering mood in those days; its armed forces were reputed to be by far the strongest in the whole of southern Africa. Even though by 1975, Prime Minister Johannes Vorster was talking about *détente,* the real, unchanged attitude came out on Jaunary 2, 1976, when Defense Minister Pieter W. Botha presented a "Defense Amendment Bill" to the House of Assembly proposing that South African troops could be conscripted for service in Africa "anywhere south of the equator," wherever South African interests were threatened! The bill as finally adopted on January 28 provided for compulsory service for South African troops, "anywhere outside

160

South Africa." Things looked great at the time Botha introduced his bill. South African troops were some 1,200 kilometers inside Angola as the result of a month-long *blitzkrieg* drive from the Namibia-Angolan border starting October 23, 1975. By the time the bill was passed, the South African column of about 5,000 men, supported by two hundred armored cars and heavy artillery, was in full flight, the myth of South African military invincibility having been destroyed. The fascist regime in Lisbon obviously could never have contemplated such a disaster in the days when the Lisbon fascists and the Pretoria racists affixed their signatures to the agreement to build Cabora Bassa!

How right the FRELIMO guerillas had been to concentrate harassment attacks on the work site and to ambush the convoys hauling material and equipment! There was not a single advantage for the Mozambique people in the construction of such a monster. According to plans published in the early stages, which made it appear that "development" of the Zambezi valley was the main aim, the project would force hundreds of thousands of Mozambican families to leave their fertile farms to be replaced by a million Portuguese. As news of the enormous quantities of power to be generated leaked out—along with the fact that it was all to be exported to the South African capitalists, and secondly only to the Portuguese to further their exploitation of Mozambique workers—Cabora Bassa became the symbol of everything that the detested Portuguese colonialists represented. This hatred was transformed into military action. The Portuguese were forced to transform the dam site into a fortress, and line the approaches with pillboxes and control points. The tug-of-war battles around the area continued until the armed struggle ended in a FRELIMO victory and the Portuguese pulled out—South Africa not having come to the rescue.

But now that Mozambique was an independent and sovereign state—what to do with such a gargantuan and freakish prize of war? Cut the losses and close it down? Exploit the fish in the lake and later on the waters for irrigation? To close it down would have caused a major crisis with Portugal because of the latter's financial obligations toward South Africa—and newly independent Mozambique was not seeking a crisis with Portugal. But there was still another reason why not only the hydroelectric station should not be closed down but why power should even be kept flowing toward South Africa. A young Angolan engineer at the transformer station expressed himself as follows:

> We have to consider that this is a very precious source of cheap electric power. We are for technical progress and this represents very advanced technology. We have to consider that it belongs to the peoples of Africa. A few years ago it seemed impossible to many of us that we would live to see the day when we would be free; when our brothers in Guiné-Bissau would be free; our brothers in Angola would be free. But it has all come about. Now we must look forward to the day when our brothers in Zimbabwe, in Namibia, and in South Africa itself, will also be free. Cheap electric power will be terribly valuable in building up all our countries. When we look back at yesterday we should be all the more confident about tomorrow.

So the work continues at Cabora Bassa and as the turbines start to turn, one after another, the power pulses down those 1,400-kilometer-long transmission lines to South Africa, the only possible client for the quantity produced. When the southern substation is completed by January, 1979, a second four-turbine substation will be built on the northern bank and then the giant complex will be considered complete. Driving up over a mountain pass, glimpses of the great gleaming stretch of water backed up behind what looked like some grotesque temple, it was impossible not to be impressed by the grandiose scale on which it had been conceived—coupled with the hope that the peoples of South Africa would also soon be free and the energy generated would be at the disposal of all the peoples of southern Africa.

It would be difficult to imagine a greater contrast than to visit in one day—both in the province of Tete—the culminating triumph of all that the old system had built in Mozambique and the modest start in forming the New Man for the New Society!

Leaving the asphalt highway which spans the 150 kilometers from Cabora Bassa to Tete, the provincial capital, we turned off into a dirt road of deep ruts and quagmires, eroded and criss-crossed by streams, with logs and branches thrown into the mud to prevent even a sturdy Land-Rover from sinking into it over its running boards. After a three-hours' hair-raising and bone-shaking drive we came to a modest collection of thatch-roofed and mud-covered frame huts which constituted the pilot school of Jecque. The low scrubby country and high tufty grasses for scores of kilometers on end had obviously been ideal for guerilla warfare, which had been waged very diligently in that region. The state of the track made it clear that it had been denied for years to the Portuguese, even though the village of Jecque was only sixty kilometers from the Rhodesian frontier.

It was around sunset on a Saturday evening when we arrived. The well-spaced school buildings were set out under tall trees, classrooms grouped toward the center, living quarters dispersed around the perimeter. Everything was well-swept, spick-and-span. The children were playing with balls made of bundles of rags. Their clothing was ragged and patched, but their faces and limbs glowed with health and cleanliness.

"What makes a pilot school different from others?" was the first question I put to Comandante Gonçalves Koliate Chahona, the school director, a tall, lean man in leopard-skin-type camouflage uniform.

Everything from building the schoolrooms and living quarters to study and work in the fields is done collectively. All problems are solved by collective discussion. If they arise among the children of a class they do their best to solve them at that level. If not among the children themselves, then between them and the teachers, and only as a last resort are the problems taken up at administration level. But at every level, it is done through discussion and so they get used, from the beginning, to running their own affairs, settling their own problems without running to the school authorities whenever a difficulty arises.

I asked what the main aim was. What type of end product did they want to turn out?

First you must understand that the school was established here in 1972. Studies and armed struggle went on simultaneously. We had to educate and struggle not only against Portuguese colonialism, but against ignorance, obscurantism, tribalism. The aim is to give the pupils not only the rudiments of general education but to inculcate in them that the highest aim is to use the knowledge they acquire to serve the people. They consciously study not to advance their own interests, which was the goal of anyone fortunate and privileged enough to get some education in the past, but in order to better serve the majority of the people. Life was so harsh, people were so downtrodden that such a concept was simply impossible under the colonialists. If you didn't fight for yourself and your family, you went under. The pupils here are already used to working in a collective way for the future socialist society, with high moral qualities, good educational standards. They are absolutely devoted to our country and people. The fact that the pupils come from every corner of the country, that they live, study, and work together, is a big help in getting rid of tribalist and racial ideas.

There were 390 pupils and twelve teachers. Subjects taught included the Portuguese language—the single national language in Angola and Mozambique—mathematics, history, geography, politics, drawing, and physical culture. There were still no textbooks—the People's Republic was not yet one year old—but teaching followed the national program approved by the Ministry of Education.

What was most impressive was that pupils with only two or three years of education—the school only taught up to the third grade—were completely at ease and self-possessed, expressing themselves without any prodding from either teachers or the director. If one judged things by the rather primitive cabins, the much-patched clothes and half-educated teachers, some visitors might laugh at the idea that this could possibly represent the future of the country. But such schools—I visited others deep in the forests of Niassa province later—are the real crucibles for forming the cadres of the new society. From here the graduates go on to special FRELIMO secondary schools from which they will emerge as highly motivated cadres for all levels of the administration.

If it was difficult to imagine anything more remote from the people than the Cabora Bassa monster, it was harder still to imagine anything closer to their daily life and needs than the Jecque-type pilot schools. If there were only a few of these in comparison to other schools, this is because there were too few cadres of the quality of Comandante Chahona to be spared. The children were somewhat special, too, all having taken part in some way in the armed struggle as combatants, transport workers, or scouts, or in some other activities suitable to their age. They had grown up in the spartan life of the forest away from oppression but also from the corruption of the Portuguese-controlled areas.

When FRELIMO was formed in 1962, there were less than 5,000 black and mestizo pupils attending primary schools in Mozambique. By the early 1970s, there were over 200,000 at school in the liberated zones. (The first pilot schools were started later.) In 1962 there were less than ten Mozambican students in Portuguese universities. Less than ten Mozambican blacks held degrees as professors of higher education during the whole period of Portuguese colonialism. To attain such status students were forced at a much earlier stage to sign away their Africanism and become *assimilados* pledged to serve Portuguese colonialism. As in Angola, only when they had renounced their Africanism could they be considered "civilized."

Within a few years hundreds and then thousands of young cadres, "immunized," as President Samora Machel expressed it, against the values and ideas of the old society, against Portuguese colonialist, tribal, and feudal concepts, will be available as the motors of the new society, conditioned to the idea of service to the people as the highest motive in life. Pupils in the pilot schools are called *continuadores*, the continuators of the revolution which their fathers and elder brothers launched. It is a name and a role that the youngsters seem happy to accept.

An element not present at the Jecque pilot school, but which I found at others, was the presence for short periods of groups of young university students doing their month's practical work, or part of it, at a pilot school, bringing with them the latest techniques in seed selection, compost fertilizers, soil testing and other knowledge which they impart to the primary school farmers. At the Eduardo Mondlane Pilot School near Mataca—(the communal village of which is described in the previous chapter)—there were nine university students from Maputo doing a month's practical work together with the pupils. Three others who were doing some historical research on the liberation struggle had come with the same group but had moved on to other areas. The group was divided into two teams, one for agriculture, one for building. "Even rabbit hutches and pigeon coops are receiving the attention of architects," said the school director, Foesa Liututu, with a smile.

These students were almost all white, because they were the only ones to have had access to pre-university education, but they seemed to have integrated with the pupils very well and, as Foesa

Liututu remarked, it was very useful in breaking down racial prejudices. For the pupils such contacts were exciting because they had their first introduction to the application of science to agriculture, and since the students brought modern musical instruments with them—guitars, flutes, mandolins—the pupils were able to get a whiff of the unpolluted aspects of urban life.

Almost all the primary-school graduates would go on to specialized FRELIMO secondary schools. From there most would be allotted by the local representative of the Ministry of Education to wherever their services were needed in Niassa province. Some would go on to higher education, but the need for cadres of their quality was so great that immobilizing too many in the universities was a luxury that could not yet be afforded.

XV Samora Machel

A short, lively man with twinkling eyes and a jaunty beard which he seems to use as a pointer, his head constantly in action when he talks. A man who smiles and laughs so abundantly, one feels that as a male nurse he must have been a good morale-booster. A man with a razor-sharp intellect and analytical mind. These were some of my first impressions of Samora Machel. The Catholic Church lost a popular priest when young Machel, after six years in a Catholic primary school, refused to go on to a seminary. By dint of his *assimilado* status and hard work, he managed to graduate from secondary school and obtain the relatively privileged status of a male nurse. This enabled him to see more of the country than his compatriots and everything he saw appalled and revolted him. One of the first eye-openers was that educational qualifications were irrelevant in approaching anything like equal status with the whites. Even for blacks and whites doing the same skilled or semi-skilled jobs, the salaries were several times higher for the whites. Racial discrimination at every level, in every field, economic as well as social, bit deeply into Machel's consciousness. The smile disappears from his face, even today, when he recalls the humiliation of it all. The miracle is that it did not turn him into a black racist, which would have been easily understandable.

> Gradually I saw that nothing could help but collective action. A man on his own could achieve nothing. At that stage—it was after 1956—I began to understand what the key problems were, the key economic and political problems, and just why it was that we Africans were disadvantaged. Then 1960 taught me more—the independence of the Congo and its tumults. I began to think seriously about the possibilities of Mozambique becoming independent. . . . Then it was that the consciousness of being oppressed, deprived, exploited, began to have its effect, as well as these ideas about independence.
>
> At that time, the Portuguese authorities were increasing their repression of all educated and literate Africans. That was something else that greatly increased our curiosity: to understand why they didn't want us to read newspapers, listen to foreign broadcasts. Yes, and then came 1961, in Angola. . . .[1]

With that sort of awakening it was natural for him to join FRELIMO soon after it was formed; and because he is a man impatient to put ideas into practice, it was natural also that he went to Algeria, in the same group as Alberto-Joaquim Chipande, to get some military training. Once the first blows had been struck at Chai and Diaca, Samora Machel entered the country with another 250 combatants and became commander of the first military base on Mozambique soil. Commander of the military forces then was Felipe Magaia. When he died, it was Samora Machel who was

167

appointed commander. Elected to FRELIMO's Central Committee at the second congress in 1968, he became president in 1969 after the assassination of Eduardo Mondlane. From then on, he led the armed struggle from inside the country.

My interview with Samora Machel—by then President of the People's Republic of Mozambique—took place on the lawn behind the former Portuguese governor's residence. The setting reminded me of my interviews with President Ho Chi Minh on the lawn behind the former French governor-general's residence in Hanoi! There was also the same informality. Shirtsleeves and no questions barred. Three chairs around a table under a sunshade which was moved as the sun rose higher in the sky. The third chair was for Jose Oscar Monteiro, Minister of State to the Presidency. Fluent in both English and French, he acted as interpreter when the President was occasionally stuck for a word in his own fluent French. It was Sunday, and in the background Samora Machel's wife, Graça Simbine, Minister of Education and Culture, was splashing about in the swimming pool with the Machel children and their friends.

My first question was based on having studied some of the President's speeches and writings—and traveling for some five weeks in the interior, especially in the old resistance bases: "The question of 'why and for whom' was posed from the beginning of your national liberation struggle. Class struggle and national struggle went on side by side. Was this due to some special conditions in Mozambique? Or could it be a model for other national liberation struggles?"

> This question opens up a whole series of questions, touching the fundamental nature of our struggle. If we speak of armed struggle— what is armed struggle? Also you have raised the question of the transformation of society; of transforming the mentality of those taking part. The aim of armed struggle is obviously to destroy the enemy. In the process we discovered the real context and definition of the enemy. The armed struggle is only one aspect of overall struggle which gives us the definition of who is the worst enemy.
>
> Was this clear from the start? It was not. At a first glance it might seem clear. Portuguese colonialism. But one had to go deeper. That the enemy was the exploiting class became clear during the overall struggle.

Suppose we had defined the enemy in a simple, restricted way—Portuguese colonialism. The Portuguese colonialists have now been defeated. But why do we have as a national slogan "*A Luta Continua*" (The Struggle Continues)? Or we could have said the enemy are the whites. The Portuguese colonialists are whites after all! But if we had accepted that—where would we be today? Against whom would we be continuing the struggle?

We unhesitatingly stated from the beginning that such definitions would be too facile—that is, to say the whites are our enemies because the colonialists are white. This would imply rejection of a deeper analysis as to who is the enemy. It would be opportunistic not to correctly define the enemy. If we define the enemy as the exploiting class it becomes clear that it is not a question of the color of the skin. There can be Portuguese exploiters and Mozambican exploiters.

We struggle for the emancipation of the workers. Is that just part of a program, or a fundamental part of the whole national liberation struggle? The war being waged was People's War. When we say People's War, we don't only mean a war waged with the participation of the people, but that the aim is for the people to have real power in their hands. This can only be done by the elimination of the exploiting class, whatever its color. That is why a correct definition of the enemy is of crucial importance.

We speak of "armed struggle serving the revolution." Why do we make a difference between armed struggle and revolution? Because we must clearly define what is armed struggle and what is revolution and put an end to the use of the word "revolution" to describe a *coup d'état* for instance. Is revolution a spontaneous uprising? No, it is part of a long process of which armed struggle is a part; it is not an automatic process. In our case it was a clear and continuing process, an ideological process.

Armed struggle becomes the highest point of political consciousness which enables us to support all sacrifices. The problem is to transform consciousness into physical action. That is when demands are made on ideology. It is at this moment in the whole process that through the intervention of ideology and political consciousness, the struggle becomes a class struggle. That is why armed struggle can create the New Man—an essential step to prepare the class origin of the new regime.

This is why we can say that the whole process started with armed struggle which transformed itself into People's War. Later when the consequences of the ideological content of People's War became clear and were accepted, it became a revolutionary People's War. It became a revolution. Why and for whom? The people!

"In your writings you have spoken of the differences between a bourgeois democratic regime such as exists in England and the fascist regime in Portugal and the effects this had on the type of independence struggles that could be waged in the British colonies and that which had to be waged in the Portuguese colonies—especially in Mozambique. Was this difference to your advantage or disadvantage?"

Because of the concrete conditions of Portuguese colonialism it was not possible to wage legal struggle. Objectively this was an advantage because legal, political struggle is a great occasion for the emergence of elitism; the formation of a "political elite," who take over as representatives of the local bourgeoisie when the colonialist bourgeoisie leave. Now we can see why the armed struggle was a highly political act. *Par excellence!*

It was also an ideological struggle. All aspects were included in that struggle, including a cultural revolution, a revolution in human relations, a revolution in our relations with other peoples. Every activity had its specific political content—just the sort of thing the bourgeoisie try to avoid. Thus we can say that the impossibility of waging legal struggle was a great contribution by the Portuguese colonialists to our struggle. It forced our political struggle to be armed struggle. This is as opposed to the concept that "politics" is the exclusive fief of a privileged ruling class in the urban centers. But to say that armed struggle is essential under such conditions is not enough. A small minority can also come to power by waging armed struggle—but with the aim of only satisfying their own class interests. It is not automatic that armed struggle always implies the participation of the people, or that even when it does, that the people really come out on top. Because of the nature of the Portuguese colonial regime we were faced with the question of whether to wage armed struggle. There could be only one answer—yes! Then—armed struggle *plus* a bourgeois revolution? There were some who also said—yes. We had to decide on armed struggle plus a people's revolution.

"To what extent are the experiences of living, fighting, and surviving in the liberated zones valid for the construction of a new society after the victory? Why, now that the whole country is liberated, do you still refer to the 'liberated zones' in the present tense?"

We had to give a concrete content to our armed struggle by the nature of our liberated zones. For us a liberated zone was not merely the physical liberation of territory, but the liberation of ways of thought; liberation from a system. At first we called them "guerilla zones." Only later did we call them liberated zones—because we became mentally liberated. Although our habits, life styles, and customs were still of the old type—we still had not formed a new consciousness to replace the old habits—we had arrived at the conclusion that the liberated zone constituted the highest point of contradictions with the old habits of the enemy, leading to the point of rupture. It was a violent rupture. In the liberated zones, because the enemy could not penetrate physically, we were waterproofed against his ideas and habits. That is why we still call provinces like Cabo Delgado, Niassa, and Tete "liberated zones." We do not say the same about Maputo, although territorially speaking, power is in our hands over the entire country. That is why we still say the liberated zones "must invade the cities."

In the liberated zones there was the concrete process of ending the exploitation of man by man. That is why, at the beginning of our talk, I said we had developed the capacity of correctly defining the enemy. It is in this that you will find the explanation for the fact that the very first measures we took after independence were to nationalize education, public health, justice, property—to a certain extent—and even funeral parlors. Because this corresponded to the struggle we waged in the liberated zones against exploitation in these fields.

We had to take a clear position on these questions. We had to have people's public health, people's education. . . . Even in the liberated zones this was not accomplished without struggle. There were those who tried to defend their privileges in these fields. It was a logical consequence of the society in which they were reared. It was also why we decided that criminality was a social, not a legal problem. That is why we associated the people with the investigation, judgment and punishment of wrongdoers, not leaving such matters in the hands of some isolated, specialized group. There were those in our ranks who asked, why be in such a hurry to nationalize these fields immediately after independence? But we had tried this out as part of our whole process in the liberated zones—and it worked. This is what we mean when we speak of the countryside "invading the cities." If we abolished prostitution and closed down the night haunts, this was because we had already done this in the liberated zones. If we gave priority to improving people's livelihoods, this was not based on an abstract notion of organization, but on very practical forms that worked in the liberated zones. There was nothing hit-or-miss about this.

The experiences of the liberated zones constitute a precious patrimony for us. Something which we have to defend and use to make a rupture, at the national level, with the old myths, values, and habits, with the structures of social life, organization, and production inherited from the colonialist society, and which still exist in our midst. Practice showed that we could solve production and other problems without huge resources or ultra-modern techniques, but merely by relying on our own strength and organization. The liberated zones were a political laboratory, a scientific laboratory, a laboratory of ideas. There we could try out what had to be done later.

"Was the timing of the nationalizations—just one month after independence—not due to the massive departure of the Portuguese and their abandonment of business enterprises and plantations?"

This had nothing to do with it. It was a question of the extension of FRELIMO power and organization to the whole country. The nationalization decrees were the means of establishing people's power and consolidating the gains of the revolution. It was an integral part of our overall program. We cannot build a new society on the structures of the old where there was exploitation and discrimination at every level.

Education, public health, property—these were key instruments of the bourgeoisie which had to be taken away from them. They were the instruments by which they hoped to retain power; to organize and consolidate their position and move into areas abandoned by the Portuguese. We had to nip such efforts in the bud. An alligator is very dangerous when he is grown up and in his own element in the middle of the river where he is stronger than us. Better to kill him on the bank when he's still young and in a place where we are stronger.

People still had in their minds the image of colonialism as the main enemy. So it was necessary to act quickly. People are still living in revolution. They feel the need to transform society. Another fundamental problem is that we are incapable of being managers of capitalism. Even if we tried we would fail.

At this he laughed heartily as if to emphasize the point that the FRELIMO leadership had no intention of trying to learn to become good managers of capitalism.

"There is a good deal of talk about the 'New Man' in the new society that is to be created. How does one define this 'New Man?'"

172

We believe that the struggle for the transformation of society must go hand in hand with the struggle for the transformation of man himself. But this is not an automatic process. It is not enough to be born into a certain type of society—to be born in the liberated zones, for instance. Some people thought the New Man would automatically emerge from the liberated zones and appear in the cities. But we explained to our students there: "The fact that you have been brought up in the liberated zone—that you have never seen a colonialist—doesn't make you a New Man. Perhaps the contrary, because you have not gone through the process of rejection. You have not been immunized against the old society."

The New Man is essentially only formed by remaining committed to struggle which is why in our schools in the liberated zones, education is linked to manual labor, and stress is placed on serving the people in a disinterested way. When someone studies, it is an effort to master knowledge in order to better serve the ordinary people. Not in order to pin a diploma on the chest and say: "I'm worth so much." Those who study should be like matches to light fires which the people can share. Study should not be used as something to divorce students from their class origins.

The New Man is born in struggle at all stages; he is dynamic, creative, capable of analysis and self-criticism, original, audacious. With a new mentality, acquired through struggle, the New Man becomes an agent of transformation and activization for social relations of a new type which will characterize the new society in all fields—production, education, culture, leadership structures, and relations with the grass roots in every field. The structures of socialism. To create such an outlook requires internal struggle which has to be systematic and organized. Not sporadic, spontaneous, emotional, but consciously planned, scientific, and systematic. But this can no longer be an individual struggle. There is no such thing as individual victory—only collective victory.

When we speak of internal struggle, this means rejecting the old values which everyone had absorbed to a greater or lesser extent—rejecting racism, tribalism, regionalism, egoism, elitism, all the various forms of subjectivism. In general we see this as a collective struggle that has to take place at the level of society and nature, as well as the individual level. It is not enough to change one aspect of society unless we change the outlook of the whole people.

We have to shape the superstructure, which is what we are doing now. This means creating a new system at the level of the superstructure. This has to be staffed by New Men with new, socialist outlooks.

As to whether the Mozambique national liberation struggle, and the first steps in building a new society, could be a model for others, Samora Machel replied briefly: "We can be a source of inspiration for other revolutions just as we drew inspiration, and continue to do so, from the struggle of other peoples. But there is no single model for other peoples. We are all models for all."

The background to the next question needs some explanation. South Africa produces about seventy per cent of the gold mined in the Western world. Not that this reflects the proportion of known gold deposits, but the fact that cheap labor in South Africa makes gold mining possible and profitable under wage and labor safety conditions unacceptable in former gold-producing countries such as the United States, Canada, and Australia. A large proportion of South Africa's gold-miners come from Mozambique. In the "bad old days" which persisted until the People's Republic was founded on June 25, 1975, the Portuguese literally sold up to 100,000 Mozambique laborers a year to the Rand gold-mining companies, pocketing the hard currency thus earned and permitting the miners to draw some starvation wages for themselves and their families.

Samora Machel drew attention to this situation in his remarkable book:

Mozambique constitutes a vast reservoir of manpower at derisory prices for the South African mining industry and the great Rhodesian plantations.

More than one million Mozambicans work in diverse sectors of activity in those two countries. Eighty per cent of foreign manpower used in the South African mines are from Mozambique. The importance of these workers can be more exactly measured if we consider the situation in the South African gold-mining industry in the Rand, where the main part of Mozambique workers are concentrated. . . .

The rentability of these mines is low. It is necessary to work 160,000 tons of earth to produce one ton of gold. In Canada, the U.S.A. and Australia, mines with a superior gold content were closed down. . . . The secret of the rentability of the South African mines is the low price of African manpower and the total disregard for the safety conditions of the workers. . . .

By virtue of agreements signed with the South African government which permitted the Rand mining companies to recruit up to 100,000 Mozambique workers every year, the colonialist government received from South Africa one billion *escudos* [approximately forty million dollars], in foreign currency, the product of taxes and wages of the workers and the receipts from the ports and railways of Lourenço Marques, used by South Africa as a complement to the purchase of workers. . . .

Mozambique workers were still going to South Africa after the country's independence, but on a voluntary basis and on terms under which they received the full value of wages paid. With unemployment high due to plants closed after the departure of their Portuguese owners, management, and technicians; with tens of thousands of Mozambicans returning from exile in Tanzania, Zambia, Malawi, and other places; and an estimated annual revenue loss of half a billion dollars for having applied the UN sanctions against Rhodesia, a cutoff of the labor supply to South Africa's gold mines would mean another heavy burden for the young People's Republic to shoulder. It could be argued that Mozambican workers are contributing to the prosperity of the South African regime. It is also argued that a hundred or so thousand militant Mozambican workers, a proportion of them indoctrinated by FRELIMO, represent a powerful reinforcement to the South African working class.

With this in mind, I put my question to Machel: "Should Mozambican miners in South Africa be regarded as an integral part of the working class there, capable of being drawn into the fierce class struggles that are beginning to develop? Or are there factors which isolate them from the mainstream of class struggle there?"

Obviously the struggle of the people of all countries is our struggle. The struggle of workers all over the world is our struggle. Such struggles are a necessary prerequisite for the life of all peoples, an essential condition for the development of society. The foreign working class does not remain aloof or neutral, just because it is foreign, from the great struggles that take place where that working class has its relations with production, where it earns its wages, where its living conditions are established. But Mozambican workers will not be decisive or the determining factor for the political and social liberation of South Africa. This can only be done by the South African workers themselves.

On the question of the struggle in South Africa, Samora Machel warned against diverting attention from the main problem to what he considered the secondary problem of *apartheid*:

> Is racism or exploitation the main question? There is a danger of losing sight of the class struggle by keeping racism in the fore. Despite different characteristics, the struggle is essentially the same as elsewhere in southern Africa; it is against the exploitation by colonialist capitalism. Racism is only a form and instrument of action. Fundamentally it is a question of oppression and exploitation. Racism gives a particular color to it; but odious and horrendous as it is, it is not the principal problem. There is a risk that fighting to end *apartheid* diverts attention from the main problem. In fact, racism is a fundamental ingredient of colonialist oppression. The result of getting the priorities wrong would make the ending of *apartheid* look like a final victory.
>
> As long as there is oppression there can never be equality. What is equality under colonial capitalism? Is the aim that all blacks should live like whites? No. The fight against *apartheid* must be seen as part of the general class struggle.

Regarding FRELIMO's attitude to the struggles going on across its borders in South Africa and Zimbabwe, President Machel was categoric:

> We cannot feel free with colonialism on our frontiers. Namibia becomes a base for South African aggression against Angolan sovereignty. Rhodesia is a base for daily attacks against the People's Republic of Mozambique. Why do they attack us? Because we are independent and have won our freedom. They want to reverse the course of history and continue to oppress us. Why is there no outcry in the West? Colonialism is a permanent crime against humanity—a cancer which corrodes daily, nourished by the blood of the poor and oppressed. Racism is a permanent crime against mankind, depriving man of his personality and dignity, humiliating him to the point where he believes he is inferior because of the color of his skin. It is hard for outsiders to imagine how we suffered—even wishing we had been born with a different-colored skin from that of our parents. Why was I born with such an unfortunate color? Only colored people can really understand the permanent affront to our human dignity. Now, here in Mozambique, we have established real equality between men. It is from this that so many Portuguese are running away. They cannot face up to real racist equality. We are the most obdurate and uncompromising enemies of racism. But we also feel

that by putting too much stress on the *apartheid* issue the danger is that revolutionary forces may be diverted into waging an anti-white campaign. That is why we say, let us define the enemy. It is not the whites; it is not a question of skin pigmentation. It is, in our area of the world, colonialist capitalist oppression.

It is known that we support the struggle of peoples everywhere fighting for independence, but especially do we support, unreservedly, the struggle of the southern African peoples against colonialism.

That these were no idle words was demonstrated time and again by concrete acts of support for the Zimbabwe freedom fighters—for which the Mozambique people paid dearly in the form of overt acts of aggression by the Smith regime in so-called punishment or "hot pursuit" raids against villages deep inside Mozambique. The FRELIMO leadership did not waver because of this. Samora Machel took the lead in helping to promote unity among the various factions in Zimbabwe, urging and encouraging them and providing material support for them to step up their armed struggle. While helping to deal with the smaller "alligator" first—Zimbabwe—just as Angola was helping to deal with Namibia, there is no question but that Samora Machel knew that Mozambique could never really relax until the biggest "alligator" of all was dealt with. The people of Mozambique were already being politically and psychologically prepared for the sacrifices that all-out support for the freedom fighters in South Africa would entail.

XVI People's Health

If there is one thing which visually and immediately distinguishes the pilot schools and their pupils from other such establishments, or children from areas not yet liberated at the moment of independence, it is the "poor but clean" atmosphere that reigns. Under their often tattered clothes, limbs and bodies are glowing with cleanliness and health. They are taught to bathe every day. Open-air bathhouses with tall reed palisades surrounding them—separate ones for the boys and girls—are a feature of every school. There are also small medical clinics, equipped well enough to administer first aid and take care of the most common ailments. These were legacies of the style of life in the liberated zones. Children elsewhere still suffered from the colonialist heritage and this could not be done away with during the first year of independence by simply issuing an administrative decree. But it is certain that wherever the pilot school graduates go, they will be proselytes of personal and public hygiene and living examples of the results. Incidentally at none of the schools which I visited did I see anyone, either pupils or staff, smoking. When I asked whether smoking was forbidden, I was told simply that the teachers and administrative staff set the example and the children had naturally followed it.

The type of conditions inherited from the Portuguese was summed up in a FRELIMO Central Committee Resolution on Public Health adopted in February, 1976, at the same time as that on communal villages. The situation described in the resolution underlines the crucial importance of the pilot schools in training future cadres totally unpolluted by colonialist-capitalist mentality. It was impossible just to take over existing administrations and cadres as they were and place them at the service of the new revolutionary regime. Also it brought out the secondary importance of fine buildings and equipment in comparison with the primary importance of forming cadres with the right outlook who, when the time came, could put the fine buildings and modern equipment to their most effective use. The two essential characteristics of public-health work in the Liberated Zones are summed up in the resolution as follows: (1) It had as its objective to serve the masses; and (2) The people themselves took part in carrying out a great number of tasks in the public-health field, helping to protect their own health.

The resolution then goes on to describe the situation as it existed in September, 1974, when agreement was reached that FRELIMO would be responsible for governing the entire country even before the formal accession to independence nine months later. FRELIMO authority, in other words, was extended to large areas that until then had been entirely under colonialist administration. The resolution continues:

> What was the main characteristic of this situation? In the first place the existing structures were oriented toward satisfying the needs of a privileged minority.
>
> On the other hand, the motive of medical aid was not to alleviate human suffering but to make profits. Under the colonial-fascist medical system—with some honorable exceptions—it was the unbridled seeking after riches which reigned. We thus inherited a completely unbalanced public-health structure.
>
> The urban areas, essentially monopolized by the colonialists, had a structure capable of providing medical assistance but only on the basis of the ability of each individual to pay. Here there were consulting offices and private clinics—places of exploitation where the patient was regarded as a source of profits. It was in such places that doctors and nurses accumulated their wealth. In the state hospitals where the less privileged went—those living in the suburbs, for instance—medical aid was precarious and patients were also treated according to their ability to pay. Patients were even classed according to the social-racist structure of colonial-capitalism, starting with the white colonialist, then the *assimilado*, down to the "native." There was a total lack of interest in the poor patient, manifested by the way in which he or she was treated by the doctor or nurse; in the lack of hygiene in the places where they were treated; and the total lack of discipline among the medical workers who treated them.

It is further pointed out that there was a high proportion of Mozambicans among the nurses—"victims of the virulent racism" that reigned in the hospital. They were not permitted to hold any responsible posts, these being exclusively reserved for the Portuguese.

> Yet, as they worked in a sector dominated by the spirit of money-making, in daily contact with doctors who were making fortunes,

they ended up by becoming infected with this mentality and started also to aspire after riches.

Due to the exploitation and discrimination of which they were victims, their consciousness was aroused as regards colonialist oppression, but their aspirations were essentially of a capitalist nature. Despite the discrimination they were still relatively privileged as compared to the broad masses of the people. Thus one can understand that their national sentiments, born of revolt against racist humiliations, did not go beyond the idea of replacing the *colons*.

Here the resolution touched on the crucial difference between the national liberation struggles waged in the Portuguese African colonies—in Mozambique and Guiné-Bissau, and by the MPLA in Angola—and the independence struggles waged in many other African colonies. The difference between revolt and revolution; between "changing the color of the bosses" and eliminating the boss concept. The tendency to see the end aim as replacing white plantation and factory owners by black ones, and white bureaucrats in leading positions by black ones, had to be fought against at every step of the way toward total independence. There are any number of examples, especially in Africa, of not only "just changing the color at the top," but of the new rulers taking over almost intact the same forces of repression—army and police—that the colonialists had used to maintain their rule. There were fierce internal struggles inside the FRELIMO leadership before such concepts were rejected. The example of the nurses is typical of the colonialist poison which infected many of them who, objectively speaking, should have been wholeheartedly on the side of the people. It would mean ignoring some of the basic constants of human nature to expect the nurses not to have been affected by the money-grabbing that went on all around them, especially as there was virtually no possibility—above all in PIDE-controlled Maputo and other major urban areas—for them to have access to any counter-influence. If that was the situation in the urban centers, one can imagine what it was in the rural areas where ninety-five per cent of the Africans lived:

The rural areas did not have any public-health structure whatsoever, because there was nothing there to enrich the doctors and nurses. "To go to the forest" was considered a punishment or very bad luck.

180

The rural population was left to itself with neither public-health organization nor guidance.

The few *colons* living there had the means to go to the urban areas where they could get whatever medical assistance they could pay for. Because nothing existed in any planned way, because there had never been any mobilization of the population to fight disease, epidemics frequently appeared that were almost impossible to control. This explains the country's high average mortality rate. Mozambique also had one of the highest infant mortality rates in the world.

While preventive medicine played an important role in the liberated zones, priority was given to curative medicine in the enemy-controlled areas, because it was only this that enabled the medical personnel to enrich themselves. The prophylactic struggle against disease still remains to be organized in the former enemy-controlled zones.

The colonial-capitalist concept of the health services is reflected also in the educational system for the public-health services. Recruitment of pupils was based on social and racial discrimination, so that the majority of qualified medical personnel are foreigners; from a social and economic viewpoint, the Mozambique nurses constitute an elite with privileged status in Mozambique society.

Conscious of the depth of the problem and of the necessity to find radical solutions to end exploitation and speculation on disease, the government of the People's Republic of Mozambique decided to nationalize medicine and forbid the exercise of medical practice for lucrative ends.

The nationalization of public health was decreed just one month after the People's Republic was set up, together with that of education, urban property, and other key areas. Obviously the nationalization measures did not suit everyone, as the resolution makes clear:

> The colonial public-health structure was shaken to its foundations. Doctors and nurses are now obliged to work exclusively for the state and to serve patients without any discrimination whatsoever.
>
> This medical system was received with great satisfaction by the people who see their aspirations satisfied, their interests defended. But many doctors and nurses do not accept it because they see themselves deprived of their means of exploitation.

Obviously it was not only in Mozambique that doctors, particularly the specialists and those with lucrative private practices, fought against nationalization of medicine. In virtually every non-socialist country where it has been introduced, there has been a vigorous backlash by the medical community intent on retaining their privilege to fleece patients. Any attempt to extend social services to benefit the majority of the population is met with the battlecry, "Our craft is in danger!"; and the methods used by sectional interests to wage the battle are often devoid of any scruples. Thus the resolution notes:

> If some doctors and nurses devote themselves with energy and enthusiasm to getting the new public-health structure working, others drag their feet. Others again, concentrated in various state hospitals and other medical institutions, create real centers of subversion, including the diffusion of reactionary slogans. Such pernicious elements encourage lack of interest in the work, especially in hospital hygiene; they foster laxity and indiscipline, and deliberately try to provoke chaos in order to prove nationalization was a mistake. Through rumors and intrigue, they agitate for the departure of the [Portuguese] doctors and, taking advantage of their daily contact with the patients, they diffuse the most diverse rumors and slanders. Racism and opportunism find a fertile soil in this atmosphere.

It was to correct all the problems and abuses manifested during the first seven months of the functioning of nationalized medicine that the Central Committee laid down the broad lines of a political and organizational struggle on the public-health front. It was the sort of approach which only a revolutionary government, certain of grass-roots support from the people, could wage. If it is grotesque to imagine such methods being used in developed Western countries, it is, unfortunately, no less grotesque to imagine it in many African countries which acquired their independence long before Mozambique. It is the typical political-ideological-educational approach of the FRELIMO of Eduardo Mondlane and Samora Machel.

> Our policy should be guided in the sense of:
> Developing intensive political work inside the hospitals with the participation of all the public health staff and the patients in order to put an end to divisionism, élitism, and racism, and create real national unity.
> Arousing the consciousness of the social tasks in which medical workers are engaged; strengthening their dedication to the cause of

building up democratic people's power by promoting the spirit of "serving the people."

Setting up structures capable of applying the line as traced by FRELIMO, so that discipline is consciously adopted as the sentinel of that political line. In this context it is especially important to create [FRELIMO] party committees in the hospitals and other medical institutions, directly linked with the party leadership and the government.

Mobilizing and organizing the people so they can participate consciously and actively in the fight against disease. We must implement the slogan: "Each of us transforms himself into an agent of public health to promote public hygiene to preserve the health of the collective and to create conditions for preparing the body for this struggle."

After winning independence, people have the right to good health, to education, to decent food and clothing. But independence was the prerequisite for all other advances. In an amazingly short period of time, as I could feel throughout my travels, FRELIMO had gained the confidence of the people in the former nonliberated areas, and above all in the rural areas. Everything that they asked people to do was so clearly in their own interests that it was easy to mobilize enthusiasm. In the big towns it was somewhat different because it was not so clearly in everybody's interests—not their short-range interests. Some intellectuals, especially those who had enjoyed a privileged social or economic status, felt veiled contempt for people who had spent all their lives in the forest and did not even know how to use a flush toilet, yet lectured them on everything from public health to political matters, up to and including how to run the country! But this was a small minority without any political base. Eventually they would either have to join in the building of the new society or be left behind in every sense.

In the meantime FRELIMO was pushing ahead with its work. On October 23, 1976, a decree was issued which stated that "all Mozambican women, regardless of their marital status or whatever work they do, are entitled to sixty days fully paid maternity leave. . . ." It can be taken from the twentieth day before the date of probable delivery and does not affect the regular annual holiday. In addition, from the fifth month of pregnancy and during the first six months after the birth, mothers are exempted from night work.

That is something so removed from the wildest dreams of any Mozambican working woman that it must have seemed little short of a miracle. What effect can the sneers and jibes of city sophisticates at the "bumpkins from the bush" have in relation to revolutionary measures which touch the very heart of people's day-to-day problems?

In a 1977 New Year's message, Samora Machel was able to announce that "due to the efforts of the government and international solidarity," the number of doctors practicing in Mozambique had risen in 1976 to three hundred—more than four times the number at the time of the Portuguese departure! And that 2,000 new primary schoolteachers had been trained, and yet another 3,000 had completed refresher courses to be oriented in the FRELIMO line in education. The number of secondary schools had increased from thirty-three to ninety-nine during the first year of independence. In addition, "1976 saw greater attendance in schools and hospitals than has ever been registered in the history of Mozambique," said the President.

FRELIMO also made patient efforts to rally to their side all who could be rallied. Being careful not to reject or waste talents that could be utilized, they allocated valuable cadres for such work of "recuperation."

At the Re-education Center at Inhussane (Inhumbane province) I was able to have a look at recuperation efforts of a more complicated nature. It was there that I met Comandante Martinis Mola Muainkongua (mentioned in the first chapter as one of the twelve who took part in the opening battle of the national liberation struggle). After a long drive through coconut groves and forests of acaju trees (which produce Mozambique's biggest foreign currency earner—cashew nuts) we stopped at a group of huts where some black-uniformed people were strolling around. "We're here," said my guide-interpreter to my great surprise. There were no guards, no barbed wire, not even an entrance gate. Comandante Martinis emerged from one of the huts, an enormous man with a tiny "peashooter" pistol on his hip. His military rank required that he wore a pistol, but it became clear that he wanted one that was as un-intimidating as possible.

After a look around a farm of about 100 hectares, which provided maize, sunflowers, tomatoes, and a wide range of vegetables for the inmates' own consumption, and a site where finishing touches were being put to the roof of a large storehouse, it was clear that the Comandante was a popular figure. He was greeted with friendly deference by all the inmates in the fields and along the dirt tracks. He explained who was being re-educated and how:

Colonialism treated everyone badly and we have to cope with the results of this. Most of the 399 here are petty criminals who turned to thievery because they had no jobs or skills. There are some who preferred robbing to any other way of making a living and a handful who were guilty of criminal assaults.

The government decided to give them a chance to learn the FRELIMO line and get rid of the old ideas which are products of the colonialist-capitalist system. It is because we regard them as victims of society that we consider that our center here is in no sense a prison. They all take part in political classes and in productive work. Great stress is also laid on the anti-illiteracy classes which they all attend.

Most of them already understand the new situation and accept the FRELIMO line. After all, they are on the receiving end of one aspect of it and many of them are well placed to make comparisons between their treatment here and what happened to them if they fell into the hands of the Portuguese police. Those who didn't understand the FRELIMO line before, now do.

Most of them are taking part in production for the first time in their lives and of course it is on a group basis. The responsible cadres only give the general orientation, they do the rest themselves. We encourage the maximum initiative from them. This introduces them to another aspect of FRELIMO policy—self-reliance. Discipline is excellent. Our staff is comprised of the commandant (myself), a political commissar and deputy political commissar, a cadre responsible for cultural and educational affairs, one for production, and another for professional training.

I asked if there were not problems with production and building activities due to the almost total lack of experience on the part of most of the inmates. Also, due to absence of guards and obstacles to escape, were there not problems of the inmates running away? And what had happened to the first "graduates"?

Those who are more advanced teach those who are backward. The first group was of 300, but most of them were free to leave after twelve months. We now have a second group of 399 which includes 99 who did not make it the first time. A few of the first group ran away and it was those who had committed the most serious offenses. But after a while they all came back—they had merely gone to see their families.

As for what happened to the first "graduates," we have not undertaken any followup. They are completely free when they leave here. By then the overwhelming majority can read and write. They can all take part in agricultural work, many others in carpentry and building. We know of some good results because some of our graduates are working in mechanical workshops in Inhumbane [the capital of the province in which the center was located—W.B.].

Comandante Martinis explained that a few of the inmates were mechanics who were allowed to go to work in Inhumbane from time to time "to keep their hand in" and to take some of the others with them for initial training. He hoped soon to set up a properly equipped workshop at the center. In fact he had discussed a number of important changes with the provincial governor a few days earlier. He advocated turning the re-education center into a fully equipped professional training school where each graduate would have mastered one profession. He also submitted plans to improve housing and give the trainees civilian-type clothing. "The governor agreed that we should do everything to avoid the idea that this is a punishment center and avoid anything that could humiliate them or offend their personal dignity. Everything should be done to recuperate them, to mold them into decent, useful citizens able to make their contribution to building up the country." To my question as to how the practitioners of one of the world's most individualistic professions—agriculture (at least as practiced in Mozambique) adapted to group work, he replied:

When they first arrive the accent is very much on political work and this helps to do away with their prejudices about collective work. Political study includes the history of the resistance struggle and its aims. They learn for the first time how we carried on the struggle; they study the essential role of the peasants in growing food, in transporting arms and other supplies. They are extremely interested in this. We tell them about the struggles inside FRELIMO and the international support we received. They are fascinated by this and their feelings of national pride start to be aroused.

Inhumbane was another example of the practical and human way in which the social evils left by the Portuguese were being healed, combined with a Vietnamese-type frugality in salvaging every possible scrap of what is considered the most precious raw material—human beings. The re-education center was an extension of the drives to bring public health and education to the most inaccessible corners of the land and this included tackling the problem of moral health. The fact that a cadre of the quality and experience of Comandante Martinis Mola Muainkongua should be in charge of the Inhussane center was a measure of the importance that the FRELIMO leadership attached to this.

XVII FRELIMO 1977

The painfully slow-but-sure, step-by-step progress of the Mozambique revolution and promises of a quickened pace to come were spelled out at FRELIMO's third congress, held in Maputo from February 3-7, 1977. The conditions under which each of the three congresses was held tell part of the story. The first (September,

1962) was held only three years after FRELIMO was founded. It had to be held on foreign soil, in what was then the British colony of Tanganyika (which, once independence was acquired, fused with Zanzibar, another newly independent British colony, to become Tanzania). The second (July, 1968) was held in the newly liberated territory of Mozambique's own Niassa province. It took place out of doors, deep in the forest with the tribune table and delegate's benches made from lengths of saplings lashed together. But the third was held in a splendid conference hall in the center of Maputo, capital of the nineteen-month-old People's Republic of Mozambique.

The universality of the guest delegations reflected FRELIMO's Vietnam-type position within the Communist world. It was rare by that time to see the Soviet Union, China, Albania and Yugoslavia sending delegates to the same Congress—or meeting anywhere else outside the United Nations. There were delegates from all countries where Communist parties held state power. Among the revolutionary parties and movements were those from Cambodia—also a rare participant by that time in events beyond her own frontiers. All former Portuguese colonies were represented—including East Timor.

The decisions of the three congresses reflect the political development which grew parallel to the armed struggle. The first decided to establish maximum unity of all sections of the population, including all tribal groupings and classes for the overthrow of Portuguese colonial rule by all means, including armed struggle. The second decided, after considerable argument, that the form of armed struggle should be Protracted Revolutionary War, and that the independence struggle was in the phase of a National Democratic Revolution. Mozambique's struggle, it was decided, was an integral part of the world struggle against imperialism.

While it is not explicitly stated in documents available from the second congress, it seems that the old problem as to whether armed struggle should be urban or rural-based was fought out, as it is being fought out today within the leadership of South Africa's African National Congress. The decision to launch armed struggle is a momentous one; to decide what form of armed struggle is hardly less so. It is crucial to success or failure. Armed struggle based on the industrial working class or on the rural peasantry?

Seizure of power in the cities with gradual extension of the struggle to the countryside as in the Bolshevik revolution or seizure of power in the countryside, gradual encirclement of the cities and their capture in the final phase as in the Chinese revolution? Pro-Soviet revolutionaries tend to favor the former, pro-Chinese the latter. It was the road chosen by the Vietnamese. The use of such terms as "Protracted Revolutionary War" and "National Democratic Revolution" shows that the advocates of the Chinese-Vietnamese rural-based war were in the majority. This was the model chosen as most appropriate for a backward people to wage anti-colonial struggle. It was at this congress also that revolutionary aims emerged and the split developed between the Eduardo Mondale-Samora Machel leadership on the one hand and the more conservative, and ultimately secessionist, leader from Cabo Delgado, Lazaro Nkavandame. Reverend Uria Simango also broke away from FRELIMO at this point for virtually the same reasons as Nkavandame.

It is a fact of life that people support national liberation struggles for different reasons and some desert whenever policy decisions conflict with their own aims and interests. Almost all sections of a colonized society can be mobilized for the overthrow of the colonial power. There will be deserters however when the question of land reform is inevitably decided in favor of "land to those who till it." Local landowners, whose concept of victory was that of adding the land from their Portuguese neighbors to their own, are liable to turn against the liberation struggle when they realize that not only will they not be expropriating their neighbor's properties but that their own may be in danger if their holdings are too big. And, while overwhelming support can be mobilized for land reform, there will be other deserters when the question of nationalizing industry is decided at some later stage of the struggle. To announce final aims—even if they have been decided by the leadership—at too early a stage would negate the possibility of mobilizing all those forces susceptible of being mobilized in the initial phases of a national liberation struggle. Not to define them at an appropriate moment would lead to disaffection by the forces on which the struggle is based and for the satisfaction of whose deepest aspirations it is being waged. Through the struggle itself political consciousness is developed to a point where the leadership can pose new problems and, if the solutions proposed are acceptable to the overwhelming majority, the leadership can be assured of mass support. It is a step-by-step process.

Thus the third congress decided that the liberation struggle could be escalated to the stage of a People's Democratic Revolution as a transitional step toward reaching a summit from which the socialist revolution could be launched.

FRELIMO, which had started like the MPLA as a front organization, had functioned as a political party much earlier than the MPLA. It was at the third congress however that, on February 3, 1977, it was formally transformed into a Marxist-Leninist, workers-peasants political party, retaining the name of FRELIMO. The Central Committee of twenty-two members elected at the second congress was replaced by one of sixty-seven members which elected an eleven-member Political Bureau, headed by Samora Machel, who was also elected party president. It includes Marcelino dos Santos, Alberto Joaquim Chipande, Joaquim Alberto Chissano and other founder members of the original FRELIMO.

In his introductory report, Samora Machel stated:

The working class is the ruling class of history. Only it is capable of engaging in the whole process of the transformation of Nature and Society and of stimulating and guiding this process. This requires a conscious and active participation in tasks at all levels of society. . . . The peasantry is the most numerous part of our population—the principal force of our country. It is the peasantry allied with the working force—the leading force—which constitute the political power base of Democratic People's Power.

FRELIMO, which started as a movement or front, had transformed itself into a Marxist-Leninist party, whereas the MPLA in Angola decided at a special Central Committee plenum (October 29, 1976) to hold a special congress in the third quarter of 1977 to form a Marxist-Leninist party. There was no question of transforming the MPLA into a party, although MPLA activists would certainly form its nucleus.

Small and medium farmers, handicraft workers, small business people, progressive intellectuals in all fields would have their role to play and would be encouraged in all activities in line with the central aim of serving the people. The specific plans outlined for every sector of economic and social life all reflected the total neglect by the Portuguese colonialists of all spheres of activity which touched the life of the people and the orgy of destruction and sabotage which preceded their departure.

During the stage of the People's Democratic Revolution, economic policy is defined as:

> Building up an independent, planned, and advanced economy capable of satisfying the elementary needs of the people and creating the conditions for moving on to the higher stage of Socialist Revolution. In our country the level of development is exceedingly low and the main obstacle to economic development is the dependency in which our economy finds itself in relation to foreign monopolies. Because of this the building up of an economy capable of satisfying the basic needs of the working people and enabling a transition to socialism necessarily implies the liquidation of colonial and neocolonial dependency in relation to imperialist states and international monopolies. . . .

Everything of any value in Mozambique was in foreign hands, and the major part, in terms of value, was not even in Portuguese hands. As part of the policy of giving major powers a vested interest in Mozambique remaining in Portuguese hands, dictator Salazar opened wide the gates to foreign investment. From the start of the colonial wars in Angola in February, 1961, until armed struggle began in Mozambique in 1964, industrial installations with a capital of two million or more dollars increased from eighty-five to 647. Between 1962 and 1969, total investments in industry more than doubled to reach a total of 526 million dollars. That all this investment was made at an accelerated rate is seen from the fact that between January and July, 1973, installations of industrial and other plants were approved to the value of 400 million dollars. Of the total investments from 1962 to mid-1973, when the military situation started to deteriorate sharply for the Portuguese, 52.3 per cent were for 180 large-scale industrial units exclusively for exports, while 47.7 per cent were for 1,724 industrial units to supply the internal market. Foreign capital greatly outweighed Portuguese capital, but whatever profits Portugal did pocket went to finance the war.

The great advantage that Portugal had to offer foreign investors was cheap labor—with salaries averaging from one to two dollars per day except in such specialized branches as oil refining—and a no-strike labor discipline imposed by the PIDE, along with other notorious forms of Portuguese repression. Trade unions, of course, had never been heard of. The extent of the foreign (from a Portuguese viewpoint) and multinational hold on the Mozambique economy can be illustrated by examining a few key industries.

The production and refining of sugar—one of the country's main exports—was monopolized by five major companies, with British companies holding a ninety per cent interest in two of them, Sena Sugar Estates and the Incomati Agricultural Society. Companhia do Buzi belonged to the Companhia de Mozambique, which in turn was controlled by the big British South Africa monopoly. The Mozambique Sugar Company was owned by French and associated interests; and MARAGRA, although nominally owned by a Portuguese monopoly, was suspected of being closely linked with the giant South African Industrial Development Corporation.

Four of the five biggest sisal and coconut plantations were dominated by British, Swiss, West German, and Dutch capital respectively; while in the fifth, Swiss, French, and Norwegian capital were combined to secure a controlling interest.

The cotton-growing and textile industries were monopolized by four major interests: British South Africa (through the Companhia de Mozambique), the Banco Português do Atlantico and the Banco Comercial de Angola, both of which are very closely linked with Barclay's Bank of England, and, finally, a Portuguese capitalist in the form of the João Ferreira dos Santos family.

Cashew nuts represent one of Mozambique's major natural resources. Over large areas of the coastal regions there are acaju forests where the nuts grow in a natural state. Four main groups monopolize the transformation into edible nuts, including the grading and packing processes. These are (1) Spence and Pierce, Ltd., a consortium of two all-British enterprises; CAJUCA, in which an Italian company holds a majority interest; (2) MOCITA, a consortium which is headed by the South African, Anglo-American Corporation (with a strong participation of Portuguese capital) but also includes the Tiger Oats and Milling Corporation; (3) an Italian firm, the Industria de Prodotti Alimentari de Bologna; and (4) SOCAJU, associated with what was then the biggest Portu-

192

guese monopoly, CUF, and the Banco Nacional Ultramarino, which, like virtually all Portuguese banks, was heavily infiltrated with foreign capital.

In the three main tea-producing companies foreign—mainly British—capital also prevailed.

Prospecting and exploitation for oil and natural gas was in the hands of exclusively American, South African, French, and West German companies. The mineral-rich province of Tete had been divided up among the Companhia Carbonifera de Moçambique, controlled by the Belgian-owned Société Minière et Géologique; the Companhia de Urânio de Moçambique, one of the British-South African Corporation's group which headed a consortium—the Companhia Mineira de Tete—including the Bethlehem Steel Company, among other non-Portuguese participants; and the Companhia Moçambique de Minas, set up by the Johannesburg Consolidated Investment Corporation and the Anglo-American Corporation.

The country's richest coal mine at Moatize, twenty kilometers northeast of the provincial capital of Tete, the Carbonifières de Mozambique, was wholly Belgian-owned. Almost sixty per cent of the coal produced—575,000 tons in 1975—was high-quality coking coal, most of it exported to Japan. And in Mozambique province, the Japanese Sumitomo Trust had secured the exclusive rights for prospecting and exploiting iron ore deposits. In other fields of exploitation of mineral wealth, British, American, Canadian, South African, even Luxembourg firms had each carved out their concessions. What they had not calculated, however, was that most of the areas which were richest in minerals were in the mountains of the northernmost provinces—the first to be liberated by FRELIMO guerillas!

The material quoted above comes from a detailed study by Samora Machel, which describes the extent of the multinational grab of Mozambique's natural resources at the pressing invitation of the Portuguese fascist government. Continuing that part of his report, Samora Machel said:

Portugal thus clearly appears as the manager for the interests of companies which are above all non-Portuguese . . . Portuguese colonialism has thus succeeded in financially exploiting its role as a parasite while at the same time trying to integrate Mozambique more directly in the plans of certain belligerent circles.

The Portuguese government and its diplomatic and propaganda machinery are constantly insisting on the necessity of integrating Mozambique into a NATO "zone of intervention." Certain American strategists would like to transform our port of Nacala, the best natural port on the African side of the Indian Ocean, into an American naval base. There are political schemes aimed at creating a military alliance between the main imperialist powers on the one hand, and on the other, Brazil, South Africa, Portugal, and its "territories" of Angola and Mozambique.

Samora Machel's analysis was written before independence was won, but he was already preparing the ground within FRELIMO and outside it for nationalization of the country's natural resources and of the business enterprises whose owners had fled, or who were sabotaging the national economy. It was clearly impossible to start economic planning or even national reconstruction when everything of value, apart from the land and its people, belonged to foreign interests.

However strenuously the Portuguese authorities tried to conceal the truth, the defeat of General Kaulza de Arriaga's "Gordian Knot" offensive and its staggering implications began to seep through to the outside world. Capital and people began to move the other way, first in a trickle, then a flow, and, finally, a flood.

It is typical that while foreign money continued to pour in, local capital started to creep out—another illustration of the fact that the great captains of finance are not all that bright. Their eyes are too closely glued to computerized projections of profits per investment to see the larger picture. They simply cannot imagine that ragged, barefooted guerillas can block their plans. Time and again, ingrained racial and class prejudices blind them to political realities. The Portuguese government was still signing authorizations to open up mines and set up industries in territory it no longer controlled, or ever could control, even while small and medium Portuguese capitalists in Mozambique were starting to transfer their capital back to Lisbon and making preparations to follow it.

The figures presented in the General Report to the Third FRELIMO Congress tell the story. The "Gordian Knot" offensive took place between May and July, 1970.

194

After the defeat of the colonial forces in Operation "Gordian Knot," capitalism, which was already entering a period of crisis, started to become ever more fearful for its future in Mozambique. The colonial bourgeoisie stepped up the flight of hard currency and started the process of economic sabotage. The exodus of *colons* also started at this period. According to colonial statistics, about 6,000 *colons* left in 1971. In 1972, about 12,500; and in 1973, some 22,000 abandoned Mozambique.

And that was before the "Captains' Coup" of April 25, 1974, in Lisbon, before the specter of independence and black rule appeared! The General Report goes on to describe the state of affairs during the Transitional Government period (September 20, 1974, to June 25, 1974), under the cover of which the Portuguese would gradually withdraw:

During the transition period the capitalists were once again forced to revise their strategy and work out new plans. They sowed panic and provoked the departure of owners of small and medium enterprises, technicians, and other qualified workers. The big capitalists who planned and directed these schemes hoped thereby to safeguard their own interests by pretending to advocate a policy of moderation and false realism, in the name of overcoming the technical and administrative shortcomings which they themselves had created. To defend their own interests either in industrial enterprises or within the state administration, they used the internal bourgeoisie, hastily formed during the final years of colonialism. They intensified the theft and unbridled destruction; cattle, tractors, machinery, heavy trucks disappeared across the frontier, or were embarked from our wharves due to the complicity of reactionary and corrupt administrative personnel. When pillage was no longer possible due to growing vigilance by the state and the working masses, the class enemies resorted to destruction. Thousands of head of cattle were slaughtered and left to rot. Essential consumer goods were hoarded, disappearing completely from the market to appear later on at fabulous prices. The ordinary trade channels, already inadequate enough, were systematically sabotaged. . . .

Subversion was organized against our country. Radio broadcasts were directed against us from abroad, counterrevolutionary pamphlets were secretly introduced. Drugs, pornography, religious propaganda of a subversive and obscurantist nature were distributed. Rumors were spread and provocations launched to accelerate the flight of technicians. Campaigns in the press systematically distorted the people's revolutionary gains to slander and discredit people's power. Armed agents with explosives were introduced to carry out criminal and terrorist activities. Outside the country, the illegal racist regime of Southern Rhodesia was once again used as an operational force to attack our country and massacre our people. . . .

The FRELIMO response to this was to rapidly extend its party and mass structures throughout the whole country and to set up *Grupos Dinamizadores* (literally, Dynamizer Groups, but which shall be referred to as Activist Groups) in every factory and enterprise and at all levels within the administration to counter enemy activities and explain the real position of FRELIMO. The General Report described them as "our fundamental weapon in fighting against all forms of economic sabotage; against all attempts to confuse, corrupt and subvert the workers." As I noticed in my travels these groups quickly acquired prestige and authority; people in factories and villages naturally turned to them when problems arose. It was also a shortcut method of building up a devoted body of mainly young people who quickly acquired experience in handling real day-to-day problems. They became vanguard units and natural transmission belts for FRELIMO policies. They blocked the attempt of the Portuguese colonialists and their internal supporters to achieve by political and economic sabotage what their armed forces had not been able to achieve on the battlefield. The "last stand" by the latter was to provoke a small military mutiny in Maputo by some four hundred soldiers and police on the night of December 17-18, 1975. They managed to seize a few buildings and fired a lot of shots in the air but it was easily put down by loyal elements of FRELIMO's armed forces vigorously supported by the Activist Groups.

A pleasant surprise for FRELIMO was the reaction of the workers to the abandonment of business enterprises. It was impossible for the government to have foreseen the scale on which it was done, nor was it technically possible to have standby management teams ready to take over. It was done spontaneously by the workers themselves. Their main interest was to not be thrown out of work. With the departure of virtually all administrative and technical personnel, they had enormous difficulties to overcome because there had been a conscious effort to keep them in ignorance of technical processes but they carried on as best they could.

The big CAJUCA factory for the processing of cashew nuts situated in the outskirts of Maputo was an interesting case in point. Foreseeing the end of cheap labor once Mozambique became independent, but unwilling to abandon such a profitable enterprise, the owners (who were mainly Italian) decided to mechanize the whole process, sacking 700 of the plant's 1,900 workers as soon as the new machines were installed. The workers advised the government that this was against the national interest. The government, without posing the question of ownership, withdrew the administrative rights of the owners and appointed an Administrative Committee, composed of three of the plant's workers.

I spoke with two of them, Luis Guila, responsible for production, and Luis José Pereira, in charge of maintenance. To my question as to what the main problems were at the beginning, Luis Guila replied:

During that first period there was plenty of confusion. No one wanted to work. They said: "We're independent now. Why should we work more than three or four hours a day?" Once our committee was set up we had lots of political work to do, explaining that we should work well, produce even more than before, because it was the whole country and not some Italian and Portuguese capitalists, which would benefit. Gradually political consciousness was raised and production went up gradually from thirty to sixty tons a day. But it was difficult because people who had never had any rights before could not understand why now that they were free we could not just halve the working hours and double the wages. We had to explain that this would sabotage the revolution and play into the hands of our enemies. Bit by bit, helped by the radio and press, there has been a real transformation in people's thinking. After the first few months, we were able to take back the 700 workers who had been sacked. A vitally important role in raising political consciousness—which is still not high enough—was played by the factory Activist Group.

Luis José Pereira explained that nine out of the ten Portuguese technicians had left and there were some complicated machines that their own workers could not handle. Otherwise production would be stepped up to one hundred tons daily—a lot of cashew nuts! Most of the finished nuts went to traditional markets in the United States, Australia, and other Western countries.

At the Maputo Metallurgical Plant, which turns out freight wagons and port handling equipment (mainly for South Africa when I visited it in May, 1976), I spoke with members of the factory Activist Group. They were in the midst of grappling with another type of problem. Like the CAJUCA plant, it was still operating on behalf of its owners but with a Portuguese manager.

> We had great difficulties at first—now we are well organized and united. We had to carry out an intensive political campaign to explain the national importance of production from this enterprise. Workers at first saw things in a very partial form, putting forward all sorts of claims that were perhaps justifiable but impractical to fulfill without harming overall interests.
>
> Last year the manager tried to divide the workers with false and demagogic offers. He promised higher wages to one group of about 150 workers in order to provoke divisions. We had to explain to them not to fall for this.

That Mozambique would pay a high price for its militant support for the Patriotic Front in Zimbabwe (Rhodesia) and the African National Congress in South Africa was obvious. But it was an acceptable sacrifice. In a statement to the diplomatic corps in Maputo on June 19, 1977, Samora Machel said that between May, 1976, and June, 1977, 1,432 civilians had been killed and 527 wounded. "There have been 143 Rhodesian acts of aggression in the year ending last March," he said, "and violations and massacres have now reached an unprecedented scale." Most of the victims were Zimbabwan refugees fleeing the war and the savage repression of the Smith regime. But in 1976, 49 soldiers of the FPLM (Mozambique People's Liberation Forces) had been killed and twenty-seven wounded in repelling these attacks. The total figures for 1977 were bound to be higher. Samora Machel was speaking just after one of the most serious attacks of the year. It started on May 29, against the town of Mapai, about one hundred kilometers inside Mozambique at an almost equal distance from the Rhodesian and South African frontiers. The town was occupied by Rhodesian forces for almost one week and destroyed before the invaders withdrew.

A far greater attack started on November 23, 1977, against a

198

refugee camp outside Chimoio, (former Vila Pery) about eighty kilometers inside Mozambique's northern Manica province. Rhodesian troops were brought in by helicopter after parachutists had secured landing sites. Jet bombers and helicopter gunships were used in the "softening up" action which preceded the invasion. Nearly one thousand civilians were killed—one hundred of them school-children when their school received direct hits from the bombers—and seven hundred were wounded seriously enough to be admitted as in-patients to the Chimoio hospital.

The Patriotic Front asserts that it has no guerilla training bases in Mozambique—they are mainly in southern Tanzania. Representatives of the UNHCR (United Nations High Commissioner for Refugees) and western journalists who visited the sites of these main attacks have confirmed that they were refugee centers. But by such actions the Smith government not only wants to punish the FRELIMO government for its total support for the Zimbabwan freedom fighters but also to further its aims of internationalizing the war. The reasoning is that if Mozambique can be provoked into requesting a Soviet-backed Cuban troop commitment—as in Angola—the West will be forced to come to Smith's rescue and thus provide the best chance for his survival. It is a forlorn hope, but one of the best he has!

At a press conference in Maputo, on September 17, 1977, a captured spy, Afonso Joane Cotoi, revealed some details of what was in store for Mozambique if Rhodesian-South African plans materialized. A Mozambican from Inhambane province, Cotoi had been recruited as a labor spy by Pretoria's intelligence services while working in a South African coal mine. From informing against his fellow-workers, he graduated as a sabotage and intelligence agent. He was taken under the wing of the "Free Africa" movement, headed by a certain Jorge Jardim—one of those extremely rich Mozambicans whose concept of liberation was that of adding expropriated Portuguese assets to his own. Quite unrepentant, Cotoi told the press that his only "regret" was that he had been captured.

> The soldiers who trained us were Rhodesians, Portuguese, South Africans and others who spoke various languages. It was very tough training, lasting the whole day with intervals for lessons. . . .
> Around the barracks there were women for us—women from

199

Portugal, from South Africa, Rhodesia and some from Mozambique.
. .

They spoke to us a lot about Jorge Jardim, saying that he was our chief and future president, that he was going to lead us to victory . . . Just as FRELIMO had kicked out the Portuguese colonialists with weapons, we would be able to kick out FRELIMO if we trained enough. They told us that Jorge Jardim was going to lead us in kicking out FRELIMO, and so we would be able to run Mozambique, and we could get very rich, occupy the chairs of the ministers and directors. We would be the owners of the factories, the farms and everything else. . . .

They told us that for us to take power it was necessary to attack and kill the main leaders and cadres of FRELIMO. They assured us that this was being set up according to plans worked out by our principal leaders, mainly Jorge Jardim . . .

Cotoi was one of a group of 105 spies and saboteurs infiltrated into Mozambique from Rhodesia at the beginning of September (1977), his group of five being landed by helicopter near Mapai. They were briefed as to the importance of gathering information in preparation for a big attack toward the end of the month. His own assignment was to watch movement of troops and supplies along roads and railways and he was given a rendezvous point where a helicopter would pick him up and whisk him back to the Rhodesian operational base. From that point on his story was rather similar to that of Nito Alves. Some kindly village folk offered him hospitality.

I found a house and asked if I could rest there, saying I had come from Maputo. They welcomed me, put a mat on the floor and told me I could sleep there. I was very tired and fell asleep, but was woken up some hours later by a group of FRELIMO fighters who had surrounded me. They asked me who I had come to see and where I came from. I showed them my documents and said that I had come from the South. They insisted on taking me with them. On the way I could see the game was up and I told them everything, that I had come from Rhodesia, that I was an agent of "Free Africa" . . .[1]

A few days after Cotoi's press conference the Rhodesian security forces launched a heavy attack with parachutists and heliborne troops, supported by jet fighter-bombers in the Mapai-Chicualacuala area where Cotoi had been operating.

Apart from coping with the military threats and other "destabilization" efforts, the FRELIMO government continued to pay a heavy price in ending the Portuguese concept of Mozambique as a service station-transit facility and source of cheap labor for South Africa. In 1975, 130,000 of about 400,000 workers in South African mines came from Mozambique. Under what is known as the Mozambique Convention the South African government paid to Portugal—later to Mozambique—a proportion of the miners' wages in gold at the official world price of forty-two dollars per ounce. The gold was then sold on the open market at three to four times that amount. In the last years of Portuguese rule the difference between the official and the real price of gold amounted to about one third of Mozambique's total exchange earnings. Compulsory recruitment was ended with independence, and the total of Mozambique miners in South Africa by the end of 1977 had dropped to 34,000. This is due to two reasons. Despite problems of unemployment the FRELIMO government discourages—but does not prevent—workers going to South Africa on a voluntary basis. As the main reason that South Africa employs foreign workers is that they are less likely to strike or engage in militant activities than local workers, the importation of possibly politically-motivated "new" Mozambicans was viewed with alarm by a security-minded South African government. Especially as the country's main wealth derives from mining. Recruitment from neighboring states—Botswana, Swaziland and Lesotho—was stepped up. The numbers imported from Rhodesia increased from 25,000 in 1976, to 40,000 in 1977. Malawi, which had imposed a ban on recruitment of labor for South Africa following an air crash in which eighty of its miners were killed, was under pressure to lift the ban and provide about 20,000 miners by 1978.

The preferential gold rate for payment to the fast-dwindling force of Mozambican miners will end in 1978, and with that will also end any incentive for the FRELIMO government to permit its nationals to continue working in South Africa.

While Mozambique still got substantial revenue from South Africa's use of Maputo's port facilities, the rapid development of the South African harbor of Richard's Bay, 320 kilometers to the south meant that that source of revenue also would soon dry up.

There have been some compensatory factors. Part of the labor force which would normally have left for the South African mines was employed in a great drive to increase the harvest of cashew nuts, now Mozambique's greatest source of foreign exchange. Compared to the 1976 harvest of 95,000 tons, it was expected the 1977 harvest would reach an all-time record of 180,000 tons. A major contribution to the take-off period of economic development was a fifty million dollar aid agreement signed in Maputo on November 7, 1977, with the Nordic countries—Sweden, Denmark, Norway, Finland and Iceland—for the financing of twenty-six projects in the field of agriculture and fisheries. The agreement is described as the biggest Nordic support to any single country in the history of Nordic aid. Spread over three years it will include support for state farms, improvement of livestock and dairy cattle breeding methods, forestry development and the training of personnel. The port facilities of Maputo and Beira are more and more being used for Mozambique's own trade with the outside world and her developing internal coastal trade.

Democratic structures were strengthened by a series of ballots which started on September 25, 1977, with the election of people's assemblies at the level of villages and small towns and ended on December 4, with the election of a 226-member People's National Assembly, the supreme legislative body. It was the first time that the African population had ever taken part in a democratic exercise of this kind. In addition to choosing people in whom they had confidence—at least at local levels—the long drawn-out electoral procedure was, as Samora Machel expressed it in his address to the first session of the national People's Assembly, on December 23, 1977: "A real school, a university in which national and class unity have been consolidated. The elections are the reality of our freedom."[2]

Mozambique faced the New Year (1978), with heightened tension on her borders, a state of war with the Smith regime and increasingly stronger invasions of her territory; a structurized party grouped around the leadership which had launched the liberation struggle fourteen years previously; an elected parliament and a government whose key members were also leaders of the FRELIMO party, and an economic plan with modest aims of two parts:

One is aimed at organizing and stimulating production of essential goods and ensuring their distribution, guaranteeing the production targets in strategic sectors, keeping the balance of payments under control and defining an adequate investment program.

The other is the central program for the activities of the state apparatus . . . to ensure that tasks are clearly defined and that the state apparatus becomes increasingly geared to the productive process . . .[3]

On December 19, 1977, Marcelino dos Santos, speaking in his capacity as Minister for Development and Economic Planning, summed up the government's attitude to economic development as: "We direct the state enterprises, we support the cooperative sector, we control the private sector." He was speaking in Tete province to announce that the Cabora Bassa hydroelectric concession and the Moatize coal mines—though remaining in private hands—would come under government control. Cabora Bassa started supplying electric power to South Africa on a regular commercial basis in April, 1977.

Huge problems but also great accomplishments. If the road ahead looked rough as 1978 loomed over the horizon, the FRELIMO leadership and the people of Mozambique could have confidence in the future by looking over their shoulders at the road travelled since FRELIMO was formed on June 25, 1962.

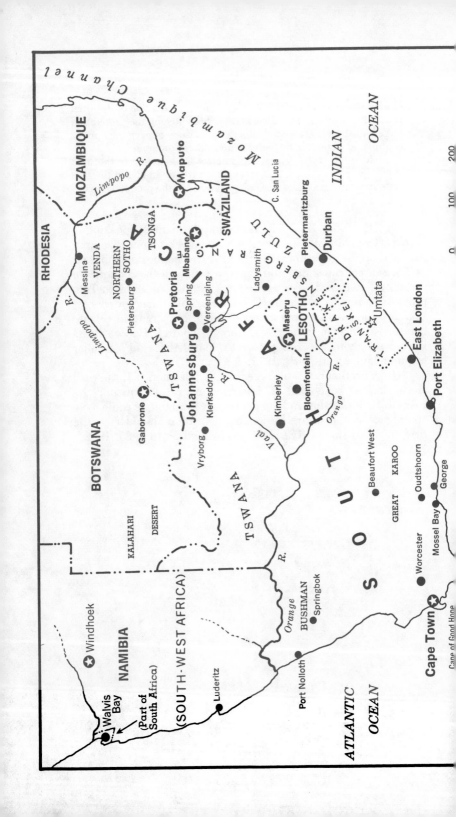

PART III

Zimbabwe (Rhodesia), Namibia and South Africa

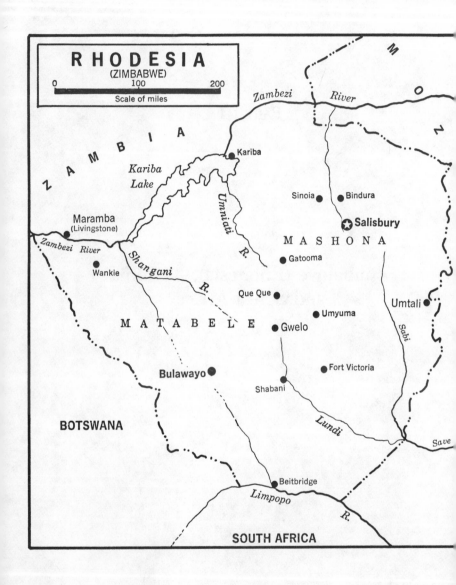

XVIII Struggle in Zimbabwe (Rhodesia)

"If we win first, our territory will be a rear base for you," said a young Zimbabwe military cadre fighting with FRELIMO guerillas in Tete province. "And if we win first," replied a FRELIMO cadre, "you can be sure that our territory will be your base." That was in 1969, and it would have been a bold man who predicted the overthrow of Portuguese fascism five years later, or that FRELIMO would be the first to win. The odds were that Ian Smith's racist government in Rhodesia would be the first to collapse. The young Zimbabwan was Josiah Tongogara, later General Tongogara, commander of the main resistance forces inside Zimbabwe.

I met him a few days after he had been released from a Zambian jail to join the ZANU-ZAPU Patriotic Front delegation to the Geneva Conference on Rhodesia (October 28-December 14, 1976).[1] Many of the veterans of armed struggle in Zimbabwe served their apprenticeship with FRELIMO forces in Tete province from 1968 onward. If the 1960s was the decade in which Britain's African colonies got their independence, the late 1950s had been a period of feverish political agitation to ensure that this came about. Among those agitating in Rhodesia from 1957 onward was young Tongogara.

> On February 29, 1959, the South Rhodesian African National Congress was banned. Under "Operation Dawn" the police made a sudden swoop and about 500 national, provincial, and district branch leaders were arrested. I managed to skip across the frontier into Zambia, where, on January 1, 1960, the National Democratic Party [NDP] was formed. I immediately joined up. In October of that year Joshua Nkomo was elected NDP president. The party quickly attracted nationalist forces formerly associated with the banned ANC, but it was in turn banned in December, 1962, when the Rhodesian Front party [later to be headed by Ian Smith] came to power and confiscated all funds and material assets. As a substitute, the Zimbabwan African People's Union [ZAPU] was immediately formed, again under the leadership of Joshua Nkomo, who at that time could operate legally in what was then Southern Rhodesia. I became a district chairman of ZAPU in Zambia.
>
> The following year ZAPU was also banned. Nkomo and the whole national executive fled the country.

At the time of which Josiah Tongogara was speaking the all-Rhodesian-Nyasaland Federation was very much a subject of the day. In 1962, the British government granted new constitutions which would ensure black majority rule to Northern Rhodesia and Nyasaland (later Malawi). It was becoming increasingly clear that Southern Rhodesia was intent on going its own way with the tacit support of elements within the British Conservative Party government. On August 8, 1963, there was a split within ZAPU. Those pressing for more vigorous action—including armed struggle—formed the Zimbabwan National Union (ZANU), headed by the Reverend Ndabaningi Sithole.[2] Its more militant program attracted young activists like Tongogara.

In 1964, I became provincial secretary of ZANU and the following year I went to Tanzania for military training. On November 11 of 1965, Ian Smith made his Unilateral Declaration of Independence, confirming indefinite racist minority rule—and our worst suspicions. In 1966, I left for advanced military training in Nanking where the Chinese comrades gave special courses in guerilla training with elements of classical warfare. Returning at the end of that year, I became chief of the Intelligence Section of the ZANU Revolutionary Council—our military planning body.

Between 1967-73, I was in charge of all military operations [directing them from 1968 onward from areas inside Zimbabwe but with easy access to a rear base in Tete province in Mozambique]. In 1973, I was appointed ZANU Chief of Defense, charged with executing overall military strategy. This task I performed until being arrested during a visit to Zambia in March, 1975, and again after my release in late October, 1976.

I asked about the Zimbabwan People's Army (ZIPA)—when and why it was formed? Outsiders who followed the Rhodesian-Zimbabwe scene had been intrigued in early 1976 by the emergence of ZIPA and a "Committee of Eighteen" which did not appear to claim allegiance to any of the known nationalist parties.

When I and the others were arrested in Zambia, there was no ZANU leadership left. After consultations which the Zambian authorities, under pressure from Tanzania and Mozambique, allowed to take place even in our place of detention, we agreed to unite the armed forces of ZANU and ZAPU to form ZIPA, under the joint direction of a committee to which each side would contribute nine members.

As to whether the fact that ZAPU military cadres tended to be trained in the Soviet Union while those of ZANU were trained in China—Tongagara himself had been back to Nanking for two refresher courses since his 1966 visit—did not pose a problem, he replied:

> This is not a big problem. Of course cadres trained in China hear plenty of adverse criticism of "revisionism" and "social imperialism"; those trained in the Soviet Union hear the same sort of things about "Maoism." But we ensure that on their return they go through a recycling and are oriented to Zimbabwe problems, to our struggle. We do not permit dissensions between others to influence our problems. We have enough of our own. At the end of a course, the Chinese usually say: "Well, we've taught you what we know. Now it's up to you to go back and apply what you have learned to your own conditions. This is the line we follow."

The development of military activities followed the course of events in the neighboring countries. Thus Zambia became independent on October 24, 1964, and, after a period of consolidation, President Kenneth Kaunda permitted the Zimbabwe guerillas to use operational and training bases inside Zambia. Thus the first armed action took place in 1966 across the Zambian border in northwestern Zimbabwe. As the FRELIMO extended their struggle into Tete province in 1968, a new base area became available there and a new front was opened up in the northeast. From then on new fronts opened up in a clockwise direction according to the battlefield fortunes of FRELIMO, the guerillas attacking from the east as FRELIMO's liberated areas expanded south, from the southeast when Mozambique attained full independence and, finally, from the southwest and west when Botswana threw in its lot with the "front-line" states (Mozambique, Zambia, Tanzania, Angola, and then Botswana) and allowed the Zimbabwe freedom fighters to install bases and sanctuaries. It took some ten years from the firing of the first shots for guerilla activity—some of it still at a very low level—to be engaged in virtually the whole perimeter area. As is inevitably the case when it comes to the crucial decision of to fight or not to fight, there are those who hesitate and draw back at the last moment.

There were plenty of sincere nationalists who reasoned that Britain, after all, was not a fascist state like Portugal. A democracy with a free press, it had yielded to outside and internal pressures to grant independence to sixteen of its seventeen African colonies. Even though Britain had no inhibitions about jailing the new leaders for "terrorist activities," the pace for demanding independence quickened! Hastings Banda of Malawi, Kwame Nkrumah of Ghana, Jomo Kenyatta of Kenya, and Kenneth Kaunda of Zambia had all tasted the bitter fruits of British colonial prisons; Sir Seretse Khama of Botswana had spent long years in exile. But in the end, independence had come about by constitutional means. Why not so in Southern Rhodesia? The banning of the South Rhodesian African National Congress acted as a catalyst for many nationalist leaders. Among them the Reverend Ndabaningi Sithole, who also turned up at the Geneva Conference claiming to represent ZANU, although he had been replaced as president by Robert Mugabe. His name, however, has its place in the history of the nationalist struggle. He described the banning of the ANC as:

> My biggest shock. . . . Over 500 national and local leaders were whisked away from their homes to jail where they were detained, some for a few months, others for many months, and still others restricted for four years. I had had great hopes for the ANC. I had been in the process of setting up branches in Chipinga district. But now the whole thing dried up in my hands. . . . The excuse given for the ban was that the ANC had a plot to kill white people in Rhodesia. Nothing could have been more incredible to me. . . . One thing that remained clear to me was that the white man was simply determined to destroy the African nationalist movement. The white man was simply determined to see white supremacy in the saddle for all time.[3]

Sithole joined the National Democratic Party as soon as it was formed and was elected its treasurer-general, which led to his being sacked by the Ministry of Education from his job as head teacher of a primary school. When the NDP was banned and ZAPU formed, he became its national chairman with Joshua Nkomo as interim president. Later, he, Joshua Nkomo, Robert Mugabe, and others were sentenced to one year in jail, followed by five more years in "detention"—covering 1964 to 1970. It was while they were in "detention" that what they had most feared and most agitated against took place—Ian Smith's Unilateral Declaration of Independence.

210

How was Ian Smith able to get away with this, in the face of British denunciation of Salisbury as a "rebel regime," the imposition of United Nations economic sanctions and other measures to isolate Southern Rhodesia from the international community? What did the Ian Smith regime have that the other sixteen British colonies, territories, and protectorates in Africa which received their independence in the 1960s did not have? The answer perhaps is chrome, that precious metal so vital for modern industry and of which Zimbabwe possesses so high a proportion of the world's known reserves. There seems to have been great reluctance on the part of Britain to take the decisive steps which would permit those reserves to fall into black hands. When the issue of making complete economic sanctions against Rhodesia mandatory was brought to the United Nations on March 17, 1970, both Britain and the United States used their vetos to nullify the resolution. The United States even violated UN resolutions by continuing under the Byrd amendment to import chrome from the rebel regime, thus greatly weakening the effect of sanctions.

The United States had divided the world up into three main sectors according to strategic raw materials which either did not exist in the industrialized northern hemisphere, or existed in insufficient quantities: Latin America, Africa, and Southeast Asia. The raw materials included copper, bauxite, cobalt, chrome, manganese, and tin. The implication was that these areas must not be permitted to fall into "non-Free World" hands. Ian Smith was not slow to pick up the cue. He was the champion of the "Free World" in Rhodesia, barring the way to "Communism," defending the "values of Christian civilization," and (in private discussions) protecting the world's richest stockpile of chrome! Only this explains the tenderness with which he was handled by Britain, which had not hesitated to send troops to put down left-wing guerillas in Malaysia (where tin was in danger) or against the "Mau Mau" in Kenya. But there was never any question of strong-arm methods against the rebel Smith regime, which at most represented some 280,000 whites as opposed to over 6 million blacks.

The result of Britain's "soft" handling of the Smith regime brought about the opposite results to those intended. It persuaded even those who could be considered "moderates," like the Reverend Sithole and Bishop Muzorewa, who headed the African National Council (temporarily set up as a legal "umbrella" under which ZAPU and ZANU could maintain contacts within Zimbabwe), that armed struggle was the only possible means of attaining independence. But however much the "moderates" verbally supported armed struggle and used the threat of it to improve their bargaining position, they were not men to go into the bush and endure the hard, dangerous life of guerilla warfare. It was only dedicated, ideologically motivated cadres who could do that. It was the old, old story of the West—and certainly the United States was deeply involved in Britain's handling of the Rhodesia situation—rejecting solutions most favorable to their interests in the hope they could pull off some better deal later on. The result was an inevitable radicalization of the struggle. The victories in Indochina, then in Angola and Mozambique, convinced Zimbabwe patriots that not only was armed struggle the only road, but that victory lay at the end of that road, even though it might be long.

While traditional nationalist leaders discussed matters among themselves—and at times with the Smith regime—and others languished in jails in Zimbabwe and even in Zambia, a younger generation pushed ahead with the armed struggle. Among these was Dzinashe Machingura, a former biochemistry student, now Deputy Political Commissar of ZIPA and one of the leading strategists of the armed struggle. He was twenty-eight years of age when he arrived for the final stage of the Geneva talks, straight from the battlefield, to reinforce the position of the Patriotic Front delegation. In a long discussion with the author which included many comparisons between the struggle in Zimbabwe and that in Vietnam—about which he was well informed—Dzinashe Machingura made the following points:

The Geneva Conference came about as the direct result of armed struggle. We have to intensify that struggle. We are no longer just fighting for majority rule but for real national independence and the transfer of power to the Zimbabwan people. From the beginning of this year [1976] we stepped up our military activities, first by infiltrating small armed units equipped with only rifles and submachine guns. But as the fighting progressed we employed bigger units of platoon- and then company-size, equipped with better and heavier weapons.

This was possible because we have the support of the mass of our people. All factors indicate that we are heading for ever-greater

212

victories. In fact we are now preparing to go over to the strategic offensive. We have reached the point where we no longer speak of "support from the masses" but of their actual participation in armed struggle.

Smith reacted to the growing support for armed struggle as minority regimes have always acted under such circumstances. On the pretext of "protecting" the villagers from "terrorists," they were to be herded into glorified concentration camps known as "protected villages." There have been "freedom villages" in Malaysia, "strategic hamlets" in Vietnam, *aldeamentos* (rural settlements) in Angola and Mozambique—all with the same objective of separating the guerilla "fish" from the "water" in which they swim. At the same time the death penalty was introduced for anyone actively aiding the freedom fighters with food or information, or passively aiding them by not reporting their presence to the nearest authorities. By mid-1976 about 500,000 of the 3,500,000 blacks living in the Tribal Trust Lands (that half of the territory which was allotted to black farmers) were locked up inside "protected villages."

A Dutch journalist, by pretending he was something else, managed to get inside some of the "protected villages" and, when we met in Mozambique, he gave me the following picture:

People from ten to twenty villages of the same ethnic grouping are concentrated in one big "protected village." Houses are huddled together and grouped around a raised watchtower. This is manned day and night by guards from the Rhodesian security forces armed with automatic rifles. There is a dusk-to-dawn curfew and any stragglers are shot on sight. The whole area is surrounded by electrified barbed wire. Electricity is used for two purposes only. To power a searchlight in the watchtower, and for the barbed wire. There are two entrance-exits and everyone is searched on entering and leaving. Overnight absences are noted and unless an absentee can give a good and authenticated reason, his name automatically goes on the black suspect list. If the villagers show too much nostalgia for their old villages and try to return, these are burned to the ground. In one "protected village" a truck with its tailgate down drove slowly through the streets with the "bag" of the previous night's curfew-breakers—half a dozen black bodies.

Obviously as in Vietnam, this also had the opposite of the intended effect. A tug-of-war started, the guerillas helping the villagers to break out, the security forces trying to round them up again. But Smith's forces were too thinly spread to keep this up for long. Kumbirai Kangai, a member of the ZANU Central Committee who also came to Geneva with the "reinforcing delegation" toward the end of the conference, said that Smith had stopped building any more "protected villages"; that they had proved the most "fertile soil" for recruiting guerilla fighters and that many of them had been "heavily infiltrated by freedom fighters." In the sparsely populated western part of the country, "protected villages" no longer existed. Smith was concentrating his efforts in the more densely populated eastern areas.

It was the failure of the "protected village" scheme which paved the way for an apparent spectacular retreat by Ian Smith. His regime in 1970 had divided the country's 97.5 million acres of land "equally" between white settlers and the black Zimbabwans. After deducting 7.5 million acres for national park land, this left 45 million acres of the best land for the 280,000 whites and 45 million acres of the poorer land for the over six million blacks. On March 1, 1977, Smith's Minister of Land and Natural Resources, Mark Partridge, introduced a bill to reduce the proportion of land set aside for the whites to a mere 500,000 acres. Twelve members of Smith's Rhodesian Front—including the powerful Deputy Prime Minister, Mr. Ted Sutton-Pryce, promptly said they would vote against the bill and were expelled from the Parliamentary Caucus. Coming on top of the removal of some of the racial discrimination measures in bars and restaurants, it was too much for the old guard to stomach. "We must move with the times. Let us do so cheerfully and intelligently, and with good hope for the future," said Mr. Partridge bravely, in introducing the bill. To the "ultras" who claimed the government was violating the very principles on which unilateral independence was based, Ian Smith replied: "In the abnormal times in which we live, party principles need updating from time to time."[4] He could not have paid a more flattering tribute to the success of the freedom fighters. Nor to the failure, one after another, of the various measures his regime had taken to try to stave off the inevitable. In this connection, I asked Dzinashe Machingura what success Smith was having with the 3,500 black

214

troops, by then mobilized into his armed forces and being increased.

> Smith no longer trusts them. All main operations are now carried out by white troops under white commanders. We have managed to win the support of most of the black troops. They contact us. Sometimes we encourage them to desert, but in some cases we tell them to stay where they are for the time being. They are well placed to tell us of enemy movements.

The ANC had obviously been a temporary makeshift to provide some representation in Salisbury. Its president, Bishop Abel Muzorewa, had never been in serious trouble with the Smith authorities but could not be involved in directing military activities. Therefore I asked Machingura whether ZIPA was intended to replace the ANC.

> Once the fighters realized the incompetence of the ANC leadership in supporting armed struggle, they decided to organize themselves, to reconstitute themselves into an army that would fight for the independence of the Zimbabwe people. The combatants from both former ZANU and ZAPU [both were supposed to have dissolved their organizations when the ANC was formed in December, 1974] agreed to form a joint military command that would lead the armed struggle. After agreeing on this, they approached the Liberation Committee of the Organization of African Unity and the front-line heads of state, who recognized and actively supported this joint command. The latter was set up on the understanding that the liberation of Zimbabwe could only be achieved through hard and protracted armed struggle. Also we agreed that the traditional leadership of the Zimbabwan independence movements had divided the people. If we were going to successfully prosecute armed struggle we could not be a party to either of the two rival ANC factions—the Muzorewa faction or the Nkomo faction. We realized that the time for personality politics had long passed. It was this approach which had divided the Zimbabwe people.

In answer to my question as to whether ZIPA should be regarded as exclusively a fighting force under the guidance of an overall political body, or whether it combined political and military functions, Dzinashe Machingura referred me to a fundamental interview he had given to the Mozambique news agency, AIM, on September 22, 1976.

> ZIPA is an army in the traditional sense of the word. But it is a unique and revolutionary army in the sense that it has a strategic role of transforming itself into a political movement. The ZIPA structure accommodates the shouldering of both the military and the political tasks of the revolution. We have a political department exclusively charged with the responsibility of shouldering the political tasks that are normally handled by a revolutionary political organization. . . .
>
> But we have to establish a formal political structure in order to give better political direction to the armed body which is now fighting inside Zimbabwe. Moves to do this are already well under way, moves to transform this organization into a revolutionary vanguard for the people's struggle.

This reply had been given before the setting-up of the formation of the Patriotic Front, formed at the urging of the front-line heads of state on the eve of the Geneva Conference, so that ZANU and ZAPU delegates would speak with one voice. Joint presidents of the Patriotic Front were Robert Mugabe, as head of ZANU, and Joshua Nkomo, head of ZAPU.[1] I asked whether this was now the "revolutionary vanguard" to which Machingura had referred.

> Many thought that the emergence of the Patriotic Front just before the Geneva Conference was a tactical move. In fact we would like to develop it into a wider front, into the basis for a National United Front. ZANU and ZAPU are the two main national liberation groups. Now that they have come together from a political viewpoint they have become the nucleus for a future United Front.

As Machingura later appeared at a press conference given in the name of the Patriotic Front, together with ZANU and ZAPU representatives, it appeared that the process of transforming the Patriotic Front into a political umbrella organization under which ZIPA would operate was developing quickly. One of the positive aspects of the Geneva Conference was that it provided a forum (or at least corridors) where ZANU and ZAPU leaders, fresh from exile, from prison, and from the battlefield, could meet for the first time in many years and hammer out new policies, forge new unity. I asked whether there were already stable liberated zones in Zimbabwe.

At this stage we speak of "semi-liberated zones." These are areas over which the enemy has no control whatsoever. Of course he can parachute some troops in and evacuate them by helicopters but he no longer tries to move in over the roads. Our political and administrative structures are not yet fully developed in these zones but the masses are fully mobilized and completely support our freedom fighters, themselves taking part in armed activities. If we announce fully liberated zones, it would present the enemy with a pretext to bomb and strafe any form of life in those areas. They already use this pretext to bomb Zimbabwe refugee camps inside Mozambique.

I asked how Dzinashe Machingura evaluated such attacks. Was Ian Smith's intelligence so faulty that he really believed the refugee camp at Nyazonia—confirmed as such by the UN representative at Maputo—was a guerilla training camp? (A total of 670 refugees had been killed in the attack.) Were the repeated thrusts into Mozambique really directed at Zimbabwe guerilla bases or at "punishing" Mozambique for its forthright and unabashed support for ZIPA and the Patriotic Front? And what was the truth behind Smith's claims of guerilla "terrorist" attacks against the African population, the murder of white clergymen, and similar reports?

One of Smith's desperate last hopes is that he can internationalize the conflict. These two questions are: (1) A ten-member co-ordinating committee was set up in January, 1977, to unify ZAPU-ZANU, with Joshua Nkomo and Robert Mugabe both members. Jason Moyo, charged with setting up the committee and who played a key role in the preparatory work was killed by a . . . letter bomb on January 22, just after the first phase of the unity talks ended. Agreement was reached that the common aims of the struggle were the destruction of colonialism, imperialism, racism, and capitalism as the first step towards building a democratic state. Long term aims envisaged the construction of a scientific socialist society. Further talks aimed at complete fusion of the two movements were scheduled and postponed several times, but finally got under way in Maputo on November 17, 1977. . . . The Smith racists hoped that FRELIMO would react to the first big attacks by a counterattack into Rhodesia. They would then have cried "Communist aggression," hoping the West would come to the rescue. This did not happen so new tactics were tried. A series of hard hit-and-run raids deep into Mozambique territory, aimed not at our bases but at strictly civilian targets in flagrant violation of Mozambique's sovereignty. These they hoped would force Mozambique to ask for Cuban and Soviet help. This would have given Smith the pretext to ask for U.S. help which, after his discussions with Kissinger, he seemed confident he could expect as long as the pretext was solidly enough founded.

Such attacks were also meant to show that to support the Zimbabwan freedom fighters and look after Zimbabwan refugees was to invite attacks by Smith's armed forces. The hope was that the People's Republic would cease its support for our guerillas because it would lose any all-out war with Rhodesia. On the second question, since the Smith regime brands us as terrorists, they have to produce something to justify this definition. We are a people's army, not terrorists. Civilians are not targets of our attacks, but the Smith regime has organized commando groups, known as the Selous Scouts, who masquerade as freedom fighters to carry out atrocities intended to discredit us at home and prepare the climate abroad to internationalize the war and stamp out "Communist terrorism." These commando terrorist actions are quite widespread, but not so much in the semi-liberated zones where we are in control and people can easily distinguish between our real freedom fighters and the bogus ones sent in by Ian Smith.

Two months after this conversation an article by David Ottaway, datelined Maputo, appeared in the *Washington Post.* It was headlined: "Rhodesian Raids May Press Mozambique to Ask Soviet Aid." The opening paragraph stated:

Western diplomats here are openly warning that the continuing forays by the Rhodesian army deep inside Mozambican territory may soon cause President Samora Machel to seek substantial Soviet and Cuban assistance to bolster this country's meager defenses. "We may see this happening much sooner than we think," a diplomat said. Some diplomats are convinced that one of the prime aims of the white-minority Rhodesian government in carrying out repeated incursions is to provoke Mr. Machel into calling for help from Cuba and the Soviet Union to strengthen Rhodesia's own bid for overt South African and U.S. backing.

The involvement of South Africa and the superpowers would have the effect of turning the struggle between whites and blacks in Rhodesia into an open East-West confrontation that could give a new lease on life to the besieged government of Prime Minister Ian Smith.[5]

The David Ottaway report also refers to "incursions by special white and black commando" units which had taken a heavy toll of lives. In this connection there was an interesting document found among the personal effects of Gustavo Marcelo Grillo, one of four American mercenaries captured in Angola, who was tried together with three other Americans and nine British in Luanda in June, 1976. Grillo was sentenced to thirty years imprisonment. The document was in the form of a circular/letter from a certain David Bufkin, a leading recruiter of mercenaries in the United States. For mercenary eyes only, the letter warned that money for Angolan operations had dried up but that Rhodesia offered good prospects. Bufkin listed the four main branches of the Rhodesian armed forces as the Regular Army, the Special Air Service (which he likened to the Green Beret special forces in the United States), the Depot Police, and a fourth group, "currently unidentified," but which Bufkin said you could only enter after having graduated through the S.A.S. "They paint themselves black, speak the language, and actually filter into the terrorist camps."

It is not too far-fetched to believe that as Machingura and other ZANU-ZAPU leaders—including Robert Mugabe and Joshua Nkomo—asserted, it was these commandos who were carrying out the indiscriminate murders. One of the attacks in which three missionaries were murdered occurred shortly after the Most Reverend Donal Lamont, Roman Catholic Bishop of Umtali near the Rhodesian-Mozambique border, was sentenced to ten years in jail for having failed to report the presence of guerillas in his episcopate and of having encouraged others to do the same. In general, as Mugabe and Nkomo pointed out, the freedom fighters had correct relations with the various religious denominations, the leaders of which frequently denounced the atrocities and iniquities of the racist regime in Salisbury. "It is the Smith regime which treats such people as enemies, not us," said Machingura.[6]

This brought us to the question of who the real enemy is. That the Smith regime was the immediate enemy was clear. But would its disappearance achieve the aims for which ZIPA and the Patriotic Front were fighting? Machingura again referred me to his AIM interview:

Our society is essentially a colonial society and, as such, we have to wage a national democratic struggle to overthrow national oppression. The national democratic resolution will serve to solve the principal contradiction in Zimbabwe, which is the domination and oppression of the vast majority of the Zimbabwan people by a small minority—a racist, reactionary clique of whites.

All those who are opposed to the liberation and independence of the Zimbabwan people are our enemies. These include the Smith racist regime, the imperialist powers that back it, puppet Africans serving the Smith regime, and all those who are opposed to the independence of the Zimbabwan people. The target of the bullets of our freedom fighters is the system of exploitation and capitalist enterprises and the armed personnel which serve to perpetuate them.

Dźinashe Machingura explained that ZIPA was already an army of several thousands and could quickly be expanded into double that size. Many hundreds had deserted from the Smith army but only a few had been able to bring weapons with them. "Some governments find it a burden to support an army only half the size of ours," he said. "We can maintain such an army because of the mass support from our people. We get food and clothing and, short of arms and ammunition, everything we need from the people. The only factor inhibiting rapid expansion of the armed forces is lack of arms."

The guerilla forces continued to expand rapidly throughout 1977, nourished by a movement away from the "protected areas." David Martin of the London *Observer* reported from Francistown in Botswana, on May 29, 1977, that African refugees were fleeing into Botswana at the rate of 800 per week. One third of them were between sixteen and twenty-five years, many of this age group demanding to join the guerillas. 12,000 such refugees had been airlifted out to Zambia during the first five months of 1977. From there, those who want to take up arms are sent to training camps, in Zambia if they are pro-ZAPU, or to Tanzania if they are pro-ZANU. In fact, as Martin pointed out, most of those coming to Botswana are from Matabeleland, just across the frontier and from where Joshua Nkomo draws his main support. A people of great warrior traditions, the young men were a precious source of recruitment for ZAPU during 1977 as Nkomo tried to increase his forces to make them numerically comparable with those of ZANU. Just prior to Martin's visit to Francistown, where the main refugee camp is situated about fifteen kilometers inside Botswana, seven Selous Scouts had infiltrated the camp and were arrested.

By mid-May, 1977, Robert Mugabe stated that ZIPA fighters were operating in over two-thirds of Zimbabwe and were fast expanding in both scope and intensity. This was confirmed in the guarded communiqués from Salisbury and by the introduction of stringent censorship of foreign correspondents' despatches in the third quarter of 1977. Even before total censorship was introduced, authentic battlefield news was almost impossible to obtain or communicate. The Australian journalist, Bruce Palling, described the situation as it was when he left Salisbury in mid-June:

> Rhodesian authorities are tightening their grip to a strangle hold over the western news correspondents trying to cover the growing guerilla war. Since UDI (Unilateral Declaration of Independence) in 1965, at least seventy correspondents have been expelled or prohibited, but lately the pressure has been intensifying to keep news reports firmly on the government side.
>
> The most effective weapon the authorities have are the tough new regulations that journalists have to sign in order to become accredited defense correspondents. At present, the Information Ministry in Salisbury grants facility trips to individual correspondents to visit the "operational area," which is, in fact, the entire countryside. In such cases, correspondents are expected to submit their reports to the Combined Operations Headquarters for censorship. Under the new scheme, the only foreign journalists based in Salisbury who will be eligible for military accreditation are those who have taken up Rhodesian residence—not a tempting course of action when all residents must do military service after two years in the country . . ."[7]

Bruce Palling states that in the four and a half years prior to his despatch, "only one correspondent has managed to witness a clash between the guerillas and the Rhodesian security forces." He also cites the case of a British-born Rhodesian journalist, representing a London newspaper, who had gone "underground" to avoid being conscripted into Smith's armed forces. For an example of the ideal type of foreign correspondent from Smith's viewpoint and how the newspaper-reading public gets its news on Rhodesia, there is a fascinating piece by British journalist Chris Mullin:

As it was in Vietnam, so it is in Rhodesia. Meikles Hotel [Salisbury] has now replaced the Continental Palace [Saigon] as the center of action. Rhodesian whites have now replaced Americans as the authors of neatly typed press handouts, laying on the occasional out-of-town junket. If anything the situation in Rhodesia is worse than that in Vietnam. For a start there are far less correspondents. Few readers of the *Daily Telegraph* will, for example, have realized that the paper's Salisbury stringer—Brian Henry—is the same as the *Daily Mail's* Peter Norman who is the same person as the *Guardian's* Henry Miller. And that all these people are in real life called Ian Mills who, as it happens, is also the BBC correspondent.

There is no suggestion that Mills is anything other than a very competent reporter. It's just that he's so busy keeping all his different outlets supplied that he simply doesn't have time for any inquiring journalism. The most he can do is to take whatever handouts are available from all sides and faithfully transmit them to his various outlets with whatever comment he can garner from his various sources over the telephone . . . [8]

An insight into the harsh reality of the situation in Rhodesia appeared in October, 1977, when Finance Minister David Smith announced that the Rhodesian dollar was to be devalued by three per cent against the South African Rand and six per cent against other currencies. Explaining the reason the Standard Bank of Rhodesia and its economic bulletin issued on October 13 stated:

There is a clear limit to the economy's ability to withstand the pressures to which it is now being subjected, with fifteen per cent of the Gross Domestic Product being devoted to the shooting and economic wars . . . Over the past year the damage to the economy has switched from being temporary in character to permanent and structural in nature . . .

By that time the war was costing almost one million U.S. dollars per day, according to the bulletin. The Gross Domestic Product would fall by seven per cent in 1977, instead of an earlier estimate by the same bank of a drop of five per cent, and in the first seven months of 1977, manufacturing production had shrunk by 5.7 per cent. Capital investment which had fallen by almost 19 per cent in 1976 was expected to fall further in 1977. Another reason cited for decreasing production was "the exodus of skilled Europeans fleeing a military and political situation which they could no longer tolerate . . ." Amongst the signs of the time quoted by the Zambia *Daily Mail*, commenting on the devaluation, its October 14 issue noted that: "One of Salisbury's biggest and newest department stores, MacKay's opened only sixteen months ago at a cost of 800,000 U.S. dollars, announced it will close after Christmas."

More than anything that the foreign correspondents were *not* allowed to report, the bulletin of the Standard Bank represented the grim shadow of events to come, the total collapse of the Smith regime. The picture it painted was completed by the statistics of rapidly increased departures over arrivals o Europeans. In the first eight months of 1977, 11,685 Europeans left the country and 3,972 had arrived which would mean a net loss of over 9,000 by the end of the year. Those who leave are those with the skills; those who arrived are the unskilled who would find it difficult to make a start in life anywhere else but in a country so desperate for European replacements as is Rhodesia. Many of them are Portuguese bitter at having lost their privileged status in the former Portuguese colonies. Their asset to Smith is that they lust after revenge by indiscriminate torture and killing of the blacks. But having lost out in their own colonies, Smith knows it is an illusion that they can make any real contribution to shoring up his condemned regime.

Chapter XIX The Geneva Conference

For the first time in thirty-seven years of reporting, including covering innumerable international conferences, I wrote a gloomy first dispatch predicting the failure of a conference before it had even started. I am normally an optimist on such matters, and used to the protracted ups and downs of negotiations such as those at Panmunjom to settle the Korean war (two years), the 1954 Geneva Conference on Indochina (three months), the Paris Peace Conference on Vietnam (four and a half years). But after having visited all the delegations before the Conference on Rhodesia started in Geneva on October 28, 1976, I wrote:

> The Zimbabwan liberation movement is relying on victory through its widening armed struggle and not the conference on black majority rule set to open here October 28. The British-sponsored negotiation effort will almost certainly fail. Its very agenda is beset with irreconcilable differences between the position of the racist Ian Smith regime and the joint Patriotic Front delegation headed by Robert Mugabe of the Zimbabwe African National Union and Joseph Nkomo of the Zimbabwe African People's Union. The Patriotic Front is negotiating in Geneva on behalf of the Zimbabwe People's Army, which is waging a guerilla war against the white settler regime in Salisbury. . . . The rock upon which the Geneva Conference appears about to crash is the "Kissinger Plan," the "package deal" product of the Secretary of State's September shuttle diplomacy efforts. Rhodesian Prime Minister Ian Smith says he bought the entire package, which he insists Kissinger assured him had been approved by the five front-line presidents.
>
> Smith asserts he is at the Geneva Conference only to implement the Kissinger deal, a blatant neocolonial scheme in which the armed power of the state would remain in the hands of the white minority. The fact that the front-line presidents (of Mozambique, Angola, Tanzania, Zambia, and Botswana) have jointly repudiated the plan, which also calls for an immediate end to armed struggle and lifting of international sanctions against Rhodesia, is attributed by Smith to a Kissinger double cross.[1]

At that time we did not know that the front-line presidents had not even seen the Kissinger plan but had been vaguely informed that the great shuttler had succeeded in persuading Smith to accept majority rule.

224

Soon after the conference started, Smith's foreign minister (and former defense minister) Pieter Van der Byl called in the press to present photos of dead and mutilated Africans as "proof" of terrorist atrocities. A big man with an oversize head and steely blue eyes, Van der Byl was soon ill at ease under a barrage of sharp questions. The sharpest was also the shortest: "Does majority rule mean one man, one vote?"

"No," snapped Van der Byl. "We stand for responsible majority rule." He refused to define this on the grounds that it might be a negotiable matter at the conference. But in the Rhodesian press room next door there was ample literature on that and related subjects.

"Responsible majority" as in force at the time the Geneva Conference started meant that Europeans, coloreds, and Asians must prove they earned an annual average of 2,772 U.S. dollars (in the Rhodesian dollar equivalent) and owned property worth 5,544 U.S. dollars. They must have completed not less than four years of secondary education. Africans must prove they earned an annual average of 924 dollars, owned property worth 848 dollars, and had completed not less than two years of secondary education "of prescribed standard." The House of Assembly—according to the Constitutional Act approved by Ian Smith's parliament on November 17, 1969—consisted of sixty-six members, of whom fifty Europeans represented their 280,000 of the population and sixteen Africans represented their 6,000,000. Only eight of the sixteen were directly elected, the remaining half to be nominated by "electoral colleges" comprised of "chiefs, headmen, and elected councillors of the African Councils in the Tribal Trust Lands in Mashonaland and Matabeleland respectively. . . ." A very original concept of "responsible majority rule." The upper house, or Senate, was comprised of twenty-three members, ten Europeans elected by the European members of the House of Assembly and ten African chiefs, chosen by an electoral college consisting of members of the Council of Chiefs. Five of these African Senators are chiefs in Matabeleland and five are chiefs in Mashonaland. What could be fairer? Numerical equality between white and black senators, and between black senators from the two predominant tribal groupings! But just in case the balance did not work, the president was empowered to appoint the remaining three Senators "acting on the advice of the Cabinet and they may be of any race."

There was no evidence throughout the Geneva Conference that Mr. Smith had departed from this original concept as to how majority rule could be exercised. In a three-paragraph statement on the first working day of the conference, Ian Smith devoted the first two paragraphs to "commiserating" with British Chairman Ivor Richard and the British government after all it had done "not only in Rhodesia but in many other parts of the world in spreading Christian civilization" for the "insults" of the nationalist speakers who had preceded Mr. Smith with their opening statements. In the third, he stated that the previous month he had announced his government's "acceptance of the joint Anglo-American proposals to settle the constitutional future of Rhodesia which were put to us by the American Secretary of State. The proposals provide for an early meeting between government representatives and Rhodesian Africans to determine the membership of the Council of State as the first step in establishing the interim government. . . ." Work on this, he indicated, should start immediately.

From the beginning to the end of the Geneva Conference the exact contents of the "joint Anglo-American proposals," and the Kissinger "package deal," were never disclosed. The conference got bogged down trying to decide whether "majority rule" would come into force in two years, as Ian Smith maintained Kissinger had proposed, or in a far shorter period, as the nationalist leaders demanded. Never had Kissinger's wizardry in the art of ambiguity and his ability to be "all things to all men" been used to greater effect in sowing bewilderment among all involved. This is how Ian Smith in a nationwide address September 24, 1976, presented the results of having been shuttled by Kissinger following the final Kissinger-Vorster-Smith meeting in Pretoria. After referring to the series of meetings and asserting that "pressures on us from the 'Free World' would continue to mount" to introduce "majority rule," Smith continued:

Dr. Kissinger assured me that we share a common aim and a common purpose, namely to keep Rhodesia in the Free World and to keep it free from Communist penetration. In this regard, of course, Rhodesia is in a key position in southern Africa. What happens here will inevitably affect the entire subcontinent. . . .

Before I spell out these proposals in detail there are some general comments I should make. The proposals represent what, in negotiating parlance, is usually called a "package deal"—which means that some aspects are more readily acceptable than others. First, on the positive side, as soon as the necessary preliminaries have been carried out, sanctions will be lifted and there will be a cessation of terrorism. Dr. Kissinger has given me a categorical assurance to this effect and my acceptance of the proposals is conditional upon the implementation of both of these undertakings. In the light of previous experience there will be some understandable skepticism regarding the undertaking that terrorism will cease, but on this occasion the assurance is given, not only on the authority of the United States government, but of the British government as well. . . .

Kissinger had had no contact whatsoever with those who directed battlefield operations, nor had he received any such assurances from the front-line heads of state; and the British government mumbled and bumbled to the effect that it had given no such assurances. Kissinger had absolutely no mandate to speak for the United Nations, which had imposed sanctions, but he had apparently mesmerized Ian Smith during the shuttling process.

Having given you the general background, I shall now read the actual terms of the proposals put to me by Dr. Kissinger. Paragraph six, relating to economic aid, is an agreed summary of a longer paper.

1. Rhodesia agrees to majority rule within two years.
2. Representatives of the Rhodesian government will meet immediately at a mututally agreed place with African leaders to organize an interim government to function until majority rule is implemented.
3. The interim government should consist of a Council of State, half of whose members will be black and half white, with a white chairman without a special vote. The European and African sides would nominate their representatives. Its functions will include: legislation; general supervisory responsibilities; and supervision of the process of drafting the Constitution.
   The interim government should also have a Council of Ministers with a majority of Africans and an African first minister. For the period of the interim government the Ministers of Defense and of Law and Order would be white. Decisions of the Council of Ministers to be taken by two-thirds majority. Its

functions should include: delegated legislative authority; and executive responsibility.

4. The United Kingdom will enact enabling legislation for this process to majority rule. Upon enactment of that legislation, Rhodesia will also enact such legislation as may be necessary to the process.

5. Upon the establishment of the interim government, sanctions will be lifted and all acts of war, including guerilla warfare, will cease.

6. Substantial economic support will be made available by the international community to provide assurance to Rhodesians about the economic future of the country. . . . The aim will be to expand the industrial and mineral production of the country. . . .

There was much more about international aid and a trust fund which would enable Rhodesia to "expand the industrial and mineral production of the country"; guarantees of investments and the "remittance overseas of an individual's liquid resources"; and other thinly veiled measures of a scheme the CIA had been trying to promote for some months prior to the Geneva Conference: the financing of whites who wanted to emigrate. Smith continued:

In our discussions in Pretoria, my colleagues and I made it clear that Rhodesians were not enamoured of schemes to buy them out—they were looking for a solution which would mean that they could go on living in their homeland. We were assured that the other parties to the proposal strongly supported this contention. Accordingly, whatever plan is produced to assist those who decide to leave, the incentive should be aimed at making it worthwhile for Rhodesians to stay.[2]

So much for what the public was told! The composition of the Council of State which would have the real power during the transition period seemed ominously similar to the existing Senate, and it was unthinkable that the nationalists—even the moderates—would agree to the army and police remaining in the same white hands as those who were doing their best to exterminate them. Or that the guerillas would lay down their arms on a vague promise of a very spurious-looking "majority rule" within two years. Or that the international community would agree to call off sanctions in exchange for a Kissinger-Smith promise!

At his Geneva hotel headquarters, Bishop Abel Muzorewa, a small, gentle owl-like man, assured me that everything—including the conference—that affects man "must be God-inspired and God-centered" and that "all man's needs must be served with Godly concern. . . . In being a militant, I am also doing God's work. . . ." More to the point, because of his good contacts in Salisbury from whence he had come directly to the conference, he had brought with him the résumé of the briefing given by Ian Smith's deputy, Ted Sutton-Pryce, to the Cabinet, on what had really been agreed with Kissinger and which would be Smith's negotiating position at Geneva. That such a document could be leaked was easily understandable after a few days at Geneva. A former prime minister, R. S. Garfield Todd, released a few months before the Geneva Conference from four years of forced residence for opposing Smith's racist policies, turned up at Geneva as a negotiations' adviser to Joshua Nkomo! A steady trickle of white Rhodesian business people visited him in his room at the Intercontinental Hotel to urge him to stand firm for real majority rule. They had no fears for a future under a black regime. Like Garfield Todd they had excellent relations with many of the militant Zimbabwan nationalists and knew they were not racists.

Although the opposition to Smith within his own government came mainly from the right, there were others who considered he was being unnecessarily pigheaded and was set on a disaster course. It was through such realists that the ten-point document came into the hands of Bishop Muzorewa. It has to be read in the light of the first five points of Smith's public version:

1. The present government will appoint the proposed Council of State which will be kept small, with an equal number of white and black members, with the Prime Minister as chairman.
2. A two-thirds majority vote must be obtained for any change in the composition of the Council of State to ensure that the whites remain in complete control.
3. Justice, Internal Affairs, Defense, and the Army and Air Force Chiefs, plus the Police, remain the same as they are now.
4. The Council of State appoints the Cabinet in which Africans will have a majority and a black chairman, but the Council of State will have to approve anything they want to change. [It is unclear whether this refers to legislative or constitutional changes or to changes in the composition of the appointed cabinet—W.B.]
5. The present government will be suspended during the period of interim government. [Bishop Muzorewa added the comment: "In fact it will be 'on ice.'"]

6. Sanctions will be lifted as soon as the Council of State is formed.
7. This all means that if after two years we do not agree on a Constitution, we can revert back and the present government will take over again.
8. Terrorism is to cease immediately.
9. Majority rule does not mean *black* majority rule. It is majority rule of the people on the voters' role, *as it is now.* [Emphasis added]
10. European secretaries of all the ministries remain the same—i.e., European.

When I asked Robert Mugabe whether these ten points corresponded to his own information about the Kissinger "package deal," he replied: "We are simply not interested in it. What has Kissinger to do with our affairs? We have not come here to discuss his ideas as to what is good for our people. Nor to negotiate with Ian Smith. We have come to negotiate with the British not the principle, but the modalities, of the transfer of power." A calm but forceful and highly impressive personality, Robert Mugabe had also been released from jail in Zambia to attend the conference. In his Geneva hotel room where he received a small group of correspondents shortly after his arrival, he replied with superb scorn to an American journalist from one of the leading newsweeklies who asked "what price" the Patriotic Front was willing to pay for independence. "You have the effrontery to ask that we should pay something to be free after eighty-six years of semi-slavery?" he said. The journalist shrunk into his seat and mumbled: "I meant in terms of facilitating the departure of those who want to leave." "Why should we want to retain people who won't accept African rule?" said Mugabe. "Some will stay—many will leave. It's a question of whether they accept whatever legal government emerges."

The great bombshell of the conference was the formation—announced only a few weeks before the delegations were due to meet in Geneva—of the Patriotic Front. Smith had great hopes of exploiting the old divisions based on personal political rivalries. But he came up against a solid wall of unity between the two most important leaders of the two most important movements. Of the four official Zimbabwan nationalist delegations at the conference, that headed by Reverend Ndabaningi Sithole counted least. Although he pretended to represent ZANU, that organization in fact had explicitly rejected his leadership. Sithole was clearly looking for outside support. I found myself in the same waiting room for an interview with Sithole with a West German correspondent from Johannesburg (who confided to me that Sithole was "the only real statesman" among the nationalists), a young American from a CIA-funded labor organization, and the Zaire ambassador to Switzerland. During my own interview there was an embarrassing moment when Reverend Sithole handed me a copy of his book, *African Nationalism.* Opening it, I found an eulogistic dedication to President Mobutu of Zaire. It was quickly retrieved and replaced by a "clean" copy! Mobutu had just "happened" to be in Switzerland during the early stages of the conference, looking for a role to play in the wings and perhaps for a client willing to serve his interests.

Apart from the ZIPA team and the ZANU-ZIPA reinforcements who came at a later stage, Robert Mugabe and Joshua Nkomo dominated the stage as far as the nationalists were concerned. They represented real power, while Bishop Muzorewa and Reverend Sithole represented positions. Nkomo, a huge man with grizzly, crewcut hair, strikes one as very shrewd, experienced and with a strong personality. He made mincemeat of some journalists who should have known better than to try to put their words into his mouth by means of barbed questions. At our first meeting, he said:

> The Patriotic Front has been set up not just to present a single ZAPU-ZANU position at this conference. We set it up, above all, to intensify the armed struggle. It is because of the battlefield successes that the British government and its allies have sensed a threat to their interests in Zimbabwe and southern Africa and have thus been compelled to bring about this conference. We have come here as a result of the sweat, blood, and toil of our people. Our delegation is here to discover whether the message of armed struggle has sunk in sufficiently to ensure the immediate and unfettered independence of the people of Zimbabwe. We consider this conference as strictly between Zimbabwans of whatever color and race on the one hand, and the colonizers, the British government, on the other. . . . We insist on the fact that Britain never ceased being the colonizer of Rhodesia and therefore must now take steps to march out of Zimbabwe through the normal decolonialization process by the end of the transitional period. The final aim is independence from Britain.

231

Referring to fears expressed in some sections of the Western press that blacks might seek revenge against white settlers once they had state power in their hands, Nkomo said:

First, our liberation struggle aims at ending all forms of racism and discrimination because of color, as well as ending economic exploitation and all forms of social privilege. Second, in the new nation of Zimbabwe color, race, or tribe cease to be the measure of value in society and, in this connection, any settler who chooses to be a Zimbabwan shall be as much of a citizen as any other. It is not our intention to substitute one form of evil for another.

An embittered Ian Smith left the conference five days after it started, saying he had "more important things to do at home." He had not been able to play the game of using one leader against the other and, moreover, Kissinger could not come out into the open and say: "Yes, Ian Smith's negotiating position is the one we agreed on." During the dreary weeks following the start of the conference, the attempts to split the delegations proceeded apace. To split the "moderates" Muzorewa and Sithole from the "militant" Mugabe and Nkomo, and to split the "moderate-militant" Nkomo from the "revolutionary-militant" Mugabe. At one point the ZANU element of the Patriotic Front was kicked out of the Intercontinental Hotel, where it had been installed together with the ZAPU element and Sithole. The pretext was that the bills—which the British government was supposed to take care of—were not being paid. The British found them cheaper lodgings at the Hotel Royal. ZAPU stayed on at the Intercontinental.[3]

On November 29, the Patriotic Front issued a communiqué protesting "divisive tactics" employed by Chairman Ivor Richard:

There have been undisguised attempts to "divide and rule." On at least two occasions, favored delegations were shown conference documents which were expressly denied to the Patriotic Front. . . . More serious perhaps is the way the conference is being conducted. Minutes of bilateral talks have not been recorded as conference documents. As a result delegations do not know what has been discussed in bilateral meetings that do not involve them. We call upon the chairman to hold more discussions in the open forum than in secret. . . .

The Patriotic Front leaders, especially those who had only recently been freed from jail, were chafing at the inaction. They wanted to end the farce and get back to the battlefield. They were uncertain as to how their fruitless diplomatic activities were viewed by their comrades in the field. It took the arrival of Mozambique Foreign Minister Joaquim Chissano in Geneva to persuade them not to stage a unilateral walkout. Chissano offered to send a planeload of leading ZANU and ZIPA militants to prove that they had the backing of the front-line combatants. On the night of December 3 there arrived three members of the ZANU Central Committee (including Josiah Tongogara, who had returned to the battlefield after the first week in Geneva) and six ZIPA commanders, including Rex Nhongo, acting commander-in-chief during Tongagara's imprisonment, and Dzinashe Machingura. It was an extremely high-level delegation, with the top military and political leaders of the ZANU-ZIPA element of the Patriotic Front. They were almost all wiped out within a few hours of their arrival. A ZANU communiqué issued on December 4 describes what happened:

> At 4:15 this morning, Comrade Rex Nhongo woke up and saw smoke and flames advancing from the door toward the center of his room. He bravely groped his way to the door and rushed out, leaving all his belongings behind. The incident was immediately reported to the hotel authorities. The fire brigade arrived after about half an hour and put out the fire which had spread all over the building. One other comrade incurred bruises as the comrades rushed out of their rooms. . . . We have no doubt that it was arson and that the act was calculated to take the lives of members of our delegation, if not to destroy the entire delegation. It was an attempt by the enemy to intimidate us so that we would soften our stand on the question of irreversible transfer of power. . . .

Virtually the whole floor of the Hotel Royal was completely gutted. Had Rex Nhongo awakened a few seconds later, it is highly possible that the entire group would have been wiped out. It was difficult for them to grasp that comfortable hotel rooms in sophisticated, neutral Switzerland could be infinitely more dangerous than battlefield bombs and shells. The Swiss police pooh-poohed the idea of arson, but came up with no convincing explanation for the fire. Ten days later the Geneva Conference was officially "adjourned" until January 17, although few had any illusions that it would be reconvened. It gave me no satisfaction at all to lead my last dispatch from Geneva:

233

The Geneva Conference on Rhodesia has broken down and the liberation struggle must now go back to the battlefield and be intensified. This paraphrases the point of view of leaders of the Zimbabwe Patriotic Front and the ZIPA in exclusive interviews with this correspondent, as they prepared to return to Africa. . . .[4]

It was Kumbirai Kangai, mentioned earlier as a member of the ZANU Central Committee, who summed up the results of the Geneva Conference for the Patriotic Front delegates. "The British say the conference is adjourned," he said, "but we think this is a diplomatic way of saying the conference has failed. A failure for the British and for Ian Smith, but not for us. In fact it was a victory for us." He went on to explain why:

We consider that at this moment there are two fronts. The battlefield inside Zimbabwe and the diplomatic front at Geneva. Here we claim a decisive victory. A couple of months ago, apparently prodded by Kissinger, who correctly foresaw the danger that Zimbabwe could become a new Mozambique or a new Angola, Smith stated that he accepted "majority rule." That was the basis of setting up the Geneva Conference, which Kissinger had not foreseen. He thought that by sleight of hand, Smith could manipulate some tribal chiefs and others known as "moderate" nationalists and claim that he had the elements of "majority rule." Once the Geneva Conference was scheduled we decided to come to see what the enemy had in mind, but also ready for serious negotiations in case of any possibility of peaceful transfer of power. In fact, it was quickly clear that Smith had come to play for time because he was hurting from our battlefield successes. Kissinger thought he only had to wave a magic wand and we—and the front-line heads of state—would be dazzled by his brilliance. In fact, Smith—and thereby Kissinger—was smoked out into the open. Before he arrived at Geneva, Smith said repeatedly he now favored "majority rule." It was quite clear to us that he was lying. He repudiated "one man, one vote" as a criterion and talked about "responsible majority rule." We managed to isolate him with regard to world public opinion.

Some people criticized us for agreeing to talks. As revolutionaries, they said, we should never have come to Geneva. But other good revolutionaries have talked and fought at the same time. Our Vietnamese comrades talked in Paris while they intensified their armed struggle. That under our constant prodding the British agreed that Zimbabwe had to have its independence, and even set a date for that independence, was a victory for us. World public opinion has accepted this and also that our interpretation of "majority rule" as

234

"one man, one vote" is a reasonable one. In fact, we no longer talk about "majority rule" because this implies a minority to be repressed. We are for the independence of all Zimbabwans and equal rights for all regardless of color.

We had to participate at Geneva to avoid deals being made behind our backs. We came to prevent the British and Smith from maneuvering to set up a puppet regime, for this was the essence of the Kissinger "plan." British annoyance that the plan failed is implicit in the statement made by British foreign secretary Anthony Crossland after the conference broke down. He said that somehow or other it had got "off course" and that plans for a "moderate regime" had been thwarted.

In the closing days of the Geneva Conference, there was a revolt within Bishop Muzorewa's ranks. It had been simmering for some time with a number of the Bishop's closest aides wanting to join the Patriotic Front at the beginning of the conference. But they were urged by Mugabe and Nkomo to stay where they were and influence the Bishop in the cause of unity. The revolt had been sparked off by a position paper submitted by Muzorewa on the opening day of the conference in which he accepted elections under the Smith regime on the basis of "one man, one vote" to elect a new prime minister. Ministries would be allocated on the basis of the proportions of votes received by the contesting parties and the prime minister alone would distribute the portfolios. As the Bishop was the only one of the nationalist leaders who had legal status, while the others were in jail or in exile, it was felt that he was intent on carving out the top position for himself and using the name of the ANC—and even the freedom fighters—to promote his personal cause. Just one week before the Geneva Conference was "adjourned," one of Bishop Muzorewa's top aides, the Reverend Canaan Banana, held a press conference in Salisbury to announce the resignation of eleven members of the national executive of the Muzorewa wing of the ANC, sometimes called the "internal ANC", and finally "UANC" (United African National Council). Four of them, including Reverend Banana, announced they were leaving for Geneva to reinforce the delegation of the Patriotic Front.

It was against this background that, at the last meeting with journalists before they returned to the battlefront via Mozambique, Kumbirai Kangai was asked to clarify the relations between the Patriotic Front and the African National Council. (In mid-

1975, Muzorewa had "expelled" Joshua Nkomo from the ANC leadership because Nkomo was pushing for a congress according to ANC statutes and Muzorewa opposed this.)

Historically speaking, the ANC was formed by ZANU-ZAPU. When Nkomo was expelled he took most of the ZAPU leadership with him. But because the ZANU element remained and Robert Mugabe could only operate in the semi-liberated zones of Zimbabwe, ZANU could continue to function partially under the ANC umbrella. Then it was discovered that Muzorewa took advantage of this to spread the rumor that he, as head of the ANC, was leader of the armed forces. In fact, he had nothing to do with the armed forces, but as he is the only one who has access and facilities to operate in Rhodesia, he could persuade many members and sympathizers that it was he who was directing the armed struggle. The ANC has no policy, no ideology, no program. Muzorewa's agreement to hold elections, even under Smith's regime, was treachery. He hoped to take advantage of Smith's ban on other leaders to have a monopoly on electioneering. In fact, ANC is practically dead now. Muzorewa will be isolated. The prestige of the Patriotic Front grows every day.

Thus, although the Geneva Conference achieved none of its stated aims, the by-products were of fundamental importance. It provided a forum for consolidation among the real national liberation militants; it brought about the exposure of those who believed it was possible to talk their way into independence and the top power positions. It projected the Patriotic Front into the unrivaled first place and provided a tribune for it to make its aims known to the outside world. Kumbirai Kangai's assessment of Bishop Muzorewa's ambitions was perfectly correct, as was demonstrated some two months later in a dispatch to the *New York Times* from Salisbury by correspondent John F. Burns. Referring to the Patriotic Front's rejection of the Kissinger-Smith proposals, Burns reported:

Mr. Smith now plans to implement the proposals in a fresh round of talks with moderate black groups, including Bishop Abel Muzorewa's United African National Council. The Prime Minister also plans a referendum among the country's 6.3 million blacks, confident that it will prove Bishop Muzorewa's group to have majority support. But U.S. officials have insisted that the plan will not

236

work, because the Patriotic Front, which claims control of the guerillas fighting the Smith government, will continue fighting.

The whole thrust of the dispatch proves Kumbirai Kangai's other point about the expanding prestige of the Patriotic Front. It was based on Foreign Minister Pieter Van der Byl's reaction to Carter administration skepticism about any settlement in Rhodesia which did not have the approval of the Patriotic Front, a view supported by Secretary of State Cyrus Vance and UN representative Andrew Young, a black who is knowledgeable about the southern African situation. Among Van der Byl's dire predictions:

Once Rhodesia's gone, you'll have a belt of Marxist states running across southern Africa—Angola, Rhodesia, Mozambique. From there they'll move north—Zambia first, then Zaire, then one by one, further north, until they have the bulk of sub-Saharan Africa.[5]

Oddly enough, he did not mention South Africa!

Little progress toward a negotiated settlement was made during the year that followed the collapse of the Geneva Conference. Anglo-American diplomacy was directed essentially at giving Smith gentlemanly prods to ensure that the "moderates" could inherit power before the battlefield "radicals" grabbed it. In a patent step to have his own tame "moderates," Smith—and according to press reports elements of the British Conservative Party—sponsored the formation of a new grouping, ZUPO (Zimbabwan United People's Organization). Heading ZUPO is Jeremiah Chirau, and together with deputy head, Kayisa Ndiwena, they are two of the five black senators who had both served in Ian Smith's Cabinet. At an inaugural press conference on December 29, 1976, they claimed the allegiance of "254 tribal chiefs and 450 headmen" and had "ample financial support from many quarters." ZUPO was formed a few days after the Geneva Conference broke down. It was with Muzorewa, Sithole and Chirau that Smith conducted negotiations based on the oft-revised Anglo-American plan during the latter half of 1977. Chirau claimed to represent the Mashona, and Ndiwena the Matabele tribal groups. One of their first common declarations was for the guerillas to lay down their arms! As distinct from Muzorewa and Sithole, they rejected elections or a referendum on the basis that their tribal authority was sufficient evidence of popular support. By such charades Smith tried to cling to power, always under the illusion that time was on his side. All he could do was to intensify repression in those areas where his regime still exercised control.

At a meeting of British Commonwealth prime ministers in London, on June 10, 1977, Joshua Nkomo urged the British government at least to intervene to stop the hanging of black nationalist leaders in Rhodesia and other atrocities of the Smith government. The *Financial Times* (London) quotes him as saying:

> "The British want to destroy the Freedom movement, to install a Government which will protect their interests". The Nationalist leader, who is in London for the Conference, said in a letter to Mr. Shridath Ramphal, the Commonwealth Secretary-General, that the Rhodesian Government was hanging many Africans every Monday on flimsy and framed-up charges, and he named fifteen men whom he said were under sentence of death in Salisbury jail . . . He said that Rhodesian troops had interrupted a traditional African ceremony at a village in the Fort Victoria area of South-east Rhodesia and had indiscriminately killed forty-five men, women and children, claiming the meeting had been organized by "terrorists".[6]

It took nine months after the Geneva breakdown for Smith to accept the principle of "one man, one vote," but with so many qualifications that the results would still conserve white majority rule, because there would be no equal value in black and white votes. The white votes would have sufficient value to ensure that over one-third of Assembly seats—and thus veto power over legislation—went to the whites. In a BBC interview on the night of September 26, 1977, after the "one man, one vote" concession had been announced, Smith was asked whether a peaceful settlement, including incorporating the guerillas in the Rhodesian army, would work. He replied:

> I don't think it would. You see there isn't really such a thing as guerilla armies. If we look at them, they're a bunch of people who have had very little training, who don't acknowledge commands, they operate in individual units, there are dozens of them all over the place . . .[7]

His solution for the guerillas was that they only had to lay down their arms, return to civilian life where they could vote in elections and even enlist as individuals in the national Rhodesian army. This was only another illustration of the dream world in which Smith lived even at the moment when the dream was about to turn into a nightmare—from his viewpoint. That the British government also lived in a dream world was clear when they appointed a Field Marshal—in this case Lord Carver—as the Resident Commissioner designate in Rhodesia to supervise the transfer of powers and negotiate the modalities for that transfer. The Field Marshal almost certainly shared Ian Smith's contempt for guerillas and it would not be surprising if he felt closer to his old Sandhurst-trained comrades-in-arms within Smith's armed forces than to black guerilla leaders. Yet it was with them and their political counterparts that any final solution would have to be negotiated—if there was still time for a negotiated solution. This point was made in a despatch from Salisbury by James MacManus in the *Guardian* (Manchester) of November 10, 1977:

> The Patriotic Front alliance challenged the powers vested in Lord Carver's potential role of Resident Commissioner, the Smith regime rejected the emphasis on a ceasefire before the formulation of a constitution, and the Zambian Government apparently dismissed the idea that elections should precede independence.
> American officials reportedly feel that the decision to place Lord Carver in charge of talks had been a disastrous error. Even British sources concede that he lacks the necessary political grasp and negotiating skills. He is said to be abrupt and abrasive in private discussions, a reflection of a direct military manner rather than any deliberate attempt at rudeness. There is also disquiet that the Field Marshal appears less than happy with the concept of a new Zimbabwe army "based on" the guerilla liberation forces.[8]

A blunt soldier, he must have reminded the Nationalists of the types who came to colonize their country at the end of the 19th century! By the time the Field Marshal was appointed the British seemed to have forgotten what their role at that stage was supposed to be. Simply expressed, it was to take back the independence which the rebel predecessors of the Smith regime had illegally appropriated to themselves and grant that independence to the representatives of the African majority. But having been invited to play that role, the British were starting to behave as if they were to reinstall their old colonial regime in Salisbury. The Patriotic

Front leaders considered themselves as the legitimate representatives of the Nationalist forces, having acquired that position by armed struggle. Their legitimacy had been recognized by the Liberation Committee of OAU. But while the abstract talks went on about what type of elections, what type of constitution, whether elections came first or a constitution, ceasefire or constitution first, and so on, the real intentions of the Smith regime were expressed in the slaughter of hundreds of African Zimbabwans in the refugee camps, continued hangings of patriots in Salisbury and the arrest of hundreds of Patriotic Front supporters all over the country.

In a latter published in *The Times* (London) on November 12, 1977, Canon L. John Collins, president of the International Defence and Aid Fund for Southern Africa, having noted the lack of progress towards a Rhodesian settlement during the Lord Carver visit, wrote as follows:

> Since April 1975, the regime has executed at least 99 people on political charges . . . The Smith regime has embarked on a countryside purge of supporters of the African National Council of Zimbabwe. Hundreds of officers at all levels from Branches to the National Assembly have been systematically arrested and detained to cripple political activity of any kind. There are 77 such members in the Marandellas Prison alone . . . [Canon Collins was referring to the umbrella organization ANC under which ZAPU-ZANU members had some legal status.] Over half a million people are estimated to have been removed from their homes into fenced camps or "protected villages" . . . In this climate of continuing political repression, it is not surprising that the liberation movements should regard with deepest suspicion proposals to retain substantial sections of the Rhodesian Army, the police, judiciary and civil service to maintain "law and order" during the transition to independence. . . .

Not only were the Patriotic Front leaders also deeply suspicious of this, but they were equally suspicious of renewed intensive efforts toward the end of 1977 at splitting the Patriotic Front; at driving a wedge between Nkomo and Mugabe, even to the extent of suggesting a separate ceasefire with the ZAPU forces. At a press conference in the Zambian capital of Lusaka, on November 11, 1977, Joshua Nkomo accused the British government of behind-the-scenes maneuvers aimed at splitting the Patriotic Front, and he produced documents which were being circulated in Britain to the effect that he was plotting to oust Mugabe from the Front.

Behind Nkomo's anger—and Mugabe's natural suspicions—was the fact that at the end of September, Zambia's president Kenneth Kaunda played host in Lusaka to a secret meeting with Ian Smith. It was their first meeting for over two years—the previous one a well-publicized affair at Victoria Falls. "It appears," reported *The Times* (London) on October 3, "that the meeting was arranged through the mediation of the head of the Lonrho organization, Mr. 'Tiny' Rowland. Lonrho has extensive interests in both Zambia and Rhodesia and has been indirectly involved in previous settlement attempts. In 1975, it provided transport and other facilities for Mr. Nkomo . . . Observers here in Lusaka today speculated whether one of Mr. Smith's motives in coming to Lusaka was to try and lure Mr. Nkomo away from the Patriotic Front . . ."

The *Sunday Times* (London) was more specific in a feature article a few days later. Depicting the unhappiness of Bishop Muzorewa, "languishing unloved in a London hotel" while the big event unfolded in Lusaka, the article continues:

> Muzorewa believes that he is the victim of an international conspiracy organized by Rowland and supported by Rowland's ally, President Kenneth Kaunda of Zambia, to install Joshua Nkomo . . . as the heir to Ian Smith . . .
>
> Muzorewa's misery springs from a secret meeting arranged by Rowland between Smith and Kaunda in the Zambian capital Lusaka two weeks ago. Both Rowland and Kaunda have for many years been prominent supporters of Nkomo, and in Salisbury, Smith, seeking to safeguard white interests under a black government, is known to regard Nkomo as the most astute black politician in the field . . .
>
> Tiny Rowland has a great deal at stake in Rhodesia. The Lonrho company there, on which the international conglomerate was founded, owns a million acres of ranches and forests and is one of the largest landowners in the country. Lonrho's gold and copper mines, under the control of local directors since Smith's declaration of independence in 1965, have helped to boost Rhodesia's sanction-breaking mineral exports of 220 million pounds a year and to keep the Rhodesian exchequer in funds . . .
>
> The nationalist leader whom Rowland has consistently supported has been Nkomo, whom he has known for twenty years. . . .[9]

Nothing could be more calculated to arouse the suspicions of the ZANU leadership and this was probably the main aim of what developed into one of those "divide and rule" attempts in which the British of all colonial powers are the most experienced. A whole spate of articles and commentaries on the theme of detaching Nkomo from Mugabe developed in the British press. Fuel was added to the fire when *The Times* (London) carried a report from Lusaka on November 12 quoting Mr. Nkomo as announcing that the Patriotic Front was "ready to meet Lord Carver and General Prem Chand, the United Nations representative in Salisbury, in Malta on November 15." The main purpose "would be to discuss the mechanism and implementation of a ceasefire. . . ." On the same day, from Salisbury, the *Guardian* (Manchester) carried a report from James MacManus, stating that the British had offered to arrange ceasefire talks between the Patriotic Front and Smith's military leaders somewhere "outside Africa." The implication that Nkomo was acting in the name of the Patriotic Front, but in fact only for the ZAPU faction, was spelled out in the following passage:

> The attraction to the Rhodesian generals was that such a move would almost certainly have formalized the split in the Patriotic Front since Mr. Mugabe's wing of the organization would have refused to attend. This would have cleared the way for the military to explore a deal with the other Front leader, Mr. Joshua Nkomo, whose guerilla forces are poised to make damaging incursions into western Rhodesia during the approaching rainy season . . .
>
> In early October a Rhodesian team flew to Zambia to meet Government officials there and members of Mr. Nkomo's Zimbabwe People's Union ZAPU.
>
> The group is said to have met its counterparts at Mfuwe in eastern Zambia where agreement was reached in principle between Mr. Nkomo's army and Rhodesian forces.[10]

Whether Joshua Nkomo was playing an agreed role within the Patriotic Front, sounding out the adversary's intentions, or instance, or not, was not clear. But there were clarifications at a summit meeting with Robert Mugabe in Maputo starting December 6. The following day President Samora Machel joined in the discussions and the day after that Joshua Nkomo announced he would not be going to London for talks with the British Foreign Secretary, Dr. Owen. At the same time President Kuanda announced he was disassociating himself from the latest Anglo-American initiative. In a change of attitude, he announced that in

Zambia's view, "the focus must be on independence first—that is the transfer of power to the majority under the leadership of the Patriotic Front . . ."

As 1977 moved into 1978, it became clearer than ever that whatever diplomatic shadow-boxing went on in London, Salisbury, Lusaka or anywhere else, the final solution was being worked out on the battlefield.

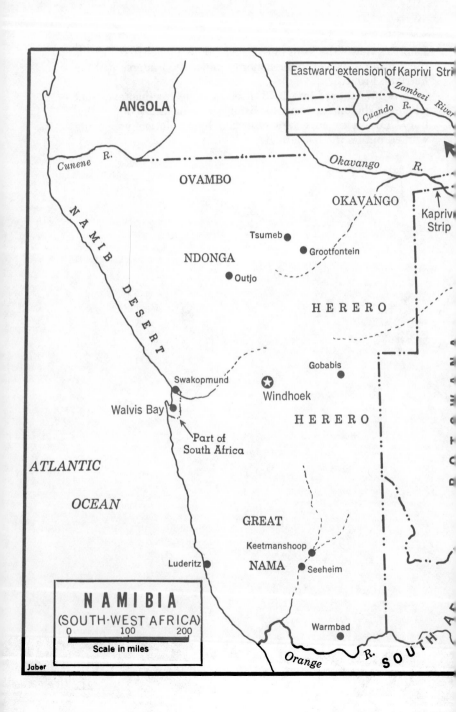

Eastward extension of Kaprivi Stri
Zambezi River
Cuando R.

ANGOLA

Cunene R.

OVAMBO

Okavango R.

OKAVANGO

Kapriv
Strip

N
A
M
I
B
DESERT

NDONGA

Tsumeb
Grootfontein

Outjo

HERERO

Swakopmund

Gobabis

Windhoek

Walvis Bay

Part of
South Africa

HERERO

ATLANTIC

OCEAN

GREAT

Keetmanshoop

Luderitz

NAMA

Seeheim

Warmbad

NAMIBIA
(SOUTH-WEST AFRICA)
0   100   200
Scale in miles

Orange R. SOUTH A

Jaber

Chapter XX The South African Volcano

The oldest of the militant nationalist movements in southern Africa is the African National Congress (ANC) of South Africa. Founded on January 8, 1912, it fathered a number of other national movements which used the same name, or variants of it. The Basutoland Congress Party, the Malawi Congress Party, the South Rhodesia African National Congress, and others. Defining the nature of the struggle in South Africa—apart from the limited aims of anti-*apartheid*—and even defining the situation, has often been something of a puzzle for outsiders. An independence struggle? But South Africa has long been independent of Great Britain, the original colonizing power. A national liberation struggle? This implies a foreign occupying power, a colonial power with all the trappings which go with it. The situation is clearly different from Rhodesia, which nationalist leaders consider a not-yet-decolonialized British colony. Would a successful anti-*apartheid* struggle against the more odious forms of racial discrimination really solve the fundamental problems in South Africa? These were questions I put to some leading ANC cadres whom I met, significantly enough, in Luanda in mid-1976, where they were setting up a permanent mission on Angolan soil.

"We consider South Africa a colonialist society," explained their leader.

> Within the frontiers of South Africa there is a colonized-type black majority oppressed by a colonialist-type white minority. We call this "colonialism of a special type." The fact that the colonialists are there, on the spot, makes our struggle more difficult. It is not as if the colonialist power was based, as of old, in Europe and its domination depended on an expeditionary corps of conscripts. The colonialists of South Africa live within the borders of South Africa and have a direct and immediate stake in the country. In general their color is white— even if they have been in the country for several generations—and the color of those they exploit and oppress is generally black.

The only identifiable cadre in the group with which I was speaking was M. P. Naicker, ANC's Director of Publicity and Information who died in London in May, 1977. The others were simply "Peter" and "Jacob," similar to the "Sam's" and "George's", I was later to meet in Mozambique. Rugged, determined men, their coal-black faces etched by suffering and struggle. Our conversation took place ten days before the explosion at the Johannesburg suburb of Soweto on June 25, 1976, when on that day alone, according to South African police statistics, 174 protesters were killed and 1,222 wounded—most of them primary- and secondary-school children—almost all of them from automatic weapons fire.

Jacob had been in Johannesburg at the time of South Africa's military debacle in Angola. I asked what the reaction had been among the African population.

Enormous! Militants who had been subdued because of the tremendous repression started to surface again. Workers and students held lightning mass rallies in support of the Angolans and Mozambicans although these are banned. They were held mainly by blacks but always with a sprinkling of whites, especially among the students. It is no secret that since it became clear that the Portuguese were going to have to get out of Angola and Mozambique, there has been a great upsurge of militancy in South Africa. Underground structures have been developed; the numbers recruited are higher than ever since the national leadership was arrested in 1963. From 1974 onward there have been repeated strikes in many industries. For a country where trade unions and strikes are illegal, this is very significant and testifies to the growing militancy of the workers. Most of the Western press has tried to write these actions off as "spontaneous." This is far from true. You don't get whole industries closing their doors "spontaneously." When one analyzes these strikes one always finds they are spearheaded by workers with trade union backgrounds. But it was the defeat of Vorster's troops in Angola which completely transformed people's thinking, especially the young people whom our traditional organizations had not been able to reach until now.

M. P. Naicker pointed out that the victories in Mozambique and Angola and the impotence of South Africa to prevent them had "changed the whole balance of forces in southern Africa" and that "progressive forces have now taken the offensive" and would never let up the pressure inside South Africa until the white colonialist minority was overthrown.

For the first time since the imperialists came, we have a genuinely friendly border—with Mozambique—as our Namibian comrades have with Angola. Before, any of our militants on the run who tried to

246

cross into Angola or Mozambique ran a big risk of being arrested by the PIDE, tortured for information, and then handed back to the South African police. Now any militant who crosses the border is received as a friend, a comrade. We can have schools and hospitals and other facilities.

I asked M. P. Naicker if there were any realistic prospects for armed struggle in South Africa now that there were friendly frontiers.

The ANC has been committed to armed struggle for a long time. If we repeat this now it is not because we want to appear fashionable, because it seems that that's what revolutionaries should do these days. Since the ANC was formed in 1912, its policies have gone through many changes. In the beginning we tried to correct the glaring injustices through memoranda and deputations to the authorities. We led mass disobedience campaigns [obviously influenced by those of Gandhi's Indian Congress party]. As we got better organized there were strikes, including big political strikes. But our leadership and the people who supported us found that each campaign was put down by brutal police suppression. The culmination of this nonviolent type of protest came with the Sharpeville massacre on March 21, 1960, when, according to official police figures, sixty-seven people were shot to death in an entirely peaceful demonstration.

For a younger generation of readers who could not know, except from history books, about this horror, nor the wave of revulsion that subsequently swept the world, it is worth recalling the background to the Sharpeville massacre. It is part of the pattern of racist barbarity which led to Soweto. On the basis that "all blacks look alike" and that they are all potential "criminals," a humiliating system of passes was introduced. It was obligatory for all males of sixteen years and over to carry a pass or be subject to immediate arrest. The modern system was introduced in 1952 and was later extended to women also. It is in the form of a small booklet and includes a residential permit issued to those who can prove residence in the same area since birth; that they have worked for the same employer there for ten years; or that they have resided in that area continuously for fifteen years. Another certificate of identification has to be signed by the pass-holder's employer every month; yet another certifies that he has paid his taxes; and there is also a curfew pass in case the pass-holder's work entails his being on the streets during curfew hours. At the time of the Sharpeville massacre, it was estimated that about half the South African police force was engaged permanently with controlling passes. The failure to produce one, or to have any of the elements out of order, was considered a criminal offense.

On March 21, 1960, the Pan-African Congress, an offshoot of the African National Congress, formed by members who objected to the latter's policy of alliance with left-wing white and Indian organizations, staged an exercise in passive disobedience. The plan was for all African pass-holders to leave their passes home, march to the nearest police station and give themselves up. On the eve of March 21, the PAC president, Mr. Mongaliso Robert Sobukwe, appealed to his followers to conduct themselves in "a spirit of absolute nonviolence"; he and fifty of his followers presented themselves at a police station in Johannesburg and were all promptly arrested. (Robert Sobukwe has been in prison or under house arrest ever since until he died of cancer at the end of February, 1978.) At Vereenigung, just fifty kilometers due south of Johannesburg, about 10,000 Africans demanded to be arrested but were dispersed by a flight of jet planes roaring low over their heads. At Sharpeville, eight kilometers north of Vereenigung, a crowd of about 20,000 grew furious when jet planes made mock bombing runs at them. In the melee that followed, the police opened fire. A post-mortem on fifty-two of the sixty-seven Africans killed, carried out by the district surgeon of Johannesburg, showed they had all been killed by bullets. Seventy per cent of them had been shot in the back.

The government rushed through emergency legislation to ban both the ANC and the PAC. A state of emergency was declared and 1,900 people were arrested. A wave of strikes followed the shootings and continued for the next three weeks, with frequent clashes with the police. The emotions aroused can be judged from the fact that at the height of the police repression a wealthy white farmer, David Pratt, tried to assassinate Prime Minister Hendrik Verwoerd by firing two shots into his head at point-blank range, but Verwoerd miraculously survived.

Among those who vigorously denounced the massacre, after having taken affidavits from one hundred hospitalized Africans, was Dr. Ambrose Reeves, the Anglican Archbishop of Johannesburg. Tipped off that he was about to be arrested for having delivered a scathing refutation of the police version at a press conference, Archbishop Reeves secretly fled the country. At a London press conference on April 22, 1960, he revealed that those Africans who had visited him after the shootings, including the two attorneys who had collected the affidavits, had all been arrested. His own life had been threatened by anonymous phone callers. Recalling all this, M. P. Naicker continued his account of subsequent developments:

> Although the ANC was not involved in the voluntary arrest demonstrations and had specifically advised ANC supporters not to participate in an action which had no hope of success, our members were very active in the strikes and agitation that followed. But the Sharpeville massacre and all our own previous activities now called for a reappraisal of the whole situation. After detailed analysis we came to the conclusion that official terrorism in South Africa could only be met by armed revolutionary action. After some initial, very severe setbacks in violent action, we drew the correct conclusions. In recent years we have been training high-level cadres for armed sturggle in many parts of the world, especially in socialist and friendly African countries. Quite a number of these are now back inside the country, preparing and strengthening the underground machinery there. Above all, the political groundwork is being patiently prepared and, when objective conditions are ripe, armed struggle will be launched. We have reached the point of no return and at our present stage of preparations, the fact of having friendly frontiers, and friends on the other sides of those frontiers of such quality as our comrades of FRELIMO and the MPLA, are factors of inestimable value. And we are confident that in the foreseeable future we will have another long and friendly frontier with liberated Namibia. We have had close relations with the SWAPO liberation movement since it was founded, as we have always had also with FRELIMO, the MPLA, and the PAIGC of Guiné-Bissau.

The initial setbacks to which Naicker had referred were mainly an action launched on December 16, 1961, and the violent repression which followed. On February 4, 1961, an armed unit of the MPLA launched the first action of the fifteen years of war which followed when it attacked Portuguese prisons and barracks in Luanda, provoking barbarous repression by the Portuguese armed forces. On December 16 of the same year, units of the *Umkhonto we Sizwe* (the Spear of the Nation), which had been set up by the ANC and the South African Communist Party, launched bomb attacks against key installations in almost every major South African city. The action showed a high degree of organization and preparation, and was intended to spark off an eighteen-month campaign of widespread sabotage. It was the first tangible result of the policy reappraisal described by Naicker. But the result, as in Angola, was crushing repression, which—as distinct from Angola—made sustained armed struggle impossible at that time. What happened is described by one of the participants:

> The organized beginnings of sabotage, and the semi-spontaneous terrorist outbursts of the PAC-inspired *Poqo* [the word was part of the "We Alone" battle cry of the PAC] in 1962 acted, however, as a spur to government counteraction, culminating in blows which led to the virtual destruction of all effective levels of leadership and organization within the country. The police raid on the Rivonia headquarters of South Africa's underground and its followup resulted in the arrest and imprisonment of almost the whole of the liberation movement's internal leadership and activist rank and file. The state security structure, refashioned to counter threatened insurgency, succeeded in silencing all liberation opposition. In the period that followed, those leaders who had previously been selected for external missions together with the MK [*Umkhonto we Sizwe*] cadres sent abroad for military training continued to make renewed efforts to get the struggle off the ground. . . .

In the same account there is another reference to the devastating effects of the Rivonia raid:

> In June, 1963, a well-prepared police raid on Rivonia resulted in the arrest of all the top leaders and the capture of valuable archives. This was followed by the roundup of numerous other members of the ANC and MK whose detention and torture under the infamous ninety-day law led to further successes by the security forces. South Africa's judicial framework, with all its inequalities, had up to then provided a degree of protection for those who fell into police hands. The new laws and interrogation techniques—learned from the French army in Algeria and from the Portuguese political police— gave the security forces a charter to force information out of those detained. Many resisted bravely but the majority who were subjected to torture, sleep deprivation, and similar methods proved unable to resist.[1]

The writer Joe Slovo is a white South African, one of those veteran militants who has now set up his headquarters in one of the "friendly" countries in the front-line areas. He is a barrister whose consistent and effective defense of the accused in political and civil rights trials in Johannesburg had led to his arrest on a charge of high treason in 1956. He was subsequently acquitted, together with the activists he was defending, and forced to leave South Africa following his detention after the Sharpeville massacre. The "infamous ninety-day law" to which he referred was the General Law Amendment Bill, introduced on April 24, 1963. The first four of its nine provisions give something of the flavor of the document. They allow for:

1. The indefinite detention of persons serving sentences for sabotage or similar crimes after the expiry of their sentence.
2. Detention in solitary confinement for ninety days, by the police, of any person considered to be capable of supplying information on subversive activities, the ninety-day period being renewable as required and no court having jurisdiction to order such a person's release.
3. The prosecution for capital offenses of persons who, while abroad, urge intervention in South Africa by force, or who received training in subversion, the penalties being the same as those for treason.
4. The checking by the postal authorities of mail for suspect material, which would be sent to the Attorney-General.[2]

It does not require much imagination to envisage what went on during the renewable ninety-day periods while the police worked over suspects "considered to be capable of supplying information." The fact that officially sixteen African detainees committed "suicide" in South African jails between March, 1976, and the end of February, 1977, and that the unofficial press tally was nineteen from June, 1976, shows that methods remain the same. The most widely publicized confirmation of what went on in South African jails was the police murder of Steven Biko on September 12, 1977. Biko was the founder and first president of the (Black) South African Students' Organization (1968-69) and was subsequently the Honorary President of the Black People's Convention. At the time of his arrest on August 18, 1977, he was

251

head of the Black Consciousness Movement. It was not until almost a month after his death that the *Rand Daily Mail* reported that a post-mortem had revealed that Steven Biko had died of "extensive brain damage and severe bruising." Because of the extent of public reaction inside and outside South Africa, and at the insistence of the Biko family, a judicial "enquiry" was held as to the circumstances leading to his death. Although the "enquiry" whitewashed the police as had been expected, enough details were revealed to horrify world opinion. On the night on which he was already dying from injury to the brain, he was transported, naked, for 700 miles in the back of a station wagon to die within a few minutes of arrival. The results of the "enquiry" only inflamed black opinion still further, convincing large sections of the population that the racist regime had to be overthrown and that all means were good to do it.

Starting in August, 1967, some ANC cadres sent abroad for military training started heading back home, getting their first baptism of fire in joint ANC-ZAPU guerilla activities in Zimbabwe. They were almost always immediately intercepted by Rhodesian and South African security forces and it seems they were mostly wiped out. Slovo writes:

> By all accounts confirmed by enemy reports, they acted with heroism and competence. But one of the prime reasons for the failure of this incursion by the joint ANC-ZAPU groups was that, within Zimbabwe, there was not the requisite level of internal organization, mass mobilization, and mass support without which armed activity may easily be strangled. For the liberation movements, the Zimbabwe incursions once again underlined the need for careful preparation of the population, and for guerilla groups to be integrated within the community rather than functioning as isolated *foci*.[3]

Slovo points out that many abstract theoretical books and articles have been written to explain the failure of armed struggle to really get off the ground in South Africa. In addition to those dwelling on the military and economic might of South Africa, the strength and invincibility of its armed forces, and the higher proportion of whites to blacks (the 1974 census listed 4,160,000 whites as against 17, 745,000 Africans, 2,306,000 "coloreds," and 709,000 Asians for a total of 24,920,000) than in Rhodesia where the ratio was twenty-five to one, much space was also devoted to variations on the theme of a lack of "psychological readiness and motivation among the Africans to use violence." Soweto certainly put an end to that argument. The heroism and spirit of self-sacrifice of pre-adolescent primary-school pupils and teen-aged secondary-school students who bore the brunt of the attack by over 1,000 police armed with modern automatic weapons and with orders to shoot to kill, was a crushing rejoinder to African "passivity." For a whole week the protests and killings continued, not only in Soweto but in other black townships—at Alexandra, also outside Johannesburg, where twelve Africans were reported killed on June 18; at Tembisa, northeast of Pretoria; at black universities in Zululand and the northern Transvaal.

The official figures of 174 blacks and two whites killed, 1,222 wounded, and 1,298 arrested which were given by James Kruger, Minister of Justice and Police, were denounced by ANC sources as far below the real total of at least 252 killed, over 2,000 wounded, and over 2,000 arrested. Kruger's report admitted that the only weapons used by the blacks were sticks, stones, and a few *pangas* (jungle knives). He claimed that two revolvers had been seized, but also admitted that no policemen had received bullet wounds.

Although the immediate issue of the demonstrations had been to protest against government decisions on the compulsory introduction of the bastard Afrikaans language—the language of *apartheid*—for teaching certain subjects in black schools, the real issue was political protest against the whole rotten racist-fascist system. The introduction of Afrikaans was a warning that the government was going to push ahead with that supreme manifestation of *apartheid*, the creation of glorified concentration-camp states known as "bantustans," which provided for the removal of the major part of the black population into areas designated by the Pretoria regime as their "homelands." It was Vorster's unique solution to "majority rule" in South Africa. Subtract enough blacks from the total population by making them into Zulu, Xhosa, Tswana, and half a dozen other separate "nationalities" who would automatically lose South African citizenship and you could make what was left into a "majority" of whites along with a few acceptable blacks, "coloreds," and Asians. Blacks needed to work the mines, staff white farms (on an average of twenty-two per farm), and work as domestics in white families would have the status of police-controlled migrant labor, their contracts renewable on a year-to-year basis, after they returned to their "bantustan" at the fulfillment of each year's contract. It was against this prospect, plus generations of repression, that the youngsters in Soweto and elsewhere throughout the country were protesting with exemplary heroism.

What did Soweto represent to the South African racists? And what did "bantustans" represent to Soweto inhabitants? Soweto was a segregated black township of about 1,000,000 people where eighty-six per cent of the houses had no electricity and ninety-seven per cent had no running water and where wage-earners were paid one-fifth of what whites were paid for doing exactly the same work. The majority of the Soweto population belonged to the Xhosa ethnic grouping. From the viewpoint of the "bantustan" policy, this meant that they were "nationals" of the Transkei, a separate state or "bantustan" arbitrarily delimited by the Pretoria authorities. Any infraction of labor discipline or of the odious pass laws still operating in June, 1976, meant deportation to the Transkei, an administrative concept totally unknown to the vast majority of Soweto residents. In any case, once the Transkei was formally "inaugurated" in October, 1976, each wage-earning Xhosa was required to go there at the end of his year's labor contract to have it renewed. As for Afrikaans, it was the language of the Boers, whereas English was the common language of South Africa. To enforce Afrikaans as a national language was to condemn the Africans to cultural and political isolation from the mainstream of current events and political tendencies. To think that school children could have no concept of such things is to ignore the influence of family conversation on such matters.

But where did the new militant upsurge come from? I find it easy to believe that the rays of hope first started to warm the hearts of the young people of South Africa because of the victories across their borders in Angola and Mozambique and above all because of the defeat of South African troops at the hands of the MPLA and their Cuban allies. For decades they had heard endless accounts from fathers and uncles of the terrible repression of any attempts to throw off the yoke of white racism. Now in their hearts they knew that their generation could take up arms and win, revenging the sacrifices and sufferings of earlier generations and securing for their own a future of freedom and human dignity.

They paid a terrible price for this exuberance, but for every youngster who fell, there must be a score who took a silent pledge to push ahead with the struggle. I am not writing in the abstract. Shortly after Soweto, I met some of the survivors who came into Mozambique looking for arms and training. Mostly they were put into schools for the time being, as is the case of the hundreds who slip across the border from Namibia into Angola. They arrive burning for action. They are cooled by the very excellent sort of advice that the Vietnamese gave to young people crying for arms and revenge after a mother or sister had been killed in a napalm raid, or raped by the Saigon fascists. "Courage" was the watchword. "But intelligent courage. Learn well how to seek revenge. Fight when possible to fight again another day! We will teach you how to be most effective."

The protests which started in Soweto continued until mid-January, 1977, by which time ANC sources estimated that at least one thousand Africans had been killed and several thousands more had been wounded. By that time the Soweto youngsters had been joined by university students and large sections of the working class. The slogans carried by the schoolchildren on that first terrible day of protest, which had included demands to disband the "bantustans," to abolish the pass system, to end the system of police control of the nonwhite population, and to permit freedom to choose place of residence and work, had become nationwide demands. The sum total of the demands was the abolition of the internal system of colonialist-capitalist oppression. A significant aspect of the developing struggle was the growing support of the "coloreds" and Asians for the demands raised at Soweto.

There is good reason to believe that Vorster was encouraged by Kissinger to think that the "bantustan" or "homelands" solution would be acceptable to the United States and many of its allies with multinational interests in South Africa. In the eight "bantustans," over eight million South Africans would become aliens. Most of them, born and brought up in the cities, where the labor of the family's breadwinners was needed by the whites, had never even seen their native villages. All of a sudden they were to have the same status as Portuguese, Italian, or any other migrants. The "bantustans" would substitute for the protective barrier or the white heartlands what Mozambique and Angola had formerly provided. They would be a recruiting ground to raise black armies to defend their "homelands" against the ANC freedom fighters, who would be projected as "invaders." Eighty-seven per cent of the total territory of South Africa would be owned by the whites and the other thirteen per cent would be divided up among the eight "bantustans." They represented the highest development of *apartheid* and also the oldest of imperialist tricks in the way of "divide and rule" tactics. Each would have its own national army and it would not be too difficult to eventually pit them against each other for control of grazing grounds, sources of water, and other essentials for survival. The slightest misdemeanor, or imagined misdemeanor, and any African could be uprooted from the only place he had ever lived in and be "deported" to his "bantustan" according to the ethnic grouping registered in his pass.

On October 26, 1976, for instance, 1,500,000 Africans automatically lost their South African citizenship and became "citizens" of the Transkei, formally declared an "independent" state with great pomp and ceremony on that date. The "ceremony" part of it was somewhat marred by the total boycott by foreign diplomats, not a single state recognizing then, or since, the Transkei's sovereignty. To complete the farce, it was announced that on the first day of independence South Africa and the Transkei had signed a "nonaggression pact." The bill under which this first "independent" "bantustan" was set up stipulated that Transkei citizens included all Xhosa-speaking persons in South Africa, as well as those speaking the related Sotho language; and that any person "culturally or otherwise associated with the Xhosa tribe" would cease to be a South African citizen as of October 26, 1976. Those who refused to accept this would become "stateless," losing the right to pursue their professions and whatever meager rights were contained as in their pass. Next on Vorster's "bantustan" program is to set up the "independent" state of Bophulhatswana for all Zulu-speaking South Africans. It already has "homeland" status and has sent representatives to Transkei "independence" ceremonies.

Although the costly violent confrontations which started with Soweto died away early in 1977, it was clear that the newly revived militancy was being channeled into political and organizational forms. The Vorster regime knew that something was simmering and bubbling away just under the surface but its security services had difficulty in putting their fingers on just what was going on. This explains the arrest and torture of Steven Biko. Before they did away with one of the most prestigious of the young African leaders, the police wanted to squeeze him dry of everything he knew about the new organizations. The regime was scared of the militancy displayed at Soweto and in the wake of Soweto. Just over a month after the murder of Steven Biko, the security forces struck again.

Following a Cabinet decision on October 18, the government declared eighteen organizations unlawful, arrested seventy leading Africans, closed down *The World*, the paper most read by the black community and the second largest in the country—arresting its editor, Percy Quoboza, as well as a number of journalists. David Woods, editor of the *Daily Dispatch*, and several white clergymen were among hundreds of others placed under house arrest or exiled from their places of residence. Among the organizations banned were the South Africans Students' Organization (SASO), the Black People's Convention (BPC), the Black Parents' Association (BPA), the Black Women's Federation, the Union of Black Journalists, the Christian Institute of South Africa and others—virtually every organization through which the black community could exercise whatever remained of democratic rights.

In justifying this greatest wave of repression since the post-Sharpeville arrests, James T. Kruger, South African Minister for Justice and the Police stated: "The unrest which took fire in the country last year and has flared up radically since, was obviously not spontaneous . . . The Government is determined to ensure that the peaceful coexistence of peoples in South Africa is not disturbed by a small group of anarchists. . . ."

The question is, what next for the South Africa's revolutionary forces? In Mozambique I met a very cheerful ANC leader, Makatini, on his return from what he considered a highly successful summit meeting of the Organization of African Unity. Three decisions particularly encouraged him. One, that the member states "admit the legitimacy of armed struggle for the seizure of power by the people"; two, that in the specific case of South Africa, there was to be no "further proliferation" of national liberation movements, recommendations for fusion between ANC and PAC having been abandoned in favor of a call for the movements to try to establish unity at the base; three, that OAU member states committed themselves not to recognize the Transkei and that any violation of this commitment "would be a betrayal not only of the struggle of the people of South Africa, but also of the entire African continent." "The ANC is committed to total liberation of the continent and will exert all efforts to consolidate the victories of Angola and Mozambique," said Makatini, "and accept them as natural allies for our own liberation."

Armed struggle is on the agenda; the question is what form should it take. One school of thought I found among some ANC leaders was that as the highest concentration of Africans is in or around the big industrial cities, armed struggle must necessarily take the form of urban guerilla warfare. To support this contention, they point to the lack of the geographic and natural conditions, such as existed in Vietnam—no thick jungle for cover, no big concentrations of peasants—necessary to wage classical guerilla warfare. To my arguments, based on my own experiences on the spot in China, Vietnam, Laos, and Korea, plus post-operational studies in Algeria, Cuba, Angola, and Mozambique, that urban guerilla warfare had not yet proved successful, there was a shrugging of shoulders and the comment: "South Africa is different." The weakness of urban guerilla warfare is obvious. The enemy is fought on his own terms, on the terrain where he is strongest and most at home; where he can concentrate his armed forces of repression, supplemented by a vast espionage network—which means he is infinitely better informed about the plans and activities of revolutionaries than they are about the plans of the enemy. Concentrating on urban guerilla warfare means abandoning one of the strongest weapons of revolutionary warfare—keeping the enemy off balance by continually confronting him with the dilemma of whether to disperse or concentrate his forces.

The obvious advantages of rural guerilla warfare are the dimensions and space within which the guerillas can operate and maintain the initiative. With a few well-planned blows at widely differing points, the enemy can be kept on the run and be drawn into situations in which he is vulnerable. "From the east today, the west tomorrow" is how Ho Chi Minh expressed it in his instructions to the Vietnam People's Army's first small guerilla group. If

258

good use is made of rural guerilla activity under centralized planning, the maximum use can be made of the magnificent back-up force which the high concentration of African labor in the industrial centers represents. At one stage this can take the form of political activity—strikes, demonstrations, student activity—to keep the local forces of repression fully occupied. When the classical stage of people's war—the encirclement of the cities by the countryside is reached—then the full potential of the urban working class can be brought into play. That such a concept also has its partisans within the ANC leadership is clear from the work of Joe Slovo, especially from the following passage:

> Guerilla warfare, almost by definition, posits a situation of vast imbalance in material and military resources between the opposing sides. . . . It is supremely the weapon of the materially weak against the materially strong. With a populace increasingly supporting and protecting it while opposing and exposing the enemy, a people's army is assured of survival and growth by skillful exercise of tactics. Surprise, mobility, and tactical retreat make it difficult for the enemy to bring its superior firepower into play in any decisive battles. No individual battle is fought under circumstances unfavorable to the guerilla. Superior force can be harassed, weakened, and destroyed. . . .[4]

This is possible only in rural guerilla warfare where mobility, advantage of knowledge of the terrain, and skillful use of movement at night, including lightning ambushes, make it impossible for the enemy to choose under what conditions each action is to be fought. It also makes it impossible for the enemy—as happened at Rivinia—to decapitate the entire revolutionary leadership in one fell swoop. Surrounded in city apartment blocks have no alternative but to shoot it out or surrender, as has happened so often in urban guerilla warfare in Latin America. Especially important in Joe Slovo's analysis—even more so, because it is clear that he will be one of those on the spot to help direct operations—is the following passage on the question of terrain:

> One of the most popular misconceptions concerning guerilla warfare is that a physical environment which conforms to a special pattern is indispensable: thick jungle, inaccessible mountain ranges, swamps, and so forth. The availability of such terrain is, to be sure, of

enormous advantage to the guerillas, especially in the nonoperational phase when training and other preparatory steps are undertaken, and no external bases are available for this purpose. . . . But guerilla warfare can, and has been, successfully waged in every conceivable type of terrain; in deserts, in swamps, in farm fields, in built-up areas, in the bush, and in countries without friendly borders. . . . In any case, in the vast expanse that is South Africa, a people's force will find a multitude of variations in topography—deserts, mountain forests, veld, and swamps. . . .[5]

After one of those innumerable "search and destroy" operations in South Vietnam when the Americans were looking for the "Vietcong Pentagon," a Vietnam veteran chuckled and remarked to me: "The Americans are always looking for our bases. Our bases are in the hearts of our people." A profound remark which the Americans were incapable of grasping until the end. It is clear that the South African freedom fighters will have no difficulty in finding bases "in the hearts of their people." The whole country is crying out for liberation.

South Africa will be liberated from its racist regime and within the generation of the Soweto martyrs. One can come to this conclusion by an analysis of political, military, psychological factors and by comparing them with similar factors that have played the decisive role in other liberation struggles. But confirmation that this is not too optimistic a judgment comes from an unusual source within South Africa itself. Professor Gideon Jacobs of the School of Business of the University of Witwatersrand, in the outskirts of Johannesburg, after a trip to the United States and other countries, returned to his university armed with a survey of South Africa as a "political risk" to prospective U.S. investors, conducted by the University of Delaware. The essence of Professor Jacob's analysis was published in the South African *Star Weekly:*

> The survey places South Africa as the highest "moderate risk" at present—with only one country, Indonesia, as a higher risk. In three years time South Africa will become a "prohibitive risk" together with Spain and Indonesia, and in seven years, the survey says, South Africa will be the highest "prohibitive risk" of all countries.
>
> Also falling into the category of "prohibitive risk" are Nigeria, Spain, Indonesia, and Kenya.

Three years ago South Africa was a recommended investment country, falling between France and Ireland, and the prohibitive risk countries then were Chile, India, Peru, Argentina, Libya, Pakistan and Portugal . . .

The University of Delaware survey is sent yearly to all American banks and prospective foreign investment companies in America.[6]

How the mighty have fallen! The professor points out that Mexico, rated as a "poor borrower," can get foreign loans at 9 per cent, whereas South Africa, by 1977, had to pay from 12 to 14 per cent, which meant that the lender could recover his principal within five to six years. A week earlier, the same *Star Weekly* had reported that in the first quarter of 1977, and for the first time, there was a net outflow of long-term capital. Foreign investors and local capitalists were losing faith in South Africa's political and economic viability. "International hostility," the paper reported on November 26, 1977, "is having a seriously adverse effect on the domestic economy and a number of steps need to be taken urgently, the Natal Chamber of Industries says in its annual report released this week."

That such a situation could have come about represents a serious misjudgment by Henry Kissinger. On the eve of Nixon taking over at the White House in 1969, Kissinger took the initiative in setting up a study group to define what U.S. policy should be in southern Africa, with main emphasis on South Africa. The study group produced NSSM (National Security Study Memorandum) 39/1969. The drafters produced five options which ranged from doing nothing to active intervention. Kissinger recommended the adoption of Option Two, which favored a policy of "communication" and "relaxation" (of the U.N.-imposed policy of "mandatory economic sanctions" against South Africa).[7] There should be an official stance of denouncing *apartheid* and other forms of racial discrimination and an unofficial policy of encouraging U.S. investments. The rationalization was that only when United States monopolies had a sufficiently high stake inside the country would they, and the administration, have leverage to force the regime to modify its racial policies! One of the guidelines given the study group was the necessity of maintaining the flow of gold from South Africa which supplied the "Free World" with over 60 per cent of its needs in gold. It would thus be essential to maintain existing racial policies if the gold was to continue to flow.

In any case, investors were not slow to take advantage of the green light. From 1969, U.S. investments in South Africa increased from 692 million dollars, 25.8 per cent of all U.S. investments in the African continent, to 1.2 billion, or 40 per cent of the total. U.S. trade with South Africa doubled during the same period with a two-to-one balance in United States' favor. Kissinger's recommendations to Nixon were based on three NSSM 39 assumptions regarding southern Africa as a whole.

(1) If violence in the area of Southern Africa escalates, U.S. interests will increasingly be threatened.
(2) The Whites are here to stay and the only way that constructive change can come about is through them . . .
(3) There is no hope for the Blacks to gain the political rights they seek through violence, which will lead only to chaos and increased opportunities for the Communists.[9]

These racist assumptions soon proved dead wrong in Angola and Mozambique; they are being proved wrong in Zimbabwe and Namibia and will be proved wrong in South Africa. The "reform by investments" strategy also proved a dismal failure. U.S. investments continued to rise until they leveled off at about 1.6 billion dollars in 1976—Vorster's repression also continued to escalate. In 1977 U.S. investments started to fall off and some important U.S. firms—Polaroid, for instance—started to pull out.

What are the factors that have caused such a dramatic reversal of South Africa's economic situation. There are pressures from student and church groups for withdrawal of their funds from banks with investments in South Africa; parliamentary pressures which have caused governments like those of Holland and Sweden to withdraw or cut back on investments and credits. There are other factors, too, which hard-headed investors have to take into account. They have to take into account the irreversible trend of world events. The fact that the United States was unable to halt the liberation of Mozambique and Angola was a sobering thought. The unrest in South Africa itself, and the Vorster regime's impotence to prevent Namibia gaining its independence in the near future have also pointed up the fragile, artificial basis of the regime. What happens to South Africa's main money-winner—gold—when miners start demanding working conditions which make it uneconomic to process 160,000 tons of earth to get one ton of gold?

Uranium? An article in the *South African Digest,* on April 15, 1977, quoted Professor Friedel Sellschop ("one of the country's top nuclear research scientists") as urging that South Africa should "exploit without delay the world's growing reliance on nuclear energy." The *Digest* claims: "It has been estimated that South Africa, with a third of the free world's uranium supply, could make more money from uranium in the next thirty years than it has made from diamonds in the last 100 years. . . ." The article goes on to describe how South Africa has developed a secret uranium-enrichment process, cheaper than elsewhere. And that "enriched uranium, due to be produced in 1984, sells at two to three times the price of natural uranium. . . ."

The catch is that South Africa's uranium mainly comes from the huge Rössing mine, the territory of which starts just east of Walvis Bay, and which in 1977 was expected to produce 5,000 of the world total of 30,000 tons of uranium produced that year. The main uranium area spreads out in a fan-shaped area from the coast between Walvis Bay and Swakopmund. In the long and fruitless negotiations that have gone on to persuade Vorster to end South Africa's illegal occupation of Namibia, his negotiators have said they would never give up the Walvis Bay enclave. Diamonds? For many years most of South Africa's gem diamonds—to the value of up to 100 million dollars a year—have come from the Oranjemund diggings along the Namibian coast starting about 100 kilometers north of the Orange river.

Much of what seemed to be the mainstay of the South African economy is thus seen to be built on shifting sands. It is certain that once a certain level of armed struggle is reached that will be backed up by industrial action and based on experiences in other countries, the miners will be in the vanguard of the struggle.

As 1977 drew to a close, the regime itself was seen to be on shifting sands. Apart from the nationwide mood of revolt among the masses, there was disaffection among elements that the Vorster regime could normally rely on to support his policies. On November 4, Gatshi Buthelezi, Chief of the Kwazulu "homeland" of the warrior Zulu people, gave an interview to the Durban *Daily News,* announcing that he now supported international sanctions against the Vorster regime. The previous day he had boycotted a meeting of regional chiefs called by Prime Minister Vorster. He was taking this stand following the wholesale arrests and banning of African organizations. It was an act of rebellion.

Vorster was on a spiral leading to disaster. His only answer to mass agitation was intensified repression which cost him friends at home and abroad and only added fuel to the fires of revolt. "Sanctions are better than blood," said Chief Buthelezi, "and the stage has now been reached where people should support such action . . . While we know that sanctions will hurt Blacks more than Whites, we should rather accept this hardship than continue to suffer wholesale arrests." After the Soweto massacre Chief Buthelezi had joined with seven of the leaders of the nine "homelands" in demanding a Round Table Conference to draft a new Constitution, a proposal which Vorster promptly rejected as "having no merit at all." Doubtless, few believe that change would come about by drafting a new constitution, but the incidents showed that black dissatisfaction had reached the highest level—in terms of personalities—that it could reach. Chief Buthelezi is considered by a very large section of black militants as being hopelessly compromised with the Vorster regime and trying to gain some credibility by occasional outbursts of nationalism. His appearance, on March 11, 1978 at the funeral of Robert Sobukwe, was denounced as an exercise in demagogy. After an angry scene in which stones were hurled at him, accompanied by epithets such as "sell-out", Chief Buthelezi withdrew.

That the South African volcano has become active again no observer of the scene can doubt, even though it is impossible to predict exactly when it will explode. Perhaps one of the most significant pointers to coming events is the fact that white departures from South Africa between January and October 1977 totalled 22,400, compared with 11,900 for the same period in 1976, while 21,000 whites entered the country—about 6,000 from Rhodesia—compared with 41,000 in 1976. Those leaving were mainly people with skills—including about 250 doctors—heading for the U.S.A., Canada, Australia, Israel and West Germany. Some whites are now suffering from the very privileges they have enjoyed until very recently. With economic recession and manpower cutbacks, employers find it financially advantageous to fire the whites and keep the blacks who do the same work for one fifth of the pay!

264

In whatever sphere one looked, whatever criteria one applied, the conclusion is inescapable: The writing is on the wall, black writing on a white wall, that the era of racist supremacy in South Africa is coming to an end.

XXI New Policies for Old?

Throughout the Senate Subcommittee Hearings (see chapter IX, "The Kissinger Version"), with the faint shadow of a new administration over the horizon, there were glimmerings of a new approach to the storms that were gathering strength in southern Africa. In any case Kissinger's innermost thinking was brought out in the following exchange with Senator Dick Clark (Dem., Iowa), who chaired the Subcommittee:

> *Clark*: . . . I guess what I am really asking is, does the United States' security depend on our becoming involved in every conflict in which

the Soviet Union is providing assistance, and, if so, are we not, in this case, allowing the Soviet Union to define American interests and in effect making us reactive in policy rather than determining our own?

Kissinger: Well, the only way you can avoid being reactive with respect to military action is to initiate it yourself.

Clark: You do not have to act at all.

Kissinger: But if you do not initiate the military actions yourself, then the decision will always be imposed on you in one way or another by the aggressive nation. . . .

It is difficult to interpret this in any other way than that Kissinger was really hurting because the United States had not jumped into Angola with a full-fledged expeditionary force before the Cubans got there! Another representative who took a dim view of the Kissinger testimony was Andrew Young of Georgia, better known later as the U.S. ambassador to the United Nations:

Young: . . . At the risk of being a little flippant, let me say that what I think we have heard is a view of Africa through the eyes of a European cold-war man. And I do not think that that is what I see in Africa through my Afro-American eyes. I do agree that we do have serious considerations to be maintained in the whole situation in southern Africa. But I do not think we can take Angola as an isolated incident and I think we make a mistake when we think that the problem we are dealing with started in January of 1975.

It may be necessary to remember that we were on the wrong side of the Angolan colonial struggle for almost fifteen years, during which time Senator Tunney on this [the Senate] side, and myself on the House side, introduced an amendment urging that none of the Portuguese weapons that we sent to Portugal for use in NATO be allowed to be transferred for use in Angola. Now that amendment was passed but was never enforced. I think the first time I heard of napalm it was being used not in Vietnam but by the Portuguese in Mozambique and Angola. In the light of that history and that wrong policy against all of our traditional values and national interests, I think, we stopped—when the Portuguese government fell—and did nothing and we created a vacuum and it was in that vacuum that Soviet interest began to expand and the situation became critical. . . .

A more precise criticism of the Kissinger analysis was offered by the testimony of Stephen R. Weissman, Associate Professor of Political Science at the University of Texas, who started by dealing severely with U.S. policy in the Congo, including CIA involvement in the murder of Patrice Lumumba, implicit backing of the Katanga secessionists, and the official U.S. rationale at the time that U.S. efforts were directed toward preventing a "Soviet" or "Communist" take-over of the Congo. Weissman continued:

> Today, in Angola, the Secretary of State defines this issue as "whether the Soviet Union, backed by a Cuban expeditionary force, can impose on two-thirds of the country's population its own brand of government." But this formulation does not even mention MPLA, the most nationally oriented and effective mass political organization in Angola's ill-prepared independence transition.
>
> Born out of discussions between Africans, Portuguese Communists, and other leftists, compelled to organize guerilla warfare against Portuguese colonialism, MPLA developed its own brand of African Marxism and a stronger politico-military organization than the Lumumbists ever had. Spurned too by the West in their long war against colonialism, MPLA leaders turned to the Soviet Union for arms and advisers. But they also received significant arms supplies from anti-Soviet Yugoslavia, food and medicine from Scandinavia, bases, sanctuaries, and other assistance from various African states— Congo-Brazzaville, Guinea, Tanzania, Zambia—and liberation movements (FRELIMO, PAIGC—Guinea—Cape Verde Independence Party). Cuban troops appeared in large numbers only as former Portuguese sergeants, Zairean regulars, and South Africans began to assist MPLA's opponents. These MPLA veterans of a long political and military battle against foreign domination have declared publicly and in internal documents that they are not Communist puppets and that they will pursue an independent foreign policy, including good relations with Western governments. The leading scholarly observers of the MPLA, John Marcum and Basil Davidson, are in agreement on this point. And they are joined, according to the *New York Times,* by the African experts of the State Department.
>
> Again, Soviet ambitions appear to have been exaggerated by U.S. officials. Neither strategic military bases nor other long-range interests compatible with Soviet satellization were mentioned in press reports of administration briefings to Congress. . . . Secretary Kissinger's version of the domino theory—that a success in Angola will encourage the Soviets to establish new patterns of dominance elsewhere—is merely an extension of the basic false premise about Angola.

Regarding relative support for the three movements inside Angola, Professor Weissman stated that the "weight of evidence is that [Holden] Roberto has been unable to extend his support beyond his ethnic group which is one of the smallest—eleven per cent—in the country. Furthermore, he has been less inclined to guerilla operations and has disdained the task of modern political education." As for Savimbi:

> Although he has based his support on a larger ethnic group than Roberto's—a third of the population—Angolan experts consider UNITA less nationally oriented than MPLA. UNITA's guerilla activities were less extensive than those of MPLA and FNLA. . . . That MPLA has probably had an edge on its opponents since the late 1960s is an indication of the internal military and political weaknesses that have beset America's Angolan protegés.

Professor John Marcum,[1] professor of politics at the University of California and a much-quoted expert on Angolan affairs, started off by stating that the Angolan war "represents a tragedy of missed opportunities" for the United States: "For fourteen years, American policy-makers paid next to no attention to the wars of independence being waged by African nationalists in Portugal's African colonies. . . ." He reproaches the policy-makers in one key document on African policy of questioning the "depth and permanence of black resolve" and remarks that the depth and permanence of fascist Portugal's resolve was never in question!

As a fellow academic he could not let Kissinger's errors of fact slip past without putting the record straight:

> I should like to comment on just a few points that the Secretary of State made in his testimony, particularly to get at some historical facts. He stated that the FNLA and UNITA played, as he put it, "a larger role than the MPLA in striving toward Angolan independence." I would suggest that that is at best partisan. Each movement had its day, each movement at various times in this struggle achieved ascendancy and then declined. I believe historically that the MPLA did at least as well as the others, though none won a clear victory.
>
> It is suggested also that the MPLA began military action against the Portuguese in the mid-1960s. In fact, fighting broke out in Angola in 1961, and both the MPLA and the UPA—Union of Angola's Peoples—which is the predecessor of the FNLA, were involved in fighting at that time. I think it is important that the historical record be accurate.
>
> At another point the Secretary of State suggested that although

various uncoordinated efforts of these movements caused difficulties, they caused no serious military threat to the domination of Portuguese military forces in Angola. He goes on to say that the overthrow of the Portuguese government in April, 1974, and subsequent growing strength of the Portuguese Communist Party apparently convinced Moscow of the revolutionary situation in Angola.

It is implicit in his statement that there is no connection between these two events. I think it is terribly important to note that an incumbent can lose without an insurgent winning militarily. This happened in Vietnam. This happened in Algeria. This happened in Angola and Mozambique. The Portuguese coup was a direct result of the wars in Africa. . . .

This was a gentle scholarly tilt at Kissinger, who, in a famous series of essays on foreign affairs, had made the correct and brilliant remark that "one of the cardinal maxims of guerilla war: the guerilla wins if he does not lose; the conventional army loses if it does not win. . . ." That was before he was appointed Nixon's national security adviser. From his later actions it is clear that he ignored this excellent formulation. Marcum continued to poke holes through what superficially had seemed the most convincing part of Kissinger's testimony:

One has only to read General Spinola's book written shortly before the coup on that, on the war that Portugal could not win, to understand the connecting links between these two events. It is not as though the Soviet Union had gotten interested in the affair only after the coup. It is also suggested by the Secretary that Soviet aid began in the fall of 1964. The Soviet Union had been helping the MPLA for most of fifteen years. Moreover, Chinese aid was coming in to the FNLA in late 1974. There are some press reports of 400 tons of Chinese arms arriving in Zaire in late 1974; they had Zaire equipment as well. And it was—and this is not mentioned in the testimony—it was in March and April that FNLA forces attacked.

Pressed by Senator Biden, who displayed throughout the hearings a healthy skepticism for the "Kissinger version," Marcum concluded his testimony with the following:

One of the points I found curious was a public statement by the State Department that it did not consult with the South Africans, that it was not informed of the intervention. And I presume it did not suggest to the South Africans that intervention would not be a good thing; it saw no evil, heard no evil, stayed away from it, which is in itself a kind of complicity. . . .

It was all very gentlemanly, Marcum's evidence, as one academic to another, but it must have left Kissinger squirming. He had been caught out in a series of what nonacademically would simply be called lies. Not just ordinary lies, but purposeful lies, aimed at dragging the United States into another Vietnam. Especially aimed at reproaching the U.S. Congress for having hampered the Executive in getting into such a war, at least financing others to internationalize the Angola war. Some readers may think this is flogging a dead horse, now that the Angolan war is over and Henry Kissinger is no longer at the State Department. The hearings, however, are worth studying for at least two reasons. The evidence of Kissinger—and that of Ellsworth—showed the contempt the Executive had for the Legislature and the type of false premises on which vital decisions were made. The hearings showed the vitality of democratic institutions in the United States once correct and courageous use is made of them. Having been one of the severest critics of most aspects of U.S. foreign policy for thirty-odd years, I am bound to admit that nowhere in either the "old world" of bourgeois democracy, or the socialist "new world" could such national self-examination—self-criticism, in fact—take place as the publication of the Pentagon Papers, the Watergate exposure, the manner of the dismissal of a vice-president and a president and the sort of probing into the conduct of foreign affairs as the hearings on Angola exemplified. All of which adds up to the conclusion that the American Founding Fathers were men of not only broad but also very far-sighted vision!

As for the "quality" of the high-level lying that went on, apart from that already quoted, there was the oft-repeated charge by Kissinger that the MPLA government was installed in Luanda by "11,000 Cuban troops and 400 Soviet advisers." Cubans claim the figure of 11,000 is inflated by "several thousands," but as they do not give a precise figure of their own this must remain a figure with a question mark. I have never met a "Soviet adviser," but I traveled with Soviet journalists—together with French, British, Italian, Yugoslav, and others—in front-line areas during the decisive battles on the Central-South fronts. We encountered Cuban artillery and tank columns and Soviet colleagues were desperately eager to interview one of the "Soviet advisers," the presence of whom had become a major topic of the Western news media. The best one of them could do was to find a Russian-speaking Cuban in a tank column taking a lunch break at the junction of the Silva Porto (Bié) Serpa Pinto road. But when he started to photograph what were indubitably Soviet tanks, his film was promptly confiscated by a higher, non-Russian-speaking Cuban officer. Discomfited, he closed his camera case and rejoined our group as we sped on to freshly liberated Bié. I cannot deny that there were Soviet advisers, I can only affirm that I never knowingly met one. Nor did Dr. Kissinger offer any substantive evidence of their presence. Colin Legum, who was rather anxious to prove outside intervention in favor of the MPLA, writes: "Although there have been a number of reports about Russian military advisers in Luanda— ranging from 200 to 400—the only hard piece of evidence is that Igor Ivanovich Uvarov, a Tass 'correspondent,' who is a leading member of the Soviet military intelligence, GRU, was active in the capital."[2] Legum cites the *Manchester Guardian,* November 20, 1975, as his source. Why there should have been "Soviet advisers" is difficult to explain. The Cubans were perfectly familiar with all the Soviet equipment being used. It was certainly not the sort of war that the Russians were used to fighting.[3]

In any case, apart from Cuban "advisers," there were just eighty-two and not 11,000 Cuban troops in Angola when the MPLA government was installed in Luanda. How many advisers? The report submitted by Deputy Defense Secretary Robert Ellsworth is more than discreet on this point. "Cuban military personnel preceded the South Africans into Angola. Since the late 1960s a permanent advisory force of approximately [deleted] Cubans had supported the MPLA. . . ." One can reasonably deduce that if the number had been impressive it would not have been deleted. On the other hand, Ellsworth is caught out in a real whopper in the same report which stated: "The South African expeditionary force totalled only some 1,000 men at its peak; it was pulled back by late January to a buffer zone of thirty miles beyond the Southwest African frontier and reinforced by another [deleted] South African troops. . . ." This was at the time that South African Defense Minister Botha was admitting to 4,000 to 5,000 South African troops concentrated in the "buffer zone."

The most moving, knowledgeable, and passionate testimony at the hearings came from the Reverend Lawrence H. Henderson, Board of World Ministries, United Church of Christ, New York:

Senators, as I see the situation, self-determination is the issue in Angola. How can Angolans determine their own future? From this distance many other issues, interests, and concerns get in the way and obscure the main issue. We can hardly see the Angolans. Our Secretary of State looks at Angola and sees a battlefield where we test our will and perhaps our material with the U.S.S.R. The media, desiring to bring Angola into focus, wear ideological glasses, seeing now through the right lens, now through the left. . . . Advocates from both right and left miss the real issue, which is Angolan self-determination. . . .

On our infrequent furloughs during our twenty-two years in Angola, we were frustrated by the ignorance of Americans who confused "Angolia," as they called it, with "Mongolia." Americans may now know that Angola exists, and many know where it is, but they're still not aware of the Angolans. . . .

The former missionary then went on to make a significant point which came from his heart as much as his head, and could only come from someone who had profound sympathy for the Angolan people's independence struggle:

Portuguese colonialism is historically responsible for the invisible status of the Angolans. Our friends and colleagues could be thrown in jail and tortured for saying: "I am Angolan." He or she was supposed to say: "I am Portuguese." Angolans fought for thirteen years for the right to say: "I am Angolan." They fought not only against Portugal, the poorest country in Western Europe, but against the United States, who supported its NATO ally, diplomatically, politically, and economically.

Recalling that the day on which he was giving evidence—February 4, 1975, the last but one of the hearings—was the fifteenth anniversary of the "attacks on the prison in Luanda, which was one of a series of events launching the war of liberation," Mr. Henderson continued:

272

Angolans decided to take things into their own hands rather than wait for someone else to rescue them from Portuguese colonialism. No Angolan political organization or activities were legally possible under the Portuguese. The liberation movements were political parties as well as military commands for guerilla units. Most importantly they were the only political instruments for Angolan self-determination. . . . Angolans, together with Mozambicans and Guineans threw off the mental shackles of colonialism, and even inspired young officers of the Portuguese army fighting in Africa to free themselves from their fascist mentality. The formation of the Portuguese Armed Forces Movement owed much to the African freedom fighters. . . .

I commend this committee and the Congress for insisting that the U.S. government withdraw from Angola. It is ironical that after a dismal record of U.S. interventions around the world to rescue beleaguered dictators, to overthrow popular regimes, and to install military juntas, the United States finally found itself backing the majority in Angola. [Mr. Henderson apparently accepted the ethnic criterion as to what constituted the majority] However, it was for the wrong reasons. We saw Angola as a battlefield in the cold war, and so we would support anyone who seemed to be opposing the U.S-.S.R. . . . We supported Portugal while she fought to maintain control of her African colonies. We are breaking sanctions to import chrome and strengthen the rebel regime in Salisbury. We have vetoed United Nations resolutions condemning South Africa's *apartheid* policy. In addition to rectifying these mistakes, we need to establish affirmative relations with the Organization of African Unity, and change our stance in the United Nations, so that we are not boasting about breaking up Third World blocs, but striving to understand the aspirations and problems of these less developed nations. . . .

The final witness was Bishop Ralph E. Dodge of the United Methodist Church, also a missionary with forty years regular contact with Angola, Mozambique, and other areas in southern Africa. He broadly agreed with the testimonies given by Marcum and Henderson with one reservation: "that Larry Henderson assumed that UNITA was the majority party and I would question that. . . ." Senator Clark closed the hearings on February 6, promising that they represented the beginning of a series of such hearings on southern Africa, based on "our firm conviction that one of the reasons we have had so much difficulty in Angola is because we have not pursued an African policy in an African context. . . ."

It is not this author's role to allot plus or minus ratings for the superpowers' performances in Africa, but it is a fact that African states give plus ratings to those who support genuine independence movements and very definite minus ratings to those who support, actively or by default, South Africa.

Inter-African solidarity and support for national liberation movements has been a notable and moving fact of African life for the past twenty-odd years, cutting across racial, religious, and ideological boundaries. As each country attains its independence, it provides bases, hospitality, sanctuaries, and other forms of aid to fraternal independence movements. It has gone that way from Cairo to the Cape, and continues to develop in that sense.

After the monarchy was overthrown in Egypt and Colonel Nasser had consolidated his power, Cairo was host to the Provisional Government of Algeria set up in Cairo in September, 1958. Tunisia and Morocco loaned their territories for bases, training, and supply facilities for the Algerian National Liberation Front. As soon as Algeria won its independence in 1962, it played host to a number of other national liberation movements, including those of the Portuguese colonies. Now that Angola has won its independence it performs the same service for the SWAPO guerillas fighting for the independence of Namibia, as Mozambique does for the ZIPA freedom fighters in Zimbabwe. Tanzania and Zambia, once they gained their independence, provided bases and training grounds for Mozambique, as Congo-Brazzaville and Guinea did for Guiné-Bissau and Angola. And as an independent Namibia and Zimbabwe will certainly do for freedom fighters in South Africa when the time comes. To pretend that this is all some Kremlin plot with Moscow pushing the buttons and pulling the levers is the height of absurdity and ignores the wind of change which started in the second half of the twentieth century in Africa, gathering hurricane force as it swept south. Moscow could push and pull as hard as it liked and nothing substantial would happen in any African state unless the people and their revolutionary leadership were ready to move. And if Moscow—in the interests of "détente" or some twist and turn in superpower relationships— tried to switch levers into reverse gear when national liberation movements wanted to press ahead, it would be a fiasco.

If Moscow—and the same applies to Peking—wants to retain credibility as a champion of the oppressed and a force for the self-determination of nations and peoples, it is bound to support those struggling for independence anywhere in the world. And in one very important aspect, the Soviet Union is freed from the sort of inhibitions which shackles U.S. freedom of action in this field. However much one may rail against Soviet "revisionism" and "social imperialism," the fact is that there are *not* some 250 Soviet private firms with a total of over a billion dollars worth of investments in South Africa clamoring to have those investments defended—by armed force if necessary.

If there are to be new U.S. policies in southern Africa and other places where people are struggling for independence, not only does the United States have to forego the old practice of imposing its bases—and puppets—in areas where it considers its interests are threatened, but it must shed the idea that the Soviet Union acts in the same way. Or that those who have accepted Soviet aid automatically become Soviet puppets. A general rule is that those who fought with arms in hand for independence are not disposed to change old masters for new ones. If a new administration in the United States had been able to bring itself to change "old policies for new ones" to support such concepts, it could have become a "stabilizing" instead of a "destabilizing" factor in newly independent countries and in those still struggling for genuine independence, economic as well as political.

There were grounds for some hopes that there would be come fundamental changes at the beginning of the Carter administration. But as time went on it was clear that policy towards southern Africa is still based on the recommendations of NSSM 39—change the style but not the content. Andrew Young was the chief instrument of a change of style and he did bring some fresh ideas and fresh language to the problems. But his action, on October 31, 1977, in applying a veto to a draft resolution before the U.N. Security Council calling for a trade embargo against South Africa, symbolized the fact that despite his change of style basic policies remained the same. The fact that Great Britain and France in turn applied vetos and that West Germany and Canada also voted against the draft resolution showed that South Africa's five biggest western investors and trading partners had no intention of sacrificing vested interests to placate world public opinion.

275

XXII The Socialist Option

"We are going to build socialism." This was the rather surprising opening remark of a night-long conversation between the author and Lopo do Nascimento, Angola's prime minister. He continued,

> I don't quite know how, but we'll do it. Socialism means a certain level of goods and services to distribute which we don't possess. But we have the will and it's what the people want.
>
> We have decreed free medicine, but we've neither doctors nor supplies. Sixty-eight doctors were left after the Portuguese exodus, over half of them in the capital. What hospitals and clinics existed outside Luanda are in ruins. Equipment, from operating theaters to X-ray machines and dental chairs, has been stolen or smashed to bits. We have decreed free education, but where are the schools, the professors, and teachers?

He went on to a classical description of the state in which a colonizing power leaves the colonized when there is no alternative but to get out. Almost universal illiteracy, virtually all administrative, professional, and technical posts monopolized by the occupiers, maximum sabotage and destruction of what could not be evacuated. In Angola's case this was compounded by foreign invaders and local puppets whose interests lay in maximum slaughter and destruction.

After 500 years of an "extraction" economy, starting with the "extraction" of slaves and ending with that of oil, diamonds, and coffee, the Portuguese had left with all the engineers and technicians needed to keep the economy going, with the doctors and teachers needed just to maintain the miserable standards of public health and education that existed; with the merchants who had monopolized the buying and selling and supply of goods in the rural areas. A whole economic infrastructure and superstructure collapsed with the mass departure of Portuguese who could not face up to a future in which the pigmentation of their skins did not automatically ensure social and economic privileges. The only possible means of transforming the wreckage that had been inherited into something which would ensure a decent and happy future for the Angolan people was to build socialism. That was the major thrust of my first hour of conversation with Prime Minister Lopo do Nascimento.

I asked if such a big leap—from a semi-slave society for many Angolans into an advanced system such as socialism represented—would not meet with considerable resistance.

There are two sectors who could oppose this. One is the small land-owning class from which I myself come. But they were practically liquidated in the 1961-62 massacres. If not by the UPA racists, then by the Portuguese. Some of the survivors still dream of getting back their properties and it is quite possible they will succeed. But as a class force they are practically finished. The second sector is that of the bureaucratic bourgeoisie allied with some of the workers' "aristocracy." These could be elements open to corruption, but not a force to oppose the socialist road. To build socialism we have to reinforce our MPLA cadres. We have to avoid the petty bourgeoisie being transformed into a bourgeoisie and thus, natural agents of imperialism. For the mass of the people—those who work with their hands in the factories and fields—there is no problem.

By fleeing the country, by abandoning their enterprises, the Portuguese forced us to take over. In some cases, we had never intended to do this. But they forced our hand. For instance, we had not intended to move into the foreign trade section too rapidly. The Portuguese had all the contacts. But they abandoned it—left it all in our hands. If the state doesn't handle it, who will? Who will sell our coffee and other products? We do not have competent cadres, but we must do it!

I asked what proportion of Portuguese had left. Ninety per cent?

More! Almost all of them. Of course this meant all technical and administrative cadres. They never trained any replacements. We are very rich in typists, but that is about all in the technical field! We have many, many problems because of this.

The big problem is the contradiction between what we want to do to solve the immediate needs of the masses, who have nothing, and our means of doing this. We also have to avoid the idea of solving exclusively urban problems—those which are in front of our eyes. Luanda is far from being Angola.

Did the Portuguese leave anything important behind in the way of industrial superstructure?

Very little. Some transformation industry, some tailoring establishments. The really profitable sectors—banking and insurance, for instance—were in the hands of the multinationals. It was not so much industrial or even financial capital that was here—it was commercial capital. Of course, there is the real estate abandoned by the Portuguese—abandoned plantations. We will take it all over and put the plantations into production. The Portuguese are already demanding compensation for what they left behind—although nobody asked them to leave. This will become a big problem between our two countries.

At that time South African troops had retreated to the border areas and Prime Minister Vorster was still talking about the need for them to remain there until they had guarantees for respect of South African "interests." Holden Roberto and Jonas Savimbi were both talking about waging guerilla warfare. What were the long-term prospects?

The South Africans were very stupid in getting involved in such an inglorious adventure. They thought because they were white they could do anything. They had intended to make a swift rush to the north, install Savimbi and Holden Roberto in Luanda and help them both to finally crush the MPLA, then pull back to the border areas and let their puppets work for them. Their arrogance was born of racist and class attitudes, but above all racist. In any case, it was Vorster who gave our government the most valid reason for asking for help elsewhere.

As for the threat of guerilla warfare, we don't expect Holden Roberto to go into the bush with a weapon in his hand. Mobutu would like to play for time while he decides what to do next. But he has plenty of problems at home and has no reason to be satisfied with Holden Roberto's performance so far!

Savimbi can make some trouble, but in the short term only. He does not have the conditions for waging guerilla war. He would need political objectives, political support—a political organization. He has none of these. He has now been pushed into a zone without population, without logistic possibilities. Will Zambia continue to support him? Not for long. Nor will South Africa.

I asked the prime minister whether he was satisfied with the results of an intense, week-long campaign to combat tribalism, racism, and regionalism.

Yes. It was very fruitful, but we must not rest on our laurels. We must maintain this campaign. The colonialists have always used such weapons to "divide and rule." Savimbi used them, Holden Roberto used them. Savimbi in particular neutralized a large part of the population in the Huambo area from supporting armed struggle with his blatant tribalism. But in the eyes of the Ovimbundu he committed the unspeakable crime of bringing in the racist South Africans. And in more conservative, traditionalist tribal circles, his crime was even greater because he and his allies were defeated in battle. He can create some troubles. Our country is vast and underpopulated. It is easy to land commando groups from planes and helicopters to carry out sabotage; but to carry out sustained guerilla operations which could threaten our government—this is impossible.

In another interview on the eve of the first anniversary of the setting up of the People's Republic, Lopo do Nascimento said:

If we consider the sectors most destroyed by the enemy and of which the re-establishment has been the most slow and difficult, we must criticize ourselves and admit that the sector of trade and supply has not developed as we had hoped. This is largely due to the interdependence of that sector on others, such as agriculture and transport. We didn't even know how the system worked.

After detailed study we discovered that supply and marketing had been basically carried out by truck-owners—who were often also the drivers—who bought goods in the rural areas from the "bush traders." During the months which preceded independence—after the date was already set for the Portuguese withdrawal—there was a massive exodus of both the "bush traders" and the owner-drivers. They took the majority of available trucks and automobiles with them, and this disrupted the transport and marketing networks.

Some agricultural products—rice, maize, and coffee, for example—were bought from the producers by specialized agencies of the colonial authorities, who had a monopoly on such transactions. The departure of their employees contributed to the breakdown of trade in such products. The producers were left without either a market or a source for agricultural implements, seeds, and fertilizers; the urban consumers had no source for essential foodstuffs; the state was deprived of a source of revenue from traditional exports. These considerable difficulties were aggravated by the destruction of road and rail bridges; of locomotives and freight cars and motor transport of all kinds. The puppets and South Africans destroyed some 130 bridges, which will seriously impede the development of communications for years to come. Of the 30,000 vehicles on our streets and roads in the last year of the Portuguese presence, less than 5,000 were left by the time we had liberated the whole country. For our coastal trade, we were left with twenty-three boats totaling 28,000 tons, which have an average age of fifteen years.

The seven major cities, including Luanda, were left with a total of 313 buses for urban service; but half of them were permanently out of action due to lack of mechanics. How could such situations be remedied without the state moving in? An enormous financial effort has been made. In 1976 debts were incurred the repayment of which will be completed only in 1982, to purchase 4,360 motor vehicles of all types, from trucks and buses to jeeps and ambulances, almost doubling the total number of motor vehicles inherited from the Portuguese. This represented an investment of over one hundred million dollars. Included in the invoices were the salaries of technicians from various firms engaged to train Angolans in handling and maintenance of the purchased vehicles. A worthwhile investment, but part of the intolerable financial burden for having been colonized.

One could see the tragic results of the lack of transport and communications in the coffee-growing centers of Uije, Negage, and others. With prices at record world levels, magnificent crops of coffee remained on the bushes because there was insufficient labor for harvesting. Plantation laborers—one small step removed from slavery—had traditionally come from the Ovimbundu people in the South, for whom Savimbi had set himself up as champion. During the Transitional Government period and the later uneasy UNITA-FNLA alliance, Savimbi had carried out a campaign to persuade the plantation laborers to return home to swell the ranks of his armed forces. But Holden Roberto's men controlled the northern airports and the migration move to the south was blocked because Roberto did not want to lose manpower and potential cannon fodder. Savimbi's agents tried other tactics. "The MPLA are pushing north from Luanda. You will all be massacred for having remained in an area under FNLA-UNITA control. Flee south while there is still time!" Many Portuguese plantation owners and managers had fled. There had been killings on a tribalist basis by the Zaire-FNLA troops. The plantation workers did not receive a *centavo* in wages during the seven months of the Zaire-ELNA military occupation nor any food from the plantation owners. Ninety per cent of them were so-called *contradados*, rounded up in their local villages in the Center-South for being "without visible means of support" and placed at the disposal of labor-contractors for the coffee plantations in the North, where they were slaves in everything but name.

I was present at a memorable and moving event in the Carmona (Uije) soccer stadium when a member of the local MPLA provincial administration tried to explain democracy and socialism to some two thousand plantation workers. The sun streamed down from a cloudless sky and the sweat poured down from coal-black faces and semi-naked bodies. They were invited to group themselves according to their provinces in the Center-South. Faces were intent but suspicious and uncomprehending. The only time they had ever been called together in the past, as some of them explained to me later, was to hear bad news, some new measures of oppression on the part of the authorities. For the first time in their lives—and never in the lives of their ancestors—they had been invited to take part in a democratic process, a decision-making process. When they had regrouped according to province, the chairman invited them to name delegates to go with him a few days later to Luanda and discuss their problems with President Neto. Nobody spoke. There were simply uncomprehending and confused expressions. "Who is prepared to speak for Benguela? For Huila?" asked the chairman. A few hands went up. The chairman asked for a name. "Is he acceptable?" "No," roared the group from Benguela, or Huila. Another name from those who had put up their hands. "Is he acceptable?" If the reply was a clear majority "Yes," he was invited to step up to the tribune to take his place alongside the chairman. After every group had made its choice, the chairman made a brief statement:

> Those who have been elected here are not to represent their own interests, but those of their fellow workers from their local regions, from the whole province for which they are elected. What has happened here this morning shows that if we organize like this to solve our problems, we can do many other things also. We will meet again this afternoon and talk with the delegates you have elected. Then we will go and report the real facts of the situation to the president. Afterward we will meet again and report on what has been decided.

The faces of this exclusively male crowd—it was forbidden to bring family members into the plantations—were still solemn and suspicious, but focused as one man on the tribune where their elected representatives stood, all hands and sheepish grins, grouped around the chairman.

> But one thing I can tell you now. We have a really independent country. It is the people who decide what is to be done. Angola is really free. Those of you who want to go home can leave. Your back wages will be paid. We would like you to stay, but it is up to you. Another thing is that the contract system is finished forever.

There was a moment of stunned silence and then pandemonium. Faces lit up. Workers hugged each other. There was no formal applause because they had never been used to it. But they poured out of the stadium in an atmosphere of good humor and animation difficult to imagine a few minutes earlier. My mind went back some twenty-odd years to the village of Hung Son in northern Vietnam, not far from where Ho Chi Minh had set up his headquarters to direct the decisive military struggle against the French colonialists. The battle of Dien Bien Phu was just starting. It was a night of drizzling rain—good protection against French night bombers. A crowd of black-clad peasants gathered around a modest campfire—a *fogueira*, as the Angolans call it. The first decisions on land reform—land to those who till it—were announced to peasants too stunned by the news to react immediately. It was only when one of the poorest landless peasants in the village staggered up to the campfire with her arms piled high with the cadastral acts of bondage to the landlords and started throwing them into the flames that the meeting was transformed into a frenzy of joy.

These are authentic moments of history which it is a privilege to share. When I related both events to Lopo do Nascimento, he smiled and said: "One has to start somewhere. At that moment, we had no money to pay their back wages. The bank vaults had all been robbed. Armed bands had collected all ready cash from shopkeepers and even small Portuguese plantation owners who wanted to pay their laborers, but at least we could show our sincerity and declare the end of slavery."

It would be pleasant to write that the plantation workers were so impressed by the decency of the new regime that they stayed on to clean up the plantations and harvest the next crop. They did not. They left by the thousands. The desire to be reunited with their families was too strong to be outweighed by completely new notions of social and political obligations. They were "slaves with the chains knocked off" and they went home. Nobody tried to stop them. The flight of labor from the coffee plantations in the critical season of 1976 was the direct result of the oppressive system that had put it there. And the inability to replace that labor with tens of thousands of politically and socially conscious volunteers was due to the sabotage of communications and transport to bring those volunteers to the spot; the inability to house and feed them or even to move the harvest to the railway and then on to the ports and coffee-starved export markets. Much of the 1976 bumper crop thus remained on the bushes.

On the other hand the government got an unexpected bonus when it was discovered that there were tens of thousands of tons of coffee remaining from the 1974 and 1975 harvests. This was partly because of the war situation and Portuguese commandeering of transport for military purposes; later the coffee was hidden from Zairean high-level looters who came with trucks to commandeer it and haul it off to Zaire—just as they had driven most Uije province cattle across the border. Portuguese owners or managers were given payment slips for whatever was taken, but these slips were never honored. Those who refused to hand over their stock were simply shot on their threshholds. This led to many ingenious methods of smuggling coffee away from the normal storage sheds.

By mid-1976, having already nationalized all the abandoned plantations, the government had set up a coffee-purchasing organization. For the first time the Angolan small-holders, who produce about forty per cent of the country's coffee, were being offered honest prices. Previously they had sold to the nearest plantation owner, who had the drying and husking equipment, for whatever he saw fit to give. Or gave coffee to the nearest grocer in exchange for food advanced during the pre-harvest period at whatever food-coffee exchange rates the grocer demanded. Now "people's shops," run by a state trading agency, which sold basic necessities at fixed prices throughout the country were starting to appear. That, plus the hard cash paid out by the state purchasing agency, whose trucks picked up the coffee from the farms, accounted for the broad smiles on the faces of the small-holders in the coffee-growing villages of Uije that I visited at the height of the 1976 harvesting season. Certainly not one in a hundred of them had ever heard of socialism but they knew they were getting a fair deal for the first time in the memory of any of them. And this was coming from the government, from the authorities, whose only role in the past, whether Portuguese or Zaire-FNLA, had been to oppress and exploit!

The Minimum Program of the MPLA, adopted at its formation on December 10, 1956, had included an eight-point policy for agrarian reform and working conditions. Among the points were those for abolishing the *contradado* system of forced labor; an eight-hour working day; distribution of land to peasants who either had none or not enough; state-guaranteed minimum wages to workers based on equal pay for equal work "regardless of sex, age, ethnic, or racial origin"; and other humane social measures such as protection for unmarried mothers and material aid to "all Angolan citizens without resources, sick or unemployed, old or disabled." Many who believed this might come true were probably written off as naïve or insane by more sophisticated compatriots. But these things did come to pass, even if it had to be on a low level of implementation. The contradiction, as Lopo do Nascimento had expressed it, between what the state would like to do and its means of doing it!

There were other contradictions. In the coffee areas, cadres of UNTA, the newly born Angolan trade unions—the true independence of which were also guaranteed under the Minimum Program—went from plantation to plantation to explain to workers their right to an eight-hour working day. They could work extra hours during the harvesting season, but only on the basis of freely negotiated arrangements with their employers—state, private, or cooperative management. The old *contradados* who had stayed on had been used to working twelve or sixteen hours a day in the harvesting season. If it was officially now eight hours, they asked, why not six or four hours? It took long patient explanations by the UNTA cadres to explain that they were now working for themselves—the state was themselves! They were building socialism. Socialism meant ever higher production.

It was all part of the birth of a new society and those suffering most from the labor pains had only a vague idea of what it was all about. Aside from a handful of the privileged ones from the old

284

days, everyone knew what they did not want. A return to the hateful, humiliating colonialist regime. But it was more difficult to be explicit as to exactly what they did want. The mere fact that the country as a whole was ninety per cent illiterate—illiteracy was virtually total in the countryside—was a terrible handicap in propagating ideas of any sort; especially so novel a one as that illiterate, ragged, barefoot peasants were being called upon to build a modern, prosperous state based on scientific socialism.

Just three months after the People's Republic was founded, a law was adopted on "State Intervention in the National Economy," the foundation stone on which the socialist system would be built. It was promulgated while military operations were in full swing in both the northern and southern extremities of the country. Continued armed struggle had to be envisaged for a long period ahead. "Destabilization" efforts had very much to be taken into consideration in economic planning! Hence the reference to a "resistance economy." Basic principles were defined as follows:

> The resistance political economy is characterized by the building of a planned economy in which three sectors will coexist: state economic enterprises, cooperative enterprises, and private enterprises.
>
> To face up to the exigencies of the resistance, the three above-mentioned sectors should be activated in such a coordinated way as to permit an increase in production of essential goods to raise people's living standards and thus ensure economic support to the anti-imperialist war. The resistance economy should rely fundamentally on our anti-imperialist national forces and thus firmly respond to the economic blockade and the systematic destruction of the national productive apparatus which the enemies of the Angolan people are trying to carry out at this moment. [The law went into effect on February 19, 1976].
>
> The creation of the material and technical base for such an economy demands an expansion of cooperative effort for the development of a state sector which will take over control of the large and medium-sized strategic industries. On the other hand, it is vital to exploit to the maximum existing resources, many of which were abandoned by the colonialists and are lying idle at this moment.

In Angola as in Vietnam, capitalist owners were frightened by specters of "bloodbaths" conjured up by President Ford and his Secretaries of State and Defense, Kissinger and Schlesinger, into abandoning their enterprises. Thus, the MPLA was forced into state management at an unnatural pace. It was either that or face total breakdown of the economy.

> The private sector in this resistance economy should be encouraged and supported by the state as long as it respects the general political-economic line worked out and defined by the MPLA.
>
> It was precisɾ ly the chaotic situation inherited from colonialism and fertilized by the imperialist war that created the urgency for immediate decisions on the nationalization of abandoned enterprises and equipment, or those belonging to traitors.
>
> The nationalized means of production will be handed over to state economic units or to agricultural and industrial economic cooperatives. In this way we can introduce democracy into the economic structures of our country, pushing ahead with a centralized plan of industrialization coordinated with the production of agricultural and small industrial cooperatives.

The law included thirty-one articles which spelled out in great detail the criteria for deciding for or against nationalization: the "type of activity, volume of employment, monopoly position in any particular branch, foreign exchange earnings, geographic location," etc., including cases "where private ownership runs counter to national interests," or cases "in which owners unjustifiably quit Angolan territory for more than forty-five days on end." In cases where nationalization was implemented, Emergency Committees were to be set up to carry out inventories of equipment, raw materials, and other assets and to ensure the functioning of the enterprises until Management Committees were organized. Compensation, in cases where the owners had not been involved in any nefarious activities, would be negotiated between the "interested parties" and the appropriate government departments.

The leading organs for state-owned enterprises were defined as (1) the Government Delegate, (2) the Management Committee, (3) the Workers' Assembly. Above these were Coordinating Committees for each branch of economic activity at national and regional levels to ensure that productive activities were in line with overall national planning. The role of the Management Committee was obviously crucial and it was these that I found in charge of the numerous nationalized coffee plantations that I visited in Uije as well as the big coffee drying and husking plants. They were composed, as the law stipulated, of an "equal number of workers appointed by the government and others elected by their fellow workers of the economic unit concerned." Those named by the government "will be chosen from workers of the units concerned or from among others of recognized competency and aptitudes even though they are not serving in the economic unit concerned." Management Committee members would continue to receive the same wages as they earned at their normal place of work and would be elected for a year at a time. Those elected by the workers could be replaced by majority decision on the proposal of the local trade union committee. Those nominated by the government could be replaced by the ministry concerned. Local trade union organizations would have a key role in the hiring and dismissal of workers and questions of working conditions—including health and safety—and in advising on promotions and professional training. The Government Delegate would be an appointee of the ministry into which a particular enterprise was integrated and could cast a deciding vote in case of a deadlock arising within the Management Committee, the membership of which should be limited to six.

Obviously a key question was that of the composition and function of the Workers' Assemblies. These were consciously designed to introduce culturally backward and illiterate workers into the practice of socialism by shortcut routes. How could it have been done otherwise? Teach them to read and write? Then study the difficult theoretical works of Marxism-Leninism? And how to apply them to Angolan conditions? They started to apply them in practice without knowing the theory. The Workers' Assemblies, as defined by the law, are to be—and have since become—of two types: the General Workers' Assembly, of which all members of any economic unit are automatically members, and Sector Assemblies in which "the workers of each department, division, service, or section of the economic unit concerned" participate if "the functions in which they are engaged are substantially differentiated" from the overall productive functions of the unit. In other words, maximum autonomy of decision is provided for at the various levels of productive activity. The Sector Assemblies meet weekly, or whenever exceptional circumstances demand. The General Assembly meets once a month, or whenever convoked by the Management or Trade Union Committees, or at the request of

287

two-thirds of the workers. At such meetings the Management Committee is bound to report on the progress of the unit in fulfilling the enterprise or state plan and the workers are expected "to exercise the right to criticism and self-criticism regarding all workers in the units, as well as the Management Committee and the Government Delegate."

Thus every nationalized enterprise—factories, plantations, public health, educational, and other services—became schools for democratic exercise in socialism.

There were plenty of problems in the execution of all this, starting with the lack of technical and administrative cadres and extending to a generalized feeling that now that the exploiters—the bosses and colonialists—had gone, why should one have to work regular hours and respond to trade union and management exhortations to produce more. It took many patient explanations and new decrees concerning work discipline and penalties for the theft or sabotage of state property to gradually create the concept of the all-Angolan importance of the work of each individual. It would have been utopian to expect that all problems would be solved by the promulgation of even the most reasonable of laws. Production dropped in many branches due to lack of experience in management, absenteeism, poor labor discipline—plus objective difficulties such as lack of finance, irregularity in supplies of raw materials, and the terrible problems of transport and communications. But to the dismay of Angola's enemies and the surprise of some of its friends, it worked. The economy creaked and groaned in many of its joints during that first year, but it did not collapse. At every level—and I could sense this in my extensive travels—even if things were tough, people knew there was a government which was theirs and was doing its best to solve their problems.

XXIII The Struggle Continues

No public meeting takes place in Angola these days without the main speaker interrupting his speech several times to shout: "A Luta . . ." to which the audience responds: "Continua!" and "A Vitoria . . ." and the response comes back with a roar: "E Certa!" (The struggle . . . continues; victory . . . is certain.) And no meeting can be concluded without many repeated affirmations of these convictions. At first this had a purely internal meaning, but gradually the wider context of continuing struggle in neighboring countries has been accepted. The invasion by South African and Zairean troops and the brutality of their behavior was a rude lesson in some of the international facts of life, especially for those who had the misfortune to be in the areas which the invaders passed through or occupied.

When the leading European colonialist powers met in what is often described as the "Scramble for Africa" Congress of Berlin (1884-85) and drew many straight lines across the map of Africa to define the frontiers of their booty, they created problems that were bound to come home to roost sooner or later. One of these was the border which divided Angola from what was then to become German-occupied Namibia, (Sudwest Afrika to the Germans). Imposed by the foremost exponent of "iron fist diplomacy" in those days, German Chancellor Prince Otto von Bismarck, it posed a problem that a latter-day Bismarck in the person of Henry Kissinger tried, but failed, to solve in the interests of the Western world.

The result of the German take-over was a most horrifying colonial war of extermination against the Herero people, who had dared to oppose their *assegai* (javelins) to the cannon of Herr Krupp in attempting to resist the colonizers. According to modern Namibian nationalists, the Herero people were reduced from several hundred thousands when the resistance war started in 1903, to about 15,000 in 1907.

After the German defeat in World War I, there was a second "Scramble for Africa" in which Namibia—under a League of Nations mandate—passed into the hands of South Africa, then acting on behalf of Great Britain. Not much of an improvement as far as the Namibian people were concerned! The League of Nations died, the United Nations was born, but South Africa clung to its mandate.

According to a Namibian legend, at the time of the Creation, God was flying over the globe deciding where to distribute what were to become the Earth's riches. By accident, he let one of the most precious bags drop, and it fell on Namibia. Gold, diamonds, copper, petroleum, and coarser treasures such as iron ore and coal—all fell on the already rich agricultural soil of Namibia. This was not helpful in persuading South Africa to relinquish its mandate. Especially after uranium—which the investors of the legend could not know about—was discovered.[1]

Appeals to the Hague Court of International Justice by countries acting in the cause of Namibian independence were without avail. But on October 26-28, 1966, the General Assembly of the United Nations, at the initiative of a number of Third World states, adopted a series of resolutions demanding that South Africa relinquish its mandate, restore the name Namibia, withdraw its occupation forces, and grant independence to the Namibian people. South Africa refused and has continued to refuse ever since. In the meantime SWAPO (Southwest African People's Organization) was formed and was recognized by the Decolonialization Committee of the United Nations as the "sole authentic representative" of the Namibian people. Numerous other resolutions calling for Namibian independence were passed at the U.N. Until the "Captains' Coup" in Portugal, it was that country, together with South Africa, which routinely opposed all such resolutions, with the United States, Britain, and France usually abstaining.

"And so," said Sam Nujoma, founder and president of SWAPO, at our memorable first meeting in Luanda at the end of February, 1976, "we came to the conclusion that armed struggle was the only way." A jovial man with a bushy beard tinged with gray, he was overjoyed with the quality of the support SWAPO was already getting from the MPLA even when South African troops were still occupying the Angola-Namibia frontier areas.

During our discussion—in which we were joined by Homateni Kaluenja, a member of SWAPO's Central Committee who had just been designated their permanent representative in Angola—I learned that there had been three distinct phases in a rapid expansion of SWAPO's armed forces. The first had been immediately after the "Captains' Coup" in Portugal when politically conscious activists realized the new perspectives that had opened up. The second was when Angola got its independence. The third was under way, and promised to be by far the most important, as the magnitude of the MPLA victory over the combination of South Africa, Zaire, FNLA, and UNITA forces started to become known. Another important factor in its growth was that the straight line which defined the old border had separated tribes, sub-tribes, and even families, who could now come together and exchange experiences. (Not to mention facilitate the infiltration of guerilla groups!) There were other advantages. For instance, although Homateni Kaluenja spoke no Portuguese, he could converse with an important minister in the Angolan cabinet who spoke no English—in their common tribal dialect. They came from opposite sides of the "straight line." Sam Nujoma said that from sources in Windhoek (the administrative capital of Namibia) they knew even from the meager details revealed at that time that the South Africans were greatly shaken by their defeat in Angola.

> They had been glorified in the West as a very powerful military force but they suffered a shattering defeat. SWAPO forces did their bit, shooting down a plane with a brigadier-general and two colonels in it. That is only part of the shape of things to come. They know that—we know it even better! We are now carrying out harassing activities within forty-five miles of Windhoek. We have no illusions. The enemy is strong and well armed. He uses the resources of our country against us. We need more sophisticated weapons to stand up to the enemy's modern arms and commando tactics. We need more international support, especially on the political front.
>
> At present the South Africans are copying American chemical warfare tactics to create a "white zone" along the whole Angola-Namibia border where nothing can live or grow. But this is terribly expensive and the frontier is impossible to police.[2]

As our conversation was interrupted to listen to an announcement over Luanda radio that President Neto was leaving for Brazzaville to hold talks with President Mobutu on the possibility of normalizing Angola-Zaire relations, I asked the SWAPO leaders if there was any basis for SWAPO-South African talks. Sam Nujoma replied that six conditions must first be met:

> South Africa must recognize the right of Namibia to self-determination and national sovereignty.
> South Africa must recognize the territorial unity and integrity of

Namibia. No "bantustans"; no separatist movements; no division of Namibia on an ethnic or tribal basis.

South Africa must withdraw all troops and security forces from Namibia territory; we cannot discuss the issues at the point of a gun.

South Africa must recognize SWAPO, as the UN and OAU have done, as the "sole authentic representative" of the Namibian people.

All political prisoners currently held in the Robben Islands penitentiary [about ten miles northwest of Capetown] and those jailed in Namibia itself must be released.

South Africa must permit all Namibians in exile to return without any threats of arrest or victimization.

As to how many political prisoners were being held, Sam Nujoma explained that the exact figure was difficult to determine. Over forty were serving life imprisonment under the "Anti-Terrorist Act" introduced in 1967, after SWAPO was formed and guerilla activity started. But every SWAPO activist, and anyone suspected of being a member of PLAN (People's Armed Forces of Namibia), whom the South African security forces had been able to lay their hands on was in prison. Nujoma had no illusions that these conditions would ever be met; the SWAPO leaders were relying on armed struggle alone to win independence. Homateni Kaluenja, who had just come from the front-line areas, explained current SWAPO military tactics:

> Thus far we have not concentrated on liberating territory or creating a liberated area. Our tactics are to hit enemy base installations and camps; force them to move about so we can ambush their convoys and keep them off balance. The three northern provinces are our main zone of operations. Many guerillas who play an active part in such harassment are getting valuable battlefield training at the same time. Once we have solid liberated areas we will start driving the South Africans south and we will never let up until they have their backs to the sea in South Africa itself. Vorster sees the danger but he doesn't dare to reveal this to the white racists. It would be too demoralizing. He has two options—to continue to live within the closed world of white racism, which he knows is doomed to extinction, or to try to come to terms with his newly independent black neighbors. . . .

What he said next was of profound significance in relation to the explosive events which took place in Soweto almost four months later. It revealed a level of information—and evaluation of that information—superior to that of the Vorster regime.

There is profound disquiet in South Africa, according to our sources. Even within Vorster's Nationalist Party. Why go to Angola? And having gone, why come back without achieving anything? These are the questions that are being asked even in the most loyal circles. But there are other much more dangerous trends for the regime. This is concentrated among black students but has also spread to some of their white counterparts. They have been watching the trend of events from Algeria to Angola and drawing their own conclusions. Our friends report on black reactions to documentaries on the Angolan war in the cinemas. Enthusiastic applause when MPLA victories are portrayed, dead silence on anything favorable to the South Africans. We are realistic. We don't envisage any "Captains' Coup" erupting in Pretoria! The South African forces must suffer far more serious defeats.

Inside Namibia we hit only at army and military installations. But this is backed up by working-class demonstrations and strikes. We do not intend to strike at civilians, but it is inevitable as our attacks develop against communications and transport, at power and other supplies, that the peaceful and comfortable lives of the whites are going to be affected. This may cause them to wake up and start putting political pressure on the Pretoria government. But we have no illusions about this. We count on our own armed struggle to liberate our own country. Certainly the fact that there is no armed struggle inside South Africa itself enables Vorster to concentrate 40,000 troops in Namibia[3]—where the total white civilian population is about 95,000—compared to about a million blacks![4] How will they cope when armed struggle starts, as it inevitably will, in South Africa itself?

It was a good question and only the future can provide the answer. But that the Vorster government was indeed shaken and nervous enough to put some pressures on the Ian Smith regime in Rhodesia to come to terms with *his blacks* is a matter for the public record. And that the multinationals were sufficiently worried about the future of their investments for Henry Kissinger to be mobilized for a last round of shuttle diplomacy in southern Africa is also on the public record.

How did SWAPO come to life and what prompted someone like Sam Nujoma to become a militant? His personal story is typical of many other leaders of the struggle in southern Africa and illustrates also that marvelous solidarity referred to earlier between personalities and movements accepted as genuinely nationalist, regardless of racial, religious, and ideological boundaries from Cairo to the Cape. Born in 1929 in a small village—Ongandjela in Ovamboland in northern Namibia—Sam Nujoma belonged to one of the typical cattle-raising families of the area.

My happiest boyhood memories were the three months between August-September and December when we lads took the cattle to the summer grazing lands, up to fifty miles away from the village. There was plenty of grass and water for the cows and we brought them back with their calves. It was a completely free and happy life. We hunted hares and antelope and lived by our own skills. Back in the village I went to a missionary school, learning to read and write—and above all—to study the Bible.

Because of family problems during World War II, he first went to live with an aunt and, when she died, with an uncle in Windhoek. The uncle arranged for him to work on the railway and to study at night school.

Working on the railway I saw oppression and racism in its fullest extent. It was an entirely South African operation. The overseers were unskilled Boers from the other side of the frontier—contemptuously called "poor whites" by those of higher status. They arrived barefoot—worse off than those of us who had families to look after our needs. But they were in complete charge of all facilities at every level. There was a "baas-boy" relationship. They were "baas" [bosses] and any African—whatever his age, education, or skill—was a "boy." They were extremely cruel and ruthless. If an African tried to give the slightest advice—"better do it this way"—based on his long technical experience, the response was inevitably: "You black bastard. You're trying to tell me—a white man!" And the "baas" would send for the police. The minimum punishment would be arrest and a terrible beating. Often the offender would be beaten to death. How could one accept such injustice? Some of us started to think that there was no reason for this to go on forever.

There were some stirrings for independence. We got some news about the Afro-Asian Conference at Bandung in 1955.

(I had attended that conference and was impressed by the frequent reference to ancient trade and cultural links between

Africa and Asia that had been interrupted when colonialism had carved out its spheres of influence on the continents of Africa and Asia and in the areas which had traditionally linked them.)

Then Ghana became independent in 1957. This made a big impression. Some of us got together and started to discuss things. If Ghana—why not us? We signed a petition and sent it to the United Nations. No results. Some of our people were working in Capetown and through them we made contact with the African National Congress and South African trade unions. They sent us some literature. Our enemy was clearly the same.

In 1959 we formed the Ovamboland People's Organization— obviously underground. Shortly after its formation we organized a boycott of all municipal facilities in Windhoek—cinemas, public baths, transport. We were protesting against racial decrees that forbade Africans from even moving through certain parts of the city. On December 10, 1959, troops and police were brought in to suppress a quite orderly demonstration. They used firearms and twelve of our supporters were killed. As president of the Ovamboland People's Organization, I was arrested. The magistrate who heard my case said: "Not guilty." But I was arrested again as I stepped out of the court and the same farce was repeated several times. "Not guilty," said one arm of the law; "Arrest him," said another. After this had happened several times, our Executive Committee decided I had better escape abroad and find a way to present our case to the United Nations. In March, 1960, I went into exile.

Then followed a saga of a battle of wits and organization between British security services working on behalf of the South African government—and on their own account—and various underground nationalist organizations in various not-yet independent British African colonies, protectorates, and other camouflaged designations of British colonial rule. Without identity, documents or money, Sam Nujoma was passed on from one organization to another from Botswana (then Bechuanaland) through Rhodesia, Zambia, Malawi, Tanzania, Uganda, and the Sudan. In Sudan, which was already independent, the newly established embassy of Ghana issued him papers enabling him to continue to the U.N., and there present a report to the Southwest Africa Committee on June 12, 1960. In the meantime the Ovamboland People's Organization had been transformed into the Southwest African People's Organization. It was in the name of SWAPO that Nujoma presented his people's case to the U.N. in late 1960. From there he went on in January, 1961, to open SWAPO offices in Cairo and other places.[5]

Sixteen years after he had eluded the daily attentions of the South African police and slipped across the frontier into Bechuanaland-Botswana, we could talk in a room at Luanda's posh Hotel Tropico of the real possibilities of ending the degradation and humiliation of alien, racist rule in his country. There were well-organized armed forces battling the South African colonialist forces south of the frontier and a secure, friendly base just to the north of it. It was similar to the situation which existed for Vietnam in 1949 after the victory of the Chinese Communists over the U.S.-backed Kuomintang opened up a friendly frontier between the Vietnam of Ho Chi Minh and the China of Mao Tse-tung.

There was not a shadow of doubt in the mind of Sam Nujoma at our first meeting in late February, 1976, or at a subsequent one nine months later, that support from Angola was total and without conditions. By then the battle had been seriously engaged. Enticements from the South African government to settle South African-Angolan problems by negotiations were countered by a principled Angolan position that there was no common frontier. Angola had a frontier with the Namibia of SWAPO, not with the South Africa of Vorster or whoever might succeed him. And Angola would support the legitimate rights of a Namibia represented by SWAPO to its full independence and sovereignty.

"Was there a particular thing which transformed you into a militant?" I put this question to Sam Nujoma, as I have to militant leaders wherever I have encountered them. "No," he replied. "It was the accumulation of oppression, humiliation, racism; the bullying attitude of South African fascists against whom we had no harsh feelings because of the color of *their* skins; their practice of flogging and otherwise torturing our compatriots. I had to leave school because of their *apartheid* language which would have set me apart from my own people. By good fortune I was able to continue my education by correspondence—up to junior certificate level. But that was exceptional. I could never accept the injustice of legally imposed superiority based on the difference of skin color." The Western world would do well to ponder on that sort of feeling; it will remain the most deep-rooted of all.

In this connection it is worth recalling that a debate raged for years in Southwest Africa on the question of flogging as a form of punishment. It had been introduced in Ovamboland (the first and largest of the so-called home territories or "bantustans") on the pretext that this was a tribal custom which must be rigorously respected! When some church people, including Bishop Leonard Auala of the Evangelical Ovambo-Kavango Lutheran Church denied under oath that tribal customs had ever permitted floggings of "more than ten strokes" while there was abundant evidence that up to thirty strokes were being administered, a puppet tribal leader was produced in court to claim there were no such limits and that in any case those being punished in such a way were only "members and supporters of SWAPO . . . flogged because they were undermining tribal custom and the authority of the headmen, which was a punishable offense." An application by Bishop Auala and the Anglican Suffragan Bishop of Damaraland, the Right Reverend Richard Wood, for an interim ban on flogging was rejected on April 17, 1974, by the Supreme Court in Windhoek on the grounds that such action "would militate against the maintenance of tribal authority." The argument of whether to flog or not to flog and if so, how many strokes, continued until May 22, 1975, when, after a continuing campaign led by bishops of varying denominations, the "prime minister" of Ovamboland, Chief Filemon Elifas, an ardent flogger of the thirty-stroke school, decreed that the flogging should no longer be done publicly but could be continued in private and that "women and political opponents of the chief" would no longer be flogged. (Bishop Wood was expelled from the territory in June, 1975.⁶) "Prime Minister" Filemon Elifas was assassinated on August 16 of the same year.

Homateni Kaluenja added that since Filemon Elifas was assassinated, "other puppets hardly dare stay in their homes at night. When they move around, it is with police or military escorts."

At another meeting with Sam Nujoma nine months later during the celebrations to mark the first anniversary of Angola's independence, he was more optimistic than ever about SWAPO's impending total victory. He had just returned from the front-line areas:

Vorster has quietly dropped the "bantustan" idea. After Elifas was killed, the South Africans spent vast sums in the Ovamboland area to buy people up—even opening free liquor shops. It only made people angrier than ever. It was such an obvious attempt to make them forget the struggle. The so-called constitutional talks in Windhoek have been a farce.[7] Even some stooge groups which originally took part have pulled out because public opinion is so strongly against them.

Young people are flocking to our ranks faster than we can arm them. Whole schools have slipped away overnight. There have been cases when teachers turned up in the morning and not a single child was there. They had gone across the border into Angola where we have set up primary and secondary schools. Teachers have often followed, partly because they are scared of being flogged or even killed by the local authorities.

Everything, including the Vorster-Kissinger intrigues, makes us more than ever convinced that intensification of the armed struggle is the only solution. The Vorster-Kissinger maneuvers were only intended to give South Africa a breathing space to consolidate and reinforce its military posture to continue the exploitation of our country by the multinationals.[8]

Referring to the Angolan independence celebrations, Sam Nujoma said: "We always stated that the Victory of the Angolan people would be our victory, but we could never imagine that within one year of the MPLA setting up the People's Republic— and when their victory was still far from complete—that our own liberation struggle could have advanced so rapidly. This is thanks to the unreserved support from our Angolan comrades."

It is this type of inter-African solidarity which sounds the death knell for the racist minority regimes in Salisbury, Windhoek, and Pretoria and other client regimes that depend on them. The victories of the peoples of Angola, Mozambique, and Guiné-Bissau which brought about the collapse of Portugal's African empire have thus radically and irreversibly transformed the situation in the rest of southern Africa. But this was a point which Vorster seemed incapable of grasping even after he had to yield to internal and external pressures and come to grips with the inevitability of Namibia's independence.

Sam Nujoma's description of the Windhoek "constitutional" talks as a farce proved to be valid. Eventually Vorster had to abandon them. Over two years after they started, a South African magazine summed up what had been accomplished at the talks until that time.

Enough has emerged from the constitutional conference at Wind-hoek to sketch a fairly detailed picture of the interim government which will rule Namibia—as South West Africa will be called—in the first five years of its independence. The announcement of the forma-tion of an interim government headed by a black president, but with a white prime minister, is thought to be a matter of days away. For the first five years, the South African government will retain execu-tive and legislative powers for defense, foreign affairs, transport, finance and exchange, inland security and telecommunications and posts. All other functions and powers will be vested in the interim government, which is likely to be headed by Dirk Mudge, an Af-rikaaner and member of the South West Africa branch of the Nationalist Party, which rules in South Africa. The president—the Herero chief Clemens Kapuuo has been tipped for the job—will be a figurehead role, confined to acting as a "symbol of unity."[9]

The Windhoek talks, usually known as the Turnhalle confer-ence because they were held in Windhoek's Turnhalle gym-nasium, were boycotted by SWAPO and other nationalist organi-zations from the beginning until they ended in admitted failure on October 12, 1977. Dirk Mudge and Clemens Kapuuo were known as Vorster's right and left hand respectively in South West Africa and Sam Nujoma had contemptuously denounced the talks as a "puppet farce."

In order to show his "democratic" approach, Vorster had his hand-picked Turnhalle group working on a post-independence constitution. And a referendum would be held in South West Africa to decide whether it was acceptable or not. The South African *Star Weekly* reported that:

> The proposed referendum will determine whether South West Af-rica/Namibia will have a constitution worked out by the Turnhalle or one imposed by the South African Government. That is the choice facing the territory's white voters. At stake is no longer the retention or sharing of power—but how to share it.
>
> If the draft constitution for interim government is rejected at the polls, the Prime Minister will impose his own—like it or not. As things stand, only South Africans will have the vote. It is of little consequence how long they have lived in the West.[10]

The referendum was actually held on May 17, 1977. Johan-nesburg Radio in its English service on the following day announced that with the results known from sixteen of South West Africa's eighteen constituencies, "more than 26,000 voters, or 95 per cent of those who went to the polls, have voted yes. . . ." It was on the basis of this farce that Vorster announced that an interim government based on the "Turnhalle constitutional plan" would be installed in Windhoek before July 1. SWAPO immediately warned that the setting up of a hand-picked puppet government would turn Namibia into a second Vietnam.

The five western powers on the U.N. Security Council (the USA, Great Britain, France, West Germany and Canada) had set up a "contact group," to ensure that they exercised some control over the situation. The group turned up in Cape Town on June 6 and, following what must have been very tough talks with the South African government, Vorster announced that he was abandoning plans for an interim government and would be appointing an Administrator-General instead to supervise a transitional period to independence. Commenting on this back-down, *The Times* (London) reported from Johannesburg:

> Shorn of its diplomatic language, it is clear from today's announcement that South Africa and more especially the Turnhalle, have made substantial compromises in the face of concerted Western pressure. Not only has the interim government idea, through which the Turnhalle hoped to establish its authority before full independence, been dropped but there has also been acceptance by the South Africans that the United Nations should play a role during the elections.[11]

The pace of support for SWAPO was beginning to quicken. The Herero tribe rejected both the Turnhalle "constitution" and president-designate Clemens Kapuuo, who claimed leadership over the Hereros. In meetings throughout the country SWAPO could muster four or five times as many supporters as the Turnhalle group. SWAPO, in other words, had nothing to fear from U.N. Security Council Resolution 385, adopted unanimously on January 30, 1977, which after condemning South Africa's "illegal occupation" of South West Africa, and its "discriminatory laws and practices," demanded the holding of free elections under UN supervision and the withdrawal of South Africa's administration.

The realism shown by the "contact group" in its pressures on Vorster was due to the belated recognition by even the leading western powers that what the African group and Third World group within the United Nations had been saying for years, was correct—SWAPO was the real representative of the South West African people. Typical of this was an article in the *Observer* (London) by Peter Temple-Morris, Conservative MP for Leominster, one of a delegation of five who visited Namibia on behalf of the Inter-Parliamentary Union.

> There is no political organization among Namibians compared to SWAPO. Whatever happens at Turnhalle, it [SWAPO] will continue to receive intense backing of the so-called "front-line" African States, Angola, Botswana, Mozambique, Tanzania and Zambia; UN money will continue to flow in for its education and social pro-grammes for thousands of Namibian exiles [mostly in Angola]; and guns and money will continue to be forthcoming from the Soviet Union and its allies . . . What we in this country must do now is to recognize SWAPO as the exclusive voice of Namibians. Until we do this, we can have little hope of influencing them . . .
>
> To recognize SWAPO is to reject whatever comes out of Turn-halle, which is seen by Africans as an attempt to gain international recognition of the Bantustan solution for Southern Africa as a whole . . .
>
> Above all we must clearly recognize that independence for Namibia is more than just a flag to put on a pole and that Namibians and their fellow Africans have the will, the money and the guns to carry on their struggle until they find a solution acceptable to them. [12]

Part of the reason for this new realism was the growing conviction that there were some highly lucrative profits to be had by cooperating with an independent Namibia. South Africa had taken great pains to hide the extent to which its revenue originated in the exploitation of Namibia. Professor Wolfgang Thomas, a member of the Turnhalle subcommittee on finance, was not only dismissed from the subcommittee but deported from the country because he asked for statistics relating to South West Africa's balance of payments and sources of revenue. Commenting on his deportation, the South African *Financial Mail* wrote that:

> Independence could have significant implications for South Africa's balance of payments, which currently benefits by an estimated 400 to 500 million rands [500 to 600 million US dollars] from South West Africa's foreign trade surplus. Is this perhaps an over-riding consid-

eration in trying to maintain an integrated central banking link between the two countries—at least during the transition period? . . . Current South West Africa merchandise imports are about 600 million rands [750 million dollars] a year, split 50-50 between South African and foreign suppliers. [Professor] Thomas believes this figure could be reduced considerably by shopping in foreign markets with low cost units and allowing goods to enter at low tariffs. It is unfair, he contends, that South West Africa has to help bear South Africa's structural balance of payments problems and be subject to imports such as a fifteen percent surcharge when its own payments situation is perfectly sound.[13]

Another report in the *Financial Mail* noted that global figures on Namibia's mineral output have been on the secret list since 1969 and that "Rio Tinto Zinc's Rossing Uranium, now the biggest single revenue earner in the territory, "operates under conditions of such secrecy that even the Administrator of South West Africa and South Africa's Minister of Mines, are obliged to sign a formal non-disclosure statement in terms of the Atomic Energy Act when they visit the mine." The paper refers to Consolidated Diamond Mines last-published report which showed revenue from diamonds in 1974 to be about 105 million dollars, with the figure for 1977 expected to be about 175 million dollars. In the meantime CDM had been absorbed into the De Beers' diamond empire. Exploitation of copper, lead, zinc, cadmium and nickel, the paper states, has gone on at an accelerated pace during the past few years in what seems to have been an effort to extract as much as possible while the territory is still in South Africa's hands. The conclusion is, however:

Taking the existing mines, but particularly Rossing, CDM, Tsumeb and Otjihase, mineral exports can probably generate enough foreign exchange earnings for the independent South West Africa/Namibia to pay its way, even before allowing for such other exports as wool, fish and fish-meal.[14]

By the end of 1977, after a full year of on-again off-again negotiations at various levels, Vorster had been winkled out of one "final position" after another, prodded by stepped-up SWAPO activity on the battlefield, and diplomatic pressures from western powers eager to prove their anti-*apartheid* sentiments and thus get off to a good start with an independent Namibia. On December 19, Britain's ambassador to the United Nations told a New York press conference that only three main questions remained to be settled: How many South African troops might remain in the Territory during the transition to independence [SWAPO maintained that 2,000 would be ample]; where those troops would be stationed; how large a U.N. presence [to supervise the elections] would be needed. "Everybody agrees now" said Ivor Richards, "that Namibia should come to independence as a unitary state, that there should be free elections prior to independence and that these elections should be monitored, supervised, observed . . . through a UN presence . . . and that whoever wins the election should be the Government of Namibia."[15]

Even if everyone did not share Ivor Richard's optimism, the signs were that Namibia would become independent during 1978 or very shortly thereafter, and SWAPO would be the elected Government of an independent Namibia. Following exactly the same tactics as Ian Smith in Rhodesia however, Vorster continued to play for time while going ahead with plans to impose an "internal settlement" on Namibia through his hand-picked stooges and a bogus "constitution" and "referendum". Thus, as part of the playing for time tactic, talks which started on February 9, 1978, at the U.N. Headquarters in New York between the five western members of the U.N. Security Council, Vorster's foreign minister, Pik Botha and Sam Nujoma were interrupted four days later when Botha suddenly flew off to Pretoria saying he had "reached the limit" of his instructions. Nujoma was being adamant on the question of an independent Namibia's sovereignty over Walvis Bay, as well as over all other economic installations "built with the blood and sweat of Namibian people with Namibian resources." Future President Sam Nujoma, of the independent People's Republic of Namibia, had every reason to be confident that the abrupt walk-out by Pik Botha from the New York meeting was symbolic of the impending departure of the South African overlords from his country. And with that another mortal blow would be struck at the last bastion of white racist supremacy on the whole of the African continent.

NOTES

PART I
Angola and After

Chapter 1 *How It Started*
1. The incident of the *Santa Maria* was the most spectacular protest action against Portugal's colonial wars until the "Captains' Coup" which overthrew the Caetano regime on April 25, 1974. Captain Henrique Galvão, originally a staunch Salazar supporter who had helped bring him to power, served the fascist regime in various capacities in Angola. In 1947, after a long term back in Portugal, he headed a mission to report on conditions in the African territories. What he found turned him into one of Salazar's bitterest enemies. His report was suppressed, but not before he managed to read it to the National Assembly. Galvão strongly condemned the system of forced labor which turned Africans into "beasts of burden," the abominable conditions of public health, the lack of education, and other vices of the Portuguese colonial system. As a result, his public career was abruptly ended. He continued his protest campaign until he was jailed for three years in 1951, but detained until 1958 under a formula of "measures of state security" which permitted indefinite renewal of detention of anyone suspected of "endangering security." He was then tried again on thirteen charges, including those of "subversion" and "incitement to revolt" and sentenced to a further sixteen years. Everyone thought that was the end of a courageous officer. But his name made world headlines on January 23, 1961, with the news of "piracy on the high seas." The 20,000-ton liner *Santa Maria* had been seized by Captain Galvão and seventy of his followers. After escaping from jail in 1959 and following a brief period of asylum in the Argentine embassy in Lisbon, Galvão had gone into exile. His first public statement was a message broadcast over the liner's radio "in the name of the Independent Junta of National Salvation, headed by General Umberto Delgado, who was fraudulently deprived of his rights by the Salazar administration." (A reference to what Galvão considered as bogus presidential elections in June, 1958, in which General Delgado stood against Salazar—the first time in thirty-two years that anyone had dared to do so.) Galvão and his supporters had boarded the liner as "tourists" at the Caribbean island of Curaçao, then taken it over after a brief gun battle. For the next ten days the *Santa Maria* zigzagged back and forth across the Atlantic, broadcast-

ing scathing attacks against the Salazar dictatorship. Finally, after some thinly veiled threats from the U.S. Navy, the *Santa Maria,* all flags and banners flying, sailed into the Brazilian port of Recife, where the 600 passengers were landed unharmed, most of them full of praise for the gallant behavior of Galvão and his band. The latter were all offered political asylum in Brazil.

2. This question is dealt with in detail in John Marcum, *The Angolan Revolution, Vol. I: The Anatomy of an Explosion,* Cambridge, Mass., and London, 1969, pp. 62-64.

Chapter 2 *Comandante Margoso's Story*

1. For a full report on the Sékou Touré speech, see *Afrique-Asie,* No. 99, December 29, 1975-January 11, 1976.

2. Pierre-Pascal Rossi, *Pour une guerre oublié,* Paris, 1969, pp. 214-15.

Chapter 3 *Holden Roberto*

1. *Remarques Congolese et Africaines,* published in Brussels as the successor to *Remarques Congoleses,* had printed in its October 14, 1964, issue what purported to be an article by a Congolese journalist on the African revolution.

2. *Afrique-Asie,* December 29, 1975-January 11, 1976.

Chapter 4 *Jonas Savimbi*

1. For a detailed account of the Alvor Agreement, see Chapter 6.

2. FLEC (Front for the Liberation of the Cabinda Enclave), the Zaire-based secessionist group, was set up in Kinshasa after the April 25, 1974, "Captains' Coup." Its president, Ranque Franque, is a close friend of President Mobutu, and the group was clearly formed to further Mobutu's plan to annex Cabinda. It quickly won the support of Spinola, then president of Portugal, and also had the backing of some French oil interests.

3. The Mbunda ethnic grouping is based in the southeast corner of Angola in areas adjoining the Zambian border and is not to be confused with the Mbundu, whose homelands are just north of Luanda.

4. Basil Davidson, *In the Eye of the Storm: Angola's People,* New York, 1972, p. 238.

5. Ibid., pp. 251-52.

6. MPLA guerilla leaders had a rich collection of *noms de guerre,* some taken from legendary leaders such as Ho Chi Minh, Che Guevara,

Chapayev. Others, like "Furioso" and "Monstro Imortal," seemed aimed at pleasing the fantasy of those who chose them.

7. Daniel Chipenda had been a close associate of Agostinho Neto and a member of the MPLA steering committee. He later broke with Neto and in early 1973 formed the "Eastern Revolt" group, recruiting guerillas from among the Mbundu people. Because he could not get recognition as one of the major national liberation movements, he threw in his lot with Holden Roberto and became assistant secretary-general of the FNLA.

8. *Depoimento* (Testimony), by Marcello Caetano, Rio and Sau Paulo, 1974, pp. 180-181. Caetano writes: "The enemy's opening of the Eastern Front constituted a tremendous preoccupation and Costa Gomes, on assuming responsibility for Angola's defence, approached the case with intelligence and decisiveness. [General] Bettencourt Rodrigues received the task . . . to pacify the region, which he did by reaching an understanding with the people of UNITA, an insurrectionary group which, under the leadership of Savimbi, operated with the disagreement of the MPLA. . . ."

Chapter 5 *The Long March of Agostinho Neto*

1. *In The Eye Of The Storm,* Basil Davidson, Penguin African Library, London, 1975, p. 224.

2. Ibid., p. 234.

3. In conversation with the author, Phnom Penh, 1966.

4. *In the Eye Of The Storm,* p. 207.

5. Following a crisis between left-wing military forces and the civilian government in Congo (Brazzaville) in July-August, 1968, Captain Marien Ngouabi, then head of a Parachutists' battalion, replaced Alphonse Massemba-Débat as Head of State. On March 18, 1977, President Marien Ngouabi was assassinated and just a week later, Massemba-Debat was executed by firing squad for allegedly master-minding the assassination. Ngouabi was replaced by one of his close supporters, Colonel Joachim Yhombi-Opango as Head of State and President of the all-powerful Military Committee.

Chapter 6 *April 25 and the Alvor Conference*

1. By an ironic twist of events, one of this author's books, *The Inside Story of the Guerilla War in South Vietnam,* which was published in Lisbon but seized by the PIDE following protests from the U.S. embassy, was used at the Portuguese military academy as a textbook for studying the type of "Vietcong" guerilla tactics that might be used in the African colonies. The net effect, as several of the AFM officers told me, was that even the most diehard officers started to ask: "If a mighty country like the

U.S.A., with all its illimitable military and economic resources, cannot win in a small country like Vietnam, how can a small and poor country like Portugal win in the vast expanses of our African territories?"

2. Kaulza de Arriaga was one of the most reactionary generals of the fascist regime, but he was also considered one of the most efficient. He withdrew his candidacy from the June, 1976, presidential elections after a Lisbon paper published proof of his involvement in atrocities while he was commander-in-chief in Mozambique.

3. The CDE (Democratic Electoral Commission), headed by the liberal Catholic economist, Professor Francisco de Moura, and the CEUD (United Democratic Electoral Commission), headed by Màrio Soares, were the closest approach to opposition formations permitted to stand candidates in the October, 1969, elections. The CEUD, which came in far behind the CED—the fascist National Union Party winning all 130 seats—later fused with the CED. After the "Captains' Coup" the CDE, which was a loose association of Socialists, left-wing Catholics, and Republicans, was broadened to include the by-then legal Communists; and the name was changed to MDP (Popular Democratic Movement). It had extremely close ties with the AFM. It was an embryonic popular front and the strongest political force in the country, until Màrio Soares decided to withdraw his Socialist Party on the grounds that the MDP had become "dominated by the Communists."

Chapter 7 *The Portuguese Exit*
1. *After Angola: The War Over Southern Africa; The Role of the Big Powers*, Colin Legum: *How the MPLA Won In Angola*, Tony Hodges, Rex Collings, London, 1976: p. 50.
2. Cf, op.cit., p. 36. (SWAPO-the South West African People's Organization had started guerilla warfare to win back South West Africa, or Namibia, from the South Africans by the time Legum and Hodges wrote their booklet.)
3. *The Guardian* (Manchester), January 26, 1976.

Chapter 8 *Enter the Cubans*
1. At the time the general Slaves' Revolt broke out in Haiti in 1791, it was estimated that of a total population of 520,000, 450,000 were slaves and another 27,500 were mulattos of slave descent. At that time the island was under French control.

Chapter 9 *The Kissinger Version*
1. This and subsequent quotes are taken from the report on the hearings before the Subcommittee on African Affairs of the Committee on Foreign

Relations, United States Senate, Ninety-Fourth Congress; Second Session on U.S. Involvement in Civil War in Angola, January 29 and February 3, 4, and 6, 1976. The report is available from the U.S. Government Printing Office.

2. São Pedro de Bassa fortress, overlooking the entrance to Luanda harbor, was the last citadel of the FNLA in Luanda. After it was stormed by the MPLA and its supporters, hundreds of corpses of MPLA activists and sympathizers were found in its vaults and in mass graves.

3. *FNLA em Angola,* a pamphlet issued by the Information Ministry of the People's Republic of Angola, October 20, 1975, in which the document as submitted to the Portuguese High Commission is published *in extenso.*

4. Jean Kay is a self-confessed professional mercenary. He has published a book about his exploits in the Yemen, the Congo, Lebanon, and Biafra; he also served with the fascist OAS in Algeria. His name flashed into the headlines of the French press in September, 1976, for his role in the theft of eight million francs (1.6 million U.S. dollars) from the aircraft construction empire of Marcel D'Assault. Ostensibly the money was to finance the Christian Phalangists in Lebanon.

5. Legum & Hodges, *After Angola,* op. cit., p. 10.

Chapter 10 *The Nito Alves Coup Attempt*

1. For the contents of this chapter, the author, who was not on the spot, is indebted to numerous telephone conversations with Sara Rodriguez of the New York *Guardian,* Augusta Conchiglia of *Afrique-Asie,* Luis de Almeida, the adviser on international affairs to Agostinho Neto, and an interview with Simon Malley, the editor of *Afrique-Asie,* following his return to Paris after long conversations with President Neto and other Angolan leaders immediately after the coup attempt.

2. Simon Malley, *Afrique-Asie,* July 11-24, 1977.

3. Sara Rodriguez, *The Guardian* (New York), June 1, 1977. As is the custom with most American newsweeklies, *The Guardian* is advance-dated. This issue was on the newsstands before the dramatic events of May 27.

4. My source for this revealing incident is a personal conversation with a member of Raoul Castro's staff.

5. Comandante "Eurico" had been my constant companion during both my first visits to Angola. He was always good-humored, efficient, and a deadly enemy of bureaucracy. My most vivid impression of him was when he vigorously battled with some of Nito Alves's security guards attempting to prevent me from entering the VIP room at Luanda airport where Agostinho Neto was briefing the press after a visit abroad. Garcia Neto had also been a helpful friend on many occasions. Saydi Mingas was one of

the most popular and efficient ministers in the post-victory government. Gato had been appointed to his functions especially to sort out the obvious sabotage at the Luanda port, from which entire cargos of consumer goods disappeared.

6. Simon Malley's interview with "Iko" was published in *Afrique-Asie*, July 11-24, 1977.

7. Sara Rodriguez, *The Guardian* (New York), June 15, 1977. (According to documents found on the chief conspirators, Sara Rodriguez and Augusta Conchiglia of *Afrique-Asie* were to be arrested and after a summary trial, executed as "imperialist spies.")

8. The "Shaba Invasion" was one of those bizarre affairs the various interpretations of which demonstrate how even major powers can get their lines crossed once they abandon the principle of objective information-gathering. China—and to a lesser extent, the United States—accused the Soviet Union and Cuba of being behind the sudden seizure of large parts of the mineral-rich Shaba province of southern Zaire, in March, 1977, by "Katangan invaders" from Angola. The Katangans, sometimes known as the Katangan "gendarmes," had crossed into Angola following Moise Tshombe's unsuccessful attempt to set up a secessionist independent state of Katanga in 1962 in what was then known as the Belgian Congo. The Katangan "gendarmes" were used by the Portuguese against the MPLA, but later many of them switched their loyalty to the MPLA. Under an agreement reached between Agostinho Neto and the president of Zaire, Mobutu Sese Seko, in February, 1976, at their meeting in Brazzaville, Katangans in Angola and Angolans in Zaire were to be given facilities to return to their homelands. That some of the Katangans took arms with them to cross a virtually uncontrolled border and linked up with armed groups already operating in Shaba province is certain. But to the author's knowledge—and after exhaustive inquiries—neither the Soviet Union, nor Cuba, nor the Angolan government was involved in any way. Cuban diplomats in Angola and Congo-Brazzaville went to extreme lengths, I have been assured, to avoid any contacts with representatives of the "Congolese National Liberation Front" (FLNC), despite an assiduous courtship by the latter. The Soviet Union was horrified about the effect that such a venture would have on its "détente" policy with the United States—and it is possible that some of their diplomats in Luanda lent a too-ready ear to the Nito Alves arguments that the MPLA leadership was involved. To emphasize the confusion regarding the "Shaba Invasion," the author, who is normally prompt to support national liberation movements, remained aloof from this one after learning that a well-known Belgian recruiter of mercenaries had contacted a compatriot well-known for her MPLA sympathies and offered "150 battle-trained mercenaries" to help the Katangans! That there are legitimate reasons for wanting to overthrow the Mobutu regime in Zaire is well known. But neither the

Soviet Union, Cuban, nor the Angolan government had any interest in supporting a revival of Katangan secessionism!

9. As recounted by Augusta Conchiglia, who interviewed Joaquina a few days after the event. *Afrique-Asie*, August 8-September 4, 1977.

10. While claims by the well-founded UNITA to contro, "half" of Angola are wildly exaggerated, UNITA does have considerable nuisance value. Although UNITA as a political force was totally discredited once it so obviously had to depend on South Africa for suport, committing the unforgivable crime of bringing in South Africa troops to massacre Angolans, it does have some military groups in the heavily-wooded areas of Huambo and Bié provinces, Savimbi's tribal stronghold areas. Before they withdrew, the South African forces established caches of arms estimated to be sufficient to keep UNITA commando groups supplied until 1978. Parallel with the diminishing arms stocks is the shrinking popular support from even areas considered most loyal to Savimbi. Tribal concepts are withering away before the unflagging campaigns against tribalism, racialism and regionalism. A real battle for "hearts and minds" is engaged. UNITA has a program on the South African "Radio Ovambo" based in Namibia with a strond tribal appeal, broadcasting in local dialects. Through its own radio and local "Action Committees," the MPLA governments counters with its all-Angolan national concepts, backed by big efforts to improve security and living standards in the UNITA-influenced areas. The other area where UNITA has a base is in camps supplied by the South Africans south of the Angolan border in Nambia. From these they can make commando raids into Angola, but their main function is to prevent SWAPO guerillas and supplies from being infiltrated into Namibia. From the Huambo-Bié bases they can also occasionally disrupt the vital Benguela railway, but in general this functions regularly from the Atlantic coast to the Zaire border.

PART II
Hurricane Mozambique

Chapter 11 *The Mozambique Detonator*
1. Basil Davidson, *The Liberation of Guiné*, London, 1969, p. 77.
2. Samora Machel, *O Processo da Revoluçao Democratica Popular em Moçambique,* (Maputo,), p. 27.

Chapter 12 *Lighting Fuses*
1. Reverend Uria Simango left FRELIMO and joined a small dissident group based primarily in Kenya; Lázaro Nkavandame later collaborated

with the Portuguese, was captured by FRELIMO forces, and at the time of this writing, is still in prison. Both men were strong opponents of the revolutionary line of Mondlane and Machel. See also Davidson, *In the Eye of the Storm,* op. cit., pp. 226-27.

Chapter 15 *Samora Machel*
1. Davidson, *In the Eye of the Storm,* op. cit., p. 171.
2. Machel, *O Processo da Revoluçao,* op. cit., p. 7.

Chapter 17 *Frelimo 1977*
1. All quotes from Afonso Joane Cotoi are taken from the *Zambia Daily Mail,* September 29, 1977.
2. *Mozambique Information Bulletin,* No. 18.
3. *Times of Zambia,* October 28, 1977.

Chapter 18 *Struggle in Zimbabwe*
1. The background to the jailing of ZANU leaders such as Josiah Tongogara, Robert Mugabe, Kumibirai Kangai, and fifty-four other cadres is long and complex. President Kenneth Kaunda of Zambia had long been restive regarding the presence of ZANU cadres and training camps on Zambian soil and his hostility grew in proportion to his positive response to overtures for "détente" from South Africa's Prime Minister Vorster. An attempt was made to capture Tongogara and some other leaders on December 9, 1974, by some armed "mutineers." Fighting took place in and around Tongogara's house, then the "mutineers" were captured and handed over to the Zambian police. Later a bomb exploded in ZANU's Lusaka headquarters, completely destroying it. On March 18, a mine exploded under the car of Herbert Chitepo, national chairman of the African National Council and its representative in Lusaka. President Kaunda accused the ZANU leadership of being responsible—a charge they hotly refuted, asserting that Chitepo was their popular leader. Since the open hostility between Kaunda and Chitepo was well known, the ZANU leaders suggested that investigations be intensified to discover the real culprit. On March 23, fifty-seven of them were arrested and some 1,200 ZANU trainees who turned up for the funeral of Chitepo were also arrested. Under intense pressure from Mozambique and Tanzania, the trainees were released nine months later, but the leaders were released only on the eve of the Geneva Conference on Rhodesia.

312

2. Later Reverend Sithole was replaced by Robert Mugabe as the head of ZANU.

3. *African Nationalism*, Ndabaningi Sithole, Oxford University Press, London, 1968 (second edition), pp. 30 & 31, and in conversation with author.

4. *International Herald Tribune* (Paris), 2 March, 1977.

5. *International Herald Tribune* (Paris), 28 February, 1977.

6. *Sunday Times* (London), 26 June, 1977.

7. *New Statesman* (London), February 25, 1977.

8. Before devaluation the Rhodesian dollar was officially worth 1.30 South African rands, 1.60 U.S. dollars and 90 pence British sterling.

Chapter 19 *The Geneva Conference*

1. *The Guardian,* New York, November 3, 1976.

2. Prime Minister's address *To The Nation,* September 23, 1976, Ministry of Information, Immigration and Tourism, Salisbury, 1976.

3. Sections of the British press, notably the *Sunday Times,* October 9, 1977, maintain that ZAPU's hotel bill at the Intercontinental—and various travels of Joshua Nkomo—were paid by Roland "Tiny" Rowland, head of LONRHO (London and Rhodesian Mining and Land Company), described as Africa's largest multinational company. The name of "Tiny" Rowland crops up continuously in behind-the-scenes moves for a settlement in Rhodesia. His special talent seems to have been in backing rising black Nationalist leaders—sometimes several in the same country—on the understanding they will favor his interests if they come to power. Among his protégés is Jonas Savimbi, of UNITA in Angola. LONRHO has enormous interests in many newly independent African countries.

4. *The Guardian* (New York), December 29, 1976.

5. Both quotes from *International Herald Tribune* (Paris) March 10, 1976.

6. *The Financial Times* (London), June 11, 1977.

7. *International Herald Tribune* (Paris) September 27, 1977, quoting a BBC (London) broadcast of the previous night.

8. *The Guardian* (Manchester) November 10, 1977.

9. *The Sunday Times* (London) October 29, 1977.

10. *The Guardian* (Manchester) November 12, 1977.

Chapter 20 *The South African Volcano*

1. *Southern Africa, The New Politics of Revolution,* Davidson, Slovo and Wilkinson, Penguin Books (African Affairs) London, 1976, pp. 180 and 192.

2. As summarized in Keelings's *Contemporary Archives*, June 29-July 6, 1963, p. 19502.

3. *International Herald-Tribune* (Paris), 25 February 1977. The most recent victim up till that time was a mulatto "who had apparently torn his blanket into strips to make a rope" according to James Kruger, Minister of Justice and the Police.
4. Davidson, Slovo and Wilkinson, op. cit., p. 194.
5. Davidson, Slovo and Wilkinson, op. cit. p. 197.
6. Davidson, Slovo and Wilkinson, op. cit. pp. 197 & 199.
7. *The Star Weekly* (South Africa), December 3, 1977.
8. On December 13, 1967, in its last resolution on South Africa prior to the study which produced NSSM 39, the U.N. Assembly had passed a resolution by eighty-nine votes to two, with twelve abstentions which included in part: (1) Condemnation of *apartheid* in South Africa as a "crime against humanity"; (2) A declaration that the situation in South Africa "constitutes a threat to international peace and security" and that "mandatory sanctions" against South Africa were the only means of achieving a peaceful solution . . . The resolution condemned those whose financial and economic support encouraged South Africa to persist in its racial policies.
9. Paraphrased from *The Kissinger Study of Southern Africa NSSM 39* (1969). Edited and Introduced by Mohamed A. El-Khawas.

Chapter 21 *New Policies for Old?*

1. This is the same John Marcum whom Savimbi had described twelve years earlier as having been engaged by Holden Roberto as his personal adviser (see Chapter 3).
2. Legum & Hodges, *After Angola,* op. cit., p. 20.
3. When one delves a little deeper, there is evidence to show that the Soviet Union was reluctant to get involved in Angola. Like the U.S. Congress, the Soviet leaders did not want to have to underwrite the staggering expense of another Vietnam. Nor did they want to fall into a confrontation with the United States, thereby putting "détente" on jeopardy. The Colombian writer, Gabriel Garcia-Márquez, after a visit to Havana in December, 1976, where he had several meetings with Castro, later wrote an 80,000-word article, large extracts of which were distributed by Prensa Latina, the official Cuban news agency. In the article, he maintains that the Central Committee of the Cuban Communist Party made its decision to send troops on November 5 as an "independent and sovereign" decision, informing the Soviet Union only after the fact. The Soviet arms which started arriving were from Cuba's own armed forces. Arms from the Soviet Union only starting arriving in Angola much later. I found plenty of well-informed people in Angola who subscribed to this view long before Garciá-Márquez wrote his article.

Chapter 23 *The Struggle Continues*

1. Namibia is a huge underdeveloped and underpopulated country of 508,000 square kilometers, half again as big as France, which is the largest European country after the Soviet Union, with 340,757 square kilometers including Corsica. Exports of copper, lead, zinc, tin, and cadmium averaged over eighty million dollars annually between 1969-73; agricultural and pastoral products, about one hundred million dollars; and fish and other marine products, just under sixty million dollars.

2. A strip of land 1,000 meters wide along the entire frontier was declared a "specially prohibited area," within which helicopter gunships and planes could fire at any human being at any time. Special commando groups were landed to shoot anyone found in this area on a "no questions asked" basis. According to the very energetic UN Commissioner for Namibia, Mr. Sean McBride, between 40,000 and 50,000 people had been forcibly removed from this area, "a gross villation of human rights" as he told a press conference in Lusaka on August 28, 1976.

3. At the Lusaka press conference mentioned above, Sean McBride said that South African forces in Namibia consisted of a motorized infantry brigade of 5,000 men; a specialized army "counter-insurgency" brigade of 5,000; a police "counter-insurgency" unit of 1,900; and a field artillery unit of 900 men. There was also a "reaction force" of 5,000 men—supposedly to deal with an enemy invasion—three anti-aircraft batteries totalling 600 men; and a paratroop battalion of 800—the whole supported by a logistics force of 26,300 men. A total of 45,500 men.

4. The 1970 census gave the total population of Namibia as 746,328, a figure which the SWAPO leaders considered far too low, especially for the African population. Partly because of natural increase since 1970, but especially because of a tendency—for taxation and other reasons— for the Namibians to conceal the true size of their familes. The breakdown according to population groups is probably correct as to their proportions. Ovambo, 342,455; white, 90,658; Damara, 64,973; Kavango, 49,577; Herero, 49,203; Nama, 32,853; colored (mainly of Asian and mixed race), 28,275; East Caprivian, 25,009; San (Bushmen), 21,909; Rehoboth Baster, 16,474; Kaokovelder, 6,457; Tswana, 3,719; and others, 14,776. In one of his reports to the UN, Sean McBride pointed out the injustice of the fact that 35,000 settlers of German origin occupied sixty-seven percent of the arable land!

5. The South African prime minister, Johannes Vorster, gave an original version of the formation of SWAPO in April 18, 1975, as an explanation as to why SWAPO was not to be invited to the "Constitutional Conference" which was "to decide the territory's future." He claimed that it had been "fathered by four Communists" in 1957. In fact it was

formed on April 19, 1960 in Windhoek, which the Namibians call Otjomuize. The aims of its founders were to use all possible avenues to achieve independence without violence. More than six years passed before the first shot was fired—on August 26, 1966—and armed struggle was launched.

6. The South African Council of Churches condemned the expulsion of Bishop Wood, noting that he would always be honored for "his courageous struggle against the barbarous practice of flogging in Ovamboland."

7. The "Constitutional Conference" had opened in Windhoek on September 1, 1975 with a farcial proportion of delegates in relation to ethnic groups. The Hereros for instance, with a census population of 49,203—but a very administration-cooperative chief, Clement Kapuuo—supplied fourty-four delegates of the original total of 135. The Ovambos, with a population of 342,455, were alloted fifteen delegates. This did not inhibit the South African foreign minister, Dr. Hilgard Muller from assuring the UN Secretary-General, Dr. Kurt Waldheim that the delegates would represent "eighty percent of the population." Boycotted by SWAPO, the conference was doomed from the start.

8. Licensing arrangements with South Africa for the export from Naimbia of copper and uranium ore, mainly by U.S., British, Canadian, and Japanese firms, was denounced by U.S Commissioner for Namibia Sean McBride as being illegal according to United Nations resolutions. But according to Homateni Kaluenja, multinational investments continued to flow into Namibia via South Africa at the rate of about fifty million dollars annually during the first half of the 1970's, sixty percent of it for "quick returns" in the mining industry.

9. *To The Point*, March 7, 1977.
10. *Star Weekly*, March 18, 1977.
11. *The Times*, London, June 11, 1977.
12. *The Observer*, London, March 6, 1977.
13. *Financial Mail*, April 15, 1977.
14. *Financial Mail*, May 20, 1977
15. *Windhoek Advertiser*, December 19, 1977.

INDEX

317

OTHER BOOKS OF INTEREST PUBLISHED BY URIZEN

LITERATURE

Bataille, Georges
Story of the Eye,
120 p. / Cloth $5.95

Bresson, Robert
Notes on Cinematography,
132 p. / $6.95 / paper $3.50

Brodsky, Michael
Detour, novel,
350 p. / Cloth $8.95

Cohen, Marvin
The Inconvenience of Living, fiction,
200 p. / Cloth $8.95 / paper $4.95

Ehrenburg, Ilya
The Life of the Automobile, novel,
192 p. / Cloth $8.95 / paper.$4.95

Enzensberger, Hans Magnus
Mausoleum, poetry,
132 p. / Cloth $10.00 / paper $4.95

Hamburger, Michael
German Poetry 1910-1975,
576 p. / Cloth $17.50 / paper $7.95

Handke, Peter
Nonsense & Happiness, poetry,
80 p. / Cloth $7.95 / paper $3.95

Innerhofer, Franz
Beautiful Days, novel,
228 p. / Cloth $8.95 / paper $4.95

Kroetz, Franz Xavier
Farmyard & Other Plays,
192 p. / Cloth $12.95 / paper $4.95

Shepard, Sam
*Angel City, Curse of the Starving
   Class & Other Plays,*
300 p. / Cloth $15.00 / paper $4.95

MOLE EDITIONS

Clastres, Pierre
Society Against the State,
188 p. / Cloth $12.95

Elias, Norbert
The Civilizing Process, Vol. 1 & 2,
400 p. / Cloth $15.00 each Vol.

Gibson, Ian
The English Vice,
364 p. / Cloth $12.95

Schivelbusch, Wolfgang
The Railway Journey,
275 p. / photos / Cloth $15.00

Sternberger, Dolf
Preface by Erich Heller
Panorama of the 19th Century
212 p. / Cloth $15.00

ECONOMICS

DeBrunhoff, Suzanne
Marx on Money,
192 p. / Cloth $10.00 / paper $4.95

Howard, Dick
The Marxian Legacy,
340 p. / Cloth $15.00 / paper $5.95

Linder, Marc
Anti-Samuelson, Vol. I,
400 p. / Cloth $15.00 / paper $5.95
Anti-Samuelson, Vol. II,
440 p. / Cloth $15.00 / paper $5.95

CONTEMPORARY AFFAIRS

Andrew Arato / Eike Gebhardt (Eds.)
*The Essential Frankfurt School
   Reader,*
554 p. / Cloth $17.50 / paper $6.95

Augstein, Rudolf
Preface by Gore Vidal
Jesus, Son of Man,
420 p. / Cloth $12.95 / paper $4.95

Burchett, Wilfred
Southern Africa Stands Up,
Cloth 12.95 / paper $4.95

Kristeva, Julia
About Chinese Women,
250 p. / Cloth $8.95

Ledda, Galvino
Padre, Padrone,
Cloth $9.95

Sartre, Jean-Paul
Sartre by Himself,
136 p. / photos / Cloth $10.95 / paper $3.95

Steele, Jonathan
Inside East Germany,
300 p. / Cloth $12.95

Stern, August
The USSR vs. Dr. Mikhail Stern,
420 p. / Cloth $12.95

Write for a complete catalog and send orders to:
**Urizen Books, Inc., 66 West Broadway, New York, N.Y. 10007
212 - 962-3413**